BOOKS AND SOCIETY IN HISTORY

BOOKS AND SOCIETY IN HISTORY

Papers of the

Association of College and Research Libraries

Rare Books and Manuscripts Preconference

24–28 June, 1980
Boston, Massachusetts

EDITED BY Kenneth E. Carpenter

R. R. BOWKER COMPANY
NEW YORK AND LONDON, 1983

The figure on page 6 is reprinted by permission of
Daedalus, Journal of the American Academy of Arts and Sciences,
Vol. 3, no. 3, Cambridge, MA.

Published by R. R. Bowker Company
1180 Avenue of the Americas, New York, N.Y. 10036
Copyright © 1983 by Xerox Corporation
Printed and bound in the United States of America

Library of Congress Cataloging in Publication Data
Main entry under title:
Books and society in history.
    1. Book industries and trade—History—Congresses.
2. Publishers and publishing—History—Congresses.
3. Books—History—Congresses. I. Carpenter,
Kenneth E., 1936–   . II. Association of College and
Research Libraries.
Z280.B66   1983   002   82-20565
ISBN 0-8352-1675-6

CONTENTS

III

Library History and the History of Books: Two
Fields of Research for Librarians

PREFACE

THE PRESENCE of Big Macs in Paris and Tokyo is a sign of a world culture that is unified only on the surface. Beneath are deep cultural divisions that manifest themselves in a variety of ways, including different scholarly traditions. The history of the book is one of those areas in which paths have diverged.

The major division is between the Anglo-American bibliographical approach and the French *histoire du livre*. The Anglo-American world has long asked questions that could only be answered by turning to the books themselves, and has thus pioneered in studies of the book as a physical object. The leading practitioners in this tradition have been students of literature, and Ronald B. McKerrow's famous introduction to bibliography is expressly entitled *An Introduction to Bibliography for Literary Students* (1st edition: Oxford, 1927). To be sure, the Anglo-American world has also devoted attention to the book trade, but the topics investigated have often been chosen more for the light they cast on certain great books rather than on the communications system of the society. Narrative history devoid of an analytical framework has frequently been the result.

In France, by contrast, the bibliographical scholarship of the Anglo-American world has been little practiced until recently. Sophisticated bibliographical description has generally been lacking, and the great bibliographies of early English books do not have French counterparts. Instead, studies in book history in France during the last several decades have been dominated by historians who have sought to understand the role of books in society. Lucien Febvre and Henri-Jean Martin's pioneering and magisterial *L'Apparition du livre* (Paris, 1958) marked the beginning. Succeeding studies in France have tended more than ever to be analytical and statistical, filled with mathematical formulae that are as unrevealing to the typical Anglo-American bibliographer and historian as are collational formulae to the uninitiated. The two worlds were barely on speaking terms, for they were divided by languages that appeared more difficult to master than either French or English.

In the 1970s, communication between representatives of the two traditions began. The Australian bibliographer Wallace Kirsop, in specialized studies and in his *Bibliographie matérielle et critique textuelle, vers une collaboration* (Paris, 1970), pleaded "for an auxiliary science rather neglected in the study of French letters" (p. 3). Roger Laufer's *Introduction à la textologie: vérification, établissment, édition des textes* (Paris, 1972) made accessible bibliographically based Anglo-American textual criticism.

Ideas flowed in the other direction as well. In 1976, 18 years after the original appeared, an English translation of Febvre and Martin was published. More important, several American historians, impressed by the fruitfulness of French historical studies on the role of the book, began writing *l'histoire du livre* but without the forbidding statistical apparatus. A number of papers by Elizabeth Eisenstein, Robert Darnton, and Raymond Birn were followed by publication of two important books at the end of the decade—Eisenstein's *The Printing Press As an Agent of Change: Communications and Cultural Transformation in Early-Modern Europe* (Cambridge and New York, 1979), and Darnton's *The Business of Enlightenment: A Publishing History of the Encylcopédie* (Cambridge, Mass., 1979).

Just as the French approach to the history of the book was adding vitality to historical studies in this country, so was its influence being felt in Britain and elsewhere on the Continent. Indeed, the term *histoire du livre*, with its connotation of an exclusively French approach, was being undermined by its very success. Book history undertaken with the aim of casting light on the communications system of societies and thereby furthering knowledge of cultural processes or change was in 1980 no longer an exclusively French variety of scholarship, nor were the techniques used by the French the only ones possible. In fact, as John Feather pointed out in his address before the Bibliographical Society in December 1978,* the sources available in France are different from those existing elsewhere, with the consequence that other nations cannot copy French techniques. The goal of *histoire du livre* can, however, be emulated, and the conference, whose proceedings are published here, aimed to further that goal by bringing before the participants some of the best work being done on the role of books in Western societies. The title, *Books and Society in History,* was chosen to reflect this intention.

The papers individually lived up to expectation. More than that, they showed the utility of an international approach to the history of the book. The book is, after all, an international phenomenon in a sense other than that books are everywhere present. From its conception in the mind of one individual to its communication to another who is reading it, a book may have been affected by other cultures. Not only do general intellectual currents influence what is published, but official encouragement of piracies in one area may harm the market in another; a markedly lower cost and pricing structure in one culture may deter imports from another; the tariffs

---

*Published as "Cross-Channel Currents: Historical Bibliography and *l'Histoire du Livre*," *The Library*, 6th series, 2 (1980): 5.

of one nation may affect the book production of others; censorship in one nation has repercussions on the output of others; and a flood of refugees from one culture affects the type of books produced in another. Thus, an international approach is required if one is to understand book production in even a single cultural area.

The papers and discussions also made clear that much basic work still needs to be done. Students of the history of the book are stopped again and again by an absence of data, most importantly by a lack of knowledge of what was actually published. The field to be cultivated is vast and requires laborers with many different skills. Moved by an awareness of this and by a sense of the importance of the tasks before us, Paul Raabe drafted a statement that was revised and endorsed by the conference speakers, the Executive Committee of the Rare Books and Manuscripts Section, and by its parent body, the Board of Directors of the Association of College and Research Libraries. Published as the Boston Statement on the History of the Book, it warrants reprinting here (see p. xi), for it conveys the sense of a field that is now unified as never before and that can, with adequate support, greatly help us understand the forces that have shaped our societies.

Acknowledgments

A glance at the geographic distribution of the list of speakers shows that funding was necessary to make the conference possible. Fortunately, the idea of an international conference was first broached during the Rare Books and Manuscripts Section (RBMS) conference in New Haven in 1978, at a time when it was clear that the conference had generated a substantial surplus. Officers of the section asked the Board of Directors of the Association of College and Research Libraries for permission to use part of the surplus to fund an international conference, and the support of that body is gratefully acknowledged. Thanks are due officers of RBMS during the years 1978 to 1980, especially Terry Belanger, Marjorie G. Wynne, and Peter E. Hanff. The editor is also grateful to the Center for the Book at the Library of Congress, which made possible a planning meeting that was most helpful in shaping the program.

Kenneth E. Carpenter

Cambridge, Massachusetts
September 1982

A STATEMENT ON THE
HISTORY OF THE BOOK

FROM JUNE 24 TO 28, 1980, the Rare Books and Manuscripts Section of the Association of College and Research Libraries, a division of the American Library Association, held an international conference in Boston, Mass., U.S.A., on the theme of Books and Society in History. Over 275 people attended. Papers were presented by scholars from four different countries. The speakers at the conference, from both the historical and library professions, drafted the following statement on the history of the book, the term "book" encompassing manuscripts and printed works of all varieties, with the expression "history of the book" meaning all aspects of the history of production, publication and distribution, from the stage of authorship on through to the impact of books on readers and, ultimately, on society.

The history of the book is fundamental to the historical study of society, but we are far from understanding the factors that have shaped the writing and the dissemination of books. These factors have changed over time and have varied from one cultural area to another; hence the impact of the book has also been ever-varied and changing.

The attempt to understand the influence of changes in book production and dissemination is peculiarly demanding. In the first place, one needs to know the basic facts of what was printed, by whom and for whom. Detailed bibliographic studies, dictionaries of printers, and inventories of both public and private libraries are among the time-consuming, exacting and fundamental studies that are needed. In addition, since the book is by its nature a cultural force that transcends national boundaries, both the design and compilation of basic tools require international cooperation. Likewise, analysis based on the fundamental tools must be on an international basis if one is to understand how national differences in book production and dissemination have affected the various cultural areas. The conference in Boston has shown the utility of such comparative studies.

In view of the new tools which make possible the gathering of fundamental data, and in light of the rapid progress which has been made in the development of methods of analysis, we call on researchers to make renewed efforts; we invite the contributions of others in all countries, whether or not represented at the conference; we appeal to library directors and all others responsible for manuscripts and books in our libraries to support activities in the field of the history of the book; and, finally, we ask funding agencies in our various countries—governments, foundations and other institutions—to support basic projects as well as seminars, workshops, and conferences on an international level.

The speakers at the conference were: Frédéric Barbier, France; James J. Barnes, U.S.A.; Raymond Birn, U.S.A.; Robert Darnton, U.S.A.; Elizabeth L. Eisenstein, U.S.A.; Bernhard Fabian, West Germany; John P. Feather, Great Britain; Henri-Jean Martin, France; Katharine F. Pantzer, U.S.A.; Paul Raabe, West Germany; and G. Thomas Tanselle, U.S.A.

Boston, Massachusetts
June 28, 1980

LIST OF CONTRIBUTORS

FRÉDÉRIC BARBIER, formerly director of the municipal library of Valenciennes, is now a research associate at the Centre national de la recherche scentifique. In additon to numerous articles, he is the author of *Trois cents ans de librairie et d'imprimerie: Berger-Levrault* (Geneva, 1980). His current project is a comparative history of the book in France and Germany in the nineteenth century.

JAMES J. BARNES holds degrees from Amherst College, Oxford University, and Harvard University, as well as an honorary degree from the College of Wooster. For the past 20 years, he has taught modern European history at Wabash College, and is currently Hadley Professor of History and chairman of the department. Over the years, he has written several books and numerous articles on various aspects of the Anglo-American book trade in the nineteenth and twentieth centuries. Most recently he and his wife, Patience P. Barnes, coauthored a volume on the different translations of Hitler's *Mein Kampf* that appeared in Britain and America during the 1930s. They continue to be intrigued by the ways in which authorship, publishing, public opinion, and the conditions of a given time interact.

RAYMOND BIRN has been a member of the University of Oregon's Department of History since 1961. He is the author of two books, *Pierre Rousseau and the Philosophes of Bouillon* (Geneva, 1964) and *Crisis, Absolutism, and Revolution: Europe 1648–1789/91*, as well as around a dozen scholarly articles dealing with the history of French journalism and the book trade. He is currently focusing his research upon the clandestine book trade and censorship in eighteenth-century France.

KENNETH E. CARPENTER, formerly curator of the Kress Library at the Harvard Business School, is now Research and Publications Librarian in the Harvard University Library. He is working on a bibliography of pre-1850 translations of economic literature, of which some preliminary results have been published as *Dialogue in Political Economy: Translations from and into German in the 18th Century* (Boston, 1977) and "The Bibliographical Description of Translations," *Papers of the Bibliographical Society of America* (3rd quarter, 1982).

ROBERT DARNTON received degrees from Harvard University and Oxford University, where he was a Rhodes scholar. Currently professor of history at Princeton University, he has published widely on various aspects of the cultural history of eighteenth-century France, including *The Business of Enlightenment: A Publishing History of the Encyclopédie, 1775–1800* (Cambridge, Mass., 1979) and *The Literary Underground of the Old Regime* (Cambridge, Mass., 1982). He has been the recipient of numerous prizes, of which the most recent was the 1982 MacArthur Prize.

ELIZABETH L. EISENSTEIN, holds the Alice Freeman Palmer Chair of History at the University of Michigan. Her most important publication is *The Printing Press As an Agent of Change* (Cambridge, 1979, 2 vols; paperback ed. 1980). She was awarded a Guggenheim fellowship for 1982 and is spending the academic term 1982–1983 as a fellow at the Center for Advanced Study in the Behavioral Sciences in Palo Alto, California.

BERNHARD FABIAN is professor of English at the University of Münster, West Germany. His fields of interest are bibliography, literary theory, eighteenth-century English literature and Anglo-German cultural relations. Recent publications include a contribution to the Rosenbach Lectures (published in *The Widening Circle*, Philadelphia 1976) and a reprint collection of the Frankfurt and Leipzig Book Fair Catalogs, 1564–1800. Current work includes a bibliographical catalog of German translations and reprints of British authors, 1680–1810.

JOHN P. FEATHER is a lecturer in the Department of Library and Information Studies at Loughborough University, England. He formerly worked in Special Collections at the Bodleian Library, and was the first Munby Fellow in Bibliography at Cambridge University Library. He specializes in the history of the book trade in the eighteenth century, and has published many articles in *The Library, Publishing History, The Book Collector,* and elsewhere. His book on *The Provincial Book Trade in Eighteenth-Century England* will be published shortly. His current research is largely concerned with the control of the book trade in the eighteenth century, both by legislation and by its internal self-regulation.

HENRI-JEAN MARTIN is professor at the École des chartes and director of studies at the École pratique des hautes études (IVᵉ section). With Lucien Febvre, he wrote the landmark *L'Apparition du livre* (Paris, 1958), *Livre, pouvoirs et société à Paris au XVIIᵉ siècle* (Paris and Geneva, 1969), and, with A. M. Lecocq, *Livres et lecteurs à Grenoble, les registres du libraire Nicolas, 1645–1668* (Geneva, 1977). Professor Martin is co-director of *Histoire de l'édition française*, a three-volume work in progress.

KATHARINE F. PANTZER is Research Bibliographer in the Houghton Library of the Harvard College Library, where she works full time on the revision of Pollard and Redgrave's *Short-Title Catalogue* of English printed books to 1640. Volume 2 of the revision, comprising letters *I* through *Z*, was published in 1976. When the updating and editing of *A* through *H* has been completed, Volume 1 will be published; its current target date is 1985.

PAUL RAABE is director of the Herzog August Bibliothek in Wolfenbüttel and has, in that capacity, furthered the study of the history of the book by making that library's rich holdings widely known and accessible, and by sponsoring a large number and variety of publications, meetings, and research organizations. Professor Raabe has published extensively on expressionism, including *Expressionismus: Der Kampf um eine literarische Bewegung* (1965), which was translated into English as *The Era of German Expressionism* (1974). He has more recently devoted himself to the history of the book, particularly during the Enlightenment, is the author of numerous papers and is editor of *Aufklärung in Deutschland* (1979).

G. THOMAS TANSELLE, Vice President of the John Simon Guggenheim Memorial Foundation and Adjunct Professor of English and Comparative Literature at Columbia University, is the author of *Guide to the Study of United States Imprints* (1971) and a number of essays relating to historical bibliography and textual study, some of which are collected in *Selected Studies in Bibliography* (1979). His Hanes Lecture of 1981, published as *The History of Books as a Field of Study,* discusses some of the same questions as those taken up at the Boston conference.

INTRODUCTION

G. Thomas Tanselle

THAT A CONFERENCE on the topic "Books and Society in History" should have been held in 1980 came as a surprise to no one; indeed, everyone regarded it as particularly timely. The attendance and discussions there suggested a high degree of interest in the subject, and Kenneth Carpenter is to be thanked for having arranged the meetings. Why this subject is so timely is a question I should like to answer in a way that differs somewhat from the customary response though not very different perhaps from the way many of those at the conference felt. I take it to be the generally accepted view that the approach represented by a group of French historians associated with *histoire du livre* has now begun to have a wider influence and that, as far as the English-speaking countries are concerned, the recent translation of Lucien Febvre and Henri-Jean Martin's *L'Apparition du livre* into English (by David Gerard, as *The Coming of the Book*, London, 1976) and the publication of Elizabeth Eisenstein's *The Printing Press As an Agent of Change* and Robert Darnton's *The Business of Enlightenment* reflect this widened interest and at the same time have served to stimulate it. The Febvre-Martin book of 1958 is often said to have inaugurated the movement, and one hears references to the field as only two decades old. To the extent that this view is correct, the conference could perhaps be seen as a celebration of the field's coming-of-age, for by this reckoning it is only slightly beyond the proverbial twenty-first year.

I should like, however, to suggest another way of looking at the matter. Not that I wish to minimize the impact of the Febvre-Martin book, for it has clearly been an influential work, and deservedly so. Nor do I wish to deny that a French school of writers on book history exists, for it plainly does exist. (For a survey of the influence of the Febvre-Martin work and of the achievements of the past two decades, see Wallace Kirsop, "Literary History and Book Trade History: The Lesson of *L'Apparition du livre*," *Australian Journal of French Studies* 16 (1979): 488–535). But to emphasize the newness, or the uniqueness, of the approach represented by these writers is to neglect its extensive roots in bibliographical history and to ignore the complementary nature of all research into the history of books. Recognizing these relationships does not in any sense diminish the achievement of these recent writers, but rather makes clearer the importance of their contribution. To stress its differences from other work is to emphasize its partiality or incompleteness. What is significant and should be focused on instead is its strong impulse toward the integration of diverse materials into an historical picture that is broad but not superficial. The full story of the role of printed books and the book industry in human life is so complex that students of the subject cannot take all the variables into account until specialized treatments of particular aspects have been produced. Some (but by no means all) of the historical research on the book in English-speaking countries, especially among those who call themselves bibliographers, has concentrated on books as physical objects and has explored what the physical evidence reveals about the production process and the effect of that process on the texts printed in books. Although such study may have a different immediate focus from what has come to be called *histoire du livre,* the two are not independent pursuits. Each impinges on the other in so many ways that it is unproductive to think of them other than as elements in the same large process of understanding. It is from this point of view, therefore, that the 1980 conference was particularly timely, for it urged just such an integrated and international approach to book history.

The learned, detailed, and elegant papers delivered at the conference are impressive in the breadth of sources they use, in the quantity of factual detail they amass, and, above all, in the way they illustrate the relation between those details and larger social and intellectual issues. Taken together, they suggest the wide range of problems that book history must investigate, and they illustrate a number of ways of tackling those problems. All periods are touched on, from fifteenth-century monastic printing shops to the operation in the twentieth century of the Book-of-the-Month Club, with examples along the way drawn from eighteenth-century Germany and all centuries of printed book production in England and France. Some of the papers deal with broad issues and trends, illustrated with concrete examples—such as Professor Eisenstein's account of the coming of the book, Professor Martin's discussion of publishing as an agent of change in France, and Professor Barnes's exposition of certain relationships between publishing and economic fluctuations. Others concentrate on somewhat narrower topics but show in the process how this detailed knowledge bears on larger concerns, such as the studies of eighteenth-century censorship by Professor Birn and Mr. Feather and of English editions in Germany by Professor Fabian. The approaches vary from the use of demographic and other statistics by M. Barbier to the examination of the physical structure of books by Miss Pantzer. But whatever the approach or the scope, the subject in general is aspects of book distribution, of the way in which ideas in printed form get disseminated. One important sub-category of this large subject, touched on several times, is the role of censorship, and it is striking that Professor Birn and Mr. Feather, in treating two very different examples of government control, similarly recognize the expressive, as well as the repressive, aspects of such control—as when Mr. Feather shows its relation to copyright and when Professor Birn comments on the connections between censors' decisions and the ideas of the Enlightenment. This pair of papers perfectly illustrates the existence of national differences in book history and the necessity of comparative studies. Another of these subdivisions of the larger theme is the role of translation in the spread of ideas, illustrated by Professor Fabian's examination of English-language publishing in Germany and Miss Pantzer's study of the implications of the shift from law French to English in the printing of the English statutes. And to help put all this into a larger perspective, we have Professor Raabe's outline of the whole field of the historical study of books and libraries.

There is no question that these papers accomplish a great deal. But their authors would be the first to agree that specialized studies of this kind, by focusing on particular areas, have to ignore other relevant considerations that must eventually be investigated and that may then alter in some ways various conclusions now drawn. Indeed, these authors have said as much, and one of the remarkable features of this group of papers is their candid recognition of their own partial nature, of the need to bring into the picture other factors not yet investigated. Professor Barnes, for example, makes clear at the beginning of his paper that in concentrating on economic matters he is leaving out "political, social, legal, technological, and cultural" considerations, though he recognizes their importance. Professor Fabian notes that the readers of the English anthologies he describes "remain to be identified" and remarks on the deficient state of knowledge about the English-German book trade. Miss Pantzer admits that in looking at the physical structure of pardons she has not concerned herself with the historical significance of the division between proclamatory and statutory pardons. M. Barbier points out that the facts embedded in the French copyright deposit records, though fundamental, have not been organized into usable statistics that he can draw on; and despite his remarkable synthesis, he begins by saying that "a synthesis is to a large extent beyond the present state of our knowledge." Professor Martin concludes by naming several basic tasks that remain to be performed in France, such as bringing the printed material under adequate bibliographical control. Professor Eisenstein explains that her title, "From Scriptoria to Printing Shops," referring to the shops rather than the printed product, is meant to reflect an emphasis on "social and historical rather than bibliographical changes."

This latter point leads me to note that, wide-ranging as these papers are, one approach that is not much represented here is the study of the production or pre-publication history of books, the elucidation of the sheet-by-sheet printing history of a book through an analysis of the physical evidence and through recourse to any relevant archives of printers' papers—in other words, the sort of work normally associated with the English tradition of analytical bibliography. Miss Pantzer's paper is the only one directly concerned with physical evidence, and it shows clearly the way in which the structure of the printed quires of the statutes provides information relevant to understanding shifts in political, social, and legal attitudes. Analytical bibliography has sometimes been regarded, by those not immediately concerned with the editing of texts, as unduly narrow, as looking inward and leading to a dead end rather than looking outward to the broad economic and sociological concerns of book-trade history. To claim that this view is characteristic of those writing *histoire du livre* would be as unfair as it would be to ignore, in talking about the English-speaking countries, the large body of work that lies outside physical, or material, bibliography. But with this caution in mind, I believe it would not be unfair to say that in general the writers concerned with books in society have had a tendency to undervalue analytical bibliography. It is consistent with the spirit of the papers printed here to say a little more about this subject, since the papers establish the pattern of referring to related tasks that need to be worked on.

I take it to be axiomatic that the primary evidence for reconstructing the details of the printing of a book lies embedded in the printed book itself and that the reconstruction of such history provides crucial information regarding the structure and economics of the printing, and ultimately the publishing, trade. Professor Darnton recognizes, at the beginning of *The Business of Enlightenment,* the value of this approach for learning about "the work habits of skilled artisans before the Industrial Revolution"; and of course a knowledge of the economics of printing is one of the essential ingredients for understanding why certain words get printed and why they appear in a particular form—and that form in turn may have a bearing on the distribution and influence of the work. The reason physical evidence from books is sometimes neglected may be that historians and literary scholars have frequently not been trained to regard books as artifacts. Often they think of books only in terms of intellectual content, and they are inclined to regard books as secondary in importance to documentary materials as a source of historical information. But for book history, the book is central, both as a physical object and as a conveyor of ideas, because the two cannot be separated. As Professor Raabe stated in his talk at the conference (a condensed version of which appears in this volume), "the individual books are the starting point for the researcher of book history, they are what he examines from various points of view." The subject is books, and therefore the books themselves constitute the primary evidence. Naturally that evidence should be supplemented by other available sources, such as printers' records; but whenever there is a conflict between an external source and the physical evidence of the book itself, the external source must give way. Those who belittle the study of watermarks and broken types take a superficial view of bibliographical analysis. Such activity is easy enough to ridicule, but it can lead to knowledge about the sources of supply of printing materials and the routines of work in printing shops. For these reasons, the physical analysis of books is an integral part of the research that bears on the most encompassing questions concerning the role of printed books in history.

Another factor contributing to the relative neglect of analytical bibliography by some writers on the role of books in society is the context within which it has developed in English bibliography. Most bibliographical analysis, it is safe to say, has been undertaken by scholars more interested in establishing literary texts than in contributing to printing or publishing history. As a result, the analytical techniques have sometimes been regarded as equipment more appropriate to the literary scholar than to the historian. It has been pointed out that some of the detailed studies aimed at identifying the spelling and typesetting habits of individual compositors have not proved to be of much practical use in making editorial decisions, and, because they have been billed as existing solely for that purpose, they are then written off as futile exercises. But despite the exaggerated claims that some literary scholars have made for analytical bibliography as a servant of literary study, analytical bibliography stands on its own and is of interest in its own right. It can be useful in editing and textual criticism because the text of a work may have been affected by the processes it was subjected to in the printing shop (and, in later periods, in the publisher's office as well). But a knowledge of these processes is equally valuable whether or not one is engaged in editing a text. Compositor analysis of sixteenth- and seventeenth-century books, for example, has rarely been undertaken apart from a concern with editing; but there is good reason to apply it to books that one would never contemplate preparing new editions of in order to add to the knowledge of what went on in printing shops of the time. Analytical bibliography is history, not literary criticism: it marshals the primary evidence of the printed artifacts into usable form.

It is ironic that the association of analytical bibliography with editing should have been an impediment to its recognition by those engaged in *histoire du livre,* for the texts embodied in books must surely be the ultimate concern of book history. The breadth of *histoire du livre* comes from its effort to trace the effect of the printed word on the course of history. That books convey ideas is the reason for their significance to those writing *histoire du livre;* some books are artistic achievements in their form, quite apart from what the words on the pages may be saying, but *histoire du livre* is not a branch of the history of art, and this aspect of books is not what is of primary concern to these historians. They recognize, however, that they must examine the industry that produces the printed objects, for the dissemination of ideas cannot be studied apart from the physical means of dissemination and the social, political, and economic influences affecting the operation of those means. Professor Darnton puts this matter succinctly in his book when he cites one of the questions asked by *histoire du livre:* "Did the material basis of literature and the technology of its production have much bearing on its substance and its diffusion?" (p. 1) This is the same question that English bibliographers from McKerrow onward have been asking. Their goal may have been the editing of a literary text, but they have seen that they must investigate how the material processes in the transmission of a text affect the words and punctuation—that is, the content—of the text itself. Nor could their research stop at the point of the first publication of a text: in order to be in a position to evaluate variants between a first edition and later editions, they have to know the circumstances leading to the publication of those later editions. They have to determine such questions of economic and social significance as whether those editions were pirated, whether they were revised by the author, whether the revisions resulted from pressure brought to bear on the author, and so on. The influence of a work is obviously dependent on what it says, and what it says may vary from one edition—or even one impression—to another. Whether the variations are intentional or accidental, whether they are extensive or occur only in one small, but perhaps crucial, passage, they will affect readers' reactions. The international dissemination of a work through translation, a subject in which Mr. Carpenter has been particularly interested* and which enters into Professor Fabian's paper, naturally is affected by the varying quality and accuracy of the different translations. But even when one is concerned only with editions of a work in its original language, one must recognize that those editions may, and generally do, differ from one another. Professor Fabian quite rightly devotes some attention to the quality of the texts reprinted by Thurneysen. To retrieve information about edition sizes from printers' or publishers' records and to observe what works turn up in inventories of booksellers' stocks or in private collections are useful starting points, but one must also know the state of the texts in the particular editions involved. In short, all studies of the dissemination of ideas in written or printed form must be concerned at some point with textual questions.

By commenting on analytical bibliography and textual study I am not suggesting that they are more important than the investigation of printers' and publishers' papers, state archives, copyright records, inventories of book collections, licensing and censorship laws, channels of book distribution, or the social, political, and economic conditions affecting the book

---

*See his "The Bibliographical Description of Translations," *Papers of the Bibliographical Society of America,* 76 (1982): 253–271.

trade. What I am saying is that evidence external to the books themselves and evidence preserved within the books are integral parts of the whole, that each affects the other, that the history of the book is not fully told until all these matters are taken into account and made a part of the total picture. Studies of individual elements in the picture are essential, and as the body of this work grows, increasingly greater syntheses will be possible—though this process, as in any field of scholarship, is an unending one. In any field that is alive, syntheses become obsolete quickly, but their existence is also a reflection of the life and activity in a field. Syntheses help to create an audience and therefore to provide more people to perform basic research. This kind of momentum has not reached very large proportions in book history, despite, or perhaps because of, its overlapping with so many other fields. But there are signs, of which the 1980 RBMS conference is one, that the situation is changing.

The conference provided an opportunity, at what appears to be an appropriate historical moment, to remind ourselves through concrete examples of all these interconnections. The conclusion I think appropriate to draw from the papers and the discussions at the conference is that the various techniques for approaching the history of books are complementary, and that international cooperation in pursuing them is essential for two reasons: first, because the history of the book in one country cannot be effectively studied in isolation from the developments in other countries; and second, because different emphases have become traditional in the study of book history in different countries, and scholars in one tradition can only benefit by adding to their repertory of research techniques the approaches emerging from another tradition. The conference provided a focus for a general desire for cooperation that has increasingly been in the air (as evidenced, for example, by Mr. Feather's 1978 Bibliographical Society paper, "Cross-Channel Currents: Historical Bibliography and *l'Histoire du Livre*," *Library*, 6th ser., 2 (1980): 1–15). Judging from conversations of which I was aware at the conference, I think we are likely to see a succession of gatherings on this subject, of varying degrees of formality and informality, during the coming years—a trend to be encouraged both for the value of such exchanges as self-education and for the role they can play in encouraging promising scholars to enter a field that is short on personnel but rich in the number of major opportunities for research that it offers. Certainly those who were present in Boston—librarians, booksellers, historians, bibliographers, and other scholars of the book—came to see all the more clearly during this conference the ways in which they are all contributors to the same great enterprise: the effort to understand how printing has influenced the course of human history and how it has affected the position in which we now find ourselves.

I

What Is the History of Books?

Robert Darnton

HISTOIRE DU LIVRE in France, *Geschichte des Buchwesens* in Germany, "history of books" or "of the book" in English-speaking countries—its name varies from place to place, but everywhere it is being recognized as an important new discipline. It might even be called the social and cultural history of communication by print, if that were not such a mouthful, because its purpose is to understand how ideas were transmitted through print and how exposure to the printed word affected human thought and behavior during the last 500 years. Some book historians pursue their subject into the period before the invention of movable type. Some students of printing concentrate on newspapers, broadsides, and forms other than the book. The field can be extended and expanded in many ways, but for the most part it concerns books since the time of Gutenberg. It is an area of research that has developed so rapidly during the last few years that it seems likely to win a place alongside fields such as the history of science and the history of art in the canon of scholarly disciplines.

Whatever the history of books becomes in the future, its past shows how a field of knowledge can take on a distinct scholarly identity. It arose from the convergence of several disciplines on a common set of problems, all of which have to do with the process of communication. Initially, the problems took the form of concrete questions in unrelated branches of scholarship: What were Shakespeare's original texts? What caused the French Revolution? What is the connection between culture and social stratification? In pursuing those questions, scholars found themselves crossing paths in a no-man's-land located at the intersection of a half-dozen fields of study. They decided to constitute a field of their own and to include historians, literary scholars, sociologists, librarians, and anyone else who wanted to understand the book as a force in history. The history of books began to acquire its own journals, research centers, conferences, and lecture circuits. It accumulated tribal elders as well as Young Turks. And although its practitioners have not yet developed passwords or secret handshakes or spawned a distinct new generation of Ph.D.s, they can recognize one another by the glint in their eyes. They belong to one of the few sectors in the human sciences where there is a mood of expansion and a flurry of fresh ideas.

To be sure, the history of the history of books did not begin yesterday. It dates from the scholarship of the Renaissance, if not earlier, and it began in earnest during the nineteenth century, when the study of books as material objects led to the rise of analytical bibliography in England. But the current work on the history of books represents a departure from the established strains of scholarship, which may be traced to their nineteenth-century origins through back issues of *The Library* and *Börsenblatt für den deutschen Buchhandel* or theses in the École des chartes. The new strain developed during the 1960s in France, where it took root in institutions like the École pratique des hautes études and spread through publications such as *L'Apparition du livre* (1958) by Lucien Febvre and Henri-Jean Martin and *Livre et société dans la France du XVIIIe siècle* (2 vols., 1965 and 1970) by a group connected with the VIe Section of the Ecole pratique des hautes études.

The new book historians brought the subject within the range of themes studied by the "Annales school" of socioeconomic history. Instead of dwelling on fine points of bibliography, they tried to uncover the general pattern of book production and consumption over long stretches of time. They compiled statistics from requests for *privilèges* (a kind of copyright), analyzed the contents of private libraries, and traced ideological currents through neglected genres like the Bibliothèque bleue (primitive paperbacks). Rare books and fine editions had no interest for them. They concentrated instead on the most ordinary sort of books, because they wanted to discover the literary experience of ordinary readers. They put familiar phenomena like the Counter Reformation and the Enlightenment in an unfamiliar light by showing how much traditional culture outweighed the avant-garde in the literary fare of the entire society. Although they did not come up with a firm set of conclusions, they demonstrated the importance of asking new questions, using new methods, and tapping new sources.[1]

Their example spread throughout Europe and the United States, reinforcing indigenous traditions, such as reception studies in Germany and printing history in Britain. Drawn together by their commitment to a common enterprise and animated by enthusiasm for new ideas, book historians began to meet, first in cafés and then in conferences. They created new journals—*Publishing History, Nouvelles du livre ancien, Revue française d'histoire du livre* (new series), *Buchhandelsgeschichte,* and *Wolfenbütteler Notizen zur Buchgeschichte.* They founded new centers—the Institut d'étude du Livre in Paris, the Arbeitskreis für Geschichte des Buchwesens in

Wolfenbüttel, the Center for the Book in the Library of Congress. Special colloquiums—in Geneva, Paris, Boston, Worcester, Wolfenbüttel, and Athens, to name only a few that took place during the last four years— disseminated their research on an international scale. By the time of the Boston conference of June 1980, whose proceedings are published in this volume, the history of books had become a rich and varied field of study.

It proved to be so rich, in fact, that it now looks less like a field than a tropical rain forest. The explorer can hardly make his way across it. At every step he becomes entangled in a luxuriant undergrowth of journal articles and disoriented by the crisscrossing of disciplines, analytical bibliography pointing in this direction, the sociology of knowledge in that, while history, English, and comparative literature stake out overlapping territories. He is beset by claims to newness—*la nouvelle bibliographie matérielle,* "the new literary history"—and bewildered by competing methodologies, which would have him collating editions, compiling statistics, decoding copyright law, wading through reams of manuscript, heaving at the bar of a reconstructed common press, and psychoanalyzing the mental processes of readers. The history of books has become so crowded with ancillary disciplines that one can no longer see its general contours. How can the book historian neglect the history of libraries, of publishing, of paper, of type, of reading? But how can he master their technologies, especially when they appear in imposing, foreign formulations, like *Geschichte der Appellstruktur* and *Bibliométrie bibliologique?*

In order to get some distance from interdisciplinarity run riot, and to see the subject as a whole, it might be useful to propose a general model for analyzing the way books come into being and spread through society (see accompanying figure). To be sure, conditions have varied so much from place to place and from time to time since the invention of movable type that it would be vain to expect the biography of every book to conform to the same pattern. But printed books generally pass through roughly the same life cycle. It could be described as a communications circuit that runs from the author to the publisher (if the bookseller does not assume that role), the printer, the shipper, the bookseller, and the reader. The reader completes the circuit, because he influences the author both before and after the act of composition. Authors are readers themselves. By reading and associating with other readers and writers, they form notions of genre and style and a general sense of the literary enterprise, which affects their texts, whether they are composing Shakespearean sonnets or directions for assembling radio kits. A writer may respond in his writing to criticisms of his previous work or anticipate reactions that his text will elicit. He addresses implicit readers and hears from explicit reviewers. So the circuit runs full cycle. It transmits messages, transforming them en route, as they

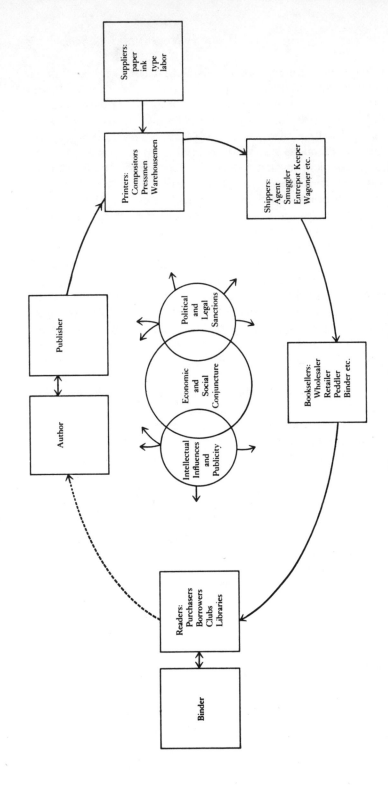

The communications circuit

pass from thought to writing to printed characters and back to thought again. Book history concerns each phase of this process and the process as a whole, in all its variations over space and time and in all its relations with other systems, whether economic, social, political, or cultural, in the surrounding environment.

This is a large undertaking. In order to keep their task within manageable proportions, book historians generally cut into one segment of the communication circuit and analyze it according to the procedures of a single discipline—printing, for example, which they study by means of analytical bibliography. But the parts do not take on their full significance unless they are related to the whole, and some holistic view of the book as a means of communication seems necessary if book history is to avoid being fragmented into esoteric specializations, cut off from each other by arcane techniques and mutual misunderstanding. The model illustrated in the diagram provides a way of envisaging the entire communication process. It should apply to all periods in the history of the printed book (manuscript books will have to be considered elsewhere), but I would like to discuss it in connection with the period I know best, the eighteenth century, and to take it up phase by phase, showing how each phase is related to: 1) other activities that a given person has underway at a given point in the circuit, 2) other persons at the same point in other circuits, 3) other persons at other points in the same circuit, and 4) other elements in society. The first three considerations bear directly on the transmission of a text; the last concerns outside influences, which could vary endlessly. For the sake of simplicity, I have reduced the latter to the three general categories circled in the center of the diagram.

Models have a way of freezing human beings out of history. To put some flesh and blood on this one, and to show how it can make sense of an actual case, I will apply it to the publishing history of Voltaire's *Questions sur l'Encyclopédie,* an important work of the Enlightenment and one that touched the lives of a great many eighteenth-century bookmen. One could enter the circuit of its transmission at any point—at the stage of its composition, for example, when Voltaire shaped its text and orchestrated its dissemination in order to promote his campaign against religious intolerance, as his biographers have shown; or at its printing, a stage in which bibliographical analysis helps to establish the multiplication of editions; or at the point of its assimilation in libraries, where Voltaire's works occupied an impressive percentage of shelf space, according to statistical studies by literary historians.[2] But I would like to consider the least familiar link in the diffusion process, the role of the bookseller, in this case Isaac Pierre Rigaud of Montpellier, and to work through the four considerations mentioned above.[3]

1. On 6 August 1770, Rigaud ordered thirty copies of the nine-volume octavo edition of the *Questions,* which the Société typographique de Neuchâtel (STN) had recently begun to print in the Prussian principality of Neuchâtel on the Swiss side of the French-Swiss border. Rigaud generally preferred to read at least a few pages of a new book before stocking it, but he considered the *Questions* such a good bet that he risked making a fairly large order for it, sight unseen. He did not have any personal sympathy for Voltaire. On the contrary, he deplored the *philosophe's* tendency to tinker with his books by adding and amending passages while cooperating with pirated editions behind the backs of the original publishers. Such practices produced complaints from customers, who objected to receiving inferior (or insufficiently audacious) texts. "It is astonishing that at the end of his career M. de Voltaire cannot refrain from duping booksellers," Rigaud complained to the STN. "It would not matter if all these little ruses, frauds, and deceits were blamed on the author. But unfortunately the printers and still more the retail booksellers are usually held responsible."[4] Voltaire made life hard for booksellers, but he sold well.

There was nothing Voltairean about most of the other books in Rigaud's shop. His sales catalogs show that he specialized somewhat in medical books, which were always in demand in Montpellier, thanks to the university's famous faculty of medicine. Rigaud also kept a discrete line of Protestant works, because Montpellier lay in Huguenot territory. And when the authorities looked the other way, he brought in a few shipments of forbidden books.[5] But he generally supplied his customers with books of all kinds, which he drew from an inventory worth at least 45,000 livres, the largest in Montpellier and probably in all Languedoc, according to a report from the intendant's subdélégué.[6]

Rigaud's way of ordering from the STN illustrates the character of his business. Unlike other large provincial dealers, who speculated on one hundred or more copies of a book when they smelled a best-seller, he rarely ordered more than a half-dozen copies of a single work. He read widely, consulted his customers, took soundings by means of his commercial correspondence, and studied the catalogs that the STN and his other suppliers sent to him (by 1785 the STN's catalog included 750 titles). Then he chose about ten titles and ordered just enough copies of them to make up a crate of fifty pounds, the minimum weight for shipment at the cheapest rate charged by the wagoners. If the books sold well, he reordered them; but he usually kept his orders rather small and made four or five of them a year. In this way, he conserved capital, minimized risks, and built up such a large and varied stock that his shop became a clearinghouse for literary demand of every kind in the region.

The pattern of Rigaud's orders, which stands out clearly from the STN's account books, shows that he offered his customers a little of everything—

travel books, histories, novels, religious works, and the occasional scientific or philosophical treatise. Instead of following his own preferences, he seemed to transmit demand fairly accurately and to live according to the accepted wisdom of the book trade, which one of the STN's other customers summarized as follows: "The best book for a bookseller is a book that sells."[7] Given his cautious style of business, Rigaud's decision to place an advance order for thirty, nine-volume sets of the *Questions sur l'Encyclopédie* seems especially significant. He would not have put so much money on a single work if he had not felt certain of the demand—and his later orders show that he had calculated correctly. On 19 June 1772, soon after receiving the last shipment of the last volume, Rigaud ordered another dozen sets; and he ordered two more two years later, although by then the STN had exhausted its stock. It had printed a huge edition, 2,500 copies, approximately twice its usual pressrun, and the booksellers had fallen all over themselves in the rush to purchase it. So Rigaud's purchase was no aberration. It expressed a current of Voltairianism that had spread far and wide among the reading public of the Old Regime.

2. How does the purchase of the *Questions* look when examined from the perspective of Rigaud's relations with the other booksellers of Montpellier? A book-trade almanac listed nine of them in 1777:[8]

Printer-Booksellers	Booksellers
Aug. Franç. Rochard	Isaac-Pierre Rigaud
Jean Martel	J. B. Faure
	Albert Pons
	Tournel
	Bascon
	Cézary
	Fontanel

But, according to a report from a traveling salesman of the STN, there were only seven.[9] Rigaud and Pons had merged and completely dominated the local trade. Cézary and Faure scraped along in the middle ranks, and the rest teetered on the brink of bankruptcy in precarious boutiques. The occasional binder and under-the-cloak peddler also provided a few books, most of them illegal, to the more adventuresome readers of the city. For example, the demoiselle Bringand, known as "the students' mother," stocked some forbidden fruit "under the bed on the room to the right on the second floor," according to the report of a raid that was engineered by the established booksellers.[10] The book trade in most provincial cities fell into the same pattern, which can be viewed as a series of concentric circles:

At the center, one or two firms tried to monopolize the market; around the margin a few small dealers survived by specializing in chapbooks and old volumes, by setting up reading clubs (*cabinets littéraires*) and binderies, or by peddling their wares in the backcountry; and beyond the fringe of legality adventurers moved in and out of the market, selling forbidden literature.

When he ordered his shipment of *Questions,* Rigaud was consolidating his position at the center of the local trade. His merger with Pons in 1770 provided him with enough capital and assets to ride out the mishaps— delayed shipments, defaulting debtors, liquidity crises—that often upset smaller businesses. Also, he played rough. When Cézary, one of the middling dealers, failed to meet some of his payments in 1781, Rigaud drove him out of business by organizing a cabal of his creditors. They refused to let Cézary reschedule the payments, had him thrown in prison for debt, and forced him to sell off his stock at an auction, where they kept down the prices and gobbled up the books. By dispensing patronage, Rigaud controlled most of Montpellier's binderies, and by exerting pressure on the binders, he produced delays and snags in the affairs of the other booksellers. In 1789 only one of them remained, Abraham Fontanel, and he stayed solvent only by maintaining a *cabinet littéraire,* "which provokes terrible fits of jealousy by the sieur Rigaud, who wants to be the only one left and who shows his hatred of me every day,"[11] as Fontanel confided to the STN.

Rigaud did not eliminate his competitors simply by outdoing them in the dog-eat-dog style of commercial capitalism of early modern France. His letters, theirs, and the correspondence of many other booksellers show that the book trade contracted during the late 1770s and 1780s. In hard times, the big booksellers squeezed out the small, and the tough outlasted the tender. Rigaud had been a tough customer from the very beginning of his relations with the STN. He had ordered his copies of the *Questions* from Neuchâtel, where the STN was printing a pirated edition, rather than from Geneva, where Voltaire's regular printer, Gabriel Cramer, was producing the original, because he had extracted better terms. He also demanded better service, especially when the other booksellers in Montpellier, who had dealt with Cramer, received their copies first. The delay produced a volley of letters from Rigaud to the STN. Why couldn't the STN work faster? Didn't it know that it was making him lose customers to his competitors? He would have to order from Cramer in the future if it could not provide quicker shipments at a lower price.

When volumes 1 through 3 finally arrived from Neuchâtel, volumes 4 through 6 from Geneva were already on sale in the other shops. Rigaud compared the texts, word for word, and found that the STN's edition contained none of the additional material that it had claimed to receive on the sly from Voltaire. So how could he push the theme of "additions and corrections" in his sales talk? The recriminations flew thick and fast in the mail between Montpellier and Neuchâtel, and they showed that Rigaud meant to exploit every inch of every advantage that he could gain on his competitors. More important, they also revealed that the *Questions* was being sold all over Montpellier, even though in principle it could not circulate legally in France. Far from being confined to the under-the-cloak trade of marginal characters like "the students' mother," Voltaire's work turned out to be a prize item in the scramble for profits at the very heart of the established book trade. When dealers like Rigaud scratched and clawed for their shipments of it, Voltaire could be sure that he was succeeding in his attempt to propel his ideas through the main lines of France's communications system.

3. The role of Voltaire and Cramer in the diffusion process raises the problem of how Rigaud's operation fit into the other stages in the life cycle of the *Questions*. Rigaud knew that he was not getting a first edition. The STN had sent a circular letter to him and its other main customers, explaining that it would reproduce Cramer's text, but with corrections and additions provided by the author himself, so that its version would be superior to the original. One of the STN's directors had visited Voltaire at Ferney in April 1770, and had returned with a promise that Voltaire would touch up the printed sheets he was to receive from Cramer and then would forward them to Neuchâtel for a pirated edition.[12] Voltaire often played such tricks. They provided a way to improve the quality and increase the quantity of his books, and therefore served his main purpose, which was not to make money, for he did not sell his prose to the printers, but to spread the Enlightenment. The profit motive kept the rest of the system going, however. So when Cramer got wind of the STN's attempt to raid his market, he protested to Voltaire, Voltaire retracted his promise to the STN, and the STN had to settle for a delayed version of the text, which it received from Ferney but with only minimal additions and corrections.[13] In fact, this setback did not hurt its sales, because the market had plenty of room to absorb editions, not only that of the STN but also one that Marc Michel Rey produced in Amsterdam and probably others as well. The booksellers had their choice of suppliers, and they chose according to whatever marginal advantage they could obtain on matters of price, quality, speed, and reliability in delivery. Rigaud dealt regularly with publishers in Paris, Lyon, Rouen, Avignon, and Geneva. He played them off against each other and sometimes ordered the same book from two or three of them so as to be certain of getting it before his competitors did. By working several circuits at the same time, he increased his room for maneuver. But in the case of the *Questions,* he was outmaneuvered and had to receive his goods from the circuitous Voltaire-Cramer-Voltaire-STN route.

That route merely took the copy from the author to the printer. For the printed sheets to reach Rigaud in Montpellier from the STN's shop in Neuchâtel, they had to wind their way through one of the most complex stages in the book's circuit. They could follow two main routes. One led from Neuchâtel to Geneva, Turin, Nice (which was not yet French), and Marseille. It had the advantage of skirting French territory—and therefore the danger of confiscation—but it involved long detours and huge expenses. The books had to be lugged over the Alps and to pass through a whole army of middlemen—shipping agents, bargemen, wagoners, entrepôt keepers, ship captains, and dockers—before they arrived in Rigaud's storeroom. The best Swiss shippers claimed they could get a crate to Nice in a month for 13 livres 8 sous per hundredweight; but their estimates proved to be far too low. The direct route from Neuchâtel to Lyon and down the Rhône was fast, cheap, and easy but dangerous. The crates had to be unsealed at their point of entry into France and inspected by the booksellers' guild and the royal book inspector in Lyon, then reshipped and inspected once more in Montpellier.[14]

Always cautious, Rigaud asked the STN to ship the first volumes of the *Questions* by the round-about route, because he knew he could rely on his agent in Marseille, Joseph Coulomb, to get the books into France without mishap. They left on 9 December 1771, but they did not arrive until after March, when the first three volumes of Cramer's edition were already being sold by Rigaud's competitors. The second and third volumes arrived in July, but they were loaded down with shipping charges and damaged by rough handling. "It seems that we are five or six thousand leagues apart," Rigaud complained, adding that he regretted not having given his business to Cramer, whose shipments had already reached volume 6.[15] By this time the STN was worried enough about losing customers throughout southern France to set up a smuggling operation in Lyon. Its agent, a marginal bookdealer named Joseph-Louis Berthoud, got volumes 4 and 5 past the guild inspectors, but then his business collapsed in bankruptcy; and, to make matters worse, the French government imposed a tax of 60 livres per hundredweight on all book imports. The STN fell back on the Alpine route, offering to get its shipments as far as Nice for 15 livres per hundredweight if Rigaud would pay the rest of the expenses, including the import duty. But Rigaud considered the duty such a heavy blow to the international trade that he suspended all his orders with foreign suppliers. The new tariff policy had made it prohibitively expensive to disguise illegal books as legal ones and to pass them through normal commercial channels.

In December 1771, the STN's agent in Nice, Jacques Deandreis, somehow got a shipment of volume 6 of the *Questions* to Rigaud through the port of Sète, which was supposed to be closed to book imports. Then the French government, realizing that it had nearly destroyed the foreign book trade, lowered the tariff to 26 livres per hundredweight. Rigaud proposed sharing the cost with his foreign suppliers; he would pay one-third of it if they would pay two-thirds. This proposal suited the STN, but in the spring of 1772, Rigaud decided that the Nice route was too expensive to be used under any conditions. Having heard enough complaints from its other customers to reach the same conclusion, the STN dispatched one of its directors to Lyon, and he persuaded a more dependable Lyonnais dealer, J.-M. Barret, to clear its shipments through the local guild and forward them to its provincial clients. Thanks to this arrangement, the last three volumes of Rigaud's *Questions* arrived safely in the summer.

It had required continuous effort and considerable expense to get the entire order to Montpellier, and Rigaud and the STN did not stop realigning their supply routes once they had completed this transaction. Because economic and political pressures kept shifting, they had to constantly readjust their arrangements within the complex world of middlemen, who linked printing houses with bookshops and often determined, in the last analysis, what literature reached French readers.

How the readers assimilated their books cannot be determined. Bibliographical analysis of all the copies that can be located would show what varieties of the text were available. A study of notarial archives in Montpellier might indicate how many copies turned up in inheritances, and statistics drawn from auction catalogs might make it possible to estimate the number in substantial private libraries. But given the present state of documentation, one cannot know who Voltaire's readers were or how they responded to his text. Reading remains the most difficult stage to study in the circuit followed by books.

4. All stages were affected by the social, economic, political, and intellectual conditions of the time, but for Rigaud these general influences made themselves felt within a local context. He sold books in a city of 31,000 inhabitants. Despite having an important textile industry, Montpellier was essentially an old-fashioned administrative and religious center, richly endowed with cultural institutions, including a university, an academy of sciences, twelve Masonic lodges, and sixteen monastic communities. As a seat of the provincial estates of Languedoc, an intendancy, and an array of courts, it had a large population of lawyers and royal officials. If they resembled their counterparts in other provincial centers,[16] they probably provided Rigaud with a good many of his customers and probably had a taste for Enlightenment literature. He did not discuss their social background in his correspondence, but he noted that they clamored for the works of Voltaire, Rousseau, and Raynal. They subscribed heavily to the *Encyclopédie* and even asked for atheistic treatises like *Système de la nature* and *Philosophie de la nature*. Montpellier was no intellectual backwater, and

it was good book territory. "The book trade is quite extensive in this town," an observer remarked in 1768. "The booksellers have kept their shops well stocked ever since the inhabitants developed a taste for having libraries."[17]

These favorable conditions prevailed when Rigaud ordered his *Questions*. But hard times set in during the early 1770s; and in the 1780s, Rigaud, like most booksellers, complained of a severe decline in his trade. The whole French economy contracted during those years, according to the standard account of C. E. Labrousse.[18] Certainly the state's finances went into a tailspin—hence the disastrous book tariff of 1771, which belonged to Terray's unsuccessful attempt to reduce the deficit accumulated during the Seven Years' War. The government also tried to stamp out pirated and forbidden books, first by more severe police work in 1771–1774, then by a general reform of the book trade in 1777. These measures eventually ruined Rigaud's commerce with the STN and with the other publishing houses that had grown up around France's borders during the prosperous midcentury years. The foreign publishers produced original editions of books that could not pass the censorship in Paris and pirated editions of books put out by the Parisian publishers. Because the Parisians had acquired a virtual monopoly over the legal publishing industry, their rivals in the provinces formed alliances with the foreign houses and looked the other way when shipments from abroad arrived for inspection in the provincial guild halls (*chambres syndicales*). Under Louis XIV the government had used the Parisian guild as an instrument to suppress the illegal trade; but under Louis XV it became increasingly lax, until a new era of severity began with the fall of Choiseul's ministry (December 1770). Thus Rigaud's relations with the STN fit perfectly into an economic and political pattern that had prevailed in the book trade since the early eighteenth century and that began to fall apart just as the first crates of the *Questions* were making their way between Neuchâtel and Montpellier.

Other patterns might show up in other research, for the model need not be applied in this manner; in fact, it need not be applied at all. I am not arguing that book history should be written according to a standard formula, but trying to show how its disparate segments can be brought together within a single conceptual scheme. Different book historians might prefer different schemata. They might concentrate on the book trade of all Languedoc, as Madeleine Ventre has done; or on the general bibliography of Voltaire, as Giles Barber, Jeroom Vercruysse, and others are doing; or on the overall pattern of book production in eighteenth-century France, in the manner of François Furet and Robert Estivals.[19] But however they define their subject, scholars of the history of the book will not draw out its full significance unless they relate it to all the elements that worked together as a circuit for transmitting texts. To make the point clearer, I will go over the model circuit once more, noting questions that have been investigated successfully or that seem ripe for further research.

1. *Authors*. Despite the proliferation of biographies of great writers, the basic conditions of authorship remain obscure for most periods of history. At what point did writers free themselves from the patronage of wealthy noblemen and the state in order to live by their pens? What was the nature of a literary career, and how was it pursued? How did writers deal with publishers, printers, booksellers, reviewers, and one another? Until those questions are answered, we will not have a full understanding of the transmission of texts. Voltaire was able to manipulate secret alliances with pirate publishers, because he did not depend on writing for a living. A century later, Zola proclaimed that a writer's independence came from selling his prose to the highest bidder.[20] How did this transformation take place? The work of John Lough begins to provide an answer, but more systematic research on the evolution of the republic of letters in France could be done from police records, literary almanacs, and bibliographies (*La France littéraire* gives the names and publications of 1187 writers in 1757 and 3089 in 1784). The situation in Germany is more obscure, owing to the fragmentation of the German states before 1871. But German scholars are beginning to tap sources like *Das gelehrte Teutschland,* which lists 4,000 writers in 1779, and to trace the links between authors, publishers, and readers in regional and monographic studies.[21] Marino Berengo has shown how much can be discovered about author-publisher relations in Italy.[22] And the work of A. S. Collins still provides an excellent account of authorship in England, although it needs to be brought up to date and extended beyond the eighteenth century.[23]

2. *Publishers*. The key role of publishers is now becoming clearer, thanks to articles appearing in the *Journal of Publishing History* and monographs like Martin Lowry's *The World of Aldus Manutius* (1979, Cornell Univ. Press), Robert Patten's *Charles Dickens and His Publishers* (1978, Oxford Univ. Press), and Gary Stark's *Entrepreneurs of Ideology: Neoconservative Publishers in Germany, 1890–1933* (1981, Univ. of North Carolina Press). But the evolution of the publisher as a distinct figure in contrast to the master bookseller and the printer still needs systematic study. Historians have barely begun to tap the papers of publishers, although they are the richest of all sources for the history of books. The archives of the Cotta Verlag in Marbach, for example, contain at least 150,000 documents, yet they have only been skimmed for references to Goethe, Schiller, and other famous writers. Fur-

ther investigation almost certainly would turn up a great deal of information about the book as a force in nineteenth-century Germany. How did publishers draw up contracts with authors, build alliances with booksellers, negotiate with political authorities, handle finances, supplies, shipments, and publicity? The answers to those questions would carry the history of books deep into the territory of social, economic, and political history, to their mutual benefit.

The Project for Historical Biobibliography at Newcastle upon Tyne and the Institut de Littérature et de techniques artistiques de masse at Bordeaux illustrate the directions that such interdisciplinary work has already taken. The Bordeaux group has tried to trace books through different distribution systems in order to uncover the literary experience of different social groups in contemporary France.[24] The researchers in Newcastle have studied the diffusion process through quantitative analysis of subscription lists, which were widely used in the sales campaigns of British publishers from the early seventeenth to the early nineteenth century.[25] Similar work could be done on publishers' catalogs and prospectuses, which have been collected in research centers like the Newberry Library. The whole subject of book advertising needs investigation. One could learn a great deal about attitudes toward books and the context of their use by studying the way they were presented—the strategy of the appeal, the values invoked by the phrasing—in all kinds of publicity, from journal notices to wall posters. American historians have used newspaper advertisements to map the spread of the printed word into the back reaches of colonial society.[26] By consulting the papers of publishers, they could make deeper inroads in the nineteenth and twentieth centuries.[27] Unfortunately, however, publishers usually treat their archives as garbage. Although they save the occasional letter from a famous author, they throw away account books and commercial correspondence, which usually are the most important sources of information for the book historian. The Center for the Book in the Library of Congress is now considering the compilation of a guide to publishers' archives. If these can be preserved and studied, they might provide a different perspective on the whole course of American history.

3. *Printers.* The printing shop is far better known than the other stages in the production and diffusion of books, because it has been a favorite subject of study in the field of analytical bibliography, whose purpose, as defined by R. B. McKerrow and Philip Gaskell, is "to elucidate the transmission of texts by explaining the processes of book production."[28] Bibliographers have made important contributions to textual criticism, especially in Shakespearean scholarship, by building inferences backward from the structure of a book to the process of its printing and hence to an original text, such as the missing Shakespeare manuscripts. That line of reasoning

has been undercut recently by D. F. McKenzie.[29] But even if they can never reconstruct an Ur-Shakespeare, bibliographers can demonstrate the existence of different editions of a text and of different issues, printings, and states, a necessary skill in diffusion studies. Their techniques also make it possible to decipher the records of printers and so have opened up a new, archival phase in the history of printing. Thanks to the work of D. F. McKenzie, Leon Voet, Raymond de Roover, and Jacques Rychner, we now have a clear picture of how printing shops operated throughout the handpress period (roughly 1500–1800).[30] More work needs to be done on later periods, and new questions could be asked: How did printers calculate costs and organize production, especially after the spread of job printing and journalism? How did book budgets change after the introduction of machine-made paper in the first decade of the nineteenth century and Linotype in the 1880s? How did the technological changes affect the management of labor? And what part did journeymen printers, an unusually articulate and militant sector of the working class, play in labor history? Analytical bibliography may seem arcane to the outsider, but it could make a great contribution to social as well as literary history, especially if it were seasoned with a reading of printers' manuals and autobiographies, beginning with those of Thomas Platter, Thomas Gent, N. E. Restif de la Bretonne, Benjamin Franklin, and Charles Manby Smith.

4. *Shippers.* Little is known about the way books reached bookstores from printing shops. The wagon, the canal barge, the merchant vessel, the post office, and the railroad may have influenced the history of literature more than one would suspect. Although transport facilities probably had little effect on the trade in great publishing centers like London and Paris, they sometimes determined the ebb and flow of business in remote areas. Before the nineteenth century, books were usually sent in sheets so that the customer could have them bound according to personal taste and ability to pay. They traveled in large bales, which were wrapped in heavy paper and were easily damaged by rain and the friction of ropes. Compared with commodities like textiles, their intrinsic value was slight, yet their shipping costs were high, owing to the size and weight of the sheets. So shipping often took up a large proportion of a book's total cost and a large place in the marketing strategy of publishers. In many parts of Europe, printers could not count on getting shipments to booksellers in August and September, because wagoners abandoned their routes to work the harvests. The Baltic trade frequently ground to a halt after October, because ice closed the ports. Routes opened and shut everywhere in response to the pressures of war, politics, and even insurance rates. Unorthodox literature has traveled underground in huge quantities from the sixteenth century to the present, so its influence has varied according to the effectiveness of the smuggling

industry. And other genres, like chapbooks and penny dreadfuls, circulated through special distribution systems. Although book historians are now beginning to clear some of the ground,[31] these special instances still need much more study.

5. *Booksellers.* Thanks to some classic studies—H. S. Bennett on early modern England, L. C. Wroth on colonial America, H.-J. Martin on seventeenth-century France, and Johann Goldfriedrich on Germany—it is possible to piece together a general picture of the evolution of the book trade.[32] But more work needs to be done on the bookseller as a cultural agent, the middleman who mediated between supply and demand at their key point of contact. We still do not know enough about the social and intellectual world of men like Rigaud, about their values and tastes and the way they fit into their communities. They also operated within commercial networks that expanded and collapsed like alliances in the diplomatic world. What laws governed the rise and fall of trade empires in publishing? A comparison of national histories could reveal some general tendencies, such as the centripetal force of great centers like London, Paris, Frankfurt, and Leipzig, which drew provincial houses into their orbits, and the countervailing trend toward alignments between provincial dealers and suppliers in independent enclaves like Liège, Bouillon, Neuchâtel, Geneva, and Avignon. But comparisons are difficult, because the trade operated through different institutions in different countries, which generated different kinds of archives. The London Stationers' Company, the Communauté des libraires et imprimeurs de Paris, and the Leipzig and Frankfurt book fairs have influenced greatly the different courses that book history has taken in England, France, and Germany.[33]

Nevertheless, books were sold as commodities everywhere. A more unabashedly economic study of them would provide a new perspective to the history of literature. James Barnes, John Tebbel, and Frédéric Barbier have demonstrated the importance of the economic element in the book trades of nineteenth-century England, America, and France.[34] But more work could be done—on credit mechanisms, for example, and the techniques of negotiating bills of exchange, of defense against suspensions of payment, and of exchanging printed sheets in lieu of payment in specie. The book trade, like other businesses during the Renaissance and early modern periods, was largely a confidence game, but we still do not know how it was played.

6. *Readers.* Despite a considerable literature on its psychology, phenomenology, textology, and sociology, reading remains mysterious. How do readers decode the signs on the printed page? What are the social effects of that experience? And how has it varied? Literary scholars like Wayne

Booth, Stanley Fish, Wolfgang Iser, Walter Ong, and Jonathan Culler have made reading a central concern of textual criticism, because they understand literature as an activity, the construal of meaning within a system of communication, rather than as a canon of texts.[35] The book historian could make use of their notions of fictitious audiences, implicit readers, and interpretive communities, but may find their observations somewhat time-bound. Although the critics know their way around literary history (they are especially strong on seventeenth-century England), they seem to assume that texts have always worked on the sensibilities of readers in the same way. But a seventeenth-century London burgher inhabited a different mental universe from that of a twentieth-century American professor. Reading itself has changed over time. It was often done aloud and in groups or in secret and with an intensity we may not be able to imagine today. Carlo Ginzburg has shown how much meaning a sixteenth-century miller could infuse into a text, and Margaret Spufford has demonstrated that still humbler workmen fought their way to mastery over the printed word in the era of *Areopagitica.*[36] Everywhere in early modern Europe, from the ranks of Montaigne to those of Menocchio, readers wrung significance from books; they did not merely decipher them. Reading was a passion long before the *Lesewut* and the *Wertherfieber* of the romantic era, and there is *Sturm und Drang* in it yet, despite the current penchant for speedreading and a mechanistic view of literature as the encoding and decoding of messages.

But texts shape the response of readers, however active they may be. As Walter Ong has observed, the opening pages of *The Canterbury Tales* and *A Farewell to Arms* create a framework that casts the reader in a role he cannot avoid no matter what he thinks of pilgrimages and civil wars.[37] In fact, typography as well as style and syntax determine the ways in which texts convey meanings. D. F. McKenzie has shown that the bawdy, unruly Congreve of the early quarto editions settled down into the decorous neoclassicist of the *Works* of 1709 as a consequence of book design rather than bowdlerization.[38] The history of reading will have to take into account the ways that texts constrain readers as well as the ways that readers take liberties with texts. The tension between those tendencies has existed wherever readers confronted books and has produced some extraordinary results, of which Luther's reading of the Psalms, Rousseau's reading of *Le Misanthrope,* and Kierkegaard's reading of the sacrifice of Isaac are but a few examples.

Though it may be possible to recapture the great rereadings of the past, the inner experience of ordinary readers will always elude us. But at least we should be able to reconstruct a good deal of the social context of reading. The debate about silent reading during the Middle Ages has produced some impressive evidence about reading habits,[39] and studies of reading societies in Germany, which proliferated there to an extraordinary degree in the eighteenth and nineteenth centuries, have shown the importance of reading in the development of a distinct bourgeois cultural style.[40] German scholars have also contributed a great deal to the study of the history of libraries and to reception studies of all kinds.[41] Following a notion advanced by Rolf Engelsing, these studies often maintain that reading habits became transformed at the end of the eighteenth century. Before this *Leserevolution* readers tended to work laboriously through a small number of texts, especially the Bible, over and over again. Afterwards they raced through all kinds of material, particularly novels and periodicals, seeking amusement rather than edification. The shift from intensive to extensive reading coincided with a desacralization of the printed word. The world began to be cluttered with reading matter, and texts began to be treated as commodities that could be discarded as casually as yesterday's newspaper. This interpretation of the reading revolution has been disputed recently by Reinhart Siegert, Martin Welke, and other younger scholars who have discovered "intensive" reading in the reception of fugitive works like almanacs and newspapers, notably the *Noth- und Hülfsbüchlein* of Rudolph Zacharias Becker, which was an extraordinary best-seller of the *Goethezeit*.[42] But whether or not the concept of a reading revolution will hold up, it has helped to align current research on reading with general questions of social and cultural history.[43] The same can be said of research on literacy,[44] which has enabled scholars to discern the vague outlines of diverse reading publics 2 to 3 centuries ago and to trace books to readers at several levels of society. The lower the level, the more intense the study has become. Popular literature has been a favorite topic of research during the last decade[45] despite a growing tendency to question both the correlation between cheap booklets like the Bibliothèque bleue and an autonomous, popular culture, and the distinctions that have been drawn between strains of "elite" and "popular" culture. It now seems inadequate to view cultural change as a linear or trickle-down movement of influences. Currents flowed up as well as down, merging and blending as they went. Characters like Gargantua, Cinderella, and Buscon inhabited literature in many forms—oral traditions, chapbooks, and sophisticated literature—and their identities changed according to nationality and genre.[46] One could even trace the metamorphoses of stock figures in almanacs. What does Poor Richard's reincarnation as *le Bonhomme Richard* reveal about literary culture in America and France? And what can be learned about German-French relations by following the Lame Messenger (*der hinkende Bote, le messager boiteux*) through the traffic of almanacs across the Rhine?

Questions about who reads what, in what conditions, at what time, and with what effect link reading studies with sociology. The book historian could learn how to pursue such questions from the works of Douglas

Waples, Bernard Berelson, Paul Lazarsfeld, and Pierre Bourdieu. One could draw on the reading research that flourished in the Graduate Library School of the University of Chicago from 1930 to 1950 and that still turns up in the occasional Gallup report.[47] And as an example of the sociological strain in historical writing, one could consult the studies by Richard Altick, Robert Webb, and Richard Hoggart of reading (and nonreading) in the English working class during the last two centuries.[48] All this work opens onto the larger problem of how exposure to the printed word affects the way people think. Did the invention of movable type transform the human mental universe? There may be no single, satisfactory answer to that question, because it bears on so many different aspects of life in early modern Europe, as Elizabeth Eisenstein has shown.[49] But it should be possible to arrive at a firmer understanding of what books meant to people. Their use in the taking of oaths, the exchanging of gifts, the awarding of prizes, and the bestowing of legacies would provide clues to their significance within different societies. The iconography of books could indicate the weight of their authority, even for illiterate laborers who sat in church before pictures of the tablets of Moses. The place of books in folklore and of folk motifs in books shows that influences were reciprocal when oral traditions came into contact with printed texts, and that books need to be studied in relation to other media.[50] The lines of research could lead in many directions, but they all should issue ultimately in a larger understanding of how printing has shaped our attempts to make sense of the human condition.

One can easily lose sight of the larger dimensions of the enterprise, because book historians often stray into esoteric byways and unconnected specializations. Their work can be so fragmented, even within the limits of the literature on a single country, that it may seem hopeless to conceive of book history as a single subject, to be studied from a comparative perspective, across the whole range of historical disciplines. But books themselves do not respect limits, either linguistic or national. They have often been written by authors who belonged to an international republic of letters, composed by printers who did not work in their native tongue, sold by booksellers who operated across national boundaries, and read in one language by readers who spoke another. Books also refuse to be contained within the confines of a single discipline when treated as objects of study. Neither history nor literature nor economics nor sociology nor bibliography can do justice to all the aspects of the life of a book. By its very nature, therefore, the history of books must be international in scale and interdisciplinary in method. But it need not lack conceptual coherence, because books belong to circuits of communication, which operate in consistent patterns, however complex they may be. The present volume represents an attempt to understand the complexities and to show how this new variety of history is advancing on several fronts in several countries.

NOTES

1. For examples of this work, see, in addition to the books named above, Henri-Jean Martin, *Livre, pouvoirs et société à Paris au XVIIe siècle (1598–1701)*, 2 vols. (Geneva, 1969); Jean Quéniart, *L'Imprimerie et la librairie à Rouen au XVIIIe siècle* (Paris, 1969); René Moulinas, *L'Imprimerie, la librairie et la presse à Avignon au XVIIIe siècle* (Grenoble, 1974); and Frédéric Barbier, *Trois cents ans de librairie et d'imprimerie: Berger-Levrault, 1676–1830* (Geneva, 1979) in the series Histoire et civilisation du livre, which includes several monographs written along similar lines. Much of the French work has appeared as articles in the *Revue française d'histoire du livre*. For a survey of the field by two of its most important contributors, see Roger Chartier and Daniel Roche, "Le livre, un changement de perspective," *Faire de l'histoire* (Paris, 1974) 3: 115–136; and Roger Chartier and Daniel Roche, "L'Histoire quantitative du livre," *Revue française d'histoire du livre*, no. 16 (1977): 3–27. For sympathetic assessments by two American fellow travelers, see Robert Darnton, "Reading, Writing, and Publishing in Eighteenth-Century France: A Case Study in the Sociology of Literature," *Daedalus* (Winter 1971): 214–256; and Raymond Birn, "*Livre et société* after Ten Years: Formation of a Discipline," *Studies on Voltaire and the Eighteenth Century* 151 (1976): 287–312.

2. As examples of these approaches, see Theodore Besterman, *Voltaire* (New York, 1969), pp. 433–434; Daniel Mornet, "Les enseignements des bibliothèques privées (1750–1780)," *Revue d'histoire littéraire de la France* 17 (1910): 449–492; and the bibliographical studies now being prepared under the direction of the Voltaire Foundation, which will replace the outdated bibliography by Georges Bengesco.

3. The following account is based on the 99 letters in Rigaud's dossier in the papers of the Société typographique de Neuchâtel, Bibliothèque de la ville de Neuchâtel, Switzerland (henceforth referred to as STN), supplemented by other relevant material from the vast archives of the STN.

4. Rigaud to STN, 27 July 1771.

5. The pattern of Rigaud's orders is evident from his letters to the STN and the STN's Livres de Commission, where it tabulated its orders. Rigaud included catalogs of his major holdings in his letters of 29 June 1774 and 23 May 1777.

6. Madeleine Ventre, *L'Imprimerie et la librairie en Languedoc au dernier siècle de l'Ancien Régime* (Paris and The Hague, 1958), p. 227.

7. B. André to STN, 22 August 1784.

8. *Manuel de l'auteur et du libraire* (Paris, 1777), p. 67.

9. Jean-François Favarger to STN, 29 August 1778.

10. The procès-verbal of the raids is in the Bibliothèque nationale, Ms. français 22075, fol. 355.

11. Fontanel to STN, 6 March 1781.

12. STN to Gosse and Pinet, booksellers of The Hague, 19 April 1770.

13. STN to Voltaire, 15 September 1770.

14. This account is based on the STN's correspondence with intermediaries all along its routes, notably the shipping agents Nicole and Galliard of Nyon and Secrétan and De la Serve of Ouchy.

15. Rigaud to STN, 28 August 1771.

16. Robert Darnton, *The Business of Enlightenment: A Publishing History of the Encyclopédie 1775–1800* (Cambridge, Mass., 1979), pp. 273–299.

17. Anonymous, "Etat et description de la ville de Montpellier, fait en 1768" in *Montpellier en 1768 et en 1836 d'après deux manuscrits inédits,* ed. by J. Berthelé (Montpellier, 1909), p. 55. This rich contemporary description of Montpellier is the main source of the above account.

18. C. E. Labrousse, *La crise de l'économie française à la fin de l'Ancien Régime et au début de la Révolution* (Paris, 1944).

19. Ventre, *L'Imprimerie et la librairie en Languedoc;* François Furet, "La 'librairie' du royaume de France au 18e siècle," *Livre et société* 1 (1965): 3–32; and Robert Estivals, *La statistique bibliographique de la France sous la monarchie au XVIIIᵉ siècle* (Paris and The Hague, 1965). The bibliographical work will be published under the auspices of the Voltaire Foundation.

20. John Lough, *Writer and Public in France from the Middle Ages to the Present Day* (Oxford, 1978), p. 303.

21. For surveys and selections of recent German research, see Helmuth Kiesel and Paul Münch, *Gesellschaft und Literatur im 18. Jahrhundert. Voraussetzung und Entstehung des literarischen Marktes in Deutschland* (Munich, 1977); Franklin Kopitzsch, ed., *Aufklärung, Absolutismus und Bürgertum in Deutschland* (Munich, 1976); and Herbert G. Göpfert, *Vom Autor zum Leser* (Munich, 1978).

22. Marino Berengo, *Intellettuali e librai nella Milano della Restaurazione* (Turin, 1980). On the whole, however, the French version of *histoire du livre* has received a less enthusiastic reception in Italy than in Germany: see Furio Diaz, "Metodo quantitativo e storia delle idee," *Rivista storica italiana* 78 (1966): 932–947.

23. A. S. Collins, *Authorship in the Days of Johnson* (London, 1927); and A. S. Collins, *The Profession of Letters (1780–1832)* (London, 1928). For more recent work, see John Feather, "John Nourse and His Authors," *Studies in Bibliography* 34 (1981): 205–226.

24. Robert Escarpit, *Le littéraire et le social. Eléments pour une sociologie de la littérature* (Paris, 1970).

25. Peter John Wallis, *The Social Index. A New Technique for Measuring Social Trends* (Newcastle upon Tyne, 1978).

26. William Gilmore is now completing an extensive research project on the diffusion of books in colonial New England. On the political and economic aspects of the colonial press, see Stephen Botein, " 'Meer Mechanics' and an Open Press: The

Business and Political Strategies of Colonial American Printers," *Perspectives in American History* 9 (1975): 127–225; and Bernard Bailyn and John B. Hench, eds., *The Press and the American Revolution* (Worcester, Mass., 1980), which contain ample references to work on the early history of the book in America.

27. For a general survey of work on the later history of books in the United States, see Hellmut Lehmann-Haupt, *The Book in America* (New York, rev. ed., 1952).

28. Philip Gaskell, *A New Introduction to Bibliography* (New York and Oxford, 1972), preface. Gaskell's work provides an excellent general survey of the subject.

29. D. F. McKenzie, "Printers of the Mind: Some Notes on Bibliographical Theories and Printing House Practices," *Studies in Bibliography* 22 (1969): 1–75.

30. D. F. McKenzie, *The Cambridge University Press 1696–1712*, 2 vols. (Cambridge, 1966); Leon Voet, *The Golden Compasses*, 2 vols. (Amsterdam, 1969 and 1972); Raymond de Roover, "The Business Organization of the Plantin Press in the Setting of Sixteenth-Century Antwerp," *De gulden passer* 24 (1956): 104–120; Jacques Rychner, "A l'ombre des Lumières: coup d'oeil sur la main d'oeuvre de quelques imprimeries du XVIIIᵉ siècle," *Studies on Voltaire and the Eighteenth Century* 155 (1976): 1925–1955; and Jacques Rychner, "Running a Printing House in Eighteenth-Century Switzerland: The Workshop of the Société typographique de Neuchâtel," *The Library*, 6th ser., 1 (1979): 1–24.

31. For example, see J.-P. Belin, *Le commerce des livres prohibés à Paris de 1750 à 1789* (Paris, 1913); Jean-Jacques Darmon, *Le colportage de librairie en France sous le second empire* (Paris, 1972); and Reinhart Siegert, *Aufklärung und Volkslektüre exemplarisch dargestellt an Rudolph Zacharias Becker und seinem 'Noth- und Hülfsbüchlein' mit einer Bibliographie zum Gesamtthema* (Frankfurt am Main, 1978).

32. H. S. Bennett, *English Books & Readers 1475 to 1557* (Cambridge, 1952); H. S. Bennett, *English Books & Readers 1558–1603* (Cambridge, 1965); L. C. Wroth, *The Colonial Printer* (Portland, 1938); Martin, *Livre, pouvoirs et société;* and Johann Goldfriedrich and Friedrich Kapp, *Geschichte des deutschen Buchhandels*, 4 vols. (Leipzig, 1886–1913).

33. Compare Cyprian Blagden, *The Stationers' Company, A History, 1403–1959* (Cambridge, 1960); Martin, *Livre, pouvoirs et société;* and Rudolf Jentzsch, *Der deutschlateinische Büchermarkt nach den Leipziger Ostermesskatalogen von 1740, 1770 und 1800 in seiner Gliederung und Wandlung* (Leipzig, 1912).

34. James Barnes, *Free Trade in Books: A Study of the London Book Trade since 1800* (Oxford, 1964); John Tebbel, *A History of Book Publishing in the United States*, 4 vols. (New York, 1972–1981); and Frédéric Barbier, *Trois cents ans de librairie et d'imprimerie.*

35. See, for example, Wolfgang Iser, *The Implied Reader: Patterns of Communication in Prose Fiction from Bunyan to Beckett* (Baltimore, 1974); Stanley Fish, *Self-Consuming Artifacts. The Experience of Seventeenth-Century Literature* (Berkeley and Los Angeles, 1972); Stanley Fish, *Is There a Text in This Class? The Authority of Interpretive Communities* (Cambridge, Mass., 1980); Walter Ong, "The Writer's Audience Is

Always a Fiction," *PMLA* 90 (1975): 9–21; and, for a sampling of other variations on these themes, Susan R. Suleiman and Inge Crosman, *The Reader in the Text: Essays on Audience and Interpretation* (Princeton, 1980).

36. Carlo Ginzburg, *The Cheese and the Worms. The Cosmos of a Sixteenth-Century Miller* (Baltimore: The Johns Hopkins University Press, 1980); Margaret Spufford, "First Steps in Literacy: The Reading and Writing Experiences of the Humblest Seventeenth-Century Spiritual Autobiographers," *Social History* 4 (1979): 407–435.

37. Walter Ong, "The Writer's Audience Is Always a Fiction," pp. 9–21.

38. D. F. McKenzie, "Typography and Meaning: The Case of William Congreve," *Wolfenbütteler Schriften zur Geschichte des Buchwesens* 4 (1981): 81–125.

39. See Paul Saenger, "Silent Reading: Its Impact on Late Medieval Script and Society," *Viator*, forthcoming.

40. See Otto Dann, ed., *Lesegesellschaften und bürgerliche Emanzipation: Ein europäischer Vergleich* (Munich: C. H. Beck, 1981), which has a thorough bibliography.

41. For examples of recent work, see Paul Raabe, ed., *Öffentliche und private Bibliotheken im 17. und 18. Jahrhundert: Raritätenkammern, Forschungsinstrumente oder Bildungsstätten?* (Bremen and Wolfenbüttel, 1977). Much of the stimulus for recent reception studies has come from the theoretical work of Hans Robert Jauss, notably *Literaturgeschichte als Provokation* (Frankfurt am Main, 1970).

42. Rolf Engelsing, *Analphabetentum und Lektüre. Zur Sozialgeschichte des Lesens in Deutschland zwischen feudaler und industrieller Gesellschaft* (Stuttgart, 1973); Rolf Engelsing, *Der Bürger als Leser: Lesergeschichte in Deutschland 1500–1800* (Stuttgart, 1974); Siegert, *Aufklärung und Volkslektüre;* Martin Welke, "Gemeinsame Lektüre und frühe Formen von Gruppenbildungen im 17. und 18. Jahrhundert: Zeitungslesen in Deutschland," in *Lesegesellschaften und bürgerliche Emanzipation*, pp. 29–53.

43. As an example of this alignment, see Rudolf Schenda, *Volk ohne Buch* (Frankfurt am Main, 1970); for examples of more recent work, see Rainer Gruenter, ed., *Leser und Lesen im achtzehntes Jahrhundert* (Heidelberg, 1977) and Herbert G. Göpfert, ed., *Lesen und Leben* (Frankfurt am Main, 1975).

44. See François Furet and Jacques Ozouf, *Lire et écrire: l'alphabétisation des Français de Calvin à Jules Ferry* (Paris, 1978); Lawrence Stone, "Literacy and Education in England, 1640–1900," *Past and Present* 42 (1969): 69–139; David Cressy, *Literacy and the Social Order: Reading and Writing in Tudor and Stuart England* (Cambridge, 1980); Kenneth A. Lockridge, *Literacy in Colonial New England* (New York, 1974); and Carlo Cipolla, *Literacy and Development in the West* (Harmondsworth, 1969).

45. For a survey and a synthesis of this research, see Peter Burke, *Popular Culture in Early Modern Europe* (New York, 1978).

46. As an example of the older view in which the Bibliothèque bleue serves as a key to the understanding of popular culture, see Robert Mandrou, *De la culture popu-*

laire aux XVIIe et XVIIIe siècles. La Bibliothèque bleue de Troyes (Paris, 1964). The more current view, which recognizes more nuances in the study of popular culture, is well represented by Roger Chartier, *Figures de la gueuserie* (Paris, 1982).

47. Douglas Waples, Bernard Berelson, and Franklyn Bradshaw, *What Reading Does to People* (Chicago, 1940); Bernard Berelson, *The Library's Public* (New York, 1949); Elihu Katz, "Communication Research and the Image of Society: The Convergence of Two Traditions," *American Journal of Sociology* 65 (1960): 435–440; and John Y. Cole and Carol S. Gold, eds., *Reading in America 1978* (Washington, D.C., 1979). For the Gallup report, see American Library Association, *Book Reading and Library Usage: A Study of Habits and Perceptions* (Chicago, 1978). Much in this older variety of sociology still seems valid, and it can be studied in conjunction with the current work of Pierre Bourdieu; see especially Pierre Bourdieu, *La distinction: Critique sociale du jugement* (Paris, 1979).

48. Richard D. Altick, *The English Common Reader. A Social History of the Mass Reading Public 1800–1900* (Chicago, 1957); Robert K. Webb, *The British Working Class Reader* (London, 1955); and Richard Hoggart, *The Uses of Literacy* (Harmondsworth, 1960; 1st ed., 1957).

49. Elizabeth L. Eisenstein, *The Printing Press as an Agent of Change*, 2 vols. (Cambridge, 1979). For a discussion of Eisenstein's thesis, see Anthony T. Grafton, "The Importance of Being Printed," *Journal of Interdisciplinary History* 11 (1980): 265–286; Michael Hunter, "The Impact of Print," *The Book Collector* 28 (1979): 335–352; and Roger Chartier, "L'Ancien Régime typographique: Réflexions sur quelques travaux récents," *Annales; Economies, sociétés, civilisations* 36 (1981): 191–209.

50. Some of these general themes are taken up in Eric Havelock, *Origins of Western Literacy* (Toronto, 1976); Jack Goody, ed., *Literacy in Traditional Societies* (Cambridge, 1968); Jack Goody, *The Domestication of the Savage Mind* (Cambridge, 1977); Walter Ong, *The Presence of the Word* (New York, 1970); and Natalie Z. Davis, *Society and Culture in Early Modern France* (Stanford, 1975).

II

[1] From Scriptoria to Printing Shops: Evolution and Revolution in the Early Printed Book Trade

Elizabeth L. Eisenstein

A FEW PRELIMINARY comments should precede the discussion of the fifteenth-century movement "from scriptoria to printing shops." A consideration of the general issues associated with evolutionary and revolutionary trends is in order here, since I use the term "revolution" to designate two rather different processes. First there is the conventional use of the term to describe any relatively abrupt and decisive change. In this sense we may say that the fifteenth-century transition from script to print constituted a communications revolution. The replacement of hand copying by printing as the *chief* mode of book production in the West (and I emphasize "chief" to account for the persistence of hand copying) occurred in so many locations in Western Europe in such a short time that it has to be designated by the term "revolution"—even at the risk of some semantic confusion.

For the term "revolution" may also be used to designate a long-range, irreversible process—a process whose effects become more pronounced the longer it goes on. This is the sense that governs references to an industrial revolution or to a demographic revolution. This is the sense that led Raymond Williams to entitle his study of the growth of literacy *The Long Revolution*,[1] and this sense also seems applicable to changes wrought by printing. When we consider the rate at which printed materials have been accumulating since the fifteenth century, it seems evident that a long-range, irreversible process has been at work. After 500 years, problems of overload have become more acute than they were a century ago, and it seems likely that the same problems will weigh even more heavily on future generations than they do upon our own.

In this regard, the typographical revolution, which started in the fifteenth century, bears a close resemblance to the agricultural revolution that started in the eighteenth century. In both cases old problems of scarcity were solved, only to be replaced by new problems of glut. The ten farmers required to feed one townsman in the Middle Ages may be likened to the ten scribes required to furnish Chaucer's fourteenth-century clerk of Oxford with the twenty books he wanted to fill his shelves.

During the millennia that intervened between the invention of writing and the introduction of printing in the West, it never took fewer than ten scribes to feed one clerk. The production, collection, and circulation of books were subject to an economy of scarcity, and tasks of preservation were naturally of paramount concern. Within a century after the installation of printing shops in Western Europe, a new economy of abundance began to make its presence felt. A landmark in this process, which reversed earlier trends, is the universal bibliography compiled by Conrad Gesner and published by Christopher Froschauer in Zurich in 1545. Gesner's *Biblioteca Universalis* excluded all vernacular publications but attempted to list all Latin, Greek, and Hebrew printed works. Making use of booksellers' lists and publishers' catalogs, the author managed to track down roughly a third of actual output. Gesner's bibliography, which went through several editions and expanded with each one, was not only the first, it was also the last attempt to encompass the entire output of the Commonwealth of Learning within the confines of one work. New specialized bibliographies multiplied at such a rate that bibliographies of bibliographies had to be compiled, and the end of this somewhat regressive sequence is surely not yet in sight.

The end of the long revolution cannot be foreseen, but its beginnings can be ascertained. They lie in the interval between the 1460s and 1480s when European printing shops first appeared. To gain some perspective on present problems, we need to take a closer look at the factors that encouraged the rapid spread of printing and the growth of allied trades in Western Europe during early modern times.

I take fifteenth-century Western Europe for my point of departure despite the often-held opinion that one ought to begin instead with China, where the first printed products were turned out. I wish I knew more about Asian printing (especially about the Korean use of movable type), but based on what little I know, I do not think that our current problems of overload started outside the West. It is instructive to look outside the boundaries of Western Christendom, if only in order to learn that the mere introduction of a new technology tells us little about the uses to which it will be put. No doubt the difference between gradual development in Asia and rapid exploitation in the West has something to do with the difference between ideographic and alphabetic systems of writing.

But other considerations are also pertinent. All the diverse "factors," whether political, economic, intellectual, or other, have to be considered in any causal analysis. Religion, in particular, should not be overlooked. There were some non-Asian societies in which alphabets were used, but printers were assigned a relatively inglorious position and forbidden to apply their art to sacred texts. In all regions governed by Islam, prohibitions against printing the Koran were in effect. (Printing was introduced in Constantinople by Jews who set up a non-Muslim press.[2]) But of course other variables were also significant. In Eastern Christendom, religious printing was sanctioned and indeed sponsored by the church. Yet, in contrast to the West, Russian printers started almost a century after Gutenberg and thereafter maintained a very sluggish pace. Only within Western Christendom was the wooden handpress, once invented, so energetically exploited by so many freewheeling entrepreneurs.

Denys Hay observes: "Some inventions have taken centuries to be adopted and even more have taken several generations . . . printing was an exception. It spread with phenomenal speed and by the 1490s each of the major states had one important publishing centre and some had several."[3] Printing spread in this manner nowhere else in the world. In explaining why this happened, moreover, the role of a few major states seems less significant than the role played by many minor ones.

Most histories of printing follow the convention of organizing developments around the rise of the major nation states. This procedure works well enough for nineteenth-century developments, but it is likely to skew patterns when applied to the earlier, more cosmopolitan age of the handpress. The major centers of book production down through the eighteenth century were not congruent with the major political capitals—Paris, Berlin, Vienna, Rome, Madrid, and London. The great printing centers were also great commercial centers such as Venice, Antwerp, and Amsterdam.[4] Indeed, nation building worked at cross-purposes with the rapid expansion of early modern printing industries. The rise of a few large, well-consolidated, dynastic states was less helpful than the presence in late medieval Europe of numerous small principalities, bishoprics, communes, free cities, and other assorted quasi-independent political units. Through the eighteenth century rulers of small principalities continued to invite printers to set up shop within their walls and thus provide revenues and publicity—fill town coffers and satisfy civic pride.[5] The absence of any powerful central authority, whether embodied in an emperor or pope, the prolonged rivalry between the pope and other rulers, quarrels among diverse rulers themselves—the fragmentation of political authority, in short—provided opportunities for printers to play one power against another while extending large trade networks from the shelter provided by small walled towns.

Of course, economic developments ought to be coupled with political ones. Late medieval particularism had to be combined with early modern capitalism in order to produce conditions favorable to rapid expansion of the printing trade. Among the cultural and intellectual factors that contributed to the rapid growth of Western printing industries, Italian humanism is often singled out. The important role played by book-hunting literati in stimulating elite patronage is undeniable. But in my view, the most dynamic impetus to the development of printing was supplied by Christian evangelism. I will comment later on the tradition of "an apostolate of the pen," which goes back to Cassiodorus; let me note here that evangelical impulses and missionary drives were extended enormously after the printer replaced the stationer or scribe.

These comments suggest that one must understand the age of scribes in order to understand the spread and rapid development of early printing. In this sense I agree with those who adopt an evolutionary model of change and stress how ripe conditions were in late medieval Europe. The absence of any powerful central authority was, after all, a heritage from the pre-Gutenberg age. So too were the far-flung networks and sophisticated systems of financing developed by late medieval merchants engaged in the wholesale cloth trade. Textile manufacture, moreover, was linked to rag paper production. The way in which printing firms were set up by lay urban entrepreneurs also owed much to precedents established by the earlier manuscript book dealers. There are obviously important links between the stationer who acted as publisher of university textbooks, and the printer who later served in the same capacity (and sometimes in the same location—on the rue St. Jacques in Paris, for example).

But all revolutions have preconditions as well as precipitants. The expansion of a regular manuscript book trade and of a literate laity, together with the prior introduction of paper and oil-based ink, of credit, and of the requisite metallurgical techniques, may be regarded plausibly as preconditions for the revolution that was to come. Although the prolonged persistence of publishers in locations such as the rue St. Jacques provides evidence of continuity, there were significant differences between the stalls of the late medieval stationer and the printing houses that were established later in the same locations. The latter tended to develop a more diversified publication program and to serve a more diversified clientele. Even while holding offices as university book providers, the new master printers also acted as independent entrepreneurs. They cultivated the patronage of others, including officials, and sometimes set up branch offices outside university towns. They even dispensed patronage themselves by providing jobs, room, and board to impecunious students and clerks. They gathered under one roof a larger and more diversified labor force than had the stationers and thus encouraged new forms of social and intellectual interchange.

Within university precincts, the printing shop emerged—as the stationer's stall had not—as a rival center of advanced study that challenged the intellectual supremacy of the graduate faculties of theology, medicine, and law. Outside university towns, publishing centers were relocated, a point that is sometimes overlooked. Thus it has been argued that fifteenth-century book production was scarcely affected by printing—a conclusion based on evidence of the low output of a printer in Bruges.[6] But in the 1470s Bruges was already declining as a center of book production and was being treated as a potential market by a Florentine merchant who had books printed in Venice loaded onto galleys bound for London and Bruges.[7]

Furthermore, publishing and selling were only two of the activities that occupied that protean figure, the early master printer. He was the successor not only of the stationer but also quite often of the copyist or scribe. Lehmann-Haupt's fine monograph on Peter Schoeffer permits us to observe the activities of a Mainz printer who had been a Paris scribe. The two figures seemed to work in contrasting milieux, subject to different pressures and with different goals. Many of Schoeffer's pioneering activities prefigured the shift from printing as a retail trade to printing as a wholesale industry, a transition that led the printer to turn peddler and to launch what soon became an annual book fair at Frankfurt. "For a while the trade in printed books flowed within the narrow channels of the manuscript book market. But soon the stream could no longer be contained." New distribution outlets were located; handbills, circulars, and sales catalogs were printed, and the books themselves were carried from the Rhine across the Elbe, west to Paris, south to Switzerland. The new printers' drive to tap markets coincided with efforts to hold competitors at bay by offering better products or, at least, by printing a prospectus to advertise the firm's "more readable" texts, "more complete and better arranged" indexes, "more careful proofreading" and editing. The patronage of officials who served archbishops and emperors was solicited, not so much because they were potential bibliophiles or even potential censors, but rather because they controlled a steady flow of orders for printing ordinances, edicts, bulls, indulgences, broadsides, and tracts. By the end of the century, Schoeffer had risen to a position of eminence in the city of Mainz. He commanded a "far-flung sales organization," had become a partner in a joint mining enterprise, and had founded a printing dynasty. His supply of types and staff of compositors and pressmen went to his sons upon his death, and the Schoeffer firm continued in operation through the next generation.[8]

As the foregoing may suggest, there are many points of possible contrast between the activities of the Mainz printer and those of the Paris scribe. Competitive and commercial drives were not entirely absent among the lay scribes who were hired by mendicant orders, or the semilay copyists who belonged to communities founded by the Brethren of the Common Life. But those drives were muted in comparison with the later efforts of Schoeffer and his competitors to recoup initial investments, pay off creditors, use up reams of paper, and keep pressmen employed. Indeed, the rapid establishment of presses in fifteenth century Venice produced

> a mad scramble in which numerous competitors trampled one
> another underfoot for a vision of prosperity that few ob-
> tained. . . . Rather more than 100 printing companies have
> been identified in Venice up to 1490; 23 were still active during
> the following decade; only 10 survived the century.[9]

Useful data on the difficulties experienced by one early master printer are offered by Giovanni Mardersteig's *Remarkable Story of a Book Made in Padua in 1477.*[10] In this account, we are told a success story, for the master printer Petrus Maufer managed to surmount all obstacles, including strikes, in order to finish printing an edition of a large (1,000-page, double-column) folio volume containing a commentary on Avicenna. Between May 1477, when the first reams of paper were obtained, and December 1477, when the last sheet came off the press, 6,800,000 characters were set in type, four presses had been put in operation and, according to the printer's boast, "not a working day had been wasted."

Almost exactly 300 years later, from June to November 1778, a similar story unfolded, as recounted in Robert Darnton's study of the wage book of the Société typographique de Neuchâtel.[11] Because of the fine detail that this eighteenth-century wage book provides, we are able to learn much more than Mardersteig tells us about the disorderly behavior of individual journeymen and the extent to which problems of labor management were compounded by absenteeism and erratic work habits. In spite of the 300 years that had intervened, the two accounts are nevertheless similar. When it came to problems of financing, labor management, and marketing, the master printers of 1477 were closer to their successors in the trade in 1788 than they were to their contemporaries who handled the manuscript book trade. The fifteenth-century stationer or manuscript book dealer did not have to worry about idle machines or striking workers. Indeed, it has been suggested that the mere act of setting up a press in a monastery or in affiliation with a religious order was a source of disturbance, bringing "a multitude of worries about money and property" into a realm previously reserved for meditation and good works.[12]

Before we examine the implications of this last suggestion, it should be noted that a significant portion of book production in Western Europe had moved out of monasteries well before Gutenberg's time. The creation of new teaching and preaching orders who served the needs of medieval townspeople had led to a reorganization of book manufacture and supply. Some scholars now even use the term "revolution" to describe what happened to book production in certain twelfth-century towns.[13] With the establishment of lay stationers to serve the needs of friars and university faculties, the copying of books became a kind of cottage industry. There developed a kind of putting-out system under which different portions of the text were farmed out to different copyists, all of whom were paid piecemeal rates. Recent research has called into question previous notions that certain lay scriptoria were attached to late medieval manuscript booksellers' shops. The classic case—one that is repeated in standard accounts—cites the example of Vespasiano da Bisticci, who allegedly set 45 scribes to work turning out 200 books for Cosimo de Medici in less than two years; this account turns out to be wrong on every count. Vespasiano provided only 111 books, some of which he bought; the process took six years, not less than two; and most of the scribes he employed were "moonlighting" notaries who copied for Vespasiano in their spare time. There was no "back room" in Vespasiano's shop where scribes gathered to copy texts.[14] In addition to exercising great caution in referring to lay scriptoria in the later Middle Ages, one must also be very careful about defining any long-term trends, for the effects of the so-called twelfth-century book revolution were neither as widespread nor as lasting as one might expect. University book production was restricted to university towns; patterns that were clear in the thirteenth century tended to get smudged by the end of the fourteenth. During the last century before the advent of printing, conditions were especially anarchic, and the system of "the pecia," or controlled piecemeal copying, seems to have been no longer used.

That medieval trends have to be traced very cautiously is also shown by the fate of monastic scriptoria. Although the twelfth-century book revolution is said to have lead to the decline of these scriptoria, by the fifteenth century, they were once again flourishing. Fifteenth-century abbots were asked whether it was permissible to copy books on holy days and wrote treatises echoing the "praise of scribes" by early Christians.

The most intriguing example of the "praise of scribes" genre, often cited as a curiosity in books on early printing, is *De Laude Scriptorum* by Joannes Trithemius (or Tritheim), abbot of Sponheim. He is sometimes called the "father of bibliography" and was an ardent bibliophile.[15] Trithemius exhorted his monks to carry on despite the invention of printing. Among other arguments (such as keeping idle hands busy, the intrinsic value of diligence and devotion, the knowledge of holy books acquired by copying), the abbot somewhat illogically compared the word written on parchment, which would last 1,000 years, with the word printed on paper, a writing material that had a shorter life. I call the comparison illogical because the difference between perishable paper and trustworthy skin was really irrelevant to the difference between printing and writing. Why was printing on parchment ruled out? Vellum copies of the Gutenberg Bible show that printing on skin was practiced in the abbot's day. Thus, we may assume the abbot was simply echoing a long-lived "praise of scribes" theme. A similar comparison of papyrus with skin was sounded by St. Jerome. It is possible, of course, that Trithemius was seriously concerned as a bibliophile about the increased use of paper, which was encouraged by printing. But he himself clearly favored presswork, for he had the very work in which he praised scribes printed in Mainz in 1494. He used one Mainz printing shop so often that it has been called the Sponheim Abbey Press. In his later writing, the abbot repeatedly paid tribute to the wonderful art of printing, "devised in the city of Mainz in Germany near the Rhine and not as certain men say falsely in Italy, . . ." and he cited his own conversations with Peter Schoeffer concerning the role of Gutenberg as inventor and of Fust as financial backer of the first press. One of Trithemius' last contributions as a chronicler also enabled Peter Schoeffer's son to pay filial tribute to his father and grandfather (Johann Fust) as the first authors of the art of printing and to render homage once again to the city of Mainz as the birthplace of the press.[16]

Thus, the abbot of Sponheim contributed one of the last works in "praise of scribes" and one of the first in praise of printing. He bridged the world of the monastic scriptorium in Sponheim and that of emerging printing shops in Mainz and Basel. It is intriguing that a northern churchman such as Trithemius should be so much more receptive to printing than a Florentine humanist bookdealer such as Vespasiano. The abbot was by no means the only churchman to link scriptoria with printing shops. Many early presses were set up in monasteries, convents, and abbeys. The celebrated edition of Marsiglio Ficino's Latin translation of Plato, of which 1025 copies were produced in 1483, came from the Florentine convent of San Jacopo de Ripoli, where nuns ran the presses. The monastery of St. Barbara in Cologne employed printers from 1475. And the Brethren of the Common Life throughout the Low Countries set up presses to take over the work of scribes.[17]

Thus, although the rise of the lay stationer in the twelfth century needs to be fully acknowledged, it would be unwise to rule out the coexistence of monastic scribes. The latter acquire added significance when we compare the fate of printing in Western Christendom with its fate in other regions. The enthusiastic Christian response to printing can be explained in part by the religious command to spread "glad tidings" far and wide. Also noteworthy is the fact that copying books was prominently featured among duties of the monk in fulfilling the evangelical mission. Insistence on preaching by the pen characterized Western monasticism since the days of Cassiodorus, who urged monks

> to preach unto men by means of the hand, to untie the tongue
> by means of the fingers . . . to fight the Devil . . . with pen and
> ink. Every word of the Lord written by the scribe is a wound
> inflicted on Satan. . . . Though seated in one spot, the scribe
> traverses diverse lands through the dissemination of what he
> has written.[18]

This advice held a special significance for members of those ascetic orders who had shunned pulpit oratory and could only "preach with their hands." "Since we cannot preach God's words by mouth," wrote a twelfth-century prior of his order, which was sworn to silence, "let us preach it with our hands. Every time we write a book, we make of ourselves heralds of the Truth. . . ." Without leaving the cloister, wrote Peter the Venerable, also in the twelfth century, a member of a silent order could journey far over land and sea; "without opening his mouth, he could make the Lord's teaching resound in the ears of the nations."[19] The carrying power of the written word, its potential as a mass medium, continued to be celebrated by Christian monks right up to the time when the first modern mass medium did appear. When Luther later hailed printing as "God's highest act of grace, the last flame before the extinction of the world," he was not introducing a new Protestant concept but was instead ringing variations on a long-lived monkish theme.

The enthusiastic welcome given to printing by Christian churchmen was by no means confined to abbots and monks. Preachers eager to extend the audience for their sermons, prelates trying to raise funds for crusades, reformers attempting to educate the clergy—all agreed with Cardinal Nicholas of Cusa that printing should be described as a divine art. Martin Lowry's recent biography of Aldus Manutius is a splendid study.[20] But Lowry's thesis that Aldus was the first to make printing acceptable to snobbish, disdainful humanists needs to be qualified by the recognition of the ready acceptance this "divine" art found among Renaissance popes and prelates. Well before Aldus established his shop, printing was already held up as an indication of the superiority of Western Christendom over the infidel Turk.[21] Even the earliest censorship edicts praise the invention of printing as God-given before proceeding to note the need for controlling its possible abuse.[22]

There is a certain irony in the enthusiastic reception accorded to printing by the Church. Despite all the early presses that were established under the aegis of the Church, the changed mode of book production dealt a relatively swift blow to ecclesiastical influence. (Not that the pulpit ever became unimportant. On the contrary, from Savonarola to John Wesley to Billy Graham and on to Oral Roberts, Christian evangelism and the development of new mass media have gone hand in hand.) But the press did replace church doors as the chief organ of publicity. News and entertainment were increasingly handled under lay auspices, and the cultural supremacy of Rome was gradually undermined.

An instructive contrast may be drawn between the first Italian presses and those that closed the age of incunabula. The first presses were established by two German printers, Sweynheim and Pannartz, under church patronage (in a German Benedictine monastery supervised by a Spanish cardinal). When Sweynheim and Pannartz left the monastery at Subiaco, they went to papal Rome. Their firm did not prosper, however, and Rome never did become a major printing center.[23] Here again is evidence of a revolutionary relocation, for the papal court previously had been a major copying center, if not the major copying center, in Western Christendom. But the expanding printing industry required much larger markets than the church alone could provide. The flourishing centers of printing were, by the end of the fifteenth century, outside the direct control of Rome. Of the numerous presses operating in Venice, very few were run by individuals who felt subservient to popes or cardinals, Dominican inquisitors, or faculties of theology. Instead, authors were prodded by Venetian printers to exploit popular lay themes:

> Blistering criticism of the papal court went uncensored. Insult, slander, even obscenity against friars and priests were so common that anti-clericalism became a literary convention . . . authors avoided only criticism of things Venetian.[24]

As one might expect, scholars became somewhat bolder about denouncing clerical monopolies on learning when benefices were no longer their chief means of support and a new kind of lay patronage could be obtained.

Collaboration with printers made it possible for a new generation of literati to behave as did the German pamphleteers who ridiculed the professors of Cologne. Like the "obscure men" who plagued Johann Reuchlin, the learned doctors at the Sorbonne soon became prime targets for Erasmian satire and Rabelaisian mirth. Not only had lay erudition overtaken that of schoolmen, but new opportunities were opened simultaneously for "lowborn adventurers of the pen." Obscure young monks, like Erasmus and Rabelais, could rise in the world without staying in clerical orders. They could find more congenial work in printing shops and thus exploit fully the talents that won them patrons and fame. The young monk François Rabelais could win freedom from monastic discipline by finding work with a Lyonnaise printer while going through medical school. He later secured a post as a municipal physician on the basis of the editorial work on ancient medical texts that he did for Gryphius. That he found this new, irreverent métier especially rewarding is suggested by his extravagant boast that "more copies of *Gargantua* were sold in two months than Bibles in ten years."[25]

As a friendless young canon from Rotterdam, Erasmus also avoided having to defer to clerical superiors by availing himself fully of the new forms of patronage to be obtained through publication. After reading P. S. Allen's account of the obscure young Dutchman who tried every shift—pushing his name onto a blank space in a French scholar's book, currying favor with a kindly printer only to drop him when a better deal could be arranged—one finds it hard to reconcile the obnoxious young man on the make with the dignified "Prince of Humanists" that the Republic of Letters came to revere.[26] Hundreds of complimentary copies given Erasmus by his printers were used by the wily author to fool potential patrons who, thinking themselves dedicatees, provided hundreds of pensions in return.[27] It is almost as difficult to imagine Thomas à Kempis adopting a similar stratagem as it is to envisage Erasmus serving meekly as a copyist in Deventer after completing his schooling there. At all events, Erasmus showed how men of letters could be emancipated from the status of client—even before anyone had dreamed of an author's copyright or royalties. By garnering favors and pensions from innumerable lords and ladies, he freed himself from dependency on any single one and could use his considerable powers of persuasion to win support for causes that he himself held dear.

The age of Erasmus, according to Trevor-Roper, was a "golden age" for European intellectuals because it "lay between the European discovery of printing and the discovery of its antidote, the Index Librorum Prohibitorum."[28] Actually, the Index served rather more as a stimulant than as an antidote, for these lists of banned books supplied Protestant printers with opportunities to profit from publicity even while attracting those Catholic purchasers who were able and willing to pay black market prices to obtain forbidden fruit.

The religious divisions of the sixteenth century helped to further the expansion of the printing industries and paved the way for Erasmus's successors to triumph over censorship and, ultimately, to obtain legal recognition of author's rights. The age of Erasmus was rather more of an awkward age than a golden one for authors, who were poised uncertainly between diverse forms of patronage. Nevertheless, collaboration with printers in the age of the handpress did lead in the end to the emergence of those modern forms of authorship with which we are familiar today. But this aspect of the "long revolution" that started with Gutenberg may be drawing to an end. I am referring to the changes that have taken place recently on the university campus, and in college classrooms and libraries since my own student days. Commercial copy centers have begun to appear within the precincts of modern universities much as stationers' stalls had originated near medieval universities. In preparing assignments for students, teachers now have to weigh the advantages of making up special course packs against the disadvantages of infringing on copyright. Even while university libraries are also taking on the function of copy centers, professors are beginning to acquire their own word processors, which will enable them to bypass university presses and turn out justified copy in their homes. In short, we seem to be in the midst of yet another publishing revolution that very well may undermine current notions of intellectual property rights and bring us closer to the medieval experience of everyman serving as his own scribe.

Before it acquired the modern meaning of irreversible change, the term "revolution" had always implied circular movement and cyclical change. Is it conceivable that the end of the first five hundred years of printing marks the terminus of a cultural cycle and that the movement from scriptorium to printing shop will be followed by yet another shift: from printing shop to copy center, computer, or console? Whatever the next turn of fortune's wheel may bring, it seems likely that certain cultural features introduced by printing are here to stay. In particular problems of increasing overload will remain, however many new copying devices may be installed. (Indeed, the introduction of new copiers will simply make current pressures more acute.) For this reason, if for no other, it seems desirable to encourage more investigation of the communications revolution of the fifteenth century. Although the age of the wooden handpress has long been over, the cumulative process it set in motion still persists.

NOTES

1. Raymond Williams, *The Long Revolution* (New York, 1966).

2. Halil Inalcik, *The Ottoman Empire: The Classical Age 1300–1600*, trans. N. Itzkowitz and C. Imber (London, 1973), p. 174.

3. Denys Hay, "Introduction," *Printing and the Mind of Man*, ed. J. W. Carter and P. H. Muir (London, 1967), p. xxii.

4. On the geography of printing industries in the age of the handpress, see L. Febvre and H.-J. Martin, *L'Apparition du livre* (Paris, 1958).

5. See a case history presented by Raymond Birn, "Pierre Rousseau and the *philosophes* of Bouillon," *Studies on Voltaire and the Eighteenth Century* 29, ed. T. Besterman (Geneva, 1964).

6. Paul Saenger, "Colard Mansion and the Evolution of the Printed Book," *The Library Quarterly* 45 (1975): 405–418.

7. Florence Edler de Roover, "Per la storia dell'arte della stampa in Italia. . . ," *La bibliofilia* 55 (1953): 107–115.

8. Hellmut Lehmann-Haupt, *Peter Schoeffer of Gernsheim and Mainz* (Rochester, N.Y., 1950), passim.

9. Martin Lowry, *The World of Aldus Manutius: Business and Scholarship in Renaissance Venice* (Ithaca, N.Y., 1979), p. 9.

10. Trans. H. Schmoller (London, 1967).

11. Robert Darnton, *The Business of Enlightenment: A Publishing History of the Encyclopédie 1775–1800* (Cambridge, Mass., 1979), Chap. 5, pp. 220–227.

12. Wytze Hellinga, "Thomas à Kempis: The First Printed Editions," *Quaerendo* 4 (1974): 4–5.

13. This development is well summarized by K. W. Humphreys, *The Book Provisions of the Medieval Friars 1215–1400* (Amsterdam, 1964), p. 13.

14. Albinia de la Mare, "Vespasiano da Bisticci: Historian and Bookseller." Ph.D. diss., University of London, 1965.

15. See a recent edition edited by Klaus Arnold: Johannes Trithemius, *In Praise of Scribes—De Laude Scriptorum*, trans. R. Behrendt (Lawrence, Kan., 1974).

16. Pierce Butler, *The Origin of Printing in Europe* (Chicago, 1940), pp. 93 and 106–107 offer pertinent documents and references.

17. For references to other monastic presses, see E. L. Eisenstein, *The Printing Press as an Agent of Change*, 2 vols. (Cambridge, 1979), Vol. 1, p. 15, n. 39.

18. Cited by Bruce M. Metzger, *The Text of the New Testament* (Oxford, 1968), p. 18. See also Jean Leclercq, *The Love of Learning and the Desire for God*, trans. C. Misrahi (New York, 1962), p. 128.

19. *Coutumes de Gigue I, prieur de la Grande Chartreuse* (12ième Siècle BN Mss lat 4342), item #410 in *Le Livre*, catalogue of a Bibliothèque nationale exhibition (Paris, 1972), p. 134.

20. See Lowry, op. cit.

21. Geoffroy Atkinson, *Les nouveaux horizons de la Renaissance française* (Paris, 1935), p. 57.

22. Rudolph Hirsch, "Pre-Reformation Censorship of Printed Books," *The Library Chronicle* (University of Pennsylvania) 21 (1955): 100–105.

23. Clifford Maas, "German Printers and the German Community in Renaissance Rome," *The Library* 5th ser., 31 (1976): 118–126.

24. Paul Grendler, *Critics of the Italian World* (Madison, Wis., 1969), pp. 4–7.

25. Michael B. Kline, "Rabelais and the Age of Printing," *Études rabelaisiennes* 4 (Geneva, 1963), pp. 1–59.

26. P. S. Allen, "Erasmus' Relations with His Printers," *Transactions of the Bibliographical Society* 13 (October 1913–March 1915): 297–323.

27. Jean Hoyaux, "Les moyens d'existence d'Erasme," *Bibliothèque d'humanisme et Renaissance* 5 (1944): 7–59.

28. H. Trevor-Roper, "Desiderius Erasmus," *Men and Events* (English title: *Historical Essays*) (New York, 1957), p. 39.

[2] Publishing Conditions and Strategies in Ancien Régime France

Henri-Jean Martin

ALTHOUGH THE TOPIC of this chapter has been defined clearly in the title, the discussion here will not be limited to the ancien régime, for a more general consideration of publishing in more recent times may cast light on the earlier period. Moreover, my research as a medievalist and my collaboration with Roger Chartier in the publication of a multivolume collective history of publishing in France, have led me to expand the scope of my investigations. Thus, I would like to preface this chapter with some general remarks.

The various means of communication within a given society consist of a series of complementary and interacting systems. When a new form of communication becomes necessary and then appears, it tends to exceed its goal and overfulfill its function. A process of reclassification then follows, for while the old means of communication are still used, they no longer serve the same functions. What is more, each period seems to adapt the media to its own use. How each era appropriates the media differently for its own purposes is a question contemporary historians are investigating when, for example, they examine the role of oral and written transmission in propagating the Reformation in a partially literate society.[1] It has been shown that the relation between written and oral transmission is ever-changing. Over the centuries, written discourse seems to have acquired a

This chapter was originally presented in French at the symposium and was translated for this volume.

certain autonomy vis-à-vis oral discourse; it has become increasingly versatile and cannot be described by simple models and ready-made formulas.[2]

In the evolution of forms of written discourse, the various means of communication through manuscript were not eliminated by the appearance of printed matter. Rather, they continued and grew stronger. Thus, it is relevant for historians of the printed book to study the renewed use of written discourse in the Middle Ages. Long before the communication specialists of today, students of medieval manuscripts, through study of the medieval acts, attained a singularly lucid understanding of the power of the written word to further an organized and hierarchical society.[3] In societies that use written communication, the book is often regarded as the most perfect example of the organization of a society's thought. It somehow embodies the ideology of that society and transmits its message, not only through the text but through its very organization. The book thus has a symbolic value.[4]

It is of great interest, then, to compare the various steps entailed in the creation, fabrication, and reading of a manuscript with the processes involved in the creation, elaboration, and distribution of a printed book. In the latter, one sees an increased diversification of tasks and a more complex organization. It is this process that I would like to consider here.[5]

If we exclude the bookseller for the time being, it is the publisher who acts as mediator between the author, the printer, and the public. In general, a publisher's success can be attributed to a privileged relationship with one or two of these parties.[6] To illustrate this point, I would like to draw on an example from a recent dissertation on the printing-publishing firm of Berger-Levrault.[7]

The founder of the firm was Wilhelm Friedrich Schmuck of Strasbourg, who opened a modest printing establishment with presses of his own in 1681, after the city was annexed by Louis XIV. Since the family had close ties with the Jesuits, Schmuck was the natural choice for printer of the intendant of Alsace, a position that assured him a steady flow of job printing. He also published on the side various pamphlets and books for the Catholic community of Alsace, as well as theses and other documents for the university.

At the end of the ancien régime, and especially during the Revolution and the Empire, the Levrault family, who were the heirs of Schmuck and by then were solidly integrated in the liberal bourgeois community, encountered a set of very favorable circumstances. To their printing office they added a typefoundry and a paper mill located in the Vosges. They furnished the army of the Rhine with paper, and they printed administrative documents and later became the official printers for the Grande Armée. In the Napoleonic era, as the Levrault family traveled through Germany in the footsteps of the imperial troops, they were able to establish a network for the export of French books. Their position as printer for the army allowed them the financial means to do more substantial publishing and also led them to begin a tradition of publishing military works, among which was *Fil de l'épée* by Captain de Gaulle (1932). Yet, their main activity had always been printing administrative forms—to this day they print the innumerable forms for social security—and their publishing activities were of secondary importance to the financial well-being of the firm.

This example invites reflection on the role of official and administrative printing in the development of typography. When we examine the initial production of Mainz that has reached us and attempt to visualize that which has not, it appears that the first objective of Gutenberg and his journeymen was not to produce new books or even Bibles but rather to devise a process for the reproduction of calendars, indulgences, and, of course, liturgical books.[8] Printing presses have been used at all times for the production of utilitarian documents. This was particularly true of ancien régime France, where, as early as the sixteenth and possibly even the fifteenth centuries, a multitude of small printing shops were established to serve prelates, magistrates, and governmental bodies.[9] Although official documents were their basic means of support, those printers did produce other works; and, at a time when barter was the predominant form of trading, the goods had to be exchangeable. Thus, the printers tended to publish not only texts of local interest but also works capable of appealing to people beyond their region. Church and government authorities, in addition to the small circle of their representatives and associates, were the main source of manuscripts.

However, since the publication of any work of substance has always required a large investment, most printers of that period were mere artisans in the service of "capitalist" booksellers. In France, there are only a handful of exceptions to this rule.

The first of these exceptions were the "humanist printers." Almost all of these individuals were somehow associated with chancelleries, for example, as clerks. Calligraphers as well as philologists, they paid particular attention to punctuation and to the layout of their texts.[10] With the appearance of type, which somehow came between them and their public, they were forced to work very closely with printers, if only to arrive at a certain level of standardization. Thus, close associations were formed in which printers played the dominant role. In most other cases, the master printers had strictly typographical tasks, in addition to the hiring and firing of hands.[11] The bookseller-publishers had the other functions. Booksellers who did not have the capital to carry on business in this manner often operated from the borders of the kingdom and published prohibited texts. We encounter such cases during the Reformation and the Enlightenment.

Another type of exception is the printer, who, thanks to official support, became a publisher. At the end of the seventeenth century, when, for political and economic reasons, the royal authorities limited the number of printing shops in France, those who were protected by the administration were most often printers for the king[12] and thus became all the more influential in the trade. Such was the case with the Coignard family, publishers of several editions of the multivolume *Dictionnaire* of Moréri between 1707 and 1725. But the most interesting case in this regard is that of Le Breton.[13] He was the grandson of the bookseller Houry, who, having married the chambermaid of the chancellor's wife, secured through the chancellor's influence the privilege for the *Almanach royal*. Le Breton was the first printer to the king and had a very well-equipped printing shop. Then the privilege for the *Almanach* passed by bequest to another member of the family, and Le Breton, in order to keep his presses rolling, embarked on printing the *Encyclopédie*. Thus, the basis of his business shifted from official support to relationships with the literary world.

Let us examine another model—the publishing firm born out of a bookselling establishment. Very early, booksellers settled in provincial France, and quite often, the necessities of exchange forced them to become publishers. One of them, Jean Nicolas the Younger, whose father was originally from Oisans, must have started out as a peddler. Established in Grenoble opposite the courthouse, Jean served a well-defined clientele composed of members of the high courts, their officers, and others who gravitated toward them. He played the role of banker, or rather, usurer, and was also a special supplier for the army. His shop sold feathers, registers, and white paper. He sent for novelties from Lyon and Paris, which he exchanged until the time of the Fronde for gloves and chamois skins from the neighboring Alps, or else for reams of paper from the mills of the area. He published texts dealing with local historical figures that were written by the "intellectuals" of the town, such as the knight Bayard or the high constable de Lesdiguières. However, these publications could not balance his account with Paris, and, after having exhausted his credit, he turned to counterfeit editions.[14]

The major part of book production has, however, basically consisted of large-scale publishing of books for the urban elite. In this type of publishing, privileged relationships formed the basis for many a firm's success. A postrevolutionary example was Monsieur Hachette.[15] A pupil of the École normale supérieure and a liberal, as were all his companions under the Restoration, Louis Hachette did not succeed in becoming a professor, for the university was under the control of Monsignor Freyssinous. Instead, he became a bookseller-publisher, adopting the motto "sic quoque docebo." Using to full advantage the process of stereotyping, he started out by publishing manuals of high quality for elementary and secondary schools. The protection of Guizot, who became minister of public instruction after the revolution of 1830, ensured Hachette's success. His former comrades from the École normale supérieure were his best suppliers of texts for dictionaries and pedagogical treatises. He had the foresight to found a number of periodicals, and this helped him to establish close ties with public school principals and teachers, who wanted schoolbooks to be representative of the ardent bourgeois ideology and pedagogical thinking of the time. Hachette's friends also constituted a powerful and vigilant group that was capable of affecting votes on the education budget; clearly, this worked to his benefit. A later enterprise was the establishment of a network of railroad station bookshops, for which Hachette successfully created several book series, among which were the pink collection for children and the blue collection, the ancestor of the blue guides. This second enterprise was also based on the publisher's privileged position—within the distribution structure, in this case. To this day, Hachette's successors have continued to play an essential role in the distribution of books and periodicals.

Did some bookseller-publishers of the ancien régime have comparable experiences? This question should be answered very cautiously, above all because the means of distribution in the ancien régime were different. However, the fifteenth-century firm of Barthélémy Buyer is an earlier example of successful publishing as a result of an existing distribution structure. Barthélémy Buyer, descended from a family of haberdashers, was established in Lyon, a city that was well situated at the center of a network of roads and rivers and that hosted trade fairs. Buyer had two specialties: the publication of legal treatises that were intended primarily for export to the south of Europe and translations of moralizing and pious works. He obtained the texts of the latter mainly from the bourgeois and trading cities of southern Germany and published them as illustrated books for distribution in the cities of France.[16] After Buyer's death, the major bookseller-publishers of Lyon formed partnerships and continued to exploit the Italian and Spanish markets in a similar fashion. They even managed to renew their trade by putting themselves at the service of the Counter Reformation. After this source of commerce disappeared, they started, in the eighteenth and the beginning of the nineteenth centuries, an import-export business between the Protestant regions of northern Europe and the Catholic south, where they had been established for centuries.[17]

Other examples of firms that monopolized sections of the market with the help of official bodies come to mind. Jean Petit the Elder (1495–1535) was a powerful bookseller-publisher of the pre-Reformation period who contributed to the publication of thousands of works, of which many were often important, and who benefited from his close association with the University of Paris and its professors.[18] The case of Sébastien Cramoisy (1585–1669) is better known. Cramoisy was descended from the Nivelles, a family that belonged to the Holy League and had good relations with the

Ultramontanes. Very early in his career and through his family ties, Cramoisy met Richelieu and came to be trusted by the royal administrators, in particular by Chancellor Séguier. As a result, within a few years, he became the official printer for the French Jesuits (together with Cardon from Lyon) and for several other religious orders. While he was printer for the archbishop of Paris, he also became the principal printer for the king.[19] His position as director of the Imprimerie royale added even more to his prestige and influence. As head of a group in which his family members occupied the key positions, he monopolized the publication of liturgical books and works by the leading clergymen. Although this might seem somewhat paradoxical at first glance, he also became one of the main publishers of Gallican treatises. Like Hachette, Cramoisy was at the service of an administration and helped spread its ideology.

In examining various firms, one is struck by the difficulties that large publishers encountered when they attempted to depart from the framework they inherited from their founders. In order to gain access to the humanist market, Petit preferred to associate himself with a newcomer, Josse Bade (Jodocus Badius Ascensius, in the Latinized form), rather than to try alone or to completely integrate Bade's enterprise in his own. In similar fashion, Hachette preferred to buy out or to collaborate periodically with other, well-established firms. However, Petit's business disintegrated with the advent of the Reformation; Cramoisy's firm stagnated and then went bankrupt at the time of the revocation of the Edict of Nantes (1685); and today Hachette encounters difficulties that, in my opinion, are related to changes in educational practices as well as to the appearance of a new type of "literature." These cases show that reliance on a particular system of distribution makes innovation especially difficult.

Just as privileged relationships are important to the financial success of firms, so do they play a significant role in the selection of manuscripts for publication. In the early decades of printing, when most texts were either in ecclesiastical libraries or in the private collections of the nobility, it is likely that certain printers were closely connected with religious orders. This was particularly the case in Germany, but in France, too, the bookseller-publishers must have had some ties with the nobility of their region.[20] Other questions pertaining to manuscript acquisitions include, how did bookseller-publishers succeed in turning some texts into bestsellers, and how did the Parisian Antoine Vérard manage to become "literary counselor," a position that was to assume much importance for the future of French letters? These subjects are treated by work in progress.[21]

Leaving aside problems for future investigation, I would like to examine the cohesive relationship that existed between authors and the public during the early years of printing by drawing on the example of the reading public of Grenoble in the seventeenth century. Comprising a group of about 1,000 people in a city of some 15,000 inhabitants, the audience of readers included some of the local gentry and, above all, members of the high courts, holders of minor offices, lawyers, clerks of all kinds, and, of course, the clergy. Access to books was thus reserved to those of higher rank, whose power rested precisely on knowledge and authority derived from the printed word. Excluded from the circle of readers were tradesmen, masters, and stewards, who went to the bookseller Nicolas only to buy the paper and blank registers they needed for their trade. Quite characteristically, merchants bought books only when they became well established in the community or when they wanted their sons to move upward in social rank.

Thus, the reading public was both homogeneous and hierarchical. Viewed as a circle, it had at its center the presidents of the courts and certain rich magistrates—in short, people who quite often had literary pretensions. They employed learned people who had no financial resources, such as chaplains, tutors, and sometimes secretaries, to help them write. The names under which their works appeared were selected according to the occasion and standards of propriety. In addition, there were people like Nicolas Chorier, a friend of Molière, who attempted to live more or less independently by practicing law, while using his literary talents to write histories as an avocation. Socially, such individuals were in a category apart. Quite often, those of high rank and learning carried on a scientific or literary correspondence with residents of other towns. As members of the fraternal republic of letters, they helped propagate its news. They met at the courthouse, in the chambers, or at the theater, when, for example, the Illustre Théatre was passing through. Above all, however, they gathered in the salons and, during the summer months, at their country retreats in the area of the Côte-Sainte-André, where an active group of literati exchanged epistles and verses.[22]

For the residents of Grenoble, the private library was a privilege reserved to those in high office and, therefore, a status symbol to which many aspired. But those who bought books were avid readers as well. Grenoble, however, was merely a provincial city, and the mores of its leaders only reflected such Parisian models as, for example, the circle of Chancellor Séguier. Richly bound and occasionally stamped with the coat of arms, the Chancellor's books were kept in galleries. Symbols of cultural attainment, these volumes reflected the order of the world.

Neither religious differences (Grenoble had a strong Protestant minority) nor the opposing beliefs and codes of behavior of the devout and the free-thinker alike were allowed to interfere with social relations. On the contrary, the interruption of such relations brought about denunciations after the revocation of the Edict of Nantes (1685). In this milieu, hypocrisy

vis-à-vis members of the Order of the Holy Sacrament was, understandably, the rule. Dispute and opposition were channelled in the direction of
manuscripts or clandestinely printed works. Despite these undercurrents,
the provincial academies flourished by formalizing a system that, for the
most part, was already functioning informally. Through the academies a
process was organized, as Daniel Roche has shown, for the selection and
integration of new ideas and talented individuals.[23]

In such tightly knit groups, the main vehicle of communication was still
the manuscript. The catalogs of French libraries show that their holdings
were composed largely of such documents. Unfortunately, no systematic
study has been devoted to them, with the exception of the work of Ira O.
Wade. Wade has shown that clandestine literature was reproduced and
distributed in manuscript form during the first part of the eighteenth century through the work of copyists, who sometimes were actually grouped
into workshops.[24]

It is important to remember that many written works were originally
oral communications. This is particularly true of the period that concerns
us: Its persistent use of rhetorical forms of speech, both in the theater and
in sermons and discourses of all kinds, was vitally important to the social
life of the time. Likewise, theological treatises often were given originally
as lectures. Another example from a completely different field is the body
of poetry that was composed to be read on social occasions or in the
salons, where conversation itself was a kind of literary exercise.

We should not forget that spiritual treatises and manuals of devotion
were frequently elaborated and "tested" over a long period before the
church hierarchy authorized their printing. In the fields of theology, politics, and law, the private libraries of religious orders, presidents of the high
court, and the clergy served as documentation centers. There, copyists of
all kinds gathered notes, compiled documents, composed memoirs on current issues, or copied others they had found.[25] Our knowledge of the initial
distribution of many literary tracts of the period allows us to conclude that
they were intended for circulation in manuscript form within a very small
circle. Finally, the archives of the academies in the eighteenth century were
filled with memoirs, only a handful of which have been published.

As the foregoing makes clear, the milieu in which booksellers and
printers worked shaped their activities. The best example of a bookseller-
publisher that played an essential role within a well-defined, creative circle
is the late nineteenth-century firm Librairie Champion, which was situated
in the vicinity of the Institut de France, 15 quai Malaquais, and later at 9
quai Voltaire. The founder, Honoré Champion (1846–1913), was the son of
a wine merchant, originally from Burgundy, who had settled in Bercy, near
Paris. Champion's education had been "modern," for he had studied at the
Collège Turgot, where neither Greek nor Latin was taught. He had had to

work from the age of thirteen or fourteen, first as an apprentice at the librairie Dumoulin, on the quai des Grands Augustins. Originally from Normandy, his employer was the official bookseller for the Imperial Society of Paleographers and Antiquaries, many of whose members spent much time at the bookshop, where they felt at home. Sundays, Champion would go to M. de Sainte-Beuve's, where he worked at putting books back in order for 10 sous. All this took place at a time when interest in the fields of history and philology was being renewed in France through contact with German thought. Champion's great opportunity came as a result of the confidence he managed to inspire in the rising stars of this movement: Paul Meyer, Gaston Paris, Léopold Delisle, Charles Morel, Herman Zotenberg, Siméon Luce, and Auguste Longnon. Champion's bookshop, like that of Anatole France's father, became a meeting place for intellectuals.

Some of these people were a part of life at the bookshop. Louis Teste, a writer for the *Gaulois* who knew so much about Stendhal at a time when only a narrow circle of adepts revered the master, conversed with Riou de Maillou, a disciple of Auguste Comte. Arbois de Jubainville talked about the Celtic family, the language of the Francs, the druids, or animal-shaped gods. Courajod, still all excited by one of the famous lectures at the École du Louvre, berated the architecture of the time, its ridiculous excesses, it absurdities. Auguste Longnon, caustic and concise, told of the development of France. M. de Pimodan, ex-officer and poet, son of a papal guard, and sensitive to the cold and distinguished, was the representative of the faubourg Saint-Germain. Anatole France came to enjoy the atmosphere, which was so similar to that of his father's shop. There were young people, like Funck-Brentano, who had just defended his thesis at the École des chartes; elders such as Siméon Luce, Tourneux, and Biré; and newcomers to the literary scene such as Charles Maurras and Marcel Schwob. Lenôtre accompanied Victorien Sardou, and Hérédia. Auguste Lesouëf, almost blind, left the manuscripts, books, and treasures that crowded his apartment on the boulevard Beaumarchais in order to come to listen to the conversation, which he interrupted from time to time with that ironic wit of an old Parisian.

The shop on the quai Voltaire was also a meeting place and center of genealogical studies for the old provincial families. I recall the brothers de Barthélémy; the duke of la Trémoille, who was the typical French aristocrat, elegant and carefree; the two Voguë; and the de Panges. In the Collection Bleue,

Honoré Champion's pride, were published the writings of the duke d'Aumale, the duke de Broglie, the duke of la Trémoille, and the marquis de Voguë. Every year, Champion published the *Annuaire de la noblesse* by the viscount Reverend, who was no viscount at all, but a genuine gentleman and critic.[26]

Champion illustrates how a bookseller can occupy a central position among a group of writers and scientists. This appears to happen more easily when the texts to be published appeal to a small and specialized audience and, above all, when they are scientific in nature and require very careful proofreading. This was the case, three centuries earlier, with the humanist printers Robert Estienne and Sébastien Gryphe (Gryphius in the Latinized form). Their clientele did not outnumber that of Champion, who often published his books in editions of five hundred copies. One can reconstitute the group by looking closely at the names of authors, writers of prefaces, dedications, and front matter in these publishers' editions. The publication of a substantial part of the chronological series of the bibliography of sixteenth-century Parisian booksellers and printers is eagerly awaited, since it will permit systematic study of the literary circles, their interaction, and their reliance on certain booksellers during the Renaissance and the beginning of the Reformation.

Due to tight administrative organization and the rigidly hierarchical state of society, the classical age of the seventeenth century seems to have been the period in which bookseller-publishers had the least influence on creative milieux. Most often, scholars were members of a religious order that was affiliated with a bookseller. Among the gentry, it was customary to look down at booksellers as mere merchants, to refer to them condescendingly as "bonshommes," or to be indignant when they were too successful. In the cities and at the court, it was in good taste to treat literature as just another pastime and to pretend, when one wrote something, that only the judgment of friends and relatives actually mattered. Confined to their tiny shops, the booksellers of the Palais attempted to turn their stores into meeting places.[27] But, as a rule, they just followed the trends of the circles for which they worked.

Under the influence of several new factors, relations between booksellers and authors changed during the eighteenth century. Some of the *philosophes* became literally objects of adulation and were paid very highly for their work. French booksellers of that period, however, seem to have played no role in the process of creation, unlike their counterparts of the sixteenth century. Authors now expected to be paid, a fact that complicated somewhat their relationships with publishers. Moreover, authors writing in French were dispersed by then all over Europe, as were their publishers and printers. This forced prospective publishers to employ informers to seek manuscripts. The Société typographique of Neuchâtel, for example, hired as a scout Mauvelain de Troyes, a literary adventurer who is the subject of a recent study by Robert Darnton.[28] Also of particular interest is the apparently unique role played by Prosper Marchand, which was recently brought to light by C. M. G. Berkvens-Stevelinck. This ex-bookseller carried on a wide-ranging correspondence throughout Europe with authors in search of a publisher. He took it upon himself to offer manuscripts to booksellers, in particular those in Amsterdam, where he lived. A confidential intermediary and prototype of the modern-day literary agent, he struck many deals and often himself prepared texts for printing. He functioned as an "intellectual partner" to booksellers and printers, who, without him, might not have been able to make wise selections or adequately prepare texts for publication.[29]

Among the factors that shape publishing are innovations that occur in a field and make it a popular subject. Recently in France, we have seen this phenomenon in the case of the "nouveaux philosophes" or the "nouvelle histoire." The result is usually the appearance of a new type of publisher, accompanied at times also by a new type of publication that is often illustrated.

Representative of this new type of publisher was Jules Hetzel.[30] Born in 1814 to a midwife and a master saddler for the first regiment of the light cavalry, Pierre Jules studied at the Collège Stanislas, a religious institution. After abandoning his law studies, he became a clerk at Paulin's, a bookseller with republican leanings, who, in collaboration with his neighbor Dubochet, published the beautiful, illustrated works so fashionable at the time, such as *Gil Blas* and *Don Quichote*. Hetzel, who had no funds when he first became his employer's associate, later took over the shop. He had gained the support of the Parisian clergy through his friendship with the abbé Affre, who later became the archbishop of Paris. He started out by publishing a luxurious book of hours and *De Imitatione Christi* by Thomas à Kempis. Then he undertook the publication of composite works such as *Scènes de la vie privée et publique des animaux* and *Diable à Paris,* the conception of which was almost entirely his own. He would solicit texts from such famous writers as Balzac, George Sand, Alfred de Musset, and Dumas, who consented rather willingly to a task that was limited in scope and also well paid. Then he had the manuscripts illustrated by famous artists such as Granville. At the same time, he attempted to develop the field of children's books, which, until then, had been neglected in France, by asking for texts from the same collaborators.

Hetzel started his career at a time when French publishers were attempting to gain a wider audience for their books and periodicals. All his life he experimented with new techniques. He was one of the first to use steam presses for his best publications, and he introduced new methods of color illustration with the help of his old schoolmate, the printer Silberman from Strasbourg. He made systematic use of industrial board binding. Although he resorted to selling by subscription and by installment, both of which methods were current at the time, he was also among those who attempted competitive pricing. Also, he preferred the smaller 18°, or Charpentier, format to the larger octavo format, referred to as "cabinet des lecteurs." He published the complete works of successful authors such as Balzac and George Sand. At first he encountered difficulties, but his innovative efforts later paid off when it became fashionable to buy small illustrated fascicles, printed in two narrow columns, for 4 sous.

In 1848, a difficult year for the publishing trade, Hetzel encountered new problems and almost went bankrupt. Then his republican convictions and his collaboration with the republican government led to his exile in 1851. As a refugee in Brussels, he worked for Victor Hugo and published a collection of major French authors that was intended exclusively for the foreign market. In the absence of an international copyright law, he could have followed the Belgian practice of pirating books, but instead he paid the authors royalties on their works. Allowed to return to France in 1859, Hetzel had such a reputation in the literary world that he was easily able to regain financial backing, in particular from the paper manufacturers. He then launched a popular edition of 130,000 copies of *Les misérables,* became the "creator" of Jules Vernes and the publisher of Erckmann-Chatrian and Alphonse Daudet, and managed in some cases to dispose of enormous pressruns. After having specialized in the popular editions of the major Romantic writers, he discovered some lesser but still sound talents that proved to be just as lucrative. He exploited the fashion for books illustrated with wood engravings and managed to create a new publishing field with albums for children. It came as no surprise when Hachette later purchased the enterprise Hetzel had left to his son, for it was well attuned to the ideology of the Third Republic.[31]

Would it seem too farfetched to consider a man like Jean de Tournes the Elder an equivalent to Hetzel, as far as editorial practices are concerned? Jean de Tournes I, probably born in Lyon in 1504 to a goldsmith, was a compositor and among the most competent of Gryphe's collaborators. At Gryphe's, he met Étienne Dolet, with whom he became friends. In 1542, almost at the same time as Dolet, he became a bookseller-publisher. The times were particularly difficult for the printing trade in Lyon, for the journeymen were struggling against their masters.[32] An object of much protection, Jean's press was endowed with an evangelical, almost reformational orientation. Forced to be cautious after Dolet's arrest, he shifted the focus of his publishing activities toward the literary field, in which he set for himself definite goals. While Gryphe had published primarily Latin and Greek texts, Jean turned his enterprise to French translations of fashionable, classical Spanish and Italian texts. At a time when national literatures were in the process of formation, he published the poets of the Lyon school, such as Maurice Scève, Louise Labbé, and Pernette Du Guillet. Since Neoplatonism was a source of inspiration for writers and artists, he reproduced translations of fables and ancient myths. He paid particular attention to illustrations because his clientele included people who had just acceded to the book culture. By substituting hard woods for softer ones, he was instrumental in improving woodcutting techniques and thus was able to illustrate his books with fine cuts designed by the famous Bernard Salomon. His illustrated history of the Bible and his edition of Ovid's *Metamorphoses* were enormously successful and influential.

What conclusions can we draw from the comparison of such diverse periods? We find both constants and marked differences in the way enterprises were started and in the role booksellers and publishers played in the creative process.

The constants, of course, are striking. Generally speaking, the launching of a firm is a one-step process that is based on an idea and the prospective exploitation of this idea. A bookseller's or publisher's real capital is not money, but rather relationships and abilities that inspire confidence. However, the value of such relationships and talents becomes clear only in periods when innovation is possible. This is in part why I have relied on nineteenth-century examples. In that period the initiative of publishers is quite evident, as shown in the case of Hachette or of Hetzel. On the other hand—and this does not seem too extravagant a claim—it seems that publishing firms emerge periodically in France that rely on the main ideology of the time: Jean Petit in the sixteenth century; in the seventeenth, Sébastien Cramoisy as well as Horace Cardon of Lyon; at the end of the eighteenth century, Panckoucke (whom we will consider later); and in the nineteenth, Louis Hachette. Thus, it seems that the book has been used as an ideological tool in the hands of certain social groups, a fact that is more apparent in French society than it is in others.

The process of creative change is clear. Initially, the bookseller who speculates on an idea, does so on the basis of trust and relationships, and is usually more or less aligned to a group whose ideals and hopes he shares. His success, then, also belongs to that group, for that success depends on the responsiveness of an audience. Once this is accomplished, however, the publisher tends to become integrated into the system and becomes conservative; thus, innovative and aggressive practices become the exception. The publisher has then become the reflection of an ideology, or, more simply put, he has become "academic," in the pejorative sense of the term.

If similarities do exist, there are also many differences between booksellers of the ancien régime and the great publishers of the later periods. As a rule, the cohesive and hierarchical nature of the elitist society under the ancien régime allowed little initiative to the booksellers who were at its service. Even more than today, the writing of a work had the concrete result of advancing its author socially. The doors to a religious or civil career were open to him; the example of Racine has been described in the now classic work of Raymond Picard.[33] A recent thesis on literary life in Paris in the year 1644 shows clearly that only a handful of authors attempted to live from their pen alone.[34] Without delving into the very complex problems of literary careers, patronage, and authors' rights, we note here that the rules of publishing in France, from the point of view of overall book production, changed only very slightly up to the Enlightenment and even the Revolutionary period.

Moreover, distribution in the early period differed radically from our contemporary system. This was particularly true in France, where the functions of publisher and bookseller were differentiated much later than they were in England. In their respective eras, the several types of booksellers we have described formed different distribution networks that were intended to answer the needs of the public and to cover the national territory. Finally, periods of innovation alternated with periods of conservatism, depending on the political and economic situation. Hence, it is necessary to comment briefly on these political, economic, and intellectual factors.

First, let us state the basic rules of publishing, which were as valid for the bookseller of yesterday as they are for the publisher of today. In order to produce a work at a competitive price, the publisher must issue a sufficient number of copies to meet fixed costs (for example, the cost of authors' rights, composition, correction, layout, presswork, and illustration). During the early period and until the eighteenth century, an edition of about 1,000 to 1,500 copies could cover these costs adequately. To issue larger editions, the bookseller-publisher would have had to commit additional capital; this was undesirable, however, because the resources would not then have been available for issuing other editions of successful books.

Working with a financial goal in mind, the publisher usually has to aim not at maximum distribution but rather at maximum profit. In a society in which those of high social standing are also the wealthiest, the logical strategy is to start out with deluxe editions and, after the original market is saturated, to follow up with more economical products.

In contrast to the first edition, it is easy to reduce costs on succeeding versions. Even if resetting of type is necessary, a page-for-page reprint does not involve author's corrections or layout costs. And when paper and binding are the main elements in production costs, type can be set more tightly and paper or skins of lower quality can be used.

These, then, are the factors that have determined both the division of labor in publishing and the market for books. Only certain rules and ethical practices differentiate the earlier book trade from today's publishing. At first, booksellers found it absolutely normal to pirate their colleagues' editions. Only fear of reprisal restrained them from doing so and, in times of crisis, even this deterrent proved insufficient. Although no legal solution was ever reached at the international level, the central government attempted to normalize the situation with a system of privileges.

Against this background, let us attempt to trace the evolution of the French publishing trade, as it was affected by political and economic factors. At first, the market open to booksellers and printers seemed unlimited. They fulfilled the great demand for elementary school books, satisfied the large audience for Books of Hours, produced spiritual works for the convents and illustrated books of religious instruction, and reproduced popular tales for the layman. At this early stage, printing must have accomplished for its age what television did in its early days: It unified its audience by reinforcing certain trends and by eradicating barriers that were perpetuated by the circulation of specialized manuscripts within exclusive and well-defined groups.

At first glance, then, the printing press seems to have been a conservative force. In some cases, it even caused what Michelet referred to as "unexpected survival." But, as with other media, printing soon entered a new phase. With the impetus of small creative groups, typography became diversified and allowed for the dissemination and crystallization of ideas. The period of the humanist printers was then followed by the Reformation. At this point, another factor came into play, for the dynamics of early capitalism stimulated bookseller-publishers to innovate in their attempt to widen the audience for books in this particularly favorable period of the Renaissance. At the most concrete level, the new stimuli led to the birth of the modern book, with all the profound modifications this involved in terms of normalization, accessibility, and aesthetic renewal. To stimulate the market, bookseller-publishers turned to Latin and then Greek texts, which were followed later by a renewal of publishing in the vernacular as national literatures began to emerge. This period also witnessed the appearance of new illustrated works (emblem books, in particular), the popularization of some aspects of humanistic thought, and the revision of scientific ideas, particularly in the natural sciences.[35] Finally, it seems that a process of diversification of the reading public had begun already at that early stage, and that new methods of distribution may have been created.

The constant appearance of new texts and of new, revised editions brought about the problem of literary property—hence, the need for regulations and the creation of a system of privileges. In turn, the conflict between intellectual and religious ideas manifested a deep and impassioned schism in society and ultimately brought about censorship. As a preventive measure, a system of prior approbations was developed, and this led to the

establishment of clandestine and peripheral presses that defied French cen-
tralization. These ruptures in society were all the more brutal in the book
trade, which was already divided between masters and journeymen, who
belonged to different and opposing social groups. The absolute monarchy
attempted to solve the problem through the Edict of Moulin in 1563 and
again in 1566. From then on, at least in theory, all new manuscripts had to
be submitted to the chancellor, who alone was authorized to grant the
petitioner a printing permit and a privilege. The privilege gave exclusive
rights to publish and distribute the work in question over a limited period
of time, and the responsibility for enforcing a privilege, in case of dispute,
devolved on the royal administration.

These regulations went into effect at a time when the Catholic reaction
was taking shape with the Council of Trent. The reaction of this "silent
majority" soon resulted in the massacre of Saint Bartholomew's Day (1572)
and its aftermath in the provinces. After the civil war ended and the tur-
moil was brought under control, the civil and religious authorities regained
their power. The system of privileges then became more than a system of
censorship; it evolved into a means of economic pressure through the
granting of monopolies. At this point, the time was ripe for Cramoisy and
his organization. Because this period witnessed a resurgence of religious
feeling in the Catholic community, the humanistic trend was replaced by a
renewed interest in theological and spiritual matters. International in character, this movement was all the more powerful for being led by the
religious orders, whose members wrote most of the polemical works that
filled the monastic libraries and that played such an important role in the
struggle against the Protestants. The readers of these Counter Reformation
tracts were the faithful, who let their choices be guided by the advice of
their confessors. Even the government, its institutions, and its officials
participated in this movement. Possibly to the detriment of the book world
as a whole, it brought success to some and caused the undoing of many
free thinkers.

The Catholic Reformation movement was so strong that it continued
until the revocation of the Edict of Nantes (1685), and its effects could still
be felt around 1740.[36] Yet, as early as 1635–1650, signs of its slackening
foretold the downfall of the great Catholic publishing tradition. The German fairs lost some of their luster as international events; the main cities
waged war against each other with counterfeit editions; and the Dutch,
who had served as agents between France and the German-speaking areas,
found themselves on the side of the French. The age of the Elzeviers and
their imitators had come.

It was time for a renewal. The religious market had been saturated, and
so bookseller-publishers turned to secular works. As the economic recession worsened, publishers turned increasingly to the use of small formats.

This phenomenon may well have affected mental attitudes, for precisely at the time of the publication of Descartes's *Discours de la méthode* (1637), expressions such as "abridgement," "shortcut," and "an easy method" were frequently used on the title pages of Parisian editions. It is well known that during the reign of Louis XIV, the character of the erudite scholar was disparaged, while the attributes of the gentleman were commended. It was toward the gentleman that Barbin, for example, geared his publishing output.

Characteristically, the central authorities reacted almost immediately to the decline of the Catholic publishing tradition and the increase in secular works. As early as 1635, Chancellor Séguier put into effect the system of preventive censorship. He enlisted as readers of manuscripts people he knew and trusted, in particular, secretaries of the king. The creation of the Académie française (1635) and of the Imprimerie royale (1640) were in line with this policy. When examined carefully, the majority of administrative measures seem to have favored a handful of Parisian bookseller-publishers who were aligned with the monarchy and so were granted monopolies. Prominent among them was Sébastien Cramoisy. During the reign of Louis XIV, the policy of preventive censorship resulted in the elimination of the concept of a public domain and led to the granting of perpetual privileges to a few bookseller-publishers and their descendants. Following the Fronde (1648–1653), during which journeymen managed to survive by publishing a multitude of unauthorized pamphlets, the government deemed it necessary to reduce the number of printing shops and to concentrate the book trade.

In practice, the main result of this policy was to strengthen the division of labor among the different kinds of bookseller-publishers. The presses just outside French borders produced those works that could not be published in France; also, their counterfeit editions ensured the dissemination of French literature both abroad and within France.

Inside the country, Paris dominated the trade more than ever. The Parisian publishers produced traditional works and innocuous novelties and occasionally brought out works with a regional appeal. In fact, Parisian bookseller-publishers could not take full advantage of the monopolies they held, since provincial presses systematically pirated new editions; they marketed counterfeit editions of lower quality at a lower price to a regional clientele, which was not as wealthy, but was less demanding. This, of course, caused the Parisians a serious loss of income, for which they attempted to compensate by not paying authors the appropriate honoraria.[37] This situation was relatively simple at the end of the seventeenth century, but grew more complex during the next century. In Paris, well-established booksellers and printers—a handful of families in all—went so far in their efforts to maintain their privileges as to stop taking on apprentices. Although the well-established publishers made considerable amounts of money, their situation became increasingly difficult with the appearance of a heterodox or semiheterodox production that they could not control. The different forms of "permissions tacites" deprived them of new works, which they would have published in the normal course of events. As a result, their participation in the enormous expansion of the book trade during the Enlightenment was paradoxically limited. They were powerless to stop the "bookseller-peddlers," whose numbers multiplied in their own city. Some of these peddlers actually managed to emerge from their underground existence to trade openly, thanks to the protection of certain elements in the government. This trend eventually led to the breakdown of the traditional system in 1777.[38]

In spite of the tremendous growth of the book trade during the Enlightenment, that period does not differ basically from the seventeenth century in terms of large projects that were undertaken, such as the *Encyclopédie* and the *Histoire naturelle* by Buffon, which recently have received much scholarly attention. From a strictly material point of view, the publishers of the Counter Reformation often embarked on comparable tasks, such as multivolume sets of patristic works, documents of the Church councils, or the *Byzantine du Louvre,* a celebrated series of Byzantine texts published by the Imprimerie royale. Even by eighteenth-century standards, the large Benedictine collections were a considerable enterprise, and publishing the works of Montfaucon was such a large task that it led to the introduction of the subscription method at the time of the system of John Law in the late 1710s.[39]

Long before the Enlightenment, the major European publishers were subjected to stiff competition, difficult negotiations, and bitter battles over market share. These, however, were not factors that brought about change. In all the cases I have mentioned, the bookseller-publishers belonged to the ideological mainstream of the period. They met with the approval of the government and Church and enjoyed all the benefits this blessing could bring in terms of clientele. As a result, they worked at their leisure, whereas the large publishing projects of the Enlightenment, which were destined for the most part to replace those we have just described (in particular the *Dictionnaire* by Bayle), were awaited impatiently by a society that was already undergoing profound change.

In the years preceding the Revolution, a new clientele was formed of laymen who could afford to buy by the tens of thousands the volumes of the *Encyclopédie* or the works of Buffon. Advertising emerged as an important element in the accelerated dissemination of new ideas, for no means were spared to reach this clientele.

These new factors were compounded by additional and more rapid means of communication that permitted, for example, quick transfers of

funds. All these changes enabled those bookseller-publishers of the Enlightenment who dared skirt the law to make spectacular and highly speculative moves. One such example, the Société typographique of Neuchâtel,
has been covered by Robert Darnton; another example I will mention is
the bookselling-publishing operation of the Cramers, who belonged to
Geneva's high society. Their association with Voltaire caused them to alter
drastically their fairly traditional business practices. They eliminated their
traditional stock and proceeded to launch their editions in close succession.
When, for example, they put a new work of Voltaire on the market, their
edition was purposely kept small so that it would be exhausted within a few
days. Then, instead of reprinting, they left the field and allowed counter-
feiters from all over Europe to compete for the market. In this manner,
they were able to recoup their initial investment almost immediately and
realize a substantial profit, all without risk.

How does Panckoucke, the publisher of the *Encyclopédie,* figure in this
context? It is clear that his earlier experiences helped him to establish
contacts and build relationships based on confidence. Like others, he also
seems to have built the foundation of his empire all at once, with the help
of funds and protectors who remain unknown. But unlike Cramoisy, for
example, whose main source of texts was the Jesuits, Panckoucke paid
authors who supplied him with manuscripts. There came a time when, as
with Jean de Tournes or Hetzel, success was more a function of exploiting
a trend or popularizing an ideology than publishing original material. To
reach his clientele, Panckoucke used a variety of advertising practices, and
he was the first, at least in France, to regroup several firms under a common direction. He succeeded in the seemingly impossible task of serving
the cause of the Enlightenment while at the same time remaining under the
protection of the government. A symbol of the ambiguity of the period, he
was a progressive who opposed revolution.

Having considered publishing for the elite, I would like to comment
briefly on the relationship of the uneducated classes to the book or, more
generally, the printed medium. This difficult problem was first studied by
Mandrou and since then has inspired some penetrating thought in the
works of Davis and Eisenstein.

We know for a fact that the modest printing shops of the kind I described earlier produced a multitude of small publications that are now
either lost or buried, uncataloged in libraries. Occasionally, some documents have allowed us to establish the existence of such publications. The
inventories of deceased bookseller-publishers of Troyes show that the
Bibliothèque bleue also contained some elementary school books, or rather
pamphlets, most of which have now disappeared. Reports of police investigations disclose that, over a long period of time, a quantity of tracts in
civilité type were printed north of the Loire. From a manuscript at the

Bibliothèque nationale we know that in the period preceding the Revolution small traditional works of devotion were published in great numbers
in Normandy and elsewhere.[40] Moreover, outlets for the sale of books,
such as haberdasheries, seem to have multiplied all over the French countryside as early as the sixteenth century. Studies still in progress also reveal
that the practice of peddling started much earlier than had been thought.
The early book peddlers, who were sometimes natives of the same village,
would follow identical routes year after year, carrying their wares of prints
and tracts.

In this light, what was novel about the eighteenth century was the increased rate of literacy.[41] An interesting document in this regard is the
account book of Pierre Héron, a bookseller-binder from Langres. Son of a
master cobbler from Dijon, Héron married Denise Diderot, the first cousin
of the *philosophe*. The lesser of two book dealers in Langres around 1770, he
often sent for works from Lyon and Paris to satisfy the demands of his
learned clientele. Among these works were a half-dozen copies at most of
the *Encyclopédie,* and hundreds, if not thousands, of theological and legal
treatises. Yet Héron's business actually was based on the sale of tens of
thousands of almanacs, Books of Hours, and devotional manuals, which he
received from Troyes, or from Neufchâteau, where about 100,000 copies of
L'Ange conducteur, a rather large and traditional prayer book, were printed.
Since the sixteenth century, the readers of this type of book had been the
master craftsmen, the notaries of market towns, the most educated of the
villagers, and the best of husbandmen.[42] One can well understand how they
might have grown weary of this traditional material and aspired to something new in the period preceding the Revolution.

To put the foregoing in a clearer perspective, it would be essential to
become better acquainted with the holdings of the numerous and geographically dispersed French libraries. Unfortunately, such a task cannot be
accomplished, for France suffers from a combination of ailments—its very
wealth of materials, its lack of the proper bibliographical spirit, a certain
indifference on the part of university officials toward the problem of cataloging, and a lack of specialization in its libraries. For my part, I dream of
the time when it will be possible to determine what has been printed in
certain major cities and to sort out this material with the help of the
computer. Also, it would be very interesting to determine the relative
importance of new editions and reprints in various periods. In spite of
recent publications, even the history of the literary trade remains to be
written in France. One can certainly dream of grand surveys that encompass all the authors of a given period, possibly along the lines of the
Dictionnaire des journalistes, edited by Jean Sgard. We have all read with the
greatest interest Darnton's monographs on some literary adventurers of the
end of the ancien régime. I would like to see the same kind of research

applied to the seventeenth century, my own area of specialization, for some similar characters were already influential at the end of the 1600s. Only then could we attempt a comparative history of publishing.

In the meantime, it would be of great interest to compare the histories of publishing in various countries during certain periods, such as the years 1645–1655, the period around 1700, and the Enlightenment. Eventually, comparative historical studies would identify similarities and differences in terms of the evolution of production, the regulation of the trade, and the plight of authors. Much work remains to be done, especially if we are to attempt to integrate into these studies developments in the all-important Latin countries of southern Europe.

NOTES

1. N. Z. Davis, *Les cultures du peuple; rituels, savoirs et résistances au 16ᵉ siècle* (Paris, 1979). I will not mention here those classics in the fields of communications that have contributed to the general direction of these reflections. Instead, I will cite only two French works that have directly influenced me: A. Moles, *Sociodynamique de la culture* (Paris, 1967); and J. Cazeneuve, *La société de l'ubiquité* (Paris, 1972).

2. H.-J. Martin, "Pour une histoire de la lecture," *Revue française d'histoire du livre*, no. 16 (1977): 583–609. Certain of the views expressed here will be elaborated upon in the book that I am preparing, *La civilisation écrite*.

3. I will cite only one example from the literature: A. de Bouard, *Manuel de diplomatique française et pontificale. I. Diplomatique générale* (Paris, 1929). For a later period, an apt characterization of the power of the scribe appears in A. Dumas, "L'action des secrétaires d'état sous l'Ancien Régime," *Annales de la Faculté de droit d'Aix-en-Provence*, N.S. vol. 67 (1954): 5–92. Obviously, one could vastly multiply such examples.

4. See, for example, J. Baudrillard, *Pour une critique de l'économie politique du signe* (Paris, 1972).

5. What I have attempted to put forth here has been shaped by analyses of the editorial functions of contemporary France. I have found particularly useful the work of J. Breton, *La littérature et le reste . . . Elements de bibliologie contemporaine* (Paris: École nationale supérieure de bibliothécaires, Centre de Paris, 1978), of which two fascicles have appeared. J. Breton is preparing a dissertation on this subject.

6. Breton, op. cit., fascicle I, chap. 2.

7. F. Barbier, *Trois cent ans de librairie et d'imprimerie. I. Berger-Levrault, 1676–1830* (Geneva, 1979); and F. Barbier, "Le monde du livre à Strasbourg de la fin de l'Ancien Régime à la chute de l'Alsace française," thesis of the third cycle, University of Paris, 1980. See also F. Barbier, *Histoire d'un imprimeur: Berger-Levrault, 1679–1976* (Paris, 1976).

8. The fact that the first presses so often began by printing liturgical works was not only a consequence of the demand for such works, based on orders from bishops and monasteries. It also reflects the fact that the liturgy, above all else, brought unity to the society. See, for example, Anselmo de Oliveira Soares, "Les origines de l'imprimerie au Portugal," thesis of the third cycle, University of Paris IV, 1980; and above all, R. Kevorkian, "Les débuts de l'imprimerie arménienne," thesis of the third cycle, University of Paris IV, 1980.

9. In addition to the classic *Gallia typographica* by G. Lepreux (Paris, 1909–1914), 10 vols., see, for example, L. Desgraves, *Étude sur l'imprimerie dans le Sud-Ouest de la France, aux XVᵉ et XVIᵉ siècles* (Amsterdam, 1968). The *Répertoire bibliographique des livres imprimés en France au XVIᵉ siècle* (Baden-Baden, 1968–) obviously can record only what has been passed down to us. It would, therefore, be of great interest to complete the record by studying documents in the archives about the printing shops. For the later period see also the thesis at the École nationale des chartes by Cl. Lannette-Claverie, "L'enquête de 1701 sur l'état de la librairie dans le royaume" (1964), in *École nationale des chartes, Positions des thèses soutenues par les élèves de la promotion de 1964* (Paris, 1964), pp. 77–84. See also the same author's "La librairie française en 1700," *Revue française d'histoire du livre*, no. 3 (1972): 3–43.

10. In addition to forthcoming publications by Jean Vezin, see the report of the research conferences of the École pratique des hautes études, IVᵉ section, in its *Annuaire 1977–78* (Paris, 1978), pp. 583–595. On the first efforts of the Parisian printers, see J. Veyrin-Forrer, *Aux origines de l'imprimerie française: L'atelier de la Sorbonne 1470–1473* (Paris, 1973), pp. 33–51; see also Dumas, op. cit.

11. Cl. Lannette-Claverie, "Les tours de France des imprimeurs et des libraires à la fin du XVIIᵉ siècle," *Revue française d'histoire du livre*, no. 6 (1973): 207–233.

12. See H.-J. Martin, *Livre, pouvoirs et société à Paris au XVIIᵉ siècle (1598–1701)*, Vol. 2 (Paris, 1969). We know that the "imprimeurs du Roi" were often large booksellers whom the authorities meant to favor.

13. On Le Breton, see M. A. Merland and J. Reyniers, "La fortune d'André-François Le Breton, imprimeur et libraire de l'Encyclopédie," *Revue française d'histoire du livre*, no. 22 (1979): 61–90.

14. H.-J. Martin, A. M. Lecocq, H. Carrier, and A. Sauvy, *Livres et lecteurs à Grenoble: les registres du libraire Nicolas 1645–1668*, 2 vols. (Geneva, 1977).

15. J. Mistler, *La Librairie Hachette* (Paris, 1964). One must regret that the author made little use of the account books of Hachette, for they existed then but have since been destroyed. Since that date, however, Hachette has established a model archival program and has been liberal in allowing researchers to consult its earlier contracts and records pertaining to pressruns since 1860. Among the first results of the use of such documents is C. Amalvi, *Les héros de l'histoire de France* (Paris, 1980), which contains part of a thesis at the École des chartes.

16. H.-J. Martin, "Le rôle de l'imprimerie lyonnaise dans le premier humanisme français," in Stage international d'études Humanistes, 14th, Tours, *L'humanisme français au début de la Renaissance* (Paris, 1973), pp. 81–91.

17. R. Chartier, "Livre et espace: circuits commerciaux et géographie culturelle de la librairie lyonnaise au XVIII^c siècle," *Revue française d'histoire du livre*, no. 1–2 (1971): 77–108.

18. Publication of the *Bibliographie des impressions parisiennes du XVIe siècle*, based on the notes of Philippe Renouard, is forthcoming. In the interim, see the papers of this scholar in the Réserve des imprimés of the Bibliothèque nationale. F. Marin has completed a revised biography of Jean Petit the Elder in an appendix to his thesis, "Jacques Kerver libraire parisien du XVI^c siècle, 1535–1585" at the École des chartes; see *Positions . . . 1980*, pp. 111–118; this work will be published in the future.

19. H.-J. Martin, *Livre pouvoirs et société,* and D. Pallier, *Recherches sur l'imprimerie à Paris pendant la Ligue (1585–1594)* (Paris, 1976).

20. For Germany, see *Mittelalterliche Bibliothekskataloge Deutschlands und der Schweiz,* 4 vols. (Munich, 1918–1979). In France, it seems that the Lyonnaise book-sellers often borrowed their texts from members of the entourage of the court of Savoy or the court of Moulins. The work of D. Coq, *Répertoire des livres en français publiés au XVe siècle,* should reveal more precise information upon its publication (1985?).

21. H.-J. Martin, "Culture écrite et culture orale, culture savante et culture populaire dans la France d'Ancien Régime," *Journal des savants* (1975): 225–282.

22. On the patronage of Chancellor Séguier, see Y. Nexon, "Le mécenat du chancelier Séguier; recherches sur un hôtel parisien au XVII^c siècle, l'activité d'un cercle littéraire et religieux et son influence," thesis, École des chartes, 1976; see *Positions . . . 1976,* pp. 121–130. See also S. Colnort-Bodet, "A travers les commensaux du chancelier Séguier: allégorie sur la théorie du mediateur," in *Actes du 100 congrès national des sociétés savantes, Paris, 1975, Section d'histoire moderne et contemporaine* (Paris, 1977), pp. 325–340.

23. D. Roche, *Le siècle des lumiéres en province: Académies et académiciens provinciaux (1680–1789),* 2 vols. (Paris, 1979).

24. Ira O. Wade, *The Clandestine Organization and Diffusion of Philosophical Ideas from 1700 to 1750* (Princeton, N.J., 1938).

25. There are multiple examples of this phenomenon, but I will cite only a few at random. On religious documentation, see, for example, the penetrating study of B. Neveu, "La vie érudite à Paris à la fin du XVII^c siècle d'après les papiers du P. Léonard de Sainte-Catherine (1695–1706)," *Bibliothèque de l'Ecole des chartes* 124 (1966): 432–511. The collections of Fontanieu, Morel de Thoisy, or Châtre de Cangé, which are kept in the Bibliothèque nationale, seem to be characteristic of the interests of "hauts fonctionnaires," but one could also mention in this regard the lawyer Moreau and the Administrative Library that he undertook to form for the Contrôle général des finances. Examples of the distribution of works in manuscript form are innumerable. See, for example, the introduction to Marguerite de Navarre, *L'Heptámeron,* ed. M. François (Paris, 1960); Bibliothèque nationale, *Malherbe et les poètes de son temps* (Paris, 1955); J. Lagny, "Sur un manuscrit contenant des oeuvres de Saint-Amant," *Revue d'histoire littéraire de la France* 78 (1978): 255–259 (note on a

manuscript of Conrart); Mme. de Lafayette, *Vie et oeuvre de la princesse Henriette d'Angleterre,* ed. M. Th. Hipp (Geneva, 1967); B. Petit, "La première version imprimée de la 'comtesse de Tende,'" *Revue d'histoire littéraire de la France* 72 (1972): 117–119; La Rochefoucauld, *Réflexions ou sentences et maximes morales,* ed. D. Secrétan (Geneva, 1967). It seems to me that systematic work in this area would be most valuable.

26. Cited in J. Monfrin, *Honoré Champion et sa librairie, 1874–1978* (Paris, 1978), pp. 32–33. My comments regarding Honoré Champion, whose papers are in the Archives de France, are based on Monfrin's study.

27. G. E. Reed, *Claude Barbin, libraire de Paris sous le règne de Louis XIV* (Geneva and Paris, 1974).

28. R. Darnton, "Trade in the Taboo: The Life of a Clandestine Book Dealer in Prerevolutionary France," in *The Widening Circle,* ed. Paul Korshin (Philadelphia, 1976), pp. 11–84.

29. C. M. G. Berkvens-Stevelinck, *Prosper Marchand et l'histoire du livre* (Bruges, 1978), pp. 44–77.

30. A Parmenie and C. Bonnier de la Chapelle, *Histoire d'un éditeur, P. J. Hetzel (Sthal)* (Paris, 1953); Bibliothèque nationale, *De Balzac à Jules Verne: un grand éditeur du XIXe siècle: P. J. Hetzel* (Paris, 1966); N. Petit, "Un éditeur au XIXe siècle: Pierre-Jules Hetzel (1814–1886) et les éditions Hetzel (1831–1914)," thesis of the École des chartes, 1980; see *Positions . . . 1980,* pp. 129–134.

31. The personal papers of Hetzel are now in the Bibliothèque nationale, but the archive of Librairie Hachette has a good part of the contracts.

32. A. Carter, M. Audin, and E. Vial, *Bibliographie des éditions des de Tournes, imprimeurs lyonnais,* 2 vols. (Paris, 1937–1938; reprinted, Geneva, 1971). On Dolet, we cite especially the recent book of Cl. Longeon, *Bibliographie des oeuvres d'Etienne Dolet, écrivain, éditeur et imprimeur* (Geneva, 1980). Claude Longeon insists correctly that the general privilege that François awarded to Dolet, doubtless at the instigation of Cardinal de Tournon, in fact deprived the theologians and the Parlement of their preventive censorship function. Although we do not know who the silent partner of Jean de Tournes was, we know for a fact that Dolet's partner, Héluin Dulin, was an ardent reformer. One wonders whether the establishment of the enterprises of Tournes and Dolet may have been aided by the attitude of their comrades, the journeymen printers of Lyons, who were then engaged in a struggle with their patrons.

33. R. Picard, *La carrière de Jean Racine* (Paris, 1956).

34. A. M. Bertrand, "Recherches sur l'édition et les milieux littéraires parisiens en 1644," thesis of the École des chartes, 1975; see *Positions . . . 1975,* pp. 11–14.

35. E. L. Eisenstein, *The Printing Press as an Agent of Change,* 2 vols. (Cambridge, 1979).

36. F. Furet, "La 'librairie' du royaume de France au 18e siècle," in *Livre et société dans la France du XVIIIe siècle* (Paris and La Haye, 1965–1970), Vol. 1, pp. 3–32.

37. M. Zephyr, "Les libraires et imprimeurs parisiens dans la seconde moitié du XVIIIe siècle (1750–1789)," thesis of the École des chartes, 1974; see *Positions* . . . *1974,* pp. 241–249.

38. Much remains to be done before we can understand French-language publishing of this period; see Robert Darnton, "Reading, Writing and Publishing in Eighteenth-Century France: A Case Study in the Sociology of Literature," *Daedalus* (1971): 214–256. Concerning the regulations of 1777, I have attempted to set the record straight in "La librairie française en 1778–1788," *Dix-huitième siècle* 11 (1979): 87–112.

39. H.-J. Martin, "Les bénédictins, leurs libraires et le pouvoir. Notes sur le financement de la recherche au temps de Mabillon et de Montfaucon," in *Mémorial du XIVe centenaire de l'abbaye de Saint-Germain-des-Prés* (Paris, 1959), pp. 273–287.

40. J. Brancolini and F. Bouissy, "La vie provinciale du livre à la fin de l'Ancien Régime," in *Livre et société dans la France du XVIIIe siècle* (Paris and La Haye, 1965–1970), Vol. II, pp. 3–35.

41. On peddling, see, in addition to footnote 38, M. Grivel, "Le commerce de l'estampe à Paris au XVIIe siècle," thesis of the École des chartes, 1980; see *Positions* . . . *1980,* pp. 81–90. See also A. Sauvy, "Noël Gilles dit La Pistole, 'marchand foirain libraire roulant par la France dans par la France,'" *Bulletin des bibliothèques de France* 12 (1967): 177–190. Anne Machet, in her doctoral thesis, "Censure et livres interdits à Venise dans la deuxième partie du dix-huitième siècle" (1978), gives information on "esclavons" peddlers who were tied to the "Bizoards" in the Besançon region, in the Mediterranean basin, and in South America.

42. On Pierre Héron, see M. Marsol, "Un oublié: Pierre Héron, 'marchant libraire' à Langres en Bassigny (1756–1776)," *Bulletin d'histoire moderne et contemporaine* 11 (1978): 33–74.

[3]   Printing the English Statutes, 1484–1640: Some Historical Implications

Katharine F. Pantzer

IN THE COURSE OF MY work on the revision of Pollard and Redgrave's *Short-Title Catalogue*[1] (STC), the relentless flow of the alphabet carried me in the spring of 1979 to letter *E,* where official and semiofficial publications are gathered under the heading "England." The quantity of entries here—nearly 10 percent of all STC entries—is rendered even more daunting by the intricacy of the texts and the variety of the sub-headings under which they are arranged. What preliminary reconnoiter-ing I had done through the years in checking lists of accession reports or sale catalogs had convinced me that the section of statutes was the most baffling and that it would be well to get it out of the way first. Although I have not yet completely extricated myself from their prickly grasp, in the effort to cope with the statutes I have amassed a good deal of material and come to some tentative conclusions that cannot be ac-commodated easily in STC itself, and these I share with you now. They are made from a bibliographer's point of view and primarily concern what was printed, when and why it was printed, why it took a particu-lar form, and similar matters. I shall unavoidably have to deal with occasional technical historical matters, and although I am quite sure my explanations will not be as accurate as a historian's would be, I hope they come close enough to provide a reasonable background for the points I wish to make about printing.[2]

The matters that came before Parliament for consideration were of two main kinds: public bills, which usually affected the country as a whole, and private bills, which sought to benefit localities, groups, or individuals, including bills introduced on behalf of the crown. If these were passed by both the House of Lords and the House of Commons and received the royal assent, they became public and private acts. Before 1490 acts determined to be public underwent a twofold transformation: "Petitioning formulae had to be removed or changed into enacting formulae, and the English petition had to be translated into the French of the statute."[3] As a result, the ultimate distinction of "public" up to this time was not so much the content of an act but its selection for transformation into law French, for only such acts formed the statute of the session and did not require special pleading in the law courts. From 1490 the essential distinction was no longer the language but rather the appearance of acts in print.[4] In this chapter I have used the term "statute" in its collective sense, meaning *all* the public acts of a session; individual acts are referred to as "acts."

Statutes are law and naturally of prime interest to lawyers. Indeed, the lawyers' interest was so strong that their specialized language, law French, was maintained as the language of statutes long after English had become the common tongue. Some possible effects of this language on the printing of statutes are discussed in section I below, with an analysis of the last three statutes in law French in Appendix A. In addition to their interest to lawyers, statutes are also relevant to administrators and to citizens. In time two basic forms of publication evolved. Lawyers and administrators needed something that could be kept for reference, and the statute of each session was printed for them in folio. The development of this book form is treated in section II and summarized in Appendixes B and C; it is complicated by the fact that certain acts—subsidies and pardons—usually received different treatment from the acts forming the main statute. For the general public initial notification was the overriding concern, and the printing of acts as broadsides, to be proclaimed and posted throughout the country, was the solution for a considerable portion of the period under study. What I have been able to gather about this form of publication is outlined in section II and Appendix D.

This whole early phase of statute printing, over a period of 157 years from 1484 through 1640, is somewhat clouded by the hazards of survival. In addition, the folios and broadsides that remain are essentially *silent* witnesses, and the testimony I have elicited from them may not be correct in all respects. Nevertheless, for other scholars to make a proper cross examination, it is necessary to summon as many witnesses as possible. Those assembled below make an interesting and occasionally curious group.

I

When was the first statute printed and why? Although "why?" may seem to be an unnecessary question, I hope before long to show that there is some justification for it. "When?" is a rather more straightforward question. The first to be printed was that of the only Parliament of Richard III, which was in session from 23 January to 22 February 1484.[5] It was printed in London by William de Machlinia probably not very long afterward. De Machlinia undoubtedly stemmed from Malines, or Mechlin, in the Low Countries, and he first comes to our notice in 1481 or 1482 in London, where he apparently began in partnership with John Lettou and later continued to print on his own. The staple of his presses was legal printing: Sir Thomas Littleton's work on land tenures, an abridgment of the statutes, a few yearbooks—that is, reports of law cases—from the late years of Henry VI's reign. These were all works of practical value to lawyers and were in the language that had been used for pleading in the law courts for more than 200 years and would continue to be used, except for a brief intermission from 1650 to 1660, again for more than 200 years: law French.[6]

Undoubtedly the reason for the choice of de Machlinia as printer of the statute of Richard III's Parliament was not so much that its text was law but that its language was this same law French. Figure 1 reproduces the first page. As is clear, the heading is in Latin, the rest in law French. While the ceremonial opening phrases can be made out without too much difficulty: "Richard, by the grace of God King of England and of France and lord of Ireland, third since the Conquest. . . ," the substance of the text beginning with chapter 1 is altogether more impenetrable and, in fact, would have been nearly as impenetrable to the ordinary citizen in 1484![7] For the interesting point is that the business of Parliament by this date— the bills submitted, the debates, and so on—was conducted in English. Indeed, so thoroughly does English permeate the scene by this time that the great historian of English law, W. S. Holdsworth, could say in 1923: "In Richard III's reign we get the first English statutes."[8] But those "first" English statutes are in law French, the official, operative language into which the English public acts were translated. Furthermore, the public acts passed by the first two Parliaments of Henry VII were also turned into law French. There is no evidence that either of these two statutes of Henry's was printed in law French, and my own feeling is that they were not. They were later eventually turned back into English, with some alteration and rearrangement from manuscript copies in law French, and printed by Caxton in 1490 along with the statute of Henry's third Parliament.

It is now time to explore the question of why Richard's statute was printed. The law texts that de Machlinia had printed previously were works

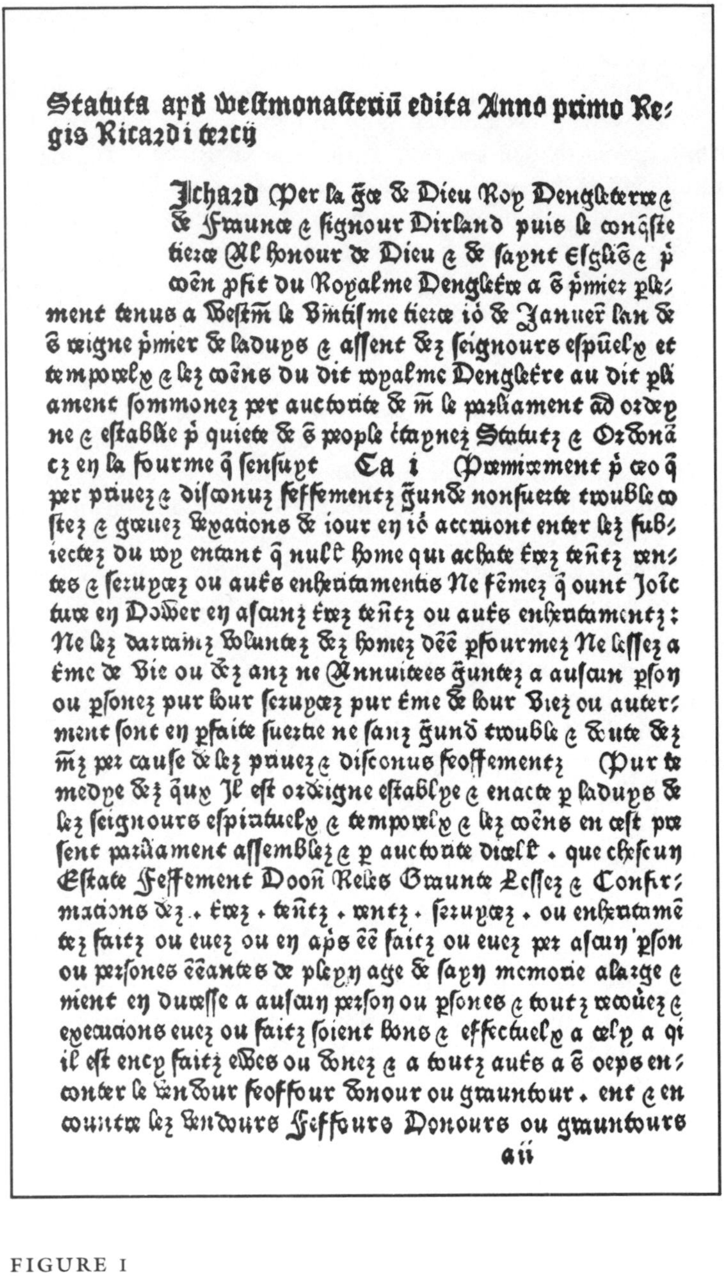

Statuta apð Weſtmonaſteriũ edita Anno primo Regis Ricardi tercij

Ichard Per la grꜩ ⁊ Dieu Roy Dengletꝛrꝛ ⁊ ⁊ Frauncꝛ ⁊ ſignour Dirland puis le conqſtꝛ tierꝛ Al honour ð Dieu ⁊ ⁊ ſaynt Eſgliſꝛ ⁊ p̄ wēn p̄fit du Royalme Dengletꝛ a ð p̄mier p̄lꝛment tenus a Weſtm̄ le Bñtiſme tierꝛ jo ⁊ Januer lan ð ð reigne p̄mier ð laduys ⁊ aſſent ðꜩ ſeignourꝛ eſp̄uelꝛ et temporelꝛ ⁊ leꜩ wēns du dit ropalme Dengletꝛe au dit p̄lament ſommoneꜩ per auctoritꝛ ⁊ m̄ le p̄rliament ꝺꝺ orðꝛne ⁊ eſtabliꝛ p̄ quietꝛ ⁊ ð people ꜩrapneꜩ Statutꜩ ⁊ Orðonã cꜩ en la fourme q̃ ſenſupt Ca i Pꝛrmixment p̄ cꝛo q̃ per priueꜩ ⁊ diſconuꜩ feffementꜩ ꝗ̃unꝺ nonſuertꝛ trouble co ſteꜩ ⁊ grꝛueꜩ ꝡꝛxaðons ⁊ iour en jo accruont enter leꜩ ſubꝛ iecteꜩ du roy entant q̃ nullꝛ home qui achatꝛ trꝛꜩ tñtꜩ rentꜩ ⁊ ſeruyꝛꜩ ou aurꝛs enꜩritamentis Ne fēmeꜩ q̃ ount Ioĩcturꝛ en Dowerꝛ en aſaunꜩ trꝛꜩ tñtꜩ ou aurꝛs enꜩritamentꜩ꞉ Ne leꜩ dartainꜩ ꝡolunteꜩ ðꜩ homeꜩ ðēē p̄fourmeꜩ Ne leſſeꜩ a ēmꝛ ð Bie ou ðꜩ anꜩ ne Annuiteꝛs ꝗ̃unteꜩ a auſain p̄ſon ou p̄ſoneꜩ pur lour ſeruyꝛꜩ pur ēmꝛ ⁊ lour Bieꜩ ou auterꝛ ment ſont en p̄faite ſuertꝛ ne ſanꜩ ꝗ̃unꝺ trouble ⁊ ꝡoutꝛ ðꜩ m̄ꜩ per cauſe ð leꜩ priueꜩ ⁊ diſconus feoffementꜩ Pur ꝛ medye ðꜩ ꝗ̃uy Il eſt orðigne eſtablye ⁊ enactꝛ p̄ laduys ð leꜩ ſeignourꝛ eſpirituelꝛ ⁊ temporelꝛ ⁊ leꜩ wēns en oeſt p̄r ſent p̄rliament aſſembleꜩ ⁊ p̄ auctorite dixlt ‧ que chꝛſcun Eſtatꝛ Feffement Doon Releꝛs Grauntꝛ Leſſeꜩ ⁊ Conſirꝛ maðons ðꜩ ‧ trꝛꜩ ‧ tñtꜩ ‧ rentꜩ ‧ ſeruyꝛꜩ ‧ ou enꜩritamē tꜩ faitꜩ ou eueꜩ ou en ap̄s ēē faitꜩ ou eueꜩ per aſaun p̄ſon ou p̄ſones ēēantꝛs ð plꝛpy agꝛ ⁊ ſapn memorie alarge ⁊ ment en durꝛſſe a auſain p̄ſon ou p̄ſoneꜩ ⁊ toutꜩ wcoũeꜩ ⁊ eperuðons eueꜩ ou faitꜩ ſoient bons ⁊ effectuelꝛ a œlp a ꝗi il eſt encp faitꜩ ewcs ou ꝺoneꜩ ⁊ a toutꜩ aurꝛs a ð oepꜩ en꞉ conter le ꝡenꝺour feoffour ꝺonour ou grauntour ‧ entꝛ ⁊ en counter leꜩ ꝡenꝺourꜩ Feffourꜩ Donourꜩ ou grauntourꜩ

a ij

FIGURE I

1 Ric. III (1484), Harvard Law School Library: Beale S96.
Type area: 21 × 12.5 cm.

by individual, although usually anonymous, authors or compilers and were intended for, and perhaps in part subsidized by, the legal profession. Joined by later legal publications, they ultimately became the body of literature covered by the law patent.[9] On the other hand, statutes were the work of Parliament, and the patent that eventually covered their printing was that of the King's Printer, whose duty it was to provide official texts for administrators and for the citizenry at large; these comprised at first statutes and proclamations, eventually Bibles, authorized liturgies, and occasional miscellaneous publications. Although it is sometimes treacherous to infer beginnings from later practice, it seems more likely than not that this difference between ordinary law texts and statutes was perceived even in 1484.

Indeed, early in the history of Parliament the necessity was recognized of disseminating statutes throughout the realm. This was done by sending a manuscript copy of the statute of the latest Parliament or session to the sheriff of each county, accompanied by a writ instructing him to proclaim it publicly in all the cities and towns, at quarter sessions, at markets and fairs, or on other occasions when people gathered together in numbers. Samples of writs issued in the years 1275, 1343, and 1362 are quoted in full in *Statutes of the Realm,* which also notes that the last writ of this sort entered on the statute rolls was in 1419.[10] Steele mentions others entered on the Parliament rolls in 1422, 1439, and 1449.[11] However, my untutored historical sallies have not turned up any recent commentary on this matter so that I am reduced to wondering: Did writs continue to be issued from 1449 to nearly the end of the fifteenth century that required the reading aloud of statutes in law French to a populace that, like Parliament itself, had come to conduct its ordinary affairs in English? Or, in spite of the fact that law French was the official language, was some kind of abridged version in English proclaimed?[12] Whether a definitive answer is possible, the matter of large-scale communication becomes vitally important when printing enters the scene.

Historians have generally considered the statute of Richard's Parliament to be beneficial and enlightened, although, as often happens with this enigmatic reign, there is dispute over whether Richard initiated any of the legislation himself. One recent historian maintains that "he was in no position to enact oppressive measures, even had he wished to do so."[13] Nevertheless, if the contents of the statute were favorable, it might well have seemed a useful tactic to disseminate copies speedily and widely by having them printed. But if this was the case, why not—at the beginning of a new reign—choose to have the statute in English, which would have made an impact on all literate men, rather than in law French, which was readable mainly by those with legal training?

If I have divined correctly one consideration in the printing of this statute—namely, the propaganda value of its contents—there may have been yet another consideration: the propaganda value of its language. At the time of Richard's Parliament, de Machlinia was perhaps just beginning work on the vast retrospective collection in law French called *Nova Statuta,* that is, statutes for the 157 years spanning the reigns of Edward III through Edward IV (1327–1483).[14] The size of *Nova Statuta*—185 sheets of paper per copy, by far the longest work de Machlinia ever printed—suggests it must have taken about a year to print. "Lxv bokes called the Newe Statutez" figured in a legal dispute that had come up twice in the London Sheriffs' Court before a request for a writ of certiorari was granted that removed the case to Chancery and assigned a hearing for the day after Ascension.[15] The only possible dates for this hearing during Richard's reign were 31 May 1484 and 16 May 1485. A request for certiorari usually received a quick response, but the length of time the case might have spent in the Sheriffs' Court is indeterminable. One could venture a guess that a minimum of three months elapsed between the date set for the hearing and the original dispute, which involved delivery of copies that were almost certainly bound volumes. A hearing date of 1485 seems plausible and also seems to find support in the appearance of some copies of *Nova Statuta,* in which the final quires show offset, show-through, and smudging from a poor quality of ink.[16] Such flaws are also evident in what may be de Machlinia's latest works.

In any event, perhaps printing Richard's statute in law French was intended as a means of demonstrating the continuity of his reign: The language of his statute was the same as that of statutes dating from the reign of Edward III. A similar desire to latch on to tradition may have influenced the decision to keep law French as the language of the statutes of Henry VII's first two Parliaments. By this time, however, it seems to have been realized that printing them had nothing extra to offer and that the traditional scribal bureaucracy could produce all the copies needed.[17]

George Painter has speculated that the reason the collection of the statutes of Henry's first three Parliaments (printed in 1490) was in English was that "Caxton not only lacked the specialist knowledge of law French, but possessed no type with the repertoire of special contractions which was considered necessary for such texts whether in manuscript or in print. Caxton was now the only printer in England; so, if Henry's laws were to be printed at all, they must be in English."[18] But de Machlinia was still in London in mid-June 1486,[**] more than three months following the dissolution of Henry's first Parliament on 4 March.[19] More to the point, special sorts were not actually necessary to print law French. The main font used for Richard's statute was cut by Johan Veldener and used by him and by Johannes Brito in the Low Countries.[20] De Machlinia used one extra abbreviation not found in Veldener or Brito works, a final *f,* for example, on b2^r line 6 of the statute, where "de*f*" means "defendant"; but since de Machlinia printed other law books in fonts without this abbreviation,[21] it cannot be considered a requisite for printing law French. As a result, I believe that Painter's statement must be turned around: It was the decision to have statutes in English that really made printing them worthwhile; printing Richard's statute in law French was an innovation that failed.[22]

In Appendix B are listed all known separate editions of statutes through Henry VII's reign. Although the dates of the fifteenth-century editions will require further refinement by Doctors Hellinga and Needham, it seems clear that no edition contemporary with the close of Parliament in 1492 and 1497 survives. These are both quite brief statutes, and earlier editions may have perished. On the other hand, Elton notes that the Exchequer MS., which otherwise follows printed editions, copies from the roll of Parliament for 7 Hen. VII and omits the statute of 12 Hen. VII,[23] so that if there were contemporary editions in 1492 and 1497, they were not readily obtainable by copyists. In addition to de Worde's separate editions of these two statutes, they also appear in Pynson's *Nova Statuta*,[24] probably completed about 1501, and in all later collected editions of Henry VII's statutes.

II

By Henry VIII's reign the public acts of Parliament were printed regularly. Nevertheless, when in 1587 Christopher Barker published the first comprehensive collection of statutes on continuous signatures, entitled "The whole volume of statutes at large, which at anie time heeretofore haue beene *extant in print,* since Magna Charta,"[25] he missed some printed items of Henry VIII's Parliaments because they had not originally been included in statutes and only gradually and somewhat erratically became joined to them. These comprised a third form of legislation, the grant of money to the king in the form of subsidies.

Subsidies came in three varieties. First was one that Barker did not miss: the subsidy of tonnage and poundage collected on imports and exports, usually granted for life during the first Parliament of a reign.[26] The first printed mention of this subsidy was actually in 6 Hen. VIII, c. 14, in 1515. Tonnage and poundage had been granted in 1510 by the first Parliament[27] but not printed in that year's statute. The later act states that the customs dues had not been collected and specifically stresses the forfeiture of goods for nonpayment. It is reasonable to infer that the 1515 act was passed so that it could be printed along with the other public acts of that year's session and thus become a matter of public record. In later reigns the tonnage and poundage subsidy appears in the statute of the first year.[28] A second subsidy, granted by the clergy separately in convocation, was afterward confirmed by Parliament. The earliest example of this subsidy is in 1540,[29] when it appears in the middle of the statute along with two other acts concerning crown revenues from the clergy. This example of the clerical subsidy is in Barker's reprint and also that of 1545; not included, however, is the subsidy of 1542, which was originally printed in a separate section with the final and most interesting of the subsidies, that of the temporalty or lay people—in short, taxes for everyone.

The subsidy of the temporalty was the one I found most mysterious in the statutes of Henry VIII. It usually was not mentioned in the STC entries or present in the copies examined, but when it did occur it was sometimes printed as a broadside and sometimes in folio format. In the latter form it was usually found bound with the main statute, but it could also turn up separately in an unrelated collection. The bibliographical difficulties of this act—not only in Henry VIII's reign but later—arise for two reasons. First, it had a limited duration of usually only a year or two, although sometimes it was more; and, second, the administration had a more particular and specialized interest in seeing that news of it got out, both to the people who were to pay the taxes and to those who were to collect them.

The earliest printed copies of the lay subsidy date from the second session of 1512 (4 Hen. VIII) and survive in such fragmentary pieces that it is impossible to tell how much earlier the practice of printing them began. Figure 2 shows the sad remains of the folio edition. Of the broadside edition the British Library has most of the first sheet (probably of four) of an edition on parchment. Section III and Appendix D discuss the broadside printing of acts, but for the moment we will concentrate on those "extras" that were printed in a form matching the traditional folio statute.

Appendix C provides a chart of significant collations of statutes between 1510 and 1640. Those for Henry VIII's sessions are particularly crucial in that they show the trend toward integration of the lay subsidies into the public and permanent record. First, some general remarks are in order. For the date of the session I have given only the beginning and end, ignoring in some cases adjournments or prorogations recorded in Powicke for Henry VIII.[30] For sessions through 1601 the table of acts appears on the verso of the title page. Beginning with 13 Eliz. (1571) there is also a table of "acts not printed," which sometimes appears at the end of the statute and sometimes below the table of acts printed. These "acts not printed" are, of course, all private acts. However, some bills promoted on behalf of individuals and still more for groups and localities are printed regularly among the "public" acts, possibly by payment of an extra fee.[31] Figure 3 shows that, in addition to three latecomers to the "public" sector, there are at least two that had been there from the first edition.

Also to be considered are the collations. For any one session I have given only collations with material differences, that is, where there is additional content or a significant variation from the position of previous content. I have not given collations where the difference is only a matter of fitting the same content into a smaller number of leaves, a process that happens not infrequently. In addition, the collations in the chart tend to obscure the number of editions of each session and the length of time during which they were reprinted. The sessions of Henry VIII, for example, were reprinted on separate signatures up to about 1575, after which they move into Christopher Barker's collection of 1587. Further information on editions and on their distinguishing features[32] will not generally be available prior to the publication of volume 1 of the STC revision itself, currently estimated for 1985.

Finally, with regard to the "extras," those items enclosed completely in square brackets (mainly **T**) indicate that no contemporary edition survives, although it is reasonable to suppose they were once printed. For these and other elusive or imperfect editions of extras, I either have cited the chapter number followed by an asterisk to indicate where the text can be found in *Statutes of the Realm* or, failing that, have given the present location in my discussion below. From Edward VI onward, chapter numbers cited refer to the contemporary tables of the respective statutes.[33] Where only chapter numbers are given in square brackets, for example, the lay subsidy and pardon of 32 Hen. VIII, the act itself has no number in its heading.

Now that the limitations of Appendix C have been made clear, we can investigate the trends it illustrates. First, the subsidy of the temporalty begins its life quite separately from the main statute, is not mentioned in its table, and survives, if at all, apart from it. The Harvard binding fragment of 4 Hen. VIII is reproduced in Figure 2. We shall come to the broadside printings of this subsidy and the one of 7 Hen. VIII later.[34] The first complete surviving folio subsidy dates from 1534, 26 Hen. VIII, at the Public Record Office in London (SP 1/86, ff. 161–170).[35] In 1540 the lay subsidy is mentioned in the table for one edition, and from then on—at least in its most common form[36]—it stands a better chance for survival.

No edition of 34 & 35 Hen. VIII mentions either of the subsidies or the act for Wales in the table, although all copies of these "extras" that I know of are bound with the main statute and, in later editions, even become linked to it by signatures. A very fine and clever point is worth mentioning here: in spite of the continuous signatures, the sections—or "elements," as I tend to call them—are separately quired so that anyone who chose to dispense with the subsidies upon their expiration could do so without damaging the remaining sections. This arrangement, born of a practical acumen that was sometimes missing in later King's and Queen's Printers, was the invention of Thomas Berthelet, who served admirably as King's Printer from his appointment in 1530 to his ouster in 1547, when Richard Grafton took over the office under Edward VI.

The position of the subsidy of the clergy is not quite so clear. Twice it turns up with the main statute, in 32 and in 37 Hen. VIII, and once with the

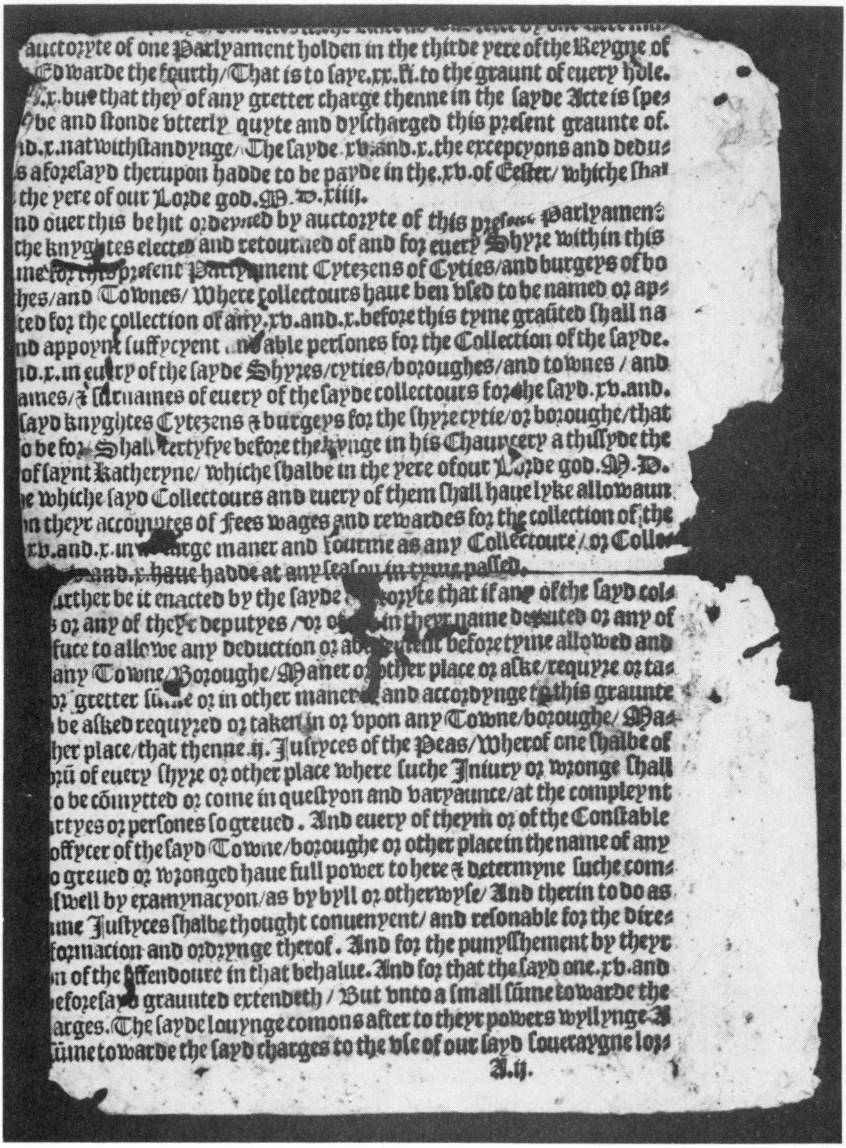
auctorytye of one Parlyament holden in the thirde yere of the Reygne of
Edwarde the fourth/That is to saye.xx.li.to the graunt of euery hole.
.x.bue that they of any gretter charge thenne in the sayde Acte is spe
be and stonde vtterly quyte and dyscharged this present graunte of.
nd.x.natwithstandynge/The sayde.xv.and.x.the excepcyons and dedu
s aforesayd therupon hadde to be payde in the.xv.of Ester/ whiche sha
the yere of our Lorde god.M.D.xiiij.
nd ouer this be hit ordeyned by auctorytye of this present Parlyament
the knyghtes electe and retourned of and for euery Shyre within this
me for this present Parlyament Cytezens of Cyties/and burgeys of bo
hes/and Townes/ Where collectours haue ben vsed to be named or ap
ted for the collection of any.xv.and.x.before this tyme graunted shall na
nd appoynt suffycyent and able persones for the Collection of the sayde.
nd.x.in euery of the sayde Shyres/cyties/boroughes/and townes / and
ames/ & surnames of euery of the sayde collectours for the sayd.xv.and.
sayd knyghtes Cytezens & burgeys for the shyre cytie/or boroughe/that
o be for Shall certyfye before the kynge in his Chauncery a thisyde the
of saynt Katheryne/ whiche shalbe in the yere of our Lorde god.M.D.
e whiche sayd Collectours and euery of them shall haue lyke allowaun
n theyr accomptes of Fees wages and rewardes for the collection of the
xv.and.x.in lyke maner and fourme as any Collectoure/or Colle
and.x.haue hadde at any season in tyme passed.
urther be it enacted by the sayde auctoryte that if any of the sayd col
s or any of theyr deputyes /or o[illegible] in theyr name deputed or any of
fuce to allowe any deduction or a[illegible] before tyme allowed and
any Towne/Boroughe/Maner or other place or aske/requyre or ta
or gretter summe or in other maner and accordynge to this graunte
be asked requyred or taken in or vpon any Towne/boroughe/ Ma
her place/that thenne.ij.Justyces of the Peas/Wherof one shalbe of
rum of euery shyre or other place where suche Iniury or wronge shall
o be comytted or come in questyon and varyaunce/at the compleynt
rtyes or persones so greued. And euery of theym or of the Constable
offycer of the sayd Towne/boroughe or other place in the name of any
o greued or wronged haue full power to here & determyne suche com
swell by examynacyon/as by byll or otherwyse/ And therin to do as
me Justyces shalbe thought conuenyent/ and resonable for the dire
formacion and ordrynge therof. And for the punysshement by theyr
n of the offendoure in that behalue. And for that the sayd one.xv.and
efore sayd graunted extendeth / But vnto a small summe towarde the
arges. The sayde louynge comons after to theyr powers wyllynge A
summe towarde the sayd charges to the vse of our sayd souerayne lor
A.ij.

FIGURE 2

4 Hen. VIII, lay subsidy (1512), Houghton Library, Harvard University: STC 9361.4.
Type area: 19.4 × 12.3 cm.

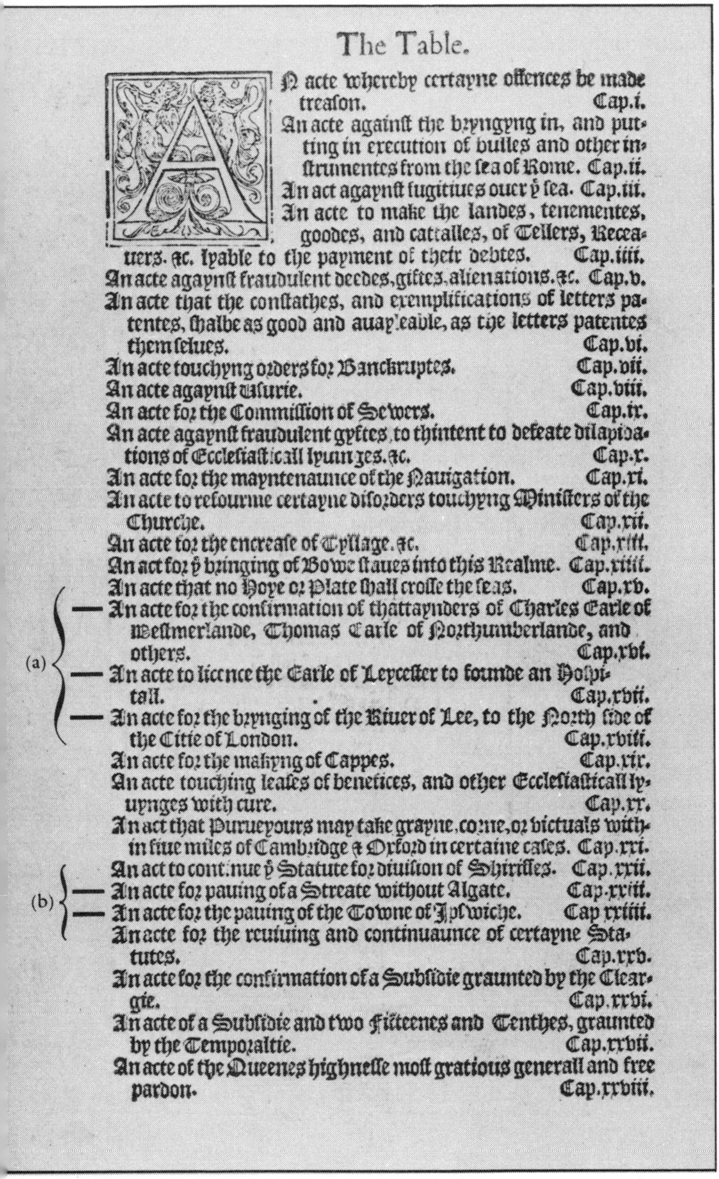

The Table.

An acte whereby certayne offences be made
treason. Cap.i.
An acte againſt the bꝛyngyng in, and putting in execution of bulles and other in-
ſtrumentes from the ſea of Rome. Cap.ii.
An act agaynſt fugitiues ouer ẏ ſea. Cap.iii.
An acte to make the landes, tenementes,
goodes, and cattalles, of Ceſſers, Recea-
uers. ꝛc. lyable to the payment of their debtes. Cap.iiii.
An acte agaynſt fraudulent deedes, giftes, alienations. ꝛc. Cap.v.
An acte that the conſtathes, and exemplifications of letters pa-
tentes, ſhalbe as good and auayleable, as the letters patentes
themſelues. Cap.vi.
An acte touchyng oꝛders foꝛ Banckruptes. Cap.vii.
An acte agaynſt Uſurie. Cap.viii.
An acte foꝛ the Commiſſion of Sewers. Cap.ix.
An acte agaynſt fraudulent gyftes, to thintent to defeate dilapida-
tions of Eccleſiaſticall lyuinges. ꝛc. Cap.x.
An acte foꝛ the mayntenaunce of the Nauigation. Cap.xi.
An acte to refourme certayne diſoꝛders touchyng Miniſters of the
Churche. Cap.xii.
An acte foꝛ the encreaſe of Tyllage. ꝛc. Cap.xiii.
An act foꝛ ẏ bꝛinging of Bowe ſtaues into this Realme. Cap.xiiii.
An acte that no Hoye oꝛ Plate ſhall croſſe the ſeas. Cap.xv.
An acte foꝛ the confirmation of thattaynders of Charles Earle of
Weſtmerlande, Thomas Earle of Noꝛthumberlande, and
others. Cap.xvi.
(a) An acte to licence the Earle of Leyceſter to founde an Hoſpi-
tall. Cap.xvii.
An acte foꝛ the bꝛynging of the Riuer of Lee, to the Noꝛth ſide of
the Citie of London. Cap.xviii.
An acte foꝛ the makyng of Cappes. Cap.xix.
An acte touching leaſes of benefices, and other Eccleſiaſticall ly-
uynges with cure. Cap.xx.
An act that Purueyours may take grayne, coꝛne, oꝛ victuals within fiue miles of Cambꝛidge ꝓ Oxfoꝛd in certaine caſes. Cap.xxi.
An act to continue ẏ Statute foꝛ diuiſion of Shiriſſes. Cap.xxii.
(b) An acte foꝛ pauing of a Streate without Algate. Cap.xxiii.
An acte foꝛ the pauing of the Towne of Jpſwiche. Cap xxiiii.
An acte foꝛ the reuiuing and continuaunce of certayne Sta-
tutes. Cap.xxv.
An acte foꝛ the confirmation of a Subſidie graunted by the Clear-
gie. Cap.xxvi.
An acte of a Subſidie and two Fiſteenes and Tenthes, graunted
by the Tempoꝛaltie. Cap.xxvii.
An acte of the Queenes highneſſe moſt gratious generall and free
pardon. Cap.xxviii.

FIGURE 3

13 Eliz. I (1571), Harvard Law School Library: Beale S290.
Type area: 23.3 × 11.8 cm. In the first two editions (a) were cc. 1, 8, 16
of the "acts not printed"; (b) were cc. 20, 21 of the acts printed.

lay subsidy, in 34 & 35 Hen. VIII. Perhaps Berthelet was still experimenting with the printing requirements of a relatively new tax. Possibly more copies were needed of that subsidy than of the main statute but considerably fewer than of the lay subsidy. Nevertheless, the gravitation of the clerical subsidy toward the end of the statute is quite evident.

Just as subsidies were granted by Parliament and by the clergy, pardons were granted by the king. Some pardons were issued simply by royal proclamation, but others became acts of Parliament. The latter, with the three exceptions noted for 22 and 23 Hen. VIII, were usually termed "free and general" pardons. These could be granted, of course, only when Parliament was in session, whereas proclamations could be used more flexibly—both in terms of the time they were issued and the offense they pardoned. There may well be further distinctions between statutory and proclamatory pardons, but my primary concern as a bibliographer rests with the physical object embodying such pardons. In the course of my work on the statutes, I first noticed the pardons as separate elements, for example, in the earliest collation for 32 Hen. VIII and the earliest collation for 1 Edw. VI. My subsequent research led me to reexamine the main statute to find earlier examples. Though not all of the pardons may be in my chart, there is a clear trend toward moving them from the end of the main statute to the end of all the acts printed. This final position very likely reflects the fact that the pardon was the last bill brought before Parliament, at the final meeting of the session.[37] Furthermore, the pardon was functionally associated with the subsidies because it, too, was in force only for a limited duration. Here again is a kind of act that might be dispensed with later.

Before we leave Henry VIII, mention should be made of the anomalous "extras," which I have called "Revenues" and "Wales." The revenue acts concern income from the king's own lands and tenants, and were private acts on behalf of the crown. The revenue act of 1515 survives in a collection of statutes of Henry VII and early Henry VIII belonging to Peterborough Cathedral and currently on deposit at Cambridge University Library (Pet.F.1.19[7]). An edition of the revenue act of 1523 printed at that time has not come to light, but the act was revived verbatim in 1536 and made perpetual. A copy of this last printing, at Dulwich College, near London, is included at the end of a copy of *The great boke of statutes*.[38] As you can see from the collations, these revenue acts, especially the earliest one, are fairly long.

The revenue act of 1515 may have been the subject of a somewhat baffling record of payment to Richard Pynson, who was King's Printer during the first part of Henry VIII's reign. The payment occurred in May 1517 and was for "printing books concerning the subsidy, £31 13s. 4d."[39] "Books" clearly refers to items in folio. The cost was enormous; for comparison, in December 1515 Pynson was paid £18 for printing all these: "100 parchment skins ınd 125 leaves [that is, sheets or broadsides] of paper of the last subsidy, ınd for printing the statutes." The session of 7 Hen. VIII ended with the lissolution of Parliament on 22 December 1515; perhaps the payment to ?ynson that month was for 6 Hen. VIII, which had been prorogued on 5 April 1515. The difference in the number of sheets printed for the two ;essions of 1515 is not that great except for the revenue act. Although the ;17 payment specifies "subsidy," does it include the main statute, the lay ;ubsidy, and the revenue act?[40] In any case, having the revenue acts printed vas considered a necessity, as the text of all three acts specified that they be ›rinted.

What I have called "Wales" in 34 & 35 Hen. VIII consists of an act :stablishing political, judicial, and administrative jurisdictions there. This nust also have been a crown act; it is listed in another document that :ouches upon statute printing, Berthelet's accounts for items bought or ›ound for the king or printed for the crown, for the period 9 December 1541 :hrough 12 June 1543.[41] On 31 May 1543—19 days after the prorogation of Parliament—Berthelet delivered to Chancery "ffourtie bookes of the Acte 'or certeyne ordenaunces in the kinges Majesties Domynion and principalitie ›f Wales, at iiij^d the pece. Summa xiij^s iiij^d."[42] It may be that the act was ›riginally printed only for distribution in Wales; at least it does not appear in :he unique copy of one early edition of the statute for 1543 (British Library: C.64.e.10(5)). This last fact led me to think that this edition of the main ;tatute was the earliest. For once "Wales" was in print, it kept being re-›rinted and was gradually moved into the main statute, thus becoming a "public" act in all but chapter number and mention in the table.

Having finished with Henry VIII's reign as far as Appendix C is con-:erned, we can now look at the succeeding reigns more briefly. There were 10 lay or clerical subsidies in Edward VI's first Parliament in 1547, although 1e was granted the usual tonnage and poundage for life. His pardon this /ear starts as a separate element without chapter number in its heading, but n the fifth edition of this session, which was printed probably about 1550, it oins the main statute and acquires the words "The .xv. Chapiter" in its 1eading.

In the next session, 2 & 3 Edw. VI, we can see the problems that arise vhen an unwary printer, Richard Grafton in this instance, does not allow 'or what I shall call the "throw-it-away syndrome." Grafton started out by ›rinting the lay subsidy separately and without chapter number for early listribution. Apparently by the time he had got to the pardon, which was ›rinted in a quire signed "d," two more acts had come up for inclusion.[43] One of these was almost certainly a genuinely public act from the begin-1ing because it increased the penalties and forfeitures specified in a previ-›us public act, 33 Hen. VIII, c.7, which was intended to prevent the export ›f certain metals. Perhaps in the mass of legislation in 1549 this first addi-

tional act was originally overlooked. The other latecomer, an act concern
ing the paving of the streets of Calais (still English territory then) is clearly
a private act made "public" at the last minute. At first these two acts were
appended to the pardon, as chapters 38 and 39, respectively. In the second
edition of the statute, which has the second collation in the chart and end
with quire M, the two acts have been moved in front of the pardon
becoming thereby chapters 37 and 38. A volume of statutes at Lincoln's Inr
contains virtually no pardons and sometimes no subsidies; presumably
both were removed at the time the individual sessions were first bound in a
collected volume and possibly they had been in some kind of temporary
bindings until then. In any case, when the owner decided to discard the lay
subsidy and the pardon, not only did the binder have to remove one leaf o
quire H but he also threw away the two unlucky and unnoticed acts tha
were between this subsidy and the pardon! Grafton was not quite thi
clumsy again.

The session of 3 & 4 Edw. VI, which lasted from 4 November 1549 to
February 1550, also granted a subsidy, but it was to be paid the following
year. The common form of the subsidy runs from D6^v to E3^r of the mair
statute, the colophon of which is dated February 1549 (old style, i.e., 1550)
The separate printing of the subsidy at the British Library that I mentioned
earlier[44] is dated 1551 and gives us the one surviving and identifiable example
of a subsidy issued separately after its inclusion in the main statute.[45]

The other two "extras" of 3 & 4 Edw. VI are even more interesting. The
separate folio edition of c.5, a statute barring unlawful assemblies, survives
at Corpus Christi College, Oxford, in two imperfect copies removed from a
binding. This edition was almost certainly not intended for perusal by
potential lawbreakers, for they would have had a broadside to look at. My
guess is that the folio act was meant for law enforcement officials whc
were of too humble a rank to need the complete statute and for whom a
slim folio would have been ideal for ready reference. "Chester" is so choice
and rare a curiosity that I have reproduced its first page as Figure 4. It is
the only act in folio I know of that was printed and yet remained a com
pletely "private" act.[46] The good mayor and aldermen of Chester made a
handsome though belated effort. They had their act printed by Grafton and
assigned a chapter number and pagination continuous with the main stat
ute. Circulation, however, was limited; the only surviving copy, bound
with the fourth edition of the statute, undoubtedly must have come from a
volume of Chester provenance!

In Mary I's reign John Cawood became Queen's Printer. The peculiar
and marked bibliographical rigidity of her statutes allows only for genera
comment. The subsidies were printed always on continuous signatures
although there must have been separate printings of at least the lay subsidy
which have entirely disappeared.[47] The folio subsidies tended to begin no

EDVARDI. VI. Fol.xxxiii,

¶An Acte, concernyng the citee of Chester, foz weares in the riuer of Dee.
¶The.xxb.Chapiter.

A moste humble wise, sheweth vnto pour royall maiestie,pour true faithful and obedient subiectes,the Maioz, Aldermen,Sherifes, Commonaltie, and Inhabitantes of pour graces citee of Chester:that where thesaid citee,is one of the auncientest Citees within pour realme, wherebp the tounes and contrees adioynyng, haue heretofoze had greate relief, commoditie, and pzofite, and is the chief kepe & defence in thofe partes,to furnish and serue pour grace in all pour affaires,and weightie businesse,into pour realme of Irelande and Scotlande, and hath no other aide oz helpe, wherebp thesaied citee is chiefly maintemed, but by the riuer of Dee,turnyng and commyng to thesaid citee , and the hauen there very shalowe and daungerous foz all shippes and vesselles , to repaire and come vnto thesaied citee,so that afwell the inhabitantes of thesame, as also straungers at this daie, with their wares and merchaundifes do not trade oz haue recourse there,as thei heretofoze wer accustomed to do, to the greate detriment of thesame. And forasmuche as diuerse persones hauyng landes adioynyng to thesame riuer of Dee,foz their pziuate lucre and commoditie,not regardyng the common weale of the whole coūtreis and citizeins, haue heretofoze made,reared, and caufed to bee fixed and set vp,in,and cleane ouer thesaied riuer of Dee, sondzie weares,goates greate hedges,piles,gates,fishe gates,nettes,and other ingines,foz takyng of fishe within thesaid riuer,and still do pzeserue,kepe,& mainteīn thesame:Bp reason wherof,the merchauntes,and other enhabitantes of thesaied citee,cannot haue recourse,ne liberall and direct passage, in,and vpon thesaied riuer,with their Cogges,krelles,Boates,fleutes, of buildyng timber,fewell,and other timber foz makyng of shippes,and vesselles foz the conueighyng and bzyngyng of thesame. and other their wares and merchaundizes bp water,in, to, and from the maine lande oz countrey, neither also the inhabitantes of the countrey there, can conueniently haue anp passage to conueigh, come , oz bzyng bp water, vp, oz doune,to,oz from thesaied citee, anp fewell,timber,cozne,oz other thyng necessarp to serue thesaied citee , but onelp bp lande , bp the whiche their trauell and recourse, bp lande to the markettes,faires, and all other tymes,the high waies and lanes, are not onelp so foule and deape, that no persone in the winter tyme,can easelp escape the anopance and daungier

a.j. therof

FIGURE 4

3 & 4 Edw. VI (1550), Act for Chester, colophon dated 1551.
Harvard Law School Library: bound with Beale S226b.
Type area: 22 × 12.8 cm.

merely mid-quire but usually mid-page. Possibly as a result, none of the copies of any of Mary's statutes that I have seen or had reports on suffers from the "throw-it-away syndrome." Did individualistic English owners find this frustrating? Or did they simply ignore the subsidies as they did many other Marian acts no longer in force? Finally, none of her sessions has a pardon. She even seems to have been fairly sparse with proclamations of pardon, since only three were recorded during her reign and all of them are known only in manuscript.[48]

Upon the accession of Elizabeth I, Richard Jugge was appointed Queen's Printer and soon took Cawood on as partner. Perhaps it was Jugge who decided to reinstate separate elements, at first only for the lay subsidy. There was no clerical subsidy or pardon in her first session, but in the next, 5 Eliz., Cawood may have had a hand in the printing since these two acts appear on continuous signatures with the main statute, and both begin mid-page. Even so, in contrast to copies of Mary's sessions, at least two statute volumes, at Westminster Abbey and the Huntington Library, display the "throw-it-away syndrome" in this session, with the clerical subsidy beginning on L4^v but all lacking thereafter. For 8 Eliz. both volumes retain the clerical subsidy so that the ravages of the syndrome were not so brutal. But in this session the pardon posed minor problems. At first it was signed to follow the clerical subsidy, but it was numbered and usually bound (in later editions also signed) as the final quire. Finally, in 13 Eliz. the two subsidies and the pardon took on a characteristic "triplet" form, at first as quite separate elements and in later editions still separable. The cadence of Clergy, Temporalty, and Pardon became so firmly established during her reign that I tend to think of it as a bibliographical "Dresden Amen"! Elizabeth was generous with her pardons, and her clerical and lay subjects were marshalled into generosity with their subsidies.

In spite of the regularity of the triplet's occurrence in Elizabeth's statutes, it was still possible for the printer to make miscalculations in the printing. As one might expect, the first miscalculation was made by a fairly new Queen's Printer. Following Jugge's death in 1577, Christopher Barker obtained the reversion of the patent and initiated the feature of having the lay subsidy on a double register (the alphabetical sequence of signatures beginning again with two letters, Aa-Cc^6 Dd^2 in this case of the first session he printed, 23 Eliz.). He got through that session all right because the clerical subsidy, although on continuous signatures with the main statute, was separately quired. Apparently this separate quiring was a happy accident, for four years later he or his shop foreman had forgotten its significance and began the clerical subsidy mid-quire in the main statute of 27 Eliz. Alas, in the Huntington Library volume this session lacks everything after H2, and H1 and H2 are separate leaves, a circumstance that poses the binder an entirely unnecessary albeit minor problem. In this statute the pardon joins the lay subsidy in the double register but remains separately quired.

The statutes of Elizabeth's last two Parliaments are of particular interest because the printer made a revealing miscalculation in 39 Eliz. and adopted an adroit maneuver for 43 Eliz. when the same thing happened again. Christopher Barker had retired in 1588 but retained his patent so that the 1598 imprint now reads "Deputies of C. Barker." This year the decision must have been made fairly early to put the clerical subsidy in the double register also. By now the order of the subsidies was firmly established: clerical before lay. Possibly the clerical subsidy was late in being formulated, or the lay subsidy was agreed to early,[49] because Barker's deputies started printing it on Bb1. When the text of the clerical subsidy did finally arrive, it turned out to be much longer than they had estimated and filled up not just six leaves or even eight, but nine. The solution finally chosen was rather inept, since it involved beginning the reprint of the lay subsidy on Bb4, but presumably the deputies thought that everyone would want the whole of that year's statute. This, however, was not universally the case. The first owners of at least this session of the two statute volumes at the Pepysian and Lambeth Palace libraries[50] were men who had acquired early editions of the lay subsidy and had no desire for the sheets of quires Cc-Ee in the normal printing of the triplet.[51] In both volumes Bb4-6 is cancelled, the early form of the subsidy is bound in place of the later one, and then both finish off with the normal pardon.

By the next Parliament, in 1601, Christopher Barker had died and his son Robert had succeeded to the patent. Perhaps Robert was cleverer than the deputies, or possibly word of customers' and booksellers' dissatisfaction had filtered back to the printing house. Whatever the reason, when in 1601 the clerical subsidy again turned out to be unexpectedly long, the overflow was printed on a quire signed "aa." As a result, the elements of the triplet were once again separable, and flexibility in the all-important matter of the lay subsidy was restored.

Under the Stuart kings, the pattern of printed statutes so thoroughly established in Elizabeth's reign began to break down. The number of sessions given in parentheses in Appendix C are the effectual sessions, i.e., those producing acts that were printed. There were other sessions that produced a great deal of wrangling but no acts. And even effectual sessions lost the old rhythm. Two statutes of James I, in 1604 and 1607, contain no subsidies or pardons; however, the statute of 1606 is more traditional in appearance and content.

In 1621 only the two subsidies passed both houses and received the royal assent. In the early nineteenth century the editors of *Statutes of the Realm* could find no text, whether printed or manuscript,[52] of the subsidies, and as late as December 1978 the typescript of the STC revision did not include them. The first to turn up, the lay subsidy, was found in a volume of James I's statutes at Lincoln's Inn by Anthony C. Taussig, a barrister in London and one of the few lawyers I know who collect law. He had had difficulty identifying editions of statutes in his own collection and, after I had sent him a copy of the old typescript of this section, he reported to me not only his own holdings but also those at Lincoln's Inn and a good portion of those at the British Library. He also turned up a second copy of the lay subsidy at the Public Record Office (SP 45/65, ff. 122–140). In March 1979 I examined the remainder of the STC statutes at the British Library, including the Elizabethan and later volumes in its Official Publications Library. To my astonishment I found both subsidies in the James I volume: BS.Ref.3, vol. 8. The work of cataloging them had been done some time ago because the pencilled "K" and entry heading were present, but no entry had been added to the general catalog. These two elusive acts of 1621 now have their rightful place in STC.

For James's last Parliament, in 1624, the main statute reappeared and there was a complete triplet; however, under Charles I disintegration set in again. In neither the effectual session of 1625 nor that of 1628 was there a pardon, and public acts other than subsidies declined to five for each session. In the Parliament beginning 3 November 1640, which came to be known as the "Long Parliament," the first act passed and given royal assent was printed by itself without title page (also discovered at Lincoln's Inn by Taussig); it was shortly after reprinted with another act and a title page dated 1640. Thus, at the very end of the period now under consideration, a new historical situation brought about a new procedure in statute printing: Henceforth the statutes were printed act by act as Parliament and king could bring themselves to reluctant agreement.

III

It is now time to consider that facet of statutes that was restored by their being in English: their proclamation. The last writ for the proclamation of statutes found by Steele during the period of statutes in law French was in 1449.[53] The next writ of this kind cited by Steele was printed along with the statute of Henry VII's last Parliament, in 1504.[54] This statute was printed by the first man to have the title of King's Printer, William Faques. Unfortunately, Faques died not long after, and the only official work to his credit other than the statute is a royal proclamation of 5 July 1504 on coinage.[55]

The writ printed in the statute is a matter of some bewilderment. The normal practice was for such writs to be written out individually by the clerks of Chancery on separate pieces of parchment. Thus the printed writ in the statute may have had no validity, and Faques possibly included it by mistake. The second puzzling feature of the printed writ is that it was addressed to the sheriff of Essex. Did Faques receive—and only temporarily have as printer's copy—the manuscript copy of the statute destined to be sent on to the sheriff of Essex for proclaiming? Were manuscript copies sent out with writs to all the sheriffs at the time Faques was printing his edition in folio? What exactly was the relationship of manuscript and printed statutes at this time?[56] Whatever significance Faques's printed writ may ultimately yield, however, it seems there is fair reason to doubt that this statute was read aloud in its entirety. The reason, of course, no longer is the language of the statute; the new reason is its length. Faques's edition had 24 leaves and would probably have required a good hour or more to proclaim.[57]

In any case, what developed in Henry VIII's reign—the earliest surviving trace dating from 1512—was a shift in the meaning of "proclaiming the statute" from an aural form to a particular visible form; that is, acts were printed as broadsides that could be fixed to posts and billboards.[58] In Appendix D are listed all the examples and references that have so far come to my attention concerning acts printed as broadsides.[59] The earliest ones are lay subsidies printed on parchment. I am not sure I have correctly identified the item for which Pynson received payment in March 1515, but it is obviously not a subsidy. The first clear instance of the publication of an ordinary public act in broadside form dates from 1529; it and others that survive from the following sessions are of such a heterogeneous nature as to imply that the practice revealed by Berthelet's accounts for 1542 and 1543 in such admirable detail was in full swing by 1529.

The act reproduced as Figure 5, 34 & 35 Hen. VIII, c.6, is typical in all respects except for its brevity. Since it is listed in Berthelet's accounts, we know that he delivered 500 copies and that they were printed on halfsheets of paper smaller than that used for some of the other acts; each copy cost a farthing, for a total cost of 10^s 5^d.[60] However, the most important feature is that, like the majority of separate subsidies and pardons in folio, the printing of which generally preceded that of the main statute, the 1543 broadside act has no chapter number. The word "Acte" in the heading is sufficient to identify it as having parliamentary authority. No regnal year or sovereign is mentioned because it would be perfectly obvious to everyone what session had just ended. All the other broadside acts in Appendix D look very much the same through at least 1558.

In 1542 Parliament was prorogued on 1 April. Nineteen days later, on 20 April, Berthelet delivered to Chancery broadside printings, described as "Actes . . . printed in proclamacons,"[61] of the first 19 of the 39 public acts of that session. Although Berthelet's records are continuous until after the close of the next session, there is nothing about delivery of broadside printings of acts 20–39. Because of the superior quality of Berthelet's accounts, we must infer that he printed no more broadside acts of the 1542

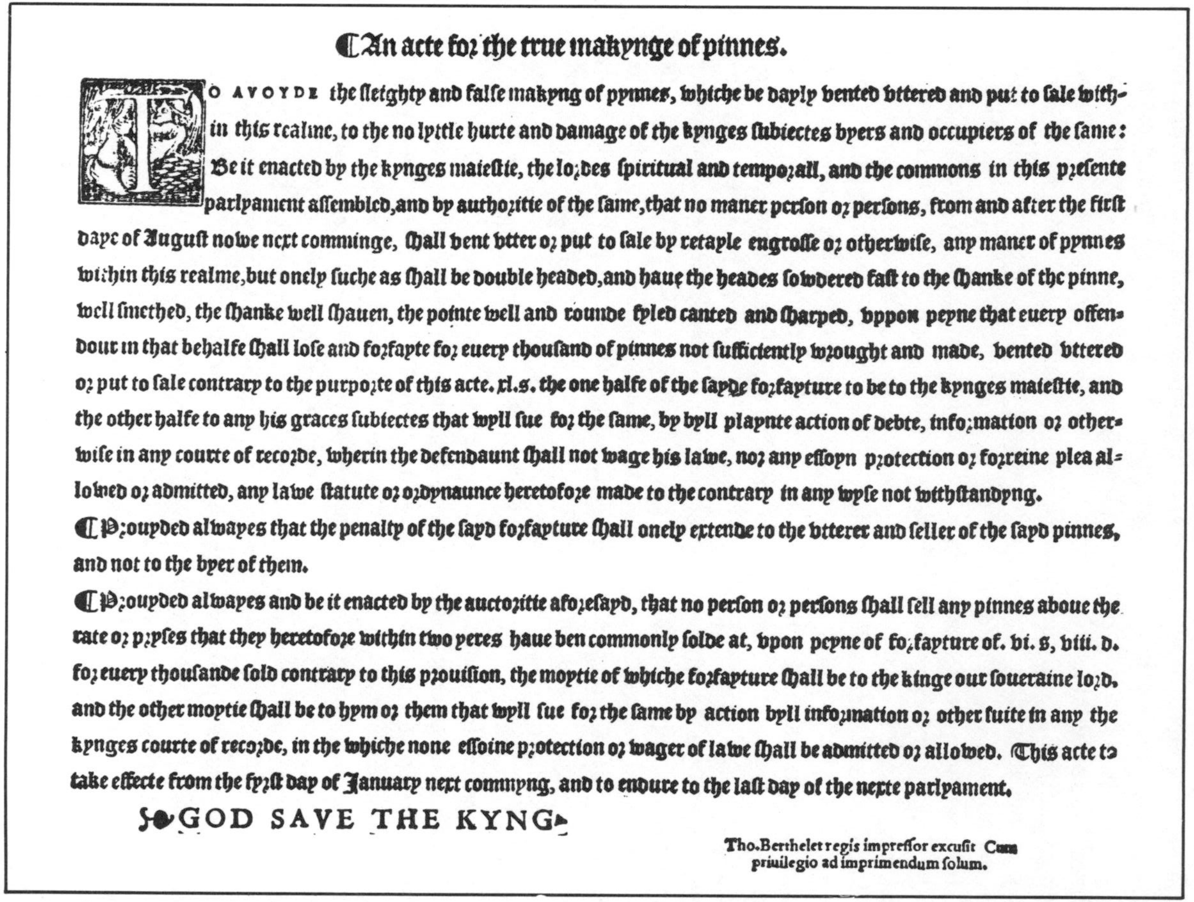

¶ An acte for the true makynge of pinnes.

FOR AVOYDINGE the sleighty and false makinge of pynnes, whiche be dayly vented vttered and put to sale within this realme, to the no lytle hurte and damage of the kynges subiectes byers and occupiers of the same: Be it enacted by the kynges maiestie, the lordes spirituall and temporall, and the commons in this presente parlyament assembled, and by auctoritie of the same, that no maner person or persons, from and after the first daye of August nowe next comminge, shall vent vtter or put to sale by retayle engrosse or otherwise, any maner of pynnes within this realme, but onely suche as shall be double headed, and haue the heades soundered fast to the shanke of the pinne, well smethed, the shanke well shauen, the pointe well and rounde filed canted and sharped, vpon peyne that euery offendour in that behalfe shall lose and forfayte for euery thousand of pinnes not sufficiently wrought and made, vented vttered or put to sale contrary to the purpose of this acte. xl.s. the one halfe of the sayde forfayture to be to the kynges maiestie, and the other halfe to any his graces subiectes that wyll sue for the same, by byll playnte action of debt, information or otherwise in any courte of recorde, wherein the defendaunt shall not wage his lawe, nor any essoyn protection or forreine plea allowed or admitted, any lawe statute or ordynaunce heretofore made to the contrary in any wyse not withstandyng.

¶ Prouided alwayes that the penalty of the sayde forfayture shall onely extende to the vtterer and seller of the sayd pinnes, and not to the byer of them.

¶ Prouided alwayes and be it enacted by the auctoritie aforesayd, that no person or persons shall sell any pinnes aboue the rate or pryces that they heretofore within thre yeres haue ben commonly solde at, vpon peyne of forfayture of. vi. s. viii. d. for euery thousande solde contrary to this prouision, the moytie of whiche forfayture shall be to the kinge our soueraine lord, and the other moytie shall be to hym or them that wyll sue for the same by action byll information or other suite in any the kynges courte of recorde, in the whiche none essoine protection or wager of lawe shall be admitted or allowed. This acte to take effecte from the first day of January next comminge, and to endure to the last day of the next parlyament.

☞ GOD SAVE THE KYNG.

Tho. Bertheleti regis impressor excusit Cum priuilegio ad imprimendum solum.

FIGURE 5. 24 & 25 Hen. VIII, c.6 (1543). Broadside form. Kent Archives Office, NR/ZPr 2s.

session. It seems likely that he printed the first batch as the text reached him but only until the final lot of acts arrived that the parliamentary officials had determined to be "public." In 1542 the 19 acts listed by Berthelet in his accounts are in the order of the folio's table. The 13 broadside acts of 1543 are the first 13 (out of 25) in the table, but this time the order in Berthelet's accounts differs from that in the table. Possibly he didn't have time to get them in the set order, or perhaps the officials hadn't yet decided on the order.

The complete 1542 statute in folio was not ready until 6 May, 16 days after delivery of the broadsides. Only 12 copies of the folio were delivered to Chancery, I assume for use by officials there. Where did the bulk of the folios go for administrative dissemination, and to what account were they charged? There may well be simple answers, which I have made no attempt to discover; what is noteworthy is that the acts "printed in proclamacons" were delivered to the clerk of the crown in Chancery (who authorized payment), exactly as if they had been royal proclamations proper, which also figure in Berthelet's accounts. Both kinds of broadsides had to go out with writs of proclamation, and Chancery was the source of writs.

In 1543, although Berthelet's accounts continue until 12 June, there is no record of his delivery of a small quantity of the folio statute. This is curious because the folio colophon is dated 1 June. On the day before, 31 May, Berthelet delivered the broadside acts. Does 1 June in his folio colophon actually mean the day he began printing the folio rather than the day he finished, or is that the day the acts comprising the statute received their official form and numbering?[62] Unfortunately, the colophon for the previous session of 1542 gives only the year and so sheds no light upon this minor perplexity of 1543.

One important matter Appendix D does not make clear is the awesome quantity of broadsides delivered on both occasions. Although a few acts were only a halfsheet, some had as many as four sheets. Ignoring the differences in the size of paper that Berthelet records (this would affect the amount of text that would fit on each sheet and also the price) but counting his "dim" as half a sheet, I calculate that on 20 April 1542 Berthelet delivered the equivalent of 14,362 full sheets of paper and on 31 May 1543 the equivalent of 9,792 full sheets. In 1542 the 17 acts of which 500 copies were printed totaled 28½ sheets a set; in 1543 a comparable set of 11 acts consisted of 19 sheets. I would imagine that broadside acts occupied most of the available posting space in the cities and towns to which they were sent!

I know of no documentary evidence for Edward's and Mary's reigns, but the surviving acts display sufficient variety to suggest that Berthelet's practice was carried on by Grafton and by Cawood. The number of complete broadside acts to survive from Elizabeth's reign is notably scanty, and two of them turn out to be in the "acts not printed" category. While this is a pleasant source of amusement for us, it probably indicates that, although the town of Lyme Regis and Sir Richard Knightley thought it advisable to have at least one copy printed, they did not consider it worth what must have been a more costly process to have the acts made fully "public." There must have been others of this sort that have not survived.

Jugge and Cawood accounts are quite rare, and among them is only one covering the close of an Elizabethan session: her first, dissolved on 8 May 1559.[63] Three broadside acts were delivered to Chancery on 14 May, followed by one royal proclamation issued and delivered on 16 May and another proclamation, without specified date of delivery, issued on 17 May. The rest of the account is torn away. Were the three acts all that were printed as broadsides, or did the proclamations only interrupt their printing so that more acts came later? In this year there were perhaps more printed; the lone survivor for 8 Eliz. shows the practice had not entirely died out by 1567. Nevertheless, this competition among proclamations for the printer's attention surely reflects competition in another domain: the amount of space available for posting. While acts had another traditional printed form, i.e., the folios, proclamations did not, and it seems likely that statutory broadsides bowed out in favor of their royal brethren.

The three remaining broadside public acts almost certainly represent specific and single decisions for publication in this form. The 1598 act against rogues and vagabonds reflects an increasing concern of Elizabeth's later reign; there were proclamations on the same subject on 9 September 1598,[64] 14 January 1600,[65] and 15 February 1601.[66] The act itself has no imprint or chapter number but does give the regnal year—possibly it was printed in connection with one of the proclamations rather than at the end of the session in February 1598. The Jacobean act of 1604 for the relief and ordering of persons infected with the plague is clearly not a contemporary printing since it is dated 1630, another year of serious plague during Charles I's reign, and it is, in fact, the latest broadside printing of an act I have come across. It specifies James's first regnal year; however, it is printed not by the King's Printer but by Robert Young, printer to the city of London. Here apparently is another example of a special allowance that was made for London, and the order to print it must have come from the lord mayor and aldermen.[67] The last example, the act of Charles's first session concerning lands in the Duchy of Cornwall, also gives the regnal year and was printed later, this time by the King's Printer in 1626, the year after the session ended. Furthermore, its imprint is in the same typesetting as a Privy Council order of 15 August 1626,[68] which would place its printing very close in time to Charles's proclamation of 13 August 1626,[69] which attempts to maximize revenues from other crown lands.

Aside from these three exceptional examples of public acts, 1567 is the latest date to which we can currently assign the practice of disseminating the complete text of public acts in broadside form. The statutory material that was commonly posted in Elizabeth's reign but later only occasionally, consisted largely of extracts from acts or abridgements, sometimes introduced by a proclamation or order that required enforcement by the justices of the peace and other local officers. The most extensive group of abridgments was of acts against excess in apparel, some of which required six sheets in shortened form.[70] The longest-lived abridgment concerned archery and unlawful games. The whole of 33 Hen. VIII, c.9, was reprinted in 1561 in broadside form and comprised five sheets. This act required the practice of archery in some form by all able-bodied men between the ages of 7 and 60, and it forbade unlawful games like bowling and dicing. Also in 1561 an epitome of this act was printed along with other abridged acts in a set of eight sheets.[71] If I estimate the date correctly, a different and separate abridgment of Henry's act was printed on one sheet as early as 1562.[72] The latest edition of this same text is dated 1632.

The repetitious nature of these proclamations of statutory abridgments suggests they fell on deaf ears, but they also held hazards for anyone who wished to obey them! A Privy Council order of 7 May 1562[73] providing abridgments on various topics, including apparel, woefully confesses that a 1533 act, 24 Hen. VIII, c.13, "remaynyng nowe in force, conteyneth so manye articles and clauses, as the same can not be conueniently abrydged, but is to be considered by readyng and perusyng the whole Act at large." Although a copy of Berthelet's original broadside printing of the act has come to light, no later reprint of the complete text in broadside form is known.[74] Perhaps we can interpret the Privy Council's comment as a hint to consult the folio statute, for only the complete text of acts had authority, and the only viable form in which they could be perused at length and at will was in folio volumes. Only the folios could encompass the richness and mass of legislation through the years, and we have seen already how the gradual development of that form of publication echoes the overall historical patterns of the period and may even afford further insight into matters of historical and political concern.

NOTES

1. *A Short-Title Catalogue of Books Printed in England, Scotland, & Ireland 1475–1640*, ed. A. W. Pollard and G. R. Redgrave (London, 1926). References below are to item numbers, the "point" numbers being provisionally assigned in the current revision of letters *A–H*; the revision of letters *I–Z* was published in 1976.

2. An earlier form of this paper had the benefit of reading by N. J. Barker of the British Library, G. R. Elton of Clare College, Cambridge, and Edith Henderson of the Harvard Law School Library. Although their generous comments have saved

me from some error, they are in no way responsible for the selection of evidence or my interpretation of it.

3. G. R. Elton, "The Rolls of Parliament, 1449–1547," *Historical Journal* 22 (1979): 10. There are many other valuable details of procedure and documents in this article.

4. ———, "The Sessional Printing of Statutes, 1484–1547," in *Wealth and Power in Tudor England,* ed. E. W. Ives et al. (London, 1978), pp. 81–82. This is another extraordinarily useful study. I have corrected a few mild aberrations in it about printing in the present paper.

5. STC 9347. See Appendix B for other bibliographical references to this and later statutes mentioned in this section.

6. David Mellinkoff, *The Language of the Law* (Boston, 1963), pp. 99, 122–130. A point in favor of law French was its precision in dealing with such technical matters as inheritance and land tenures. However, the general objection of lawyers against having law in English was akin to that of clerics against having the Bible in English: The common man would inevitably get things wrong and needed a special class to interpret matters for him. Mellinkoff notes on pp. 111–112 the abysmal failure of the Statute of Pleading in 1362 to bring the English language into law courts.

7. For the contents of this statute and of the first two of Henry VII, see Appendix A.

8. W. S. Holdsworth, *A History of English Law,* vol. 2, 3rd ed. (London, 1923), p. 480.

9. The Stationers' Register lists 26 individual items plus yearbooks entered to Richard Tottell on 18 February 1583, although he had begun printing some of them 30 years before; see Edward Arber, ed., *A Transcript of the Registers of the Company of Stationers of London 1554–1640,* 5 vols. (London, 1875–1894), 2: 419. Another belated register of law titles occurred on 5 March 1620, when 63 individual items plus the yearbooks were recorded as being in the English Stock (Arber, 3: 668–669). For further details of this stock, see *Records of the Court of the Stationers' Company 1602 to 1640,* ed. W. A. Jackson (London, 1957), pp. viii–xi.

10. *Statutes of the Realm,* 11 vols. (London, 1810–1828), 1: lxxxvi–lxxxvii.

11. Robert Steele, *A Bibliography of Royal Proclamations,* 2 vols. (London, 1910), 1:xiii. References are made in roman numerals to pages of the introduction; later references (section III) in arabic numerals pertain to item numbers in Steele's text.

12. In contrast to statutes, royal proclamations were almost exclusively in English by about 1450; see ibid., 1:xi, clxxv–clxxxii, the latter pages of which include the texts of a number of Richard III's proclamations.

13. Alison Hanham, *Richard III and His Early Historians* (Oxford, 1975), pp. 16–18, where general background on this point is also given.

14. STC 9264, Duff 378, Beale S1. A closer approximation to the true date of this collection will require more exacting bibliographical study. Nevertheless, I have looked a little into de Machlinia's output and have had the benefit of preliminary observations by Paul Needham of the Pierpont Morgan Library on the paper de Machlinia used and have exchanged ideas on his types with Lotte Hellinga of the British Library. The work of these two is still in its early stages, and my own findings here are subject to revision.

15. E. Gordon Duff, "Early Chancery Proceedings Concerning Members of the Book Trade," *The Library* 8 (1907): 408–409, 413–414. My thanks are due to Edith Henderson for help in interpreting this incident. Unfortunately, none of the persons involved in the dispute has any recorded connection with known members of the book trade. The defendant in the action that survives is "Robt Cokker of London, seriaunt," apparently not a serjeant-at-law, i.e., senior member of the legal profession. It was Cokker who had possession of the 65 copies at the outset of the dispute, and they must have represented a sizable portion of the total copies printed. What this means regarding the distribution of *Nova Statuta* is uncertain.

16. Offset is particularly noticcable, also in the preliminary table, in one of two copies at the Inner Temple Library, namely, the one without 1 Ric. III bound at the end. Of the two copies at the Harvard Law School Library, the one in a modern binding shows more offset than the one in the remnants of its original binding. The former shows traces of smudging throughout, but the difficulty seems to increase around quire kk and continues with fair consistency to the end.

17. Since there is not soon likely to be a devil's advocate on this point, I should perhaps add that if Henry's first two statutes were printed in law French, the reason no trace of copies survives may be that Caxton's collection in English made them outmoded, both because of language and, more importantly, because of the small alterations in the text noted in Appendix A.

18. George D. Painter, *William Caxton* (New York, [1977]), p. 173.

19. The latest dated text in de Machlinia's types is the bull of Innocent VIII (STC 4096, Duff 227) issued in Rome on 27 March 1486, confirming Henry's marriage to Elizabeth of York and his title and that of his heirs to the throne of England. Not until two and a half months later, on 13 June, was there a Council memorandum that "my Lord of Lincoln" was to translate it and have copies made; see *Select Cases in the Council of Henry VII*, ed. C. G. Bayne, Selden Society, 75 (London, 1958), p. 8. Steele, op. cit., 1:lxxvii, suggests "Lincoln" was probably John de la Pole, Earl of Lincoln (Richard III's nephew and choice as heir), who was present at this meeting of Henry's Council, rather than John Russell, Bishop of Lincoln (Richard's chancellor), who, although also a member of Henry's Council, was not present on this occasion. I believe that Russell, with his vastly greater ecclesiastical and legal experience, is the more appropriate candidate. Furthermore, Russell was not only an early buyer of printed books and "a keen supporter of learning and of printing" Elizabeth Armstrong, "English Purchases of Printed Books from the Continent 1465–1526," *English Historical Review* 94 (1979): 268–269, 276) but several years

before had had a Latin speech of his printed by Caxton (STC 21458, Duff 367; see also Painter's *Caxton*, pp. 94–95). The decision to have copies of the translation of the bull printed rather than written by hand was, again, more likely to have been Russell's.

20. Wytze and Lotte Hellinga, *The Fifteenth-Century Printing Types of the Low Countries* (Amsterdam, 1966), 1: 64–66; Vol. 2, plates 83–87; Veldener's types 5[B] and 5*, Brito's type 2.

21. I have belatedly noticed a composite final *f* sort in *Nova Statuta*, on E3[r] of the table, line 4 from the bottom, but its use must be quite sparing. It consists of a normal lowercase *f* followed by a thin reversed-S sort.

22. Less than 30 years after Caxton's edition, John Rastell's view was that Henry himself determined to have statutes in English: ". . . now of late days the most noble prince our late sovereign lord King Henry the vij. worthy to be called the second Solomon . . . ordained and caused that all the statutes and ordinances which were made for the common wealth of this realm in his days should be endited and written in the vulgar English tongue and to be published, declared, and imprinted so that then universally the people of the realm might soon have the knowledge of the said statutes and ordinances which they were bound to observe, and so by reason of that knowledge to avoid the danger and penalties of the same statutes, and also the better to live in tranquillity and peace . . ." (*Abbreuiacōn of statuts trāslatyd out of frēch īto ēglish*, 8°, 25 October 1519; STC 9515.5, British Library: B.E. 11/1, πA2[r–v], spelling modernized). The laudatory and enthusiastic tone is quite evident even in this brief excerpt, but Rastell was a barrister himself with many friends in the legal profession, and his opinion is likely to have been a relatively informed one. I am grateful to A. C. Taussig of London for calling this passage to my attention.

23. Elton, "Sessional Printing," p. 74, n.1.

24. STC 9265, Beale S2.

25. STC 9316, to be moved to STC 9305.3; Beale S31. Emphasis added.

26. This subsidy, which I had originally neglected to notice, was brought to my attention by Professor Elton, who also generously provided information on the other subsidies.

27. *Statutes of the Realm*, 3:21–22, c. 20*.

28. 1 Edw. VI, c.13; 1 Mary I, st.2, c.18; 1 Eliz. I, c. 19; 1 Jac. I, c.33. Under Charles this subsidy became a bone of contention. Although customs continued to be collected, Parliament did not grant the subsidy until 1641, and then only on a temporary basis and subject to renewal.

29. 32 Hen. VIII, c.23; see J. J. Scarisbrick, "Clerical Taxation in England, 1486–1547," *Journal of Ecclesiastical History* 11 (1960): 52.

30. *Handbook of British Chronology*, ed. F. M. Powicke et al. (London, 1939), pp. 349–350.

31. A fairly advanced form and continually increasing variety of fees for private acts in Elizabeth's reign are discussed by J. E. Neale, *The Elizabethan House of Commons* (New Haven, Conn., 1950), pp. 335–348, with examples of payments made primarily by the cities of London and Westminster. On p. 383 Neale says: "The one infallible distinction was that of the officials: they levied fees on private, but not on public bills." How far back in time the practice reaches is uncertain, but Elton, "Rolls," p. 7, suggests the possibility that some form of feeing may have been in existence in 1472.

32. These are both extraordinarily complex matters for statutes after Henry VIII. Indeed, the correspondence of editions in the STC revision with old STC entries and even with Beale entries is so complicated that it seemed pointless to cite STC or Beale references in Appendix C. Besides, the purpose of that appendix is to reveal bibliographical shapes, not to deal with copies or editions.

33. In a few cases the number of acts in the table is taken from a later edition when the earliest table is at variance with the number of acts printed in the text. For example, in the table of the first edition of 35 Hen. VIII there are 19 acts, including as number 18 an act for Queen Catharine Parr's jointure, usually crossed out by pen. All editions of the text and all subsequent tables have only 18 acts. Information of this sort is, again, primarily a matter of editions and will be treated in the STC revision itself.

34. Recently Dr. Dennis E. Rhodes, of the British Library, most generously brought to my attention a more substantial fragment of the subsidy of 5 Hen. VIII, which he discovered in a binding (N.7.xii) at Hereford Cathedral. He has described it in greater detail in "Four Important End-Papers in Hereford Cathedral Library," *The Library*, 4 (1982): 410–415, where Hen. VIII is misprinted Hen. VII.

35. I am grateful to Howard Jay Graham of Walla Walla, Washington, for drawing my attention to the mention of this item in S. E. Lehmberg, *The Reformation Parliament 1529–1536* (Cambridge, 1970), pp. 208–209, n.5. Mr. Graham also shared generously his wide knowledge of other historical topics relating to the statutes.

36. I specify "most common form" because for 2 & 3 and 3 & 4 Edw. VI and for 39 Eliz. stray examples of subsidies in a different collation from the "common form" survive, and they suggest that many copies continued to be issued separately. The Edwardian examples are at the British Library, in Harl. MS. 7615, fols. 14–31 and 33–36, respectively. The eccentric subsidy for 39 Eliz. survives in two typesettings, one each found taking the place of the common form of the subsidy for that year in Elizabethan statute volumes at the Pepysian Library, Magdalene College, Cambridge (Pepys 1995), and at Lambeth Palace Library (1587.47).

37. Neale, op. cit., p. 419.

38. STC 9286, Beale S25.

39. F. J. Funivall, "Pynson's Contracts with Horman and Palsgrave," *Transactions of the Philological Society* (1857), p. 374.

40. On the other hand, the late date of payment may indeed mean that only the subsidy is meant and that the large sum Pynson received reflects the quantity of

copies printed. The subsidy of 7 Hen. VIII is to a large extent a continuation of those granted in 5 and in 6 Hen. VIII, the collection of which fell far short of the amount granted (*Statutes of the Realm* 3: 104–105). The collection for the subsidy of 7 Hen. VIII was to be in two installments: the subsidy proper on 21 November 1516, and an extra fifteenth and tenth on 21 November 1517 (*Statutes of the Realm* 3:195–199, especially p. 197). Were large editions of the subsidy printed for both installments? A separate printing of 1,000 copies for the second installment of the lay subsidy of 1 Eliz. cost over £33 in 1559 (see note 45), but that was 16 leaves long. Since the subsidy of 7 Hen. VIII is comparatively brief—it would come to six or at most eight leaves in a separate printing—was it accompanied by supplementary material of some kind?

41. Arber, 2:51–60. In comparison with the records for Pynson we have just dealt with, Berthelet's accounts are a marvel of precision—another great cause of my admiration for him.

42. Arber, 2:59.

43. It may be that a stage is missing here and that the pardon was originally printed alone in a quire d+ without chapter number in the heading.

44. See note 36.

45. Having just belabored Grafton for his ineptitude, I must here say that I stand in debt to him for the dated colophon. Another example of a separate, late printing of a subsidy known only through documentary evidence is the subsidy of Elizabeth's first Parliament, which was dissolved on 8 May 1559. Sometime between 21 October 1559 and 6 January 1560 Jugge and Cawood printed "one thousand bookes of the Subsedye for the Secund payment of the same xxxiij^{li} vj^s viij^d" (Arber, 1:570). The account does not specify the date of delivery to Chancery, but the proclamations listed immediately before and after the subsidy were issued on the two dates mentioned. It is impossible to be sure which, if any, of the surviving editions of the subsidy is the one printed in late 1559 because the subsidy's collation is separate and uniform throughout all editions, and the date of its colophon does not change.

46. *Statutes of the Realm* ceases to give the text of private acts after 1539. A couple of Elizabethan broadside examples of private acts are listed in Appendix D.

47. See Appendix D under 8 Eliz. for evidence that in 1566 Jugge and Cawood were able to obtain or printed themselves the subsidy of 2 & 3 Ph. & M. in nine sheets, or 18 leaves if in folio.

48. P. L. Hughes and J. F. Larkin, ed., *Tudor Royal Proclamations,* 3 vols. (New Haven, 1965–1969), vol. 2, nos. 394, 399, 421; no. 403 slips in a mention of pardon at the end, but its main thrust is to secure the capture of Sir Thomas Wyatt.

49. J. E. Neale, *Elizabeth I and Her Parliaments 1584–1601* (London, [1957]), pp. 358–362, notes there was considerably less dispute about the subsidy in this Parliament than had been the case in 1593.

50. See note 36.

51. These quires represented 20 percent of the whole statute and accordingly a sizable portion of its cost.

52. *Statutes of the Realm* 4:1208.

53. See note 11.

54. STC 9357, Beale S106. The writ appears on A2^r above the beginning of the first act.

55. STC 7760.4, Steele 46.

56. Printed writs do rarely occur on royal proclamations. The earliest was Faques's proclamation on coinage, which began with a writ addressed to "Vic. Norff. Suff. &c.," that is, to the sheriffs of Norfolk, Suffolk, and the rest. Was this more generalized form of address an attempt to give validity to the writ as printed? Later printed writs of proclamation are all directed to the mayor and sheriffs of London. Steele (1:xii, n. 7) lists two: one of 23 October 1534 about meat prices in London (STC 7781, Steele 143) and the other of 1 May 1559 for the Merchant Adventurers (STC 7894, Steele 507). It seems likely no copies of these proclamations left London. Indeed, the former was not printed by Berthelet but probably by William Rastell, a fact that emphasizes even more clearly its local nature. A third example, a proclamation of 21 December 1562 regarding speedy payment by the queen's London tenants (STC 7954, Steele 572), reinforces the London connection; evidently this city was considered large enough to be a special case.

Circulation of a proclamation in both manuscript and printed form is confirmed by a proclamation of autumn 1536, of which 20 copies were prepared in manuscript and 300 in print. This proclamation has been reasonably identified as Steele 161 and TRP (see note 48) Vol. 1, no. 168; no printed ones survive. Mention is made of the rebellion in Lincolnshire; this was, however, an urgent situation demanding special treatment. See R. W. Heinze, *The Proclamations of the Tudor Kings* (Cambridge, [1976]), pp. 21–22; the "books of answer" to be sent out with the proclamation are apparently STC 13077.5 (formerly STC 15650), directed to the Lincoln rebels, or possibly its mate in the same Cambridge University Library volume, STC 13077, directed to the York rebels.

57. Steele, op. cit., 1:xiii, n.11, notes an attempt in 1650 under the Commonwealth to revive the practice of proclaiming acts aloud. I do not know whether it was successful, but the procedure of publishing acts individually during that period certainly makes the attempt seem possible.

58. Undoubtedly their posting was accompanied by proper ceremony and fanfare and perhaps an epitome of their contents, but I am quite sure that by 1529 at the latest, the full text of the statute was not read aloud.

59. Just over half of those listed in Appendix D—the acts in the Kent Archives Office and the East Sussex Record Office—came to my notice when I was doing some collateral reading in connection with the proclamations section of the STC revision during the summer and autumn of 1980. I have examined the East Sussex 1561 reprint of 33 Hen. VIII, c.9, but apart from the act reproduced as Figure 5 I had

not seen any of the Kent items by the time I finished revising this article. After examining microfilm, I have corrected Appendix D and added a few explanatory remarks (see note 74).

60. Arber, 2:59. Since in the original delivery of 31 May 1543 Berthelet specifies a rate of "ob. the pece," i.e., obolus or halfpenny—the price for a full sheet—perhaps the act was set in duplicate or printed by work and turn. The odd lot of 20 copies delivered on 12 June must have been cut apart because the rate is "quatern the pece" (Arber, 2:60).

61. Arber, 2:54.

62. It is not simply a matter of postdating the colophon so that payment would be charged to June rather than May, because Berthelet did not receive payment until 29 September 1543 for his deliveries during the whole 18-month period from December 1541 to June 1543: a total of £100/o/6½ (Arber, 2:50).

63. Arber, 1:564.

64. STC 8266, Steele 899.

65. STC 8271, Steele 905.

66. There are three editions: STC 8282–8284, Steele 916–918.

67. See note 56 for printed writs specifying London. I am indebted to Franklin B. Williams, Jr., of Arlington, Virginia, for pointing out the existence and location of this act, which is entered in STC among the official publications of the corporation of London.

68. STC 8838, Steele 1489.

69. STC 8837, Steele 1487.

70. Proclamations with abridgments solely on apparel were issued on 15 June 1574 (STC 8066, Steele 690), 16 February 1577 (STC 8091, Steele 717), 12 February 1580 (STC 8119, Steele 745), 13 February 1588 (STC 8168, the Harvard copy; Steele 798 is based on the mixed British Library copy), and 6 July 1597 (STC 8257, Steele 890).

71. STC 9339.5, copy in the Society of Antiquaries at the beginning of its Humphrey Dyson volume of proclamations.

72. STC 8046.5, at the Folger Library; Steele 667–674, 1059–1061, 1545–1548 are later editions.

73. STC 7951, Steele 568.

74. This statement is not entirely accurate. Although the 1533 act on apparel, c. 13, was printed by Berthelet, recent inspection of microfilm of the Kent items revealed that its imprint differed from the other two surviving broadsides of that session. 24 Hen. VIII, cc.6 and 7 have Berthelet's name in rotunda type, whereas c.13 has it in roman type, in the same typesetting as 3 Hen. VIII, c.3, on archery, and 22 Hen. VIII, c.12, on vagabonds. Enforcement of acts on these topics was ordered by a proclamation of Henry's (STC 7788, Steele 156), which has been assigned the date of

February 1536. The proclamation also has the same setting of the imprint, but in the course of reimposing it a full stop was juggled, yielding the misprint "CVM PRIVILEGI.O." There can be little doubt that the three acts were reprinted in order to be sent out with the proclamation. In the course of examining other films of broadsides with Berthelet imprints, I happened to notice that 23 Hen. VIII, c.4, on beer casks, which is cropped close so that no heading or imprint survives, had a Jugge and Cawood woodcut initial letter, datable by breaks in its border between June 1563 and June 1566. As a result, this broadside act must be counted along with 33 Hen. VIII, c.9, on archery and unlawful games, as another Elizabethan reprint. The final point the Kent film revealed was that the earliest Elizabethan broadside act extant, 8 Eliz., c.3, against export of live sheep, also cited the regnal year in its heading. Its woodcut initial and imprint do not offer conclusive evidence, but the fact that I could not find the C-shaped paragraph mark in its heading used after the proclamation of 15 July 1568 (STC 8005, Steele 629) strongly suggests that the act was printed at the end of the session in 1567. From this time on all surviving broadside acts, whether public or private, mention the regnal year.

Appendix A

THE LAST THREE STATUTES TURNED INTO LAW FRENCH

The following table is based on the order of the acts (given in column 2) as printed in *Statutes of the Realm,*[§] which follows that of manuscript copies in law French: the Exchequer MS.: E164/11 at the Public Record Office for 1 Ric. III and Petyt MS. 511/6 at the Inner Temple Library for 1 and for 3 Hen. VII. *S.R.* also prints the English text from the rolls of Parliament now at the Public Record Office: C65/114, 123–125, citing item numbers of the acts (column 1) assigned in *Rotuli Parliamentorum.*[†] The chapter numbers (column 3), also listed in *S.R.,* give the order in the earliest printed editions by de Machlinia (STC 9347) and Caxton (in STC 9348). To indicate the general contents of the acts I have added brief titles, largely adapted from *S.R.* The dates are those of the sessions.

As far as printing is concerned, there are a few points I wish to make about these statutes. For 1 Ric. III the law French versions, both manuscript and printed, agree as to order with only minor reshuffling from the order of acts recorded in *R.P.* For 3 Hen. VII the Petyt MS. statute in law French follows *R.P.* with even less variation than for 1 Ric. III and does not include the act revoking penalties, which, from its position on the roll, was evidently considered a private act promoted by the alien

---

[§] 2:477–523. Cited as *S.R.* hereafter; for the full reference see n.10 in Notes.

[†] 6 vols. [London, ca. 1767], 6: 237–408. Cited hereafter as *R.P.* I have not seen any of the manuscripts and rely for references to them on Elton, "Sessional Printing" (see n.4 in Notes), p. 74, for the Exchequer and Petyt MSS. and on Elton, "Rolls" (see n.3 in Notes), pp. 13–14, nn.53, 56, for the rolls of Parliament.

merchants themselves. Accordingly, Petyt must reflect a contemporary decision as to what acts constituted the statute in 1486.‡

Caxton's text of 1 Hen. VII, printed four years later, represents a departure from Petyt in more ways than language. It omits *Titulus regis;* it reorders the acts—not into any truly coherent order but into loose thematic groupings somewhat in the manner of Petyt for 3 Hen. VII; and it adds the private act for the alien merchants. These changes would appear to reflect a retrospective decision about the statute. Henry had been on the throne for more than four years, so perhaps *Titulus regis* was regarded as redundant for purposes of printing, whereas c.10, inasmuch as it had reference to a public act of Richard's Parliament, had "public" implications not fully realized at first.

For 3 Hen. VII, Caxton and Petyt agree quite closely; the order in *R.P.* is wildly different. Apparently the decision to use thematic groupings was taken at the time the statute was framed in law French, in late 1487 or early 1488. I have not studied the last few acts closely enough to see if Caxton's slightly different order from Petyt's represents an advance in this kind of tidiness. Petyt omits Caxton's c.14, which must have been deemed a public act (although two in this section of the roll, nos. 27 and 32 in *R.P.*, were private acts against individuals) but was to be in force only until the next Parliament, which began on 13 January 1489. Perhaps when Petyt was copied, the act had expired and was considered not worth including by whoever wrote or commissioned the MS., while Caxton's edition, going back to the statute as originally framed, did include it.

---

‡The selection of acts was the responsibility of the clerk; their translation into law French was overseen by common law judges; the engrossing of the statute on the statute roll and preparation of authentic copies was the responsibility of the master of rolls; see Elton, "Rolls," pp. 9–12, for more details, although he minimizes the role of the judges. It is not clear which of these had a hand in determining the order of acts in the statute, but it seems likely that both the clerk and the master had some involvement in the changes in Caxton's edition noted below.

---

1 RICHARD III (23 Jan.–22 Feb. 1484)

R.P. English	Exchequer MS. Law French	[De Machlinia 1484] Law French	
20	1	1	Against secret feoffments (land law)
18	2	2	Freeing subjects from benevolences
21	3	3	For bailing persons suspected of felony
22	4	4	For returning sufficient jurors
23	5	5	Validating feoffments to the use of others made by Richard before he was king
24	6	6	Regulating trials in courts of pyepowder

25	7	7	For proclamation upon fines levied
26	8	8	Regulating dyeing and clothmaking
27	9	9	Restricting freedom of trade and movement by Italian and other alien merchants, with proviso exempting alien members of the book trade
28	10	10	Against importing silks
30	11	11	Regulating prices of bowstaves
29	12	12	Against importing leather and metal wares
31	13	13	Regulating sizes of wine and oil casks
32	14	14	Regulating collections of tenths from the clergy
33	15	15	Annulling letters patent to Lady Elizabeth Grey (widow of Edward IV)

1 HENRY VII (7 Nov.–10 Dec. 1485; 23 Jan.–4 Mar. 1486)

R.P. *English* VI, p. 270	*Petyt MS.* *Law French* *Titulus regis*	*[Caxton 1490]* *English* —	
			Acknowledging Henry VII's right to the throne
66	1	1	Formedon (land law)
67	2	4	For punishing priests for unclean living
68	3	3	Regulating law courts at Calais
69	4	2	Denizens to pay customs and subsidy
70	5	8	For importing Gascon wines in English ships
71	6	5	Regulating tanners
72	7	6	Protecting Henry VII's followers from certain lawsuits
74	8	7	Against illegal hunting in forests
73	9	9	Against importing silks
20	—	10	Revoking penalties and fines imposed in 1 Ric. III c. 9 but allowing Henry VII himself to collect them or to issue letters patent or letters of safe conduct

3 HENRY VII (9 Nov.–18 Dec. 1487)

17	1	1	Establishing a subcommittee of the Council to deal with certain misdemeanors (sometimes miscalled "Court of Star Chamber")
21	2	1 (end)	Against murderers
18	3	2	Against abducting women
24	4	3	Regulating bailing by justices of the peace
20	5	4	Against fraudulent deeds of gift
29	6	5	Against usury
28	7	6	Against unlicensed exchange and rechange
33	8	7	For registering imports with Customs
34	9	8	Against export of money by alien merchants
25	10	9	Permitting Londoners to sell wares at all fairs
19	11	10	Regulating appeal by writs of error
30	12	11	Regulating export of wool by alien merchants
31	13	12 (end)	Limiting prices of longbows
26	14	13	Empowering king's officials to investigate treasonous conspiracies
23	15	12 (beg.)	Against unlawful retainers in the king's household
22	—	14	Outlawed persons may sue as feoffees in trust

Appendix B

SEPARATE EDITIONS OF STATUTES IN FOLIO THROUGH 19 HENRY VII

Regnal year	Date of Sessions§	No. of Acts Printed	Statute	Printer	STC	Duff†	Beale‡
RICHARD III 1483–1485 (1 Parliament)							
1	23 Ja.–22 Fb. 1484	15	a–b^8	[de Machlinia, 1484]	9347	379	S96
HENRY VII 1585–1509 (7 Parliaments)							
1	7 No.–10 De. 1485 / 23 Ja.–4 Mr. 1486	10	a^8 b1				
3	9 No.–18 De. 1487	14	$b1^v$–$b8$ $c1$–6	Caxton, 1490	9348	380	S97
4	13 Ja.–23 Fb. 1489 / 14 Oc.–4 De. 1489 / 25 Ja.–27 Fb. 1490	24	$c7$–8 d^8 e^{10} / a–d^6 e^8	de Worde [1496?]	9349	381	S98
7	17 Oc.–4 No. 1491 / 26 Ja.–5 Mr. 1492	7	a^6	de Worde [1496?]	9350	382	—
11	14 Oc.–21 De. 1495	27	A^8 B–E^6 / A^8 B–E^6 / A^8 B–E^6 / A^8 B–D^6	[de Worde, 1496] / [de Worde, 1496?] / [Pynson, 1496?] / [de Worde, 1500?]	9354 / 9353 / 9355 / 9352	385 / 384 / 386 / 383	— / S102 / S105 / S103
12	16 Ja.–13 Mr. 1497	6	Aa^4	de Worde [1501?]	9355.5		—
19	25 Ja.–30 Mr. 1504	24	A–C^8 / A–C^6 / 1^6 m^8 n^4	W. Faques [1504] / de Worde, 1506 / Pynson [1508?]	9357 / 9357.4 / 9356		S106 / — / S109

§Dates are from J. C. Wedgwood, *History of Parliament 1439–1509*, Vol. II (1938), pp. 475, 494, 511, 527, 542, 564, 583, 597.

†E. Gordon Duff, *Fifteenth Century English Books: A Bibliography*, [London,] 1917.

‡Joseph H. Beale, *A Bibliography of Early English Law Books*, Cambridge, [Mass.] 1926. A copy of STC 9355.5 is at King's College, Cambridge, and one of STC 9357.4 is at the Pierpont Morgan Library.

Appendix C

STATUTES IN FOLIO 1510–1640†

HENRY VIII 1509–1547 (21 Sessions)

Regnal Year	Date of Session	No. of Acts in Table	Statute	"Extras"
1	21 Ja.–23 Fb. 1510	15	$\langle$A–C^6 D^4? 4$^6\rangle$ A^6 B^4 C^2	—
3	4 Fb.–30 Mr. 1512	15	A^6 B^4 C1–5	[T: c.22*]
4	4 No.–20 De. 1512	8	C6 D–E^4	T: $\langle$A^8?$\rangle$ c.19* (See Fig. 2; also Appendix D)
5	23 Ja.–4 Mr. 1514	8	A^6 (**P** = c.8)	T: $\langle$A$^4\rangle$ B^4 = c.17*
6	5 Fb.–5 Ap. 1515	18	A–B^6 C–D^4	[T: c.26*]
7	12 No.–22 De. 1515	8	A^6 B^4 C^6 (**P** = c.8)	T: c.9* (See Appendix D) Revenues: A^6 B–D^4 = c.7*
14 & 15	15 Ap.–15 Au. 1523	14	tp + a^4 b–c^6	[T: c.16*; **P**: c.17*; **Revenues: c.15***]
21	3 No.–17 De. 1529	21	A–D^4 E^6 (**P** = c.1)	—
22	16 Ja.–31 Mr. 1531	16	A–D^6 (**P** for Clergy = c.15; **P** for Temp. = c.16)	—
23	15 Ja.–14 My. 1532	18	A–D^6	—
		19	A–D^6 E^4 (**P** for York = c. 19)	

Regnal year	Date	No.	Chapters	Notes
24	4 Fb.–7 Ap. 1533	13	A–C⁶	—
25	15 Ja.–30 Mr. 1534	22	A–G⁶	—
26	3 No.–18 De. 1534	18	A–D⁶ E⁴ (P = c.18)	T: A⁶ B⁴ = c.19*
27	4 Fb.–14 Ap. 1536	18	A–H⁶	—; Revenues: a⁶ b⁸ = c.62*
28	8 Jn.–18 Jy. 1536	18	A–D⁶ E²	—
31	28 Ap.–28 Jn. 1539	14	A–E⁶	—
32	12 Ap.–21 Jy. 1540	49	A⁸ B–L⁶ (C = c.23) + T: A⁶ B⁸ = [c.48] + P: A⁴ = [c.49]	
		48	A–M⁶ (P = [c.48] begins M4ʳ)	no T
33	16 Ja.–1 Ap. 1542	39	A–L⁶ M⁴	—
34 & 35	22 Ja.–12 My. 1543	25	A–E⁶ F⁴	T & C: A–C⁶ = [cc.27*, 28*]
			A–E⁶ F⁴	T & C: A–C⁶; Wales: A⁶ B⁸ = [c.26*]
			A–E⁶ F⁴; G–I⁶ (T & C)	Wales: A⁶ B⁸
			A–E⁶ F⁴; G–I⁶ (T & C); K⁶ L⁸ (Wales)	
			A–E⁶ F⁴; G⁶ H–I⁴ (Wales)	no T or C
35	14 Ja.–29 Mr. 1544	18	A–D⁶ E⁴, F⁴ (P = c.18)	—
37	23 No.–24 De. 1545	25	A–F⁶ (C = c.24, beg. F3ʳ) + T: A–B⁶ C⁴ = [c.25]	
		24	A–F⁶ (C = c.24)	no T

EDWARD VI 1547–1553 (5 Sessions)

Regnal year	Date	No.	Chapters	Notes
1	4 No.–24 De. 1547	15	A–E⁶ F–G⁴; A⁴ (P = [c.15])	—
			A–E⁶ F⁸ (P = c. 15, begins F6ʳ)	
2 & 3	24 No. 1548–15 Mr. 1549	39	A–G⁶ H⁴ (C = c.35; beg. G5ʳ); I–L⁶ (T = c.36); d⁶ (P = c.37)	T: a–b⁶ C⁶ = [c.36]
			A–G⁶ H⁴ I–K⁶ L⁴ M⁶ (C beg. G5ʳ; T beg. H4ʳ; P, moved to c.39, beg. M3ʳ)	

Regnal Year	Date of Session	No. of Acts in Table	Statute	"Extras"
3 & 4	4 No. 1549–1 Fb. 1550	24	A–B⁶ C⁶⁺¹ D⁶ E⁴ (T = c.23, beg. D6ᵛ); F⁴ (P = c.24)	c.5: A⁶, vs. unlawful assemblies, 1551 T: A⁴ = [c.23] 1551 Chester: a⁴ = "c.25" 1551 (Fig. 4)
5 & 6	23 Ja.–15 Ap. 1552	26	A–E⁶ F⁴	—
7	1–31 Mr. 1553	14	A–F⁶ G⁴ (T = c.12, beg. Dlᵛ; C = c.13, beg. F6ʳ); H⁴ (P = c.14)	—
MARY I 1553–1558 (6 Sessions)				
1	5–21 Oc. 1553	1	A1–3	—
1	24 Oc.–5 De. 1553	18	A4–6 B–D⁶ E⁴ (T = c.17, beg. Elʳ; Tonnage & pound-age = c.18, beg. Elᵛ)	—
1	2 Ap.–5 My. 1554	12	A–B⁶ C–D⁴	—
PHILIP AND MARY				
1 & 2	12 No. 1554–16 Ja. 1555	17	A⁶ B⁴ C–F⁶	—
2 & 3	21 Oc.–9 De. 1555	23	A–I⁶ K⁴ (C = c.22, beg. G3ᵛ; T = c.23, beg. HIᵛ)	—
4 & 5	20 Ja.–7 Mr. 1558	11	A–G⁶ (C = c.10, beg. D3ᵛ; T = c.11, beg. E2ʳ)	—
ELIZABETH I 1558–1603 (13 Sessions)				
1	23 Ja.–8 My. 1559	20	A–E⁶ F⁸, A–B⁶ C⁴ (T = [c.20])	—
5	12 Ja.–10 Ap. 1563	"31"	A–L⁶ M⁸ (C = c.29, beg. L4ᵛ; P = c.31, beg. M4ᵛ); A–B⁶ C⁸ (T = [c.30]) A–L⁶ M⁸ (ditto); N–P⁶ (T = [c.30])	—

No.	Date	No.	Description	
8	30 Sc. 1566–2 Ja. 1567	19	A–D^6 E^4 (C = c.17, beg. D3^v); A–C^6 (T = [c.18]); F^4 (P = [c.19]) / A–D^6 E^4 (ditto); F–H^6 (ditto); I^4 (ditto)	—
13	2 Ap.–29 My. 1571	25	A–F^6 G^4, A–B^4 (C = [c.23]); A–C^6 (T = [c.24]); A^{4+1} (P = [c.25])	—
		28	A–G^6 H^4, A–B^4 (C = [c.26]); A–C^6 (T = [c.27]); ¶^{4} (P = [c.28]) (See Fig. 3) / A–G^6; H^6 (C = c.26); I–L^6 (T = c.27); M^4 (P = c.28)	
14	8 My.–30 Jn. 1572	13	A–D^6	—
18	8 Fb.–15 Mr. 1576	"22" [23]	A–E^6 F^8 (C = "c.20", beg. F1^v); A–C^6 (T = [c.22]); A^6 (P = [c.23])	—
		24	A–F^6 (C = c.22, beg. E6^v); G–I^6 (T = c.23); K^6 (P = c.24)	
23	16 Ja.–18 Mr. 1581	16	A–G^4; H–I^4 (C = c.14); Aa–Cc^6 Dd^2 (T = [c.15]); ¶–¶¶^{4} (P = [c.16])	—
27	23 No. 1584–29 Mr. 1585	30	A–H^6 I^4 (C = c.28, beg. H3^v); Aa–Cc^6 Dd^2 (T = [c.29]); Ee–Ff^4 (P = c.30)	—
29	15 Fb.–23 Mr. 1587	9	A^6 B^4, Aa–Bb^4 (C = [c.7]); Cc–Ee^6 (T = [c.8]); Ff^6 (P = [c.9])	—
31	4 Fb.–29 Mr. 1589	16	A–C^6; D–E^4 (C = [c.14]); Aa–Cc^6 Dd^2 (T = [c.15]); Ee^6 (P = [c.16]) / A–C^6; D–E^4 (ditto); Aa–Cc^6 Dd^8 (T; P beg. Dd2^v) / A–C^6; no C, T, or P though they are still listed in the table	—
35	19 Fb.–10 Ap. 1593	14	A–C^6 D–E^4; ¶–¶¶^{4} (C = [c.12]); Aa–Cc^6 Dd^2 (T = [c.13]); Ee^6 (P = [c.14]) / A–D^6; E^6 F^4 G–I^6 (C; T beg. F3^v); K^6 (P)	—

Regnal Year	Date of Session	No. of Acts in Table	Statute	"Extras"
39	24 Oc. 1597–9 Fb. 1598	28	A–H⁶ I⁴; Aa–Ee⁶ (**C** = [c.26]; **T** = [c.27] beg. Bb4ᵛ); Ff–Gg⁴ (**P** = [c.28])	Bb–Dd⁶ Ee² (**T** = [c.27])
		25	A–B⁶ C–D⁴, no **C**, **T**, or **P**, which are omitted in the table	
43	27 Oc.–19 De. 1601	19	A–E⁶ F⁴, Aa⁶ aa⁴ (**C** = [c.17]); Bb–Ee⁶ (**T** = [c.18]) Ff–Gg⁴ (**P** = [c.19])	—
			A–K⁶ L⁴ (**C** beg. E5ᵛ; **T** beg. G1ᵛ; **P** beg. K4ʳ) A–D⁶ E⁴, no **C**, **T**, or **P** though they are still listed in the table	
JAMES I 1603–1624 (6 Effectual Sessions)				
1	19 Mr.–7 Jy. 1604	33	A⁶ B–I⁸	—
3	5 No. 1605–27 Mr. 1606	27	A⁴ B–I⁶, Aa⁶ Bb⁴ (**C** = [c.25]); Cc–Ff⁶ (**T** = [c.26]); Gg–Hh⁴ (**P** = [c.27])	—
4	18 No. 1606–4 Jy. 1607	13	A–G⁶ H⁴	—
7	9 Fb.–23 Jy. 1610	24	π⁴ (b)⁴ A–H⁶ (**C** = [c.22] beg. G3ᵛ); Aa–Bb⁶ Cc–Dd⁴ (**T** = [c.23]); Ee–Ff⁴ (**P** = [c.24])	—
18	30 Ja.–4 Jn. 1621	[2]	–; a⁴ b⁶ (**C**); Aa–Ee⁴ (**T**)	—
21	19 Fb.–29 My. 1624	34	π⁴ A⁴ B–I⁶ K–L⁴, a⁶ b⁴ (**C** = [c.32]); Aa–Dd⁴ Ee⁶ (**T** = [c.33]) Ff⁴ Gg⁶ (**P** = [c.34])	—
CHARLES I 1624–1649 (Beheaded) (3 Effectual Sessions through 1640)				
1	18 Jn.–11 Jy. 1625	7	π⁴ B⁴, a–c⁴ (**C** = [c.5]); Aa–Ff⁴ (**T** = [c.6]); Gg² (Act regarding bills still pending before adjournment because of plague = [c.7])	—

16   3 No. 1640–[26 Mr. 1641]   [2]   A–D² [c.1]
                                       A⁴ B⁶ C–1⁴ [cc.1–2]   —

† T Subsidy of the Temporalty (lay subsidy); C Subsidy of the Clergy; P General Pardon

Appendix D

BROADSIDE STATUTES, EITHER EXTANT OR FROM DOCUMENTARY EVIDENCE, WITH FURTHER INFORMATION ON A FEW IN FOLIO

Regnal Year	End of Session	Act No.	STC	Steele§	No. of Sheets	Comment and Locations†
HENRY VIII						
3	30 Mr. 1512	c.3	7762.7	—	2	For maintenance of archery; KAO(NR/ZPr 13); a reprint by Berthelet, 1536?
4	20 De. 1512	c.19*	7763	59	4?	Lay subsidy; L(1st sheet only, on parchment).
5	4 Mr. 1514	c.17*	—	—	4	Lay subsidy. Pynson was paid in June 1514 for 100 parchment rolls of 4 skins each (see Furnivall, note 39 in Notes, p. 374, for this and the next two references).
6	5 Ap. 1515	c.2?	—	—	1?	Enforcing statute of Winchester (1285) concerning archery. Pynson pd. Mar. 1515 for 450 skins of "the Acts or retendors of the statutes of Winchester."
		c.26≠	—	—	1?	Lay subsidy. Pynson pd. Dec. 1515 for 100 skins of parchment and 125 sheets of paper.
7	22 De. 1515	c.9*	7767.5	—	3?	Lay subsidy; CANT² (2nd? sheet only, imperfect, on parchment).

Regnal Year	End of Session	Act No.	STC	Steele§	No. of Sheets	Comment and Locations†
21	17 De. 1529	cc.8,9	7773	120	1	Against killing calves; limiting price of imported hats; both on same sheet; SHR.
22	31 Mr. 1531	c.12	7776.5	—	4½	For the poor; against vagabonds; KAO(NR/ZPr 5); a reprint, 1536?
23	14 My. 1532	c.4	7777	129	3	Regulating beer and ale casks; L⁵(imperfect); a reprint by Jugge & Cawood, 1564?
24	7 Ap. 1533	c.6	7778.4	—	1	Concerning sale of wines; KAO(Sa/ZP3/2, imperfect).
		c.7	7778.5	—	1	Continuing act against killing calves; KAO(Sa/ZP3/3, imperfect).
		c.13	7778.8	—	3½	Reforming excess in apparel; KAO(NR/ZPr 6); this act is a reprint, 1536?
25	30 Mr. 1534	c.1	7779.2	—	2	Concerning graziers and butchers; KAO(Sa/ZP3/4 and 1, imperfect).
		c.13	7779.8	—	2½	Limiting the number of sheep one can own; KAO(Sa/ZP3/5, imperfect).
		c.22	7780	136	4	Establishing the succession to the throne; L, L¹¹(20 copies).
26	18 De. 1534	c.1	7782.2	—	½	Making the king head of the church; KAO(Sa/ZP3/7, imperfect).
		c.2	7782.3	—	1	Ratifying the oath to observe the succession; KAO(NR/ZPr 9).
		c.3	7782.4	—	6	Concerning payment of First Fruits and one Tenth; KAO(NR/ZPr 10).
		c.13	7782.6	—	1	Making divers offenses treason; KAO(NR/ZPr 11).
		c.17	7782.8	—	½	No farmers of clergy to pay for their lessors' First Fruits; KAO(NR/ZPr 12).
28	18 Jy. 1536	c.7	7788.3	—	8?	Establishing the succession; KAO(Sa/ZP3/8, fragment).
33	1 Ap. 1542	cc.1–19	—	[200–218]	various	On 20 Apr. 1542 Berthelet delivered 500 copies of each act except for two that were "private" in origin: c.3 in 200 copies, regulating folding of cloth in north Wales; c.13 in 12 copies, transferring certain towns from Denbigh to Flint (Arber [note 9 in Notes], 2:54–56).

		c.9		[208]	4	For maintenance of archery; against unlawful games; for a reprint in 5 sheets see [1561] below. On 6 May 1542 Berthelet delivered 12 copies of the statute in folio (cc.1–39; Arber, 2:56).
34 & 35	12 My. 1543	cc.1–13		[229–241]	various	On 31 May 1543 Berthelet delivered 500 copies of each act except for c.12 in 50 copies, for paving streets in London and Westminster; c.13 in 50 copies, creating seats in parliament for Chester. Further odd lots of most of these delivered on 12 June 1543, the last date in the account (Arber, 2:58–60). There is no mention of the statute in folio (cc.1–25, plus subsidies and Wales) except for Wales on 31 May.
		c.6	7800.3	[234]	½	For true making of pins; KAO(NR/ZPr 21); see Fig. 5.
		c.8	7800.5	[236]	1	Regulating medicines non-surgeons may give; KAO(NR/ZPr 22).
		c.9	7800.6	[237]	2	For preserving the river Severn; KAO(NR/ZPr 23).
		c.10	7800.7	[238]	2	Regulating the making of coverlets in York; KAO(NR/ZPr 24).
35	29 Mr. 1544	c.2	7802.7	—	½	Concerning trial for treason; KAO(NR/ZPr 19).
		c.3	7803	249	1	Ratification of the king's style; CANT[2].
		c.6	7803.7	—	2	Concerning jurors; KAO(NR/ZPr 20).
37	24 De. 1545	c.7	7805.3	—	1	Abrogating 6 weeks of the session; KAO(NR/ZPr 26).
		c.15	7805.5	—	1½	Against regrating wools; KAO(NR/ZPr 27).
		c.23	7805.7	—	1½	Continuing certain acts; KAO(NR/ZPr 28).
EDWARD VI						
1	24 De. 1547	c.1	7811.2	—	3	Concerning the sacrament in both kinds; KAO(NR/ZPr 31).
		c.5	7811.5	—	2	Against export of horses; KAO(NR/ZPr 32, imperfect).
		c.12	7811.9	—	3?	Repealing certain acts on treason; CANT[2](last sheet only, imperfect).

Regnal Year	End of Session	Act No.	STC	Steele§	No. of Sheets	Comment and Locations†
2 & 3	15 Mr. 1549	c.1	7819.4	—	4?	For uniformity in divine service; HN(3rd? sheet only, imperfect, with STC 15029 printed on its verso).
		c.2	7819.6	—	3	Concerning service of captains and soldiers; NRO(Brudenell B.iii.6).
		c.19	7819.8	—	2	For abstinence from flesh in Lent; L(Harl.MS.7614, ff. 13–14).
		c.39	7819.10	—	5	Pardon; L(Harl.MS.7614, ff. 198–202).
5 & 6	15 Ap. 1552	c.2	7844.6	—	2	For relief of the poor; L(Harl.MS.7614, ff. 15–16).
		c.5	7844.8	—	2	For tillage and corn; against enclosures; s(imperfect).
		c.19	7844.10	—	1	Regulating the exchange of silver and gold; L(Harl.MS.7614, f. 412).
MARY I						
1, st.2	5 De. 1553	c.2	7852	434	2	Repealing Edwardian acts on religion; HD.
		c.3	7853	435	3	Against offending preachers; F.
		c.12	7854	436	7	Against unlawful assemblies; DNPK.
PHILIP AND MARY						
2 & 3	9 De. 1555	c.3	7867	—	1	For keeping milk cows; L, O(J).
		c.4	7866	462	8?	Concerning clerical dues and taxes; L(imperfect).
		c.6	7867.3	—	3	Limiting food, etc. sequestered by the king and queen's purveyors; L(imperfect), M(deposit).
		c.8	7867.5	—	2	For mending highways; F.
		c.9	7867.7	—	1	Voiding licenses of inns where unlawful games are played; L(imperfect), M(deposit).
		c.15	7867.9	—	2	Forbidding the k & q's purveyors to sequester food within 5 miles of Cambridge and Oxford; L(imperfect), M(deposit).

Regnal Year	End of Session	Act No.	STC	Steele§	No. of Sheets	Comment and Locations†
JAMES I						
1	7 Jy. 1604	c.31	16731.5	—	2	For relief of those stricken by plague; HD; a reprint in 1630 by R. Young, printer to the city of London.
CHARLES I						
1	11 Jy. 1625	c.2	8837.5	—	1	Authorizing leases of lands in the Duchy of Cornwall; L⁵(Procs. Car. I, no. 23). Imprint dated 1626.

§ Steele numbers in square brackets signify items known to him only by the documentary evidence.

†The following location symbols are used:

CANT² Canterbury Corporation Archives, deposited at Canterbury Cathedral
DNPK Edmund Brudenell, Deene Park, Corby, Northants.
ESRO East Sussex Record Office, Lewes
F Folger Library
HD Harvard University
HN Huntington Library
KAO Kent Archives Office, Maidstone
L British Library

L⁵ Society of Antiquaries
L¹¹ Public Record Office
L³⁰ London University
M Rylands Library
NRO Northamptonshire Record Office, Delapré Abbey
O(J) Bodleian Library (John Johnson Collection)
S William Salt Library
SHR Shrewsbury School

‡Number in the table of "acts not printed."

[4] The Beginnings of English-Language Publishing in Germany in the Eighteenth Century

Bernhard Fabian

AMONG THE HUNDREDS of thousands of items to be included in the new *Eighteenth Century Short Title Catalogue (ESTC)*, one small group of books is likely to attract special attention. Few if any of them can be considered notable as instances of fine bookmaking. The majority are shoddily printed on paper of inferior quality and are flimsily bound in wrappers. What distinguishes them is their place of publication. They are, in a familiar phrase, English books printed abroad, and their Continental imprint illustrates, as an early theorist of the *ESTC* put it, "a vital fact of history—that in 1700 an educated man could do without English, whereas in 1800 it would be essential to him."[1]

I am concerned here with a fraction of this fraction of English eighteenth-century books—those published in Germany or, more precisely, in the German-speaking area of that time. I am not yet in a position to say how large that fraction is, nor could I, in the virtual absence of any research on the subject,[2] make comparative estimates. But I feel that the evidence that has so far come to light is varied and detailed enough to warrant an attempt to outline the conditions and circumstances of the publication of this particular group of books and to indicate, at least tentatively, their role in the expansion of the English language and of English culture into Europe during the eighteenth century.

I

In 1700 the number of Germans for whom English was essential must have been negligible. Of course, as early as the thirteenth century Hamburg merchants found a rudimentary knowledge of English to be useful.[3] But farther south English was, in the strictest sense of the word, a foreign language. The times were past when, for political and religious reasons, English books like Tyndale's *New Testament* had been produced at Cologne (1525), and English pamphlets purportedly "emprented at Marlborow in the lande of Hesse" had been exported from Germany or Holland for circulation in England.[4] Nor were English books any longer available at the Frankfurt fairs, as they had been in sizable numbers—witness Georg Draudius's *Bibliotheca Exotica* (1625)—late in the sixteenth and early in the seventeenth century.[5]

By the end of the seventeenth century, Frankfurt had lost much of its former attraction and importance.[6] It had become so insignificant as a center of the international book trade that Zacharias Conrad von Uffenbach, the famous bibliophile, had to learn English from the Bible because this was the only English book obtainable in Frankfurt.[7] Even in Amsterdam he found "nothing but sermons and the like."[8] Leipzig was then rapidly establishing itself as the new center of the book trade for Germany and Central Europe,[9] but for the early years, if not decades, of the eighteenth century the Leipzig Fair catalogs do not list any English books.[10] After touring the major European countries, including England, to establish contacts with foreign scholars, Otto Mencke began editing the *Acta Eruditorum,* the German counterpart of the *Philosophical Transactions* and the *Journal des sçavans,* and found that though his contributors could write reviews in Latin, few of them could read a book in English.[11]

In the intellectual traffic between England and Germany the principal medium of communication was still Latin. It had already served as the language of the Renaissance humanists and the theologians of the Reformation.[12] The late seventeenth-century scientist found it a natural vehicle for the exchange of ideas, as the correspondence between Newton and Leibniz shows,[13] and even the mid-eighteenth-century scholar used Latin in communicating with his English friends and colleagues. Johann David Michaelis, the famous Göttingen Orientalist, thanked Robert Wood in Latin for one of the privately printed quartos of the *Essay on Homer* (1769).[14]

In 1700, it is true, the German reader could read a certain number of contemporary English authors in translation.[15] *The Pilgrim's Progress* was available in German within a few years of its publication, and by 1703 at least four translations had appeared.[16] *Mac Flecknoe* was adapted as early as 1702,[17] although satirists like Oldham and Rochester seem to have remained unknown. Dryden's plays, as well as those of other Restoration dramatists, had to wait for translation until well into the eighteenth century. It is not surprising that comparatively little English literature was available. The authors considered to be important at the time were not the purely literary authors. The German reader of the period was essentially a scholarly reader or at least a reader with strong scholarly inclinations. He would be eager to know about English historians, theologians, scientists, and philosophers, and his interest in their work increased year by year. As a member of the scholarly community in Europe, he would read these authors in Latin in editions that were either reprinted from Latin versions previously published in England or translations prepared anew for the Continental reader. Works available only in English would not reach him except in special circumstances.

To cite but a few examples, the first collection of Bacon ever published anywhere was the *Opera Omnia*, which appeared in Frankfurt in 1665.[18] Another edition of *Opera Omnia* followed in 1694, issued simultaneously in Leipzig and Copenhagen.[19] Latin versions of Boyle's works were collected as *Opera Varia* (again the first collection ever made) and appeared in Geneva in 1677.[20] The publisher was Samuel de Tournes, who specialized in this kind of literature and apparently served a fairly large Continental market.[21] Thomas Stanley's *History of Philosophy* (1655–1662) was translated into Latin on the Continent and reached the German reader from Amsterdam in 1690 and again from Leipzig in 1711.[22] Thomas Burnet's *Telluris Theoria Sacra* (1681, 1689) was distributed as a reprint from Frankfurt as early as 1691 and from Amsterdam in 1694.[23] The tradition of translating English works into Latin for distribution on the Continent, which has never been traced in detail, extended at least until the middle of the eighteenth century. As the century progressed, these translations decreased in number, and they were almost exclusively confined to the fields of science, medicine, and classical studies. One of the latest and choicest examples appears to be Colin Maclaurin's *Account of Sir Isaac Newton's Philosophical Discoveries* (1749), translated by an Austrian Jesuit from the French edition of Lavirotte and published in Vienna in 1761.[24]

To summarize, then, the first significant phase in the reception of English authors in Germany was the republication in Latin, or the translation into Latin, of seventeenth-century scholarly or scientific writers. Though of great significance, this Latin phase was only transitional. It had a catalytic effect by stimulating interest in English literature in the widest sense of the word. The scholarly reader in Germany came to realize, if only gradually and over a longer period, that in addition to Latin as the *lingua franca* of the republic of letters and French as the *lingua franca* of polite society, English was indispensable as a medium through which important scholarly and literary discoveries could be made.

II

It is fitting that the earliest of the seventeenth-century English grammars for speakers of German were written in Latin. The first, Tellaeus's *Grammatica Anglica,* appeared in Strasbourg in 1665, to be followed, in 1670, by Johann Podensteiner's *Clavis Linguae Anglicanae.*[25] Of John Wallis's well-known *Grammatica Linguae Anglicanae* (1653), the first two editions were published in England. The third, however, appeared in Hamburg in 1672 and was acknowledged by Wallis as a genuine edition.[26] Its success with the German reader was apparently considerable. Another Hamburg edition came out in 1688,[27] and as late as 1765 Wallis was reprinted in Leipzig with a false London imprint.[28]

Grammars in English and German soon followed. Among them, Johann David Scheibner's *Vpright Guide for the Instruction of the English Tongue* (1688) was the first.[29] It is an early, if not the earliest, example of late seventeenth-century English printing in Germany and indicates that the knowledge of English had not progressed very far. After the turn of the century the standard grammars began to appear, notably *A Compleat English Guide for High-Germans* (1706) by Johann König (*alias* John King), which appeared first in London and then in Leipzig, where by the middle of the century it had reached its seventh edition.[30]

Although it is difficult to classify these early grammars, they appear to have been aimed at different groups of language learners. One kind of grammar was obviously directed toward the *homme d'affaires,* the other toward the man of letters. The difference was not that the grammar for the *homme d'affaires* was written in German or English, whereas the scholar's grammar would be in Latin. Until roughly 1690, both tended to be in Latin. The difference lay in the approach: The first group of grammars was predominantly practical, whereas the other was more literary. An example of the first type was the *Grammatica Nova Anglicana* (1689).[31] In addition to the grammar proper, it provided examples of short "Dialogi Anglicani" intended to help the potential visitor. Also, it added a collection of English proverbs with Latin translations and occasionally French equivalents. At their most literary, grammars of the practical type tended to include anecdotes or prayers or other short texts. Their makeup did not change significantly during the eighteenth century. The other type of grammar is best represented by Martinus Hassen's *Selecta Anglicana, sev Varia Exempla Styli Anglicani,* which appeared in Wittenberg in 1712.[32] It was essentially a collection of English texts to which a rudimentary grammar was appended. In his long Latin introduction, the editor not only distinguished the styles of various scholarly disciplines but also gave a broad survey of contemporary English scholarship placed side by side with German scholarship. Hassen's texts are culled from Chamberlayne's *Present State of Britain,* Wood's *Athenae Oxonienses,* Abercromby's *Discourse of Wit,* Locke's *Essay Concerning Human Understanding,* and other works.

Hassen's *Selecta Anglicana* and similar works are of particular interest in the history of English-language publication in Germany. Not only are they noteworthy instances of printing in the then new foreign language (the standard of printing was fairly high in view of the general ignorance of English); they are also links between the elementary grammars of the early period and the full-scale anthologies of English literary texts that tended to supplement the grammatical handbooks of a later period and that, in turn, preceded the first attempts to reprint whole works.

Theodor Arnold, who converted Nathan Bailey's *English Dictionary* into an English-German dictionary,[33] compiled in 1725 the first anthology that can be said to contain a belletristic element, however utilitarian. Under the title of *Choice Letters,* he presented his readers with a bilingual collection of "the Elegantest of the most Elegant" letters.[34] They were partly taken from model letter writers such as John Hill's *Young Secretary's Guide* (1696) and partly from collections of literary letters such as Tamworth Reresby's *Miscellany of Ingenious Thoughts and Reflections* (1721). Arnold dedicated his anthology "to All Lovers of the English Virtue, Nation and Language" and by so doing reminds us that by 1720 the era of the seventeenth-century scholar was gradually coming to an end and a new era was about to begin: that of the eighteenth-century Anglophile.

The very next anthology, the first entirely in English, was a highly competent and professional piece of bookmaking. It appeared in Göttingen in 1737, shortly after the opening of the university. In its production two newcomers had joined forces. The publisher was Abraham Vandenhoeck, a Dutchman, who had moved his printing and bookselling business from London to Hamburg and soon after accepted an invitation to become Göttingen's university printer.[35] The compiler was a certain John Tompson, an Englishman, who had come to Germany to teach English and Italian at the University of Helmstedt in 1731 and who had been appointed instructor in English at the new University of Göttingen in 1735.[36] He remained in Göttingen for the rest of his life and was so successful as a language teacher that in 1762 the university made him *professor ordinarius*—apparently the first full professor of English ever appointed.[37]

Called *English Miscellanies,* this collection consisted "of various pieces of Divinity, Morals, Politicks, Philosophy and History, as likewise of some choice Poems." All came, as the title page has it, "out of the most approved Authors in the English Tongue"—Tillotson, Nichols, Locke, Milton, Cowley, Waller, Denham, Dryden, Buckingham, Prior, Addison, Pope, and others. In other words, Tompson had apparently taken the late seventeenth-century scholarly anthology as his model and added to it a selection of texts from the belletristic authors of the late seventeenth and early eighteenth centuries. The onetime London printer Vandenhoeck was able to give the book, and especially the title page, a suitably English look, so that the neophyte would have been assured that he possessed the essence of English literature between two covers.

English Miscellanies was the right book at the right moment, and it was bound to be a success. The number of German readers of English had decidedly increased over the past decades, and the demand for English reading matter had grown. Original English books were still, as Theodor Arnold noted in 1725, "very scarce in our Book-seller-shops."[38] Though there were a few bookshops that stocked some English books, notably the house of Grosse in Leipzig, which had issued the Fair catalogs since 1595,[39] even the center of the German book trade could not cater adequately to its clientele. As late as 1744 Luise Adelgunde Gottsched, the wife of the then high priest of German literature, had to translate *The Rape of the Lock* twice, first from French and again from English, because a copy of the English text was not initially available.[40]

The importance of Tompson's anthology can hardly be overestimated. It remained without a serious rival for nearly three decades and thus must be said to have dominated the period during which the eighteenth-century German taste in English literature was formed. When in 1766 it reached its fourth edition as a two-volume work, "carefully revised and corrected" to adapt itself to recent developments,[41] it had established for the German reader a canon of English literature. An essentially neoclassical canon, it included the major eighteenth-century authors and a few minor ones, to the exclusion of novelists who were difficult to anthologize—for example, it included Milton and Dryden but not Shakespeare and not yet Ossian.

In the wake of Tompson's *Miscellanies,* anthologies proliferated in the 1770s and 1780s. Led by *The Moral Miscellany* of 1764,[42] these collections "of some letters, anecdotes, remarks and verses" (1774),[43] of "maxims, anecdotes, fables, tales, allegories" (1782),[44] and various other pieces tried to find their readers, as did those "of the best modern English poems, chiefly didactic and descriptive" (1786)[45] or "of the most approved English poets" (1794).[46] None apparently attained the stature of Tompson's *Miscellanies,* but they all contributed to establishing the anthology as a distinct genre exclusively designed for educational use.[47]

The readers of the early anthologies remain to be identified. It is safe to assume that the majority of these readers before 1750 taught themselves English.[48] But even in the second half of the century, when institutional training had become more widely available and no other nation, as Johann Christoph Gatterer noted in Göttingen, was so keen on learning foreign languages as the Germans,[49] many acquired their knowledge of English without the assistance of a teacher. Goethe, for instance, relied on a tutor but also on Dodd's *Beauties of Shakespeare.*[50] Frau von Stein, his well-known friend, was self-taught and used Goldsmith and Shakespeare as her manuals of instruction.[51] Others profited from professional teaching. Tompson's *Miscellanies* are known to have been used in courses offered by universities and by academies for young noblemen (*Ritterakademien*).[52] Some of these institutions appear to have provided instruction to prospective learners of English as early as the late decades of the seventeenth century. Little is known about the teachers and even less about the students, but it would seem that the first full-size reprint of an English book to appear in Germany in the eighteenth century was intended for the youthful reader. It appeared as early as 1726 in Jena, where English was apparently taught from 1695,[53] and was printed "for John Meyer's widow." Strangely, but not surprisingly in view of the enormous vogue of the book throughout Europe, it was a reprint of the English translation of Fénelon's *Télémaque*. In nonidiomatic English it claimed to be "reprinted according to the *London's* Edition."[54] Nearly a quarter of a century later, in 1749, the second edition appeared. Although the publisher had fashionably translated his first names into English,[55] the note on the title page was still not idiomatic. The book claimed to be "Reprinted at the second Time according to the *London's* Edition, and carefully purg'd of the Errors of the former."

III

The reprinting of English authors on a larger scale was not undertaken before the middle of the eighteenth century, and even then the start was slow. Characteristically, the first reprints of longer works occurred in bilingual editions with parallel English and German texts. Those published in the 1740s may be taken as an indication that the transition from the anthology to the complete reprint was not an abrupt one. The earliest appears to be a printing of Pope's *Essay on Man* (1740), which accompanies the first translation of the work by Barthold Hinrich Brockes,[56] one of the significant transitional figures in eighteenth-century German literature. Brockes included extracts from Thomson, Milton, and Addison, likewise in English and German, in addition to some of his own poems. Similarly, the first reprint of Pope's *Essay on Criticism* is found in a small volume that also contains other translations and an *Essay on German Criticism* in verse by the translator.[57] In spite of the bad poetry, the essay is a good example of the kind of stimulation midcentury German writers received from translating English authors.

The bilingual editions of Pope culminated in a sumptuous quarto, published in 1759, which combined a new verse translation with what purported to be a reprint of the last revised edition of the English text.[58] Carefully designed, lavishly illustrated, and dedicated to the Countess of Saxony, this volume was obviously intended to be a deluxe edition, which the Anglophile could conspicuously display in his library or on his coffee table. It was published in the small town of Altenburg in Saxony and came from the press of Paul Emanuel Richter, who made the first sustained effort to republish English authors for the German market. Obviously the *Essay on Man* was meant to be the grand opening for a series of reprint editions of the classics of English literature. According to an announcement in the Fair catalogs, it was to be followed by an edition of the English text without the German translation.[59] However, no such edition ever appeared, and it was not until 1770 that the next English book was printed at Altenburg.

Soon after the 1759 edition by Richter (whose small but reputable publishing house was founded in 1666),[60] one of the leading publishers of the period took an interest in English authors: Friedrich Nicolai, well known as one of the dominant figures of the German Enlightenment.[61] Between 1762 and 1764, he issued *The Works of Alexander Pope* in a ten-volume reprint of Warburton's edition. Neatly done in small octavo, the reprint is preceded by an interesting announcement:

> English Literature having found these many years ago, so much lovers in Germany and the adjacent countries, I doubt not, the design i have form'd to print neat Pocket-Editions of the English Classical Writers, will be very acceptable to the learned world. I thought best, to begin my Task with the Edition of Mr. POPE'S Works, this Author being so universally esteemed by all those that have any taste of Poetry or Learning.
>
> All care possible has been taken to have this Edition correct as well, as neat, and, I hope, with so good a success, that the Reader will find but very few faults, that are of any Consequence.
>
> This Edition is more complet as the English Pocket-Editions, for it is printed on Mr. WARBURTON'S Edition in Great Octavo, and contains all his Notes and Commentaries. Yet in the English little Editions the Commentaries are left out.
>
> If this first Commencement should not wholly displease to the lovers of English Literature. The Editions of the Works of MILTON, ADDISON, THOMPSON, SHAKESPEARE,

YOUNG, PRIOR, AKENSIDE, and other classical English
Writers shall follow immediately the Edition of Mr. POPE'S
Works, and shall be printed with the same neatness and cor-
rectness, adorned too with curious cuts done by the best
hands.[62]

Not a single one of these editions was published, and many "lovers of
English literature," both in Germany and in the adjacent regions served by
the German book trade, must have been disappointed.

Although Richter and Nicolai operated on different levels, both had
obviously overestimated their market. There can be no doubt that the
demand for English books in Germany, which increased gradually during
the early decades, rose rather sharply after the middle of the century with
the large-scale assimilation of literary authors, particularly poets and novelists. But it was not until the end of the century that the number of profi-
cient readers of English became so large as to constitute a market for
multivolume editions of English authors printed in Germany. If Richter's
edition of the *Essay on Man* was too elegant and expensive to be a success,
Nicolai's multivolume edition of Pope's *Works* was definitely too big. The
public, as Nicolai told one of his correspondents, did not react favorably;[63]
the edition was still being offered for sale in 1846.[64]

After these inauspicious beginnings, the 1760s give the impression of
having been a period of publishing experiments. Various anthologies appeared, as did editions of the major and minor poets. In Brunswick, Johann
Arnold Ebert published the first volume of his bilingual edition of Young's
Night Thoughts and *Satires* (1760); in it, Young is as heavily annotated as
any ancient poet has ever been.[65] In Altona, a reprint of Young's latest
work, *The Resignation,* followed within a year of its London publication
(1763),[66] and in Leipzig the infamous pseudo-Dodsley inaugurated the long
series of German editions, frequently bilingual, of Thomson's *Seasons*
(1766).[67] In Breslau (now Polish Wrocław) an edition of Richard Glover's
Leonidas appeared in 1766.[68] Strange as it may seem, the work was regarded
highly in Germany[69] as a model of the epic poem envisaged by some
German poets, notably Klopstock.

The surprising titles during this period came from Wittenberg and
Göttingen. In Wittenberg ten successive volumes of the *Philosophical Transactions* were reprinted, with Latin prefaces, between 1766 and 1776.[70] (In the
seventeenth century a Latin translation had been published in Amsterdam
and Leipzig.[71]) In Göttingen, where the university was building the richest
collection on the Continent of contemporary and early English books,[72] one
publisher made available in 1767 three very different works: Steele's *Conscious
Lovers,* Shakespeare's *Othello,* and a selection from Thomas Percy's recently

published *Reliques of Ancient English Poetry*[73]—an unusual triad by contemporary English standards, but a good example of the frequently omnivorous consumption of English literature on the Continent.

The great period of the English reprint coincided with the last three decades of the century. In the period of peace, prosperity, and cultural expansion following the end of the Seven Years' War, a sudden outburst of literary and scholarly activity produced the literature of *Sturm und Drang* and of early German classicism. With the new literature new categories of readers emerged. The educated reader, as distinct from the earlier scholarly reader, made his appearance, and the lower-class reader began to emerge.[74] Literature gradually became synonymous with belles lettres. The literary and social influence of France subsided and the German elite turned to England as a source of inspiration, literary, political, or technological. English literature was discovered as a distinct national literature, and this created a demand for "authentic" information.[75] Some of the major critics, writing in the leading journals of the day, encouraged publishers to bring out original English works instead of the apparently faulty translations that were available in ever-increasing numbers at the semiannual fairs.[76]

Appropriately, the beginning was heralded by a work that enjoyed its greatest success not in England, but in Germany: Goldsmith's *Vicar of Wakefield*. It appeared as a reprint in Berlin in 1769 (three years after the first London edition), and within twenty years four more editions were called for, three in Berlin and one in Mainz.[77] Appropriately, too, the reprint carried on the title page a note that commended the "new edition" as one "wherein the Accent is plac'd on the most necessary words for the facility of those who are desirous to pronounce the english rightly." One copy, now in Darmstadt, was acquired by a noble lady who inscribed her name, in the still Frenchified form, as "Caroline Comtesse d'Erbach."[78] I know of no other title page that illustrates so perfectly the cultural situation of the educated German reader around 1770.

Further editions of Goldsmith soon followed. With a reprint of his *Essays* in modest octavo (1770), the firm of Richter made a second and more successful start after the failure of its 1759 edition of *An Essay on Man*.[79] The *Traveller* was published, along with *The Deserted Village*, as part of a collection of four poems.[80] *The Deserted Village* was also privately printed in Darmstadt by Johann Heinrich Merck "for a Friend of the Vicar," that is, Johann Wolfgang von Goethe.[81] With the spurious *Triumph of Benevolence* ⁺he Berlin publisher Mylius obviously wanted to capitalize on the success of his *Vicar*, but apparently no second edition of the two-volume novel was called for.[82] Finally, *The Citizen of the World* had to wait for republication until 1810.[83]

Taken as a group, the nearly twenty reprints of Goldsmith's works exhibit a pattern that appears to be characteristic, though it does not hold true for the reprint editions of all literary authors. The early editions were designed for learners of English. If they were not obviously schoolbooks, they at least smacked of the schoolbook. The reprint editions published between the mid-1770s and the early 1790s belong to a different category: They were reading editions of literary works, intended to appeal to the man of letters or at least to the educated reader. Although this type of reprint persisted into the early decades of the nineteenth century, it seems to have been superseded by new and fairly elaborate school editions. The new school texts were done on a different scale. In addition to being "accented," they provided whole chapters in translation or phonetic transcription and contained rudimentary grammars and elementary literary or linguistic introductions. The appearance of these school editions seems to indicate that the reception of certain English authors was beginning to degenerate into a school exercise. Between 1797 and 1806 three such editions of the *Vicar of Wakefield* appeared.[84] A so-called "polyglot" edition of *Rasselas,* which had an interlinear translation and a normal translation (as well as an interesting list of subscribers), suggests that Goldsmith shared this fate with at least one of his friends.[85]

Although the number of English books published in the German-speaking area increased noticeably after 1770, with a dozen or more books appearing in some years, the range of authors suitable for republication remained small. One limitation was the size of the market: Even by the end of the century the number of readers of French in Germany far exceeded the number of readers of English. The choice of suitable authors was also limited by the standard of literary taste and, above all, by the linguistic abilities of the general educated reader. As a recent learner of the language, a reader could not be expected to master texts of more than ordinary length or more than ordinary difficulty. As a result, the usual reprint tended to be a volume of moderate size—the smaller the better.

Editions of the poets came close to the ideal norm for the reprint and appeared almost yearly.[86] Thomson's *Seasons* was soon followed by Gay's *Fables* (1772)[87] and a collection of minor poems with such works as Edmund Cartwright's *Armine and Elvira.*[88] Jones's *Poems Consisting Chiefly of Translations from the Asiatic Languages* (1774),[89] Edward Moore's *Fables for the Female Sex* (1784),[90] and Prior's *Poems on Several Occasions*[91] were apparently of equal interest. The great exception was a four-volume edition of *Ossian,* of which both private press and commercial editions began to appear in 1773,[92] followed by various others, including *Tales of Ossian for Use and Entertainment* prepared in 1784 as a reader for beginners.[93] In Germany the controversy over *Ossian* was followed but apparently not fully documented, for the only reprint was of John Clark's *Answer to Mr. Shaw's Inquiry into the Authenticity of the Poems Ascribed to Ossian* (1781)—obviously a bad choice.[94]

The novelists, bulkier than the poets but more easily accessible in translation, came late and almost in reverse order of their original publication. After the *Vicar of Wakefield, Tristram Shandy* appeared in 1772.[95] Two years later an enterprising publisher brought out *Tom Jones,* but nearly a decade elapsed before *Joseph Andrews* followed.[96] The vogue of sentimentalism called for an edition of *The Sentimental Journey,* which was reprinted in 1771; in 1776 a second edition appeared, as did the first German edition of Sterne's *Letters.*[97] Mackenzie's *Man of Feeling,* Smollett's *Humphry Clinker,* and Fanny Burney's *Evelina* were also made available,[98] and in 1794 *The Castle of Otranto* appeared in a "Last Edition adorned with cuts," with the subtitle, "A Gothic Story," suitably set in Gothic letters.[99] Characteristically, Richardson's *Sir Charles Grandison* was reprinted only in excerpts.[100] However, the French translation was republished as early as 1756 for the convenience of the many German readers who then read their English authors in French.[101] There was no German edition of Defoe despite the early popularity of *Robinson* in translation.

Although Shakespeare was one of the great literary discoveries, he made his impact in translation rather than in the original English text. The series of translations that culminated in the "classic" translation by Schlegel and Tieck need not be considered here, but as background it is desirable to point out the infrequency of republications of Shakespeare during this period. The first separate English edition of one of the plays appears to have been *Julius Caesar,* which appeared ("with explanatory notes selected from Dr. Johnson's and Mr. Steeven's commentaries") in Göttingen in 1777.[102] *Macbeth* was reprinted in 1778 by another Göttingen publisher, and *Hamlet* in 1784 by a third.[103] Does the fact that three publishers tried their luck as reprinters suggest that the sales left something to be desired? In any case, the translators of Shakespeare worked from English editions (Eschenburg owned one of the later Folios),[104] but it was obvious that Shakespeare was too difficult for the general reader. No multivolume edition of Shakespeare appeared in Germany until the end of the eighteenth century.[105] Contemporary English dramatists, on the other hand, fared better. *A Collection of New Plays by Several Hands* in four volumes began to appear in 1774 and brought Richard Cumberland, Arthur Murphy, George Colman, David Garrick, Richard B. Sheridan, and others to the attention of the German reader.[106] Lillo's *London Merchant,* the model of the domestic tragedy, was not available before 1776,[107] rather late in view of Lessing's *Miss Sara Sampson* (1755).

If nearly all these works belonged to the established canon, others would seem to have been departures from it: Lady Mary Wortley Montagu's *Letters,*[108] George Keate's *Sketches from Nature Taken and Coloured in a Journey to Margate* (an imitation of the *Sentimental Journey*),[109] Adam Ferguson's *Institutes of Moral Philosophy,*[110] George Anson's *Voyage Round the*

World,[111] and John Trusler's *Principles of Politeness.*[112] Late in the 1780s, the first attempts were made to provide the German reader with light reading, and titles like *Belinda, or the Fair Fugitive* and *Louisa, or the Cottage on the Moor* made their appearance.[113] Many more of these ephemeral novels were of course devoured in translation, for reading novels was the vice of the age,[114] in Germany as elsewhere.

IV

Who were the publishers behind the reprints? There is no single answer to this question. In the first place, a small number of leading publishers must be named. In Berlin Friedrich Nicolai took a genuine interest in the distribution of English authors in Germany. His ill-fated attempt to market Pope was the first, although not the only effort he made to acquaint the German reader with English literature. In 1791 he published the first bibliography ever compiled of late eighteenth-century English literature, and again he lost money on it.[115] In Göttingen Abraham Vandenhoeck's widow, one of the most successful of eighteenth-century businesswomen (and whose firm still exists to this day as Vandenhoeck & Ruprecht),[116] presumably printed English authors both as a patriotic duty, because she was English in origin, and as a local duty, because she lived in a place that was called "Londres en miniature" on account of its excessive Anglophilie.[117] In Dresden the Walther'sche Hofbuchhandlung was a truly international publishing house, with branches in Prague and Warsaw. It issued Voltaire in French, Tasso in Italian, and Locke, Swift, and Fielding in English.[118]

Among the smaller publishers the firm of Richter in Altenburg stands out. In the early 1770s, when Paul Emanuel Richter was joined by his nephew, their business seemed to have expanded considerably. They entered the international market by importing English, Dutch, Swedish, and Italian books.[119] With more than 20 English titles published in 15 years, the Richters must be regarded as the most important reprinters of the 1770s and early 1780s.[120] Their books were favorably received, although their printing, admittedly neat, was not always found faultless.[121] Another active publisher was Johann Friedrich Schiller, a cousin of the poet, who had lived in London and acted as the London agent for the house of Weidmann in Leipzig before he became a Mainz bookseller in 1784.[122] In Berlin the Mylius'sche Verlagsbuchhandlung and the Himburg'sche Buchhandlung were engaged in the reprinting business, and likewise Victor Bossiegel (later bought up by Vandenhoeck & Ruprecht) in Göttingen, Keyser in Erfurt, Fleischer in Frankfurt, and so on. None of these reprinters contributed more than a few titles.[123]

The big Leipzig publishers abstained from reprinting, apparently for two reasons. First, reprinting was considered to be a disreputable practice.[124]

Many German books published in Leipzig appeared in pirated editions in southern Germany, so that the Leipzig publishers, led by their doyen, Philipp Erasmus Reich, were strongly opposed to reprinting as a matter of principle. Throughout the latter part of the eighteenth century reprints were barred from inclusion in the Fair catalogs.[125] Although legal authorities, notably Johann Stephan Pütter in Göttingen, did not object to the reprinting of foreign books provided the original publisher could not reasonably expect substantial sales in the country in which the reprint appeared,[126] obviously not all publishers accepted this justification of the practice.

The second reason the big Leipzig publishers disdained reprinting lay in the fact that they were among the leading international booksellers of the period. They served a large market and were apparently able to supply a considerable range of books as early as the first decades of the eighteenth century. Weidmann, for instance, had branches in Stockholm and Warsaw and thus served a market that comprised Germany, Scandinavia, the Baltic region, Poland, and Russia; its market may have extended even to some southern countries as well.[127] The Leipzig fair catalogs provide evidence that, from about 1750, English books played an increasing part in the international book trade at Leipzig.[128] The major Leipzig booksellers acted as commission agents for a number of English publishers, and apparently they found the trade in original English books, coupled with the publication of translations (which in some years accounted for as many as seven titles), a more attractive business than the publication of reprints and translations.

The various attempts to market German editions of English authors must be viewed in the context of the international book trade between England and the Continent. The structure of this trade has not been fully explored yet, but currently available statistics for the total volume of British book exports in the eighteenth century seem to indicate that the German market was a minor one for the English publisher.[129] The almost conspicuous absence of English booksellers from the Leipzig fairs suggests that although trade relations existed, the British interest in the German market was anything but intense.[130] On the German side, the book trade, although well organized internally, was provincial and not sufficiently well connected in England, France, Italy, and other countries.[131] The situation improved somewhat in the later decades of the century, but even then the Anglophile reader must have felt that the book trade between England and Germany left much to be desired. The first entirely English bookshop on the Continent, opened by an Englishman in Hamburg in 1787, was an instant success.[132]

Reprinting made up for some of the deficiencies of the book trade. If the supply of books from England had been plentiful, or at least adequate presumably no German reprints would have appeared. But the fact is that throughout the century complaints about the paucity or inaccessibility of English books were frequent.[133] The demand was often specialized and reflected the needs or interests of scholars, but it apparently exceeded the supply.[134] Although the book trade could not satisfy the requirements of each individual reader, publishers could satisfy the demand when it was sufficiently strong to make a reprint commercially viable. The size of these reprint editions varied. Sometimes 800 copies may have been sufficient, if not excessive.[135] In exceptional cases, more copies were sold. Johann Arnold Ebert's bilingual and annotated editions of Young added up to about 5,000 copies, as he proudly reported to the author.[136]

Conceivably, the many uncertainties attending the Anglo-German book trade were responsible for some of the miscalculations made by German publishers. Friedrich Nicolai was deeply distrustful of English booksellers, and his abortive attempt to create a German market for reprint editions can perhaps be attributed to his lack of trust in the trade.[137] Johann Christian Dieterich in Göttingen, an occasional publisher of reprints, misjudged the situation when, in 1783, he announced a reprint of Johnson's *English Poets* and, shortly thereafter, a huge collection of the classical poets and best prose writers of England. It was to be neatly printed on deluxe writing paper and to be edited by the distinguished Georg Christoph Lichtenberg.[138] A two-volume edition of Milton was all that appeared, and even this was a failure, as was the edition of Milton published by Richter in the same year. In May 1789 two German *littérateurs* proposed "to publish a New Edition of the best English periodical works in the original language," from the *Tatler* and *Spectator* "down to the best modern works of this kind." Once again, nothing became of the project.[139] Both schemes were stimulated by the frequent complaints about the unavailability of original English books, but the vociferousness of the few obviously made the market appear much bigger than it actually was.

The great asset of the German reprints was their low price. Johnson's *Poets* were to be sold at half the price of the original edition. It seems safe to assume that the prices of other reprints were at least as low. By German standards, and perhaps by Continental standards in general, English books were expensive. When Albrecht von Haller, the famous medical bibliographer, went to England, he found the quality of English books superior but the prices exorbitant.[140] The printing, paper, and binding of German books were generally inferior to that of imported books, but the prices were correspondingly lower and seem to have appealed to many readers for whom English authors were otherwise unobtainable or unaffordable.

English-language publication in the German-speaking area should not be regarded only as a business venture. In view of the deficiencies of the international book trade, it should also be seen as an act of cultural self-help. The practice of reprinting English authors followed the expansion of

English culture as it progressed from north to south. Almost all of the early reprint publishers were located in northern or central Germany. In the 1780s they were joined by at least one Bavarian publisher, Adam Gottlieb Schneider in Nuremberg, who published his editions of Sterne in true Shandean fashion under the imprint of Adam Theophilus Taylor, London.[141] Finally, in the 1790s the expansion reached Austria.[142] A new market for English books opened up, but it was either inaccessible or unattractive for the conventional international bookseller. As a result, Rudolf Sammer, author of an English grammar,[143] went into publishing. Just before the turn of the century, he produced a number of small duodecimos, among which was a nine-volume collection of Sterne.[144]

V

The most enterprising and successful of the late eighteenth-century reprint publishers was a Swiss, Johann Jacob Thurneysen of Basle.[145] Trained at Leipzig by Johann Gottlob Immanuel Breitkopf, a printer of international standing, Thurneysen opened a printing office at Basle in the 1770s. His first spectacular business venture was a reprint of Beaumarchais's Kehl edition of the works of Voltaire. Thurneysen sold it at half the price of the original edition and seems to have gained thereby both a substantial profit and an international reputation.

Conceived on a grand scale, Thurneysen's English project was announced as "a collection of the principal English historians, philosophers and poets." Of his advertisement—a key document in the history of English-language publishing on the Continent—no copy seems to have survived. However, from a note published by one of his business associates it is certain that a group of *littérateurs* (unfortunately anonymous) acted as an advisory board and that native speakers read the proofs.[146] As a result, Thurneysen's editions were not only carefully supervised reprints; they were, at least in some cases, edited editions that deserved to be called, for better or for worse, "new editions."

The series was launched with a reprint of Gibbon's *Decline and Fall*. The first three volumes, originally published in 1776 and 1781, appeared in 1787 and the last three, published in 1788, followed only a year later.[147] Gibbon, then in Switzerland, was impressed by so careful a piece of work, though he warned Cadell, his publisher, of "the unexpected invasion of *foreign* pirates."[148] Thurneysen reprinted the original quartos in octavo. He retained the octavo format for all his reprints, so that the more than 180 volumes he published in about fifteen years gave the impression that he was in fact forming a collection.[149]

Bolingbroke's *Letters on the Study and Use of History* was the next title followed by Robertson's *History of Charles V*, Blair's *Lectures on Rhetoric*, Ferguson's *Essay on the History of Civil Society*, Hume's *History of England*, Gillies's *History of Ancient Greece*, Middleton's *History of the Life of M. Tullius Cicero*, Smith's *Wealth of Nations*, and others.[150] With Kippis's *Life of Cook* (1788) the series was expanded to include works of current interest. In 1791 Thurneysen announced that he would also provide reprints of the most recent accounts of travels, among them Bruce's *Travels to Discover the Sources of the Nile* and Chandler's *Travels in Asia Minor*, but neither appeared.[151] Apparently the Anglophile reader preferred the classics. It was fitting that the series came to include a deluxe edition of Shakespeare (1799–1802), based on Reed's edition of 1793, and that it ended in 1803, on account of Thurneysen's premature death, with a reprint of Warton's edition of Pope.[152]

What distinguished the Basle reprints from others that appeared at the same time was not only the painstaking care with which they were produced. It was also the editorial expertise with which the books were selected and prepared for reprinting. Whenever possible, Thurneysen procured the latest revised edition of the work as his copy text. Thus Blair's *Lectures* (1788) appears to have been printed from the second edition (1785) and Burke's *Philosophical Inquiry* (1792) from the eighth or ninth edition (1776, 1782). In each case the text was carefully checked and occasional printer's errors were corrected. Frequently the accidentals of the text were slightly modernized, although in the case of Sterne's *Sentimental Journey* the older typographic style of the 1760s seems to have been retained deliberately. Of Hume's *Essays and Treatises* Thurneysen published an edition that adds to the complexities of the bibliography of Hume, for it differs in minor points from all editions which he could possibly have used as copy text.

Thurneysen's edition of George Keate's *Accounts of the Pelew Islands* provides a good example of the speed with which the publisher's advisers and printers worked. The book was published in London in 1788, and the map was dated 1 July. A copy of the book was brought from London to Switzerland, the book was reprinted, the map redrawn, the index readjusted to suit the change in format, and the reprint was offered for sale in William Remnant's English bookshop in Hamburg in June of the following year. It was announced among the new books "published in the English Dominions."[153]

The commercial success of Thurneysen's reprints must be attributed to an impressive system of distribution. Through his edition of Voltaire, Thurneysen had established business connections with the publisher and bookseller Karl Wilhelm Ettinger in Gotha in Saxony. Ettinger became Thurneysen's distributor for northern and central Germany and represented him at the Leipzig fairs.[154] It was through Ettinger and through William Remnant in Hamburg that Thurneysen's books came into the hands of many German men of letters who played a significant role in the reception of English culture in Germany. Ludwig Tieck, the translator of Shakespeare, owned a copy of Thurneysen's Shakespeare (now in the British Library).[155] Christian Garve, philosophical writer and translator of Burke, Ferguson, Hume, and Smith, bought almost the whole series.[156]

Thurneysen's reprints were also distributed in France. There are a number of imprints on which the names of Levrault in Strasbourg and of Pissot in Paris appear together with that of Thurneysen. The precise business relations between Thurneysen and his Basle associates, Legrand and Decker, have not been fully established yet, but it is clear that the distribution of the reprints in France was part of a well-devised business strategy.[157] Pissot's lot of Kippis's *Life of Cook*, for instance, was sold in Paris with the original title page, whereas Thurneysen's own lot had a cancelled title page.[158] By piecing together various fragments of evidence, future bibliographers should be able to add substantially to the story of the reception of English authors both in France and Germany.

Wherever he bought his Thurneysen reprints, the eighteenth-century Anglophile was likely to have been pleased with his purchases. Not only were the texts reliable; they also appeared in a dress that closely resembled that of the original London editions, for Thurneysen followed the style and conventions of English typography. Above all, Thurneysen's reprints were cheap. His octavo edition of Keate's *Pelew Islands* was offered in Hamburg at roughly a quarter of the price of the London quarto edition.[159] At a time when English books were excessively expensive by Continental standards, Thurneysen's offerings undoubtedly provided a service "to the friends of English literature." It is no wonder that journals from Paris to Gotha took note of almost every reprint as it came off the Basle press, and that they were full of praise. The highest praise bestowed on Thurneysen came perhaps from Göttingen, the "Londres en miniature," where one reviewer wrote that each library which contained Thurneysen's series could be considered "a sanctuary of good taste."[160]

Acknowledgment

I am indebted to the Stiftung Volkswagenwerk for the award of an Akademie-Stipendium, which gave me the opportunity to collect in various libraries some of the material on which this paper is based. I should also like to acknowledge the research assistance of Dr. Marie-Luise Spieckermann.

NOTES

1. R. J. Roberts, "Towards a Short-Title Catalogue of English Eighteenth Century Books," *Journal of Librarianship* 2 (1970): 251.

2. A bibliography of German reprints of English authors is in preparation as part of a larger bibliography to be published by Anton Hiersemann.

3. See H. P. Junker, "Englischer Unterricht, geschichtlicher Abriss," in *Enzyklopädisches Handbuch der Pädagogik*, ed. W. Rein (Langensalza, 1904), Vol. 2, p. 40.

4. See Robert Steele, "Notes on English Books Printed Abroad, 1525–48," *Transactions of the Bibliographical Society* 11 (1912): 189–236.

5. See Max Spirgatis, "Englische Literatur auf der Frankfurter Messe von 1561–1620," in *Beiträge zur Kenntnis des Schrift-, Buch- und Bibliothekswesens* 7 (Sammlung bibliothekswissenschaftlicher Arbeiten, 15) (Leipzig, 1902), pp. 37–89.

6. See Felix von Schröder, *Die Verlegung der Büchermesse von Frankfurt am Main nach Leipzig*, Volkswirtschaftliche und wirtschaftsgeschichtliche Abhandlungen, 9 (Leipzig, 1904); and Walter Fischer, *Die Abwanderung des Buchhandels von der Frankfurter Messe nach Leipzig* (Bottrop, 1934); see also Ernst Hasse, "Notizen zur Geschichte des Verfalls der Frankfurter Büchermesse," *Archiv für Geschichte des deutschen Buchhandels* 4 (1879): 221–223.

7. *Merkwürdige Reisen durch Niedersachsen, Holland und Engelland* (Frankfurt und Leipzig, 1753), Vol. 2, p. 443. Translated in part as *London in 1710: From the Travels of Z. C. von Uffenbach*, trans. and ed. W. H. Quarrell and Margaret Marc (London, 1934).

8. Ibid.

9. See, for instance, F. Hermann Meyer, "Die Leipziger Büchermesse von 1780–1837," *Archiv für Geschichte des deutschen Buchhandels* 14 (1891): 288–316; see also "Schreiben eines Buchhändlers von der Leipziger Ostermesse," *Leipziger Kalender* 9 (1912): 127–133.

10. This applies for the period from 1700 to 1725.

11. See Joachim Kirchner, "Zur Entstehungs- und Redaktionsgeschichte der *Acta Eruditorum*," in *Ausgewählte Aufsätze aus Paläographie, Handschriftenkunde, Zeitschriftenwesen und Geistesgeschichte* (Stuttgart, 1970), pp. 153–172. Kirchner refers to two letters from Mencke to Leibniz, written in October 1684 (p. 169).

12. See Karl Heinrich Schaible, *Geschichte der Deutschen in England* (Strassburg, 1885); W. D. Robson-Scott, *German Travellers to England, 1400–1800* (Oxford, 1953); William Brenchley Rye, *England as Seen by Foreigners in the Days of Elizabeth and James the First* (London, 1865).

13. See, for instance, *The Correspondence of Isaac Newton*, ed. H. W. Turnbull, 3 vols. (Cambridge, 1959–1961), especially letters no. 427 and 430; Gottfried Wilhelm

Leibniz, *Philosophischer Briefwechsel*, I (Darmstadt, 1926; reprint Berlin, Hildesheim, New York, 1972), nos. 25, 119, 127.

14. The copy is now in Göttingen University Library. The correspondence is printed in the appendix to my reprint edition of Wood's *Essay on Homer* (Hildesheim, 1976).

15. See Gilbert Waterhouse, *The Literary Relations of England and Germany in the Seventeenth Century* (Cambridge, 1914; reprint New York, 1966).

16. *Eines Christen Reise nach der seligen Ewigkeit* (Hamburg: Georg Wolff, 1684; Hamburg: Gottfried Liebernickel, 1694, 1696; Basel: Genath, 1702).

17. *Ein Heldengedicht, Hans Sachs genannt, aus dem Englischen übersetzt* (Altona, 1702). Adapted by Christian Wernicke.

18. Francofurti ad Moenum, impensis Johannis Baptistae Schonwetteri . . . , 1665. R. W. Gibson, *Francis Bacon: A Bibliography of His Works and of Baconiana to the Year 1750* (Oxford, 1950), no. 235.

19. Lipsiae, impensis Johannis Justi Erythropili . . . , 1694; Hafniae, impensis Johannis Justi Erythropili . . . , 1694 (Gibson, nos. 243a and 243b).

20. Genevae, apud Samuelem de Tournes, 1677; two issues. John F. Fulton, *A Bibliography of the Honourable Robert Boyle, Fellow of the Royal Society* (Oxford, 1932–1933; reprint 1947; 2nd ed. 1961), nos. 246 and 246A; see also p. 148.

21. For a short history of the publishing house, see John Rochester Kleinschmidt, *Les imprimeurs et libraires de la république de Genève 1700–1798* (Geneva, 1948), pp. 98–105. A nearly complete collection of De Tournes editions was acquired by Hinrich von Bülow, whose library (consisting of nearly 10,000 volumes) became the nucleus of Göttingen University Library.

22. *Historia Philosophiae Orientalis: Recensuit, ex Anglica Lingua in Latinam Transtulit, Notis &c. Auxit J. Clericus.* Amstelodami, 1690; *Historia Philosophiae . . . ex Anglico Sermone in Latinum Translata, Emendata, & Variis Dissertationibus atque Observationibus Passim Aucta. Accessit Vita Autoris.* Lipsiae, apvd Thomam Fritsch, 1711. The fourth London edition (1743) has a note on the title page: "compared throughout with . . . the Latin Translation printed at Leipsick."

23. Francofurti ad Moenum, Typis & impensis Balth. Christ. Wustii Sen. 1694. Amstelaedami, J. Wolters, 1694, 2nd ed. 1699.

24. Viennae Austriae, Typis Joannis Thomae Trattner. The translator was Gregor Falck.

25. Tellaeus, *Grammatica. . .* Argentinae, typis Carolinis, sumpt. Authoris, 1665; *Johannis Podensteiner Clavis. . .* [Wittenberg?], 1670; [another edition] [Wittenberg?], 1685. See Robin C. Alston, *A Bibliography of the English Language from the Invention of Printing to the Year 1800* (reprint Ilkley, 1974), II, nos. 344–346.

26. Hamburgi, apud Gothofredum Schultzen, 1672 (Alston, I, no. 16).

27. *Grammatica . . . Cui Subjungitur Johannis Podensteiner Clavis Linguae Anglicanae.* [Hamburg], sumtibus viduae Gotfried Schultzen, 1688 (Alston, I, no. 18). For Podensteiner, see note 25.

28. Londini et Lipsiae: Svmtibvs Io. Dodslei et Casp. Moseri, 1765 (Alston, I, no. 21). The name of Dodsley was used by Schwickert, one of the eighteenth-century Leipzig publishers. "J. Dodsley und Compagnie" became a cause célèbre when Lessing discontinued his *Hamburgische Dramaturgie* because of a reprint published by "Dodsley"; see Gustav Wustmann, "Dodsley und Compagnie," in *Aus Leipzigs Vergangenheit: Gesammelte Aufsätze* (Leipzig, 1885), pp. 236–249. There were also translations of English works with this imprint.

29. *The Vpright Guide . . . , Comprehending the Whole Ground and Rules of this Gentle Language.* Ienae, apud Johannem Bilke, 1688. Alston, II, no. 349.

30. London: W. Freeman & B. Barker, 1706. [Another edition] Leipsick: John Frederick Braun, 1715; [Another edition] Leipsick: J. F. Brown's Heirs, 1727; third edition, Leipsick: J. F. Brown's Heirs, 1734; fourth edition, Leipzig: J. F. Bkowns [sic] Heirs, 1740; fifth edition, Leipzig: Charles Ludwig Jacobi, 1748; sixth edition, Leipzig: Charles Ludwig Jacobi, 1755; seventh edition, Leipzig: Charles Lewis Jacobi's Widow, 1762 (Alston, II, nos. 359–365, 367). English grammars for Germans have chiefly been studied by phoneticists. See, for example, Otto Driedger, *Johann Königs (John King's) deutsch-englische Grammatiken und ihre späteren Bearbeitungen (1706–1802): Versuch einer historischen Behandlung* (Marburg, 1907); Walther Müller, "Theodor Arnolds englische Grammatiken und ihre späteren Bearbeitungen. Ein kritischer Beitrag zur englischen Lautgeschichte," *Die neueren Sprachen* 17 (1909), 385–402, 461–479, 533–549; Wilhelm Vietor, *Die Aussprache des Englischen nach den deutsche-englischen Grammatiken vor 1750* (Marburg, 1886).

31. Jenae, sumpt. Tobiae Ohrlingi, 1689 (Alston, II, no. 350). The author signs himself J. N. S.

32. Vitembergae, Christoph. Theophil. Lvdovicvm (Alston, II, no. 463).

33. See Martin Lehnert, "Das englische Wörterbuch in Vergangenheit und Gegenwart," *Zeitschrift für Anglistik und Amerikanistik* 4 (1956): 282.

34. *Choice Letters: Auserlesene Briefe, aus einigen von den galantesten und berühmtesten englischen Autoribus gesammelt, und ins Hochteutsche übersetzet von Aldinor.* Hanover [sic]: Nicolaus Förster und Sohn, 1725. Aldinor was used by Arnold as an anagram (see Zedler's *Universallexikon*, Supplement, 1751, II, 379).

35. See Wilhelm Ruprecht, *Väter und Söhne: Zwei Jahrhunderte Buchhändler in einer deutschen Universitätsstadt* (Göttingen, 1935); and B. Fabian, " 'London' Books?" *Factotum: Newsletter of the XVIIIth Century STC*, no. 4 (1978): 18–20.

36. Johann David Michaelis, *Räsonnement über die protestantischen Universitäten in Deutschland* (Frankfurt und Leipzig, 1773; reprint Aalen 1973), Vol. 3, 86–87.

37. Wilhelm Ebel, *Catalogus Professorum Gottingensium, 1734–1962* (Göttingen, 1962), p. 104.

38. *Choice Letters,* op. cit., p. 4.

39. The Grosse catalogs of available books are preserved as appendixes to some fair catalogs. The earliest appeared for the Easter Fair of 1732.

40. *Herrn Alexander Popens Lockenraub, ein scherzhaftes Heldengedicht* (Leipzig Bernhard Christoph Breitkopf, 1744), "Vorrede," sig. b4r.

41. Göttingen: For the Widow of Abram Vandenhoeck.

42. Leipzig and Züllichau: printed for the House of Orphans and Frommann

43. Friedrich Wilhelm Streit, *An Attempt to Facilitate the Study of the English Language by Pvblishing in the Present Cheap Manner a Collection of Some Anecdotes Remarks. . . .* Ronneburgh: printed and sold by Heinr. Gottl. Rothe.

44. J. H. Emmert, *A Collection of Maxims, Anecdotes . . . Selected from Some of the Best English Writers.* Göttingen: printed for Victorinus Bossiegel.

45. *The Poetical Library; Being a Collection of the Best Modern English Poems.* 2 vols Leipzig: printed for A. F. Boehme by I. G. Struck at Wernigerode, 1786–1787.

46. G. F. Niemeyer, *A Collection aut* [sic] *of Some of the Most Approved English Poets.* 2 vols. Vol. 1: Printed for C. Ritscher at Hannover, 1794; [another issue] Printed for Huntemann jun. at Bremen, and C. Ritscher at Hannover, 1794. Vol. 2 Hannover, for W. Pockwitz, jun. 1796. The collection is bilingual, with parallel English and German texts.

47. See, for example, Christian Ludwig Ideler and Johann Wilhelm Heinrich Nolte, *Handbuch der englischen Sprache.* Berlin: Verlag der Buchhandlung der Königl. Realschule, 1793. Revised and enlarged editions were published in 1808, 1811 1823, 1832.

48. See Junker, op. cit., p. 412.

49. *Historisches Journal* 1 (1772): 274.

50. James Boyd, *Goethe's Knowledge of English Literature* (Oxford, 1932), pp. ix–xvii

51. Wilhelm Bode, *Der weimarische Musenhof, 1756–1781,* 3rd ed. (Berlin, 1917). p. 247.

52. An example is Johann Arnold Ebert, the translator of Young, who based his courses at the Collegium Carolinum at Brunswick on it. See M. Joh. Gottl. Biedermann, *Altes und Neues von Schulsachen* (Halle, 1752–1755), Vol. 3, pp. 331–332. See also Wilhelm Aehle, *Die Anfänge des Unterrichts in der englischen Sprache, besonders auf den Ritterakademien,* Erziehungswissenschaftliche Studien 17 (Hamburg, 1938). The best general account, based on extensive study of the source material, is Konrad Schröder, *Die Entwicklung des englischen Unterrichts an deutschsprachigen Universitäten* (Ratingen bei Düsseldorf, 1969).

53. See Schröder, *Die Entwicklung des englischen Unterrichts,* pp. 182–183. The date is suggested by the appearance of Johann Jakob Lungershausen's *Nursery of Young English Trees, id est Arboreticum Anglicum.*

54. *The Adventures of Telemachus, The Son of Ulysses. . . . Done into English from the last Paris (which is the only genuine) edition, by Mr. Is. Littlebury and Mr. A. Boyer.*

55. *The Adventures of Telemachvs. . . .* Iena: For Theodore William Ernest Gvth, 1749.

56. *Hrn. B. H. Brockes . . . Aus dem Englischen übersetzter Versuch vom Menschen . . . nebst verschiedenen andern Uebersetzungen und einigen eigenen Gedichten.* Hamburg: Christian Herold, 1740.

57. *Versuch über die Critik aus dem Englischen des Herrn Pope. Nebst einem Versuche einer Critik über die deutschen Dichter, auch einer Zugabe einiger kleineren Schrifften, von M. Gottfried Ephraim Müller.* Dresden: George Conrad Walther, 1745.

58. *Essay on Man. Der Mensch ein philosophisches Gedichte.* Altenburg: Richter, 1759.

59. In the catalog for the Easter Fair of 1759 the edition is advertised as "deutsche Uebersetzung mit und ohne der englischen Urschrift" (p. 965).

60. A short history of the firm is outlined in a petition to the government of 7 May 1781, by Paul Emanuel Richter (manuscript in Historisches Staatsarchiv Altenburg, Landesregierung Sign. 8820) and in an obituary of Gottfried Richter, published in 1696. See also Marie-Luise Spicckermann, "The English Reprints of Richter at Altenburg: Some Notes and a List," *Factotum: Newsletter of the XVIIIth Century STC*, no. 7 (1979): 25.

61. See Horst Möller, *Aufklärung in Preussen: Der Verleger, Publizist und Geschichtsschreiber Friedrich Nicolai,* Einzelveröffentlichungen der Historischen Kommission zu Berlin 15 (Berlin, 1974).

62. "The Bookseller's Advertisement on this new Edition."

63. To Johann Peter Uz, 5 October 1762: "Das deutsche Publikum begünstigt meinen Anschlag auf die engländischen Schriftsteller bisher eben nicht sehr." Quoted from: Martin Sommerfeld, *Friedrich Nicolai und der Sturm und Drang: Ein Beitrag zur Geschichte der deutschen Aufklärung: Mit einem Anhang: Briefe aus Nicolais Nachlass* (Halle, 1921), p. 331.

64. See *Verlags-Katalog der Nicolaischen Buchhandlung in Berlin* (1846), p. 85.

65. Ebert's editions of Young are listed in Harold Forster, "Edward Young in Translation I," *Book Collector* 19 (1970): 481–500.

66. *Resignation. In Two Parts, and a Postscript. To Mrs. B*****. Die Verläugnung in Zwey Theilen, nebst einer Nachschrift, an Mad. B*****.* Altona [no publisher].

67. *The Seasons.* London and Leipzig: printed for J. Dodsley and C. Moser, 1766. "A New Edition. To which is Prefixed An Essay on the Plan and Character of the Poem, by J. Aikin" appeared in Leipzig in 1781 as "Printed for E. B. Schwickert." Further German editions followed, for example: Basil: printed for John Schweighauser, 1769; Hamburg: printed for J. H. and J. G. Herold, by G. F. Schniebes, 1791; Leipzig: printed for John Sommer, 1794; Leipzig: printed for Breitkopf and Haertel, 1801. Haydn's oratorio *The Seasons* was first performed in 1801.

68. *Leonidas. A Poem.* Leipzig and Breslau: printed for J. E. Meyer.

69. There is a correspondence between Glover and Johann Arnold Ebert. See *Ebert's Episteln und vermischte Gedichte,* ed. J. J. Eschenburg (Hamburg, 1795), Vol. 2, pp. 92–102.

70. *Philosophical Transactions, Giving Some Account of the Present Undertakings, Studies, and Labours of the Ingenious, in Many Considerable Parts of the World,* Vols. 47 ff. Wittenberg: by C. C. Dürr, 1766–1776.

71. *Acta Philosophica Societatis Regiae in Anglia, Anno 1665–1669* (Leipzig, 1675). The Amsterdam edition (1674 ff.) appeared in six volumes.

72. See B. Fabian, "An Eighteenth-Century Research Collection: English Books at Göttingen University Library," *Library,* 6th Ser., I (1979): 209–224.

73. Published under the general title of *Select English Plays. Volume the First, Containing Othello, the Moor of Venice. The Conscious Lovers. To Which Are Annexed Ancient and Modern Songs.* Göttingen: printed for Victorinvs Bossiegel, 1767. *The Conscious Lovers* and *Ancient and Modern Songs and Ballads* were also sold separately.

74. See Rolf Engelsing, *Analphabetentum und Lektüre: Zur Sozialgeschichte des Lesens in Deutschland zwischen feudaler und industrieller Gesellschaft* (Stuttgart, 1973).

75. See Johann Wilhelm von Archenholz, "An die Freunde der englischen Litteratur und Sprache," *Neue Litteratur und Völkerkunde* I (1787): 344–345.

76. See, for instance, Johann Heinrich Merck in *Allgemeine deutsche Bibliothek* 26, Vol. I (1775): 283.

77. "A New Edition," Berlin: Printed for August Mylius, 1769; second edition, Berlin: Sold by August Mylius, Bookseller, and printed at Altenburg by Richter, 1776; third edition, Berlin: Sold by August Mylius, Bookseller, and printed at Altenburg by Richter, 1780. "A New Edition, Corrected," Mentz [Mainz]: Printed for J. F. Schiller, 1787; fourth edition, Berlin: Printed for August Mylius, Bookseller in Brother-Street, 1789.

78. Hessische Landesbibliothek, Darmstadt; shelfmark: 52/417.

79. Altenburg: Richter. Another edition was published by Richter in 1774.

80. Altenburg: Printed for Gottlob Emanuel Richter, and committed to A. F. Boehme, Bookseller in Leipzig, 1773. With the half title: "Four poems viz.: I. Armine and Elvira. II. The Hermit of Warkworth. III. The Deserted Village. IV. The Traveller."

81. In 1772. See Hermann Bräuning-Oktavio, "Johann Heinrich Merck als Drucker, Verleger, Kupferstecher und Mäzen," *Philobiblon: Eine Vierteljahrsschrift für Buch- und Graphiksammler* 13 (1969): 99–122, 165–208; and "Goethe und Johann Heinrich Merck: Die Geschichte einer Freundschaft," *Goethe: Neue Folge des Jahrbuchs der Goethe-Gesellschaft* 12 (1950): 190.

82. 2 vols. Berlin: Sold by August Mylius, 1786.

83. 2 vols. Leipzig: Printed for G. A. Grieshammer, 1810.

84. "Accentuirt von J. Ebers," Berlin: G. C. Nauck, 1797; Francfort on the Mayn: Printed for B. Koerner, 1800; ed. Friedrich Theodor Kühne, Berlin: Heinrich Frölich, 1806.

85. Ed. Geo. Smout, 2 vols. Hamburg: bei dem Verfasser und in Commission bei Hartwig & Müller, 1826.

86. Here as elsewhere the titles quoted represent a selection.

87. Altenburg: Printed for Gottlob Eman. Richter, and committed to Adam Friedr. Boehme, bookseller in Leipzig.

88. Altenburg: Printed for Gottlob Emanuel Richter, and committed to A. F. Boehme, Bookseller in Leipzig, 1773. With the half title "Four poems" (see note 80).

89. Altenburg: By Gottlob Emanuel Richter.

90. Altenburg: printed and sold by G. E. Richter.

91. Leipzig: Paul Gotthelf Kummer, 1783. Bilingual edition.

92. *Works of Ossian*. Francfort and Leipzig: Printed for I. G. Fleischer, [1773]–1778; [another edition] 1783.

93. Nürnberg: Raspe, 1784; second edition 1794.

94. Included in *Works of Ossian*, I (1773 and 1783) (see note 92).

95. Altenburg: Printed for G. E. Richter, and committed to A. F. Boehme, bookseller in Leipzig. There were further editions by other publishers.

96. *The History of Tom Jones*, 2 vols. Dresden: Printed for G. C. Walther, 1774; *The History of the Adventures of Joseph Andrews*, 2 vols. Dresden: Printed by C. and F. Walther, 1783. For a complete list of English books published by Walther, see Curt Vinz, "Das Verlagsverzeichnis der Waltherschen Hofbuchhandlung in Dresden vom Jahre 1833," *Archiv für Geschichte des Buchwesens* 9 (1967): 156.

97. *A Sentimental Journey through France and Italy*, 2 vols. Leipzig: Committed to A. F. Boehme, 1771; "The second edition in Germany," Altenburg: Printed for Gottlob Emanuel Richter, 1776; *Letters of the Late Rev. Mr. Laurence Sterne*, 3 vols. Altenburg: Printed for Richter.

98. *The Man of Feeling*, Hamburgh: printed for Hoffmann, Bookseller, 1785; *The Expedition of Humphry Clinker*, 2 vols. Altenburg: printed and sold by Richter, 1785; *Evelina*, 3 vols. Dresden: Printed for C. and F. Walther, 1788.

99. Berlin: printed for Christ. Fred: Himbourg.

100. Johann Heinrich Emmert, ed., *The Novelist: Or, a Choice Selection of the Best Novels. Vol. I. Containing Sir Charles Grandison and Tom Jones* [*Vol. II. Containing Joseph Andrews, and Clarissa Harlowe*], Göttingen: printed for Vandenhoeck and Ruprecht, 1792–1793. A complete edition of *Clarissa* was published in Basle by Johann Jakob Thurneysen in 1792.

101. *Histoire de Sir Charles Grandison,* 7 vols. Leipsic: Chez les Herit. de M. G. Weidmann.

102. Göttingen: to be sold by A. Vandenhoeck's Widow.

103. *Macbeth.... With Explanatory Notes Selected from Dr. Johnson's and Mr. Steevens's Commentaries,* Göttingen: to be sold by I. C. Dieterich; *Hamlet.... With Explanatory Notes,* Göttingen: Printed for Victorinus Bossiegel.

104. *Verzeichniss derjenigen Bücher aus dem Nachlasse weil. Geheime-Justizraths und Professors Dr. Joh. Joachim Eschenburg, welche auktionsmässig verkauft werden sollen* (Braunschweig, 1822), p. 90.

105. *The Dramatic Works of William Shakespeare,* ed. Karl Wagner, 8 vols. Brunswick, 1797–1801.

106. Altenburg: Printed for Gottl. Eman. Richter, 1774–1778.

107. Göttingen: printed for Victorinus Bossiegel. There were earlier translations.

108. Berlin: Sold by August Mylius, 1781.

109. Dresden: by C. and F. Walther, 1784.

110. Mentz [= Mainz] and Frankfort: Printed for J. F. Schiller; and Sold by Varrentrapp jun. and Wenner, 1786.

111. Mentz [= Mainz]: Printed for J. F. Schiller, 1788.

112. 2 vols. Berlin: Printed for August Mylius in Brother-Street, 1784.

113. *Belinda...,* Halle: sold by Franck and Bispink, 1789; Elizabeth Helme, *Louisa...,* 2 vols., "the fifth edition corrected and augmented." Leipzig: Printed for Graef, 1789.

114. See Dominik von König, "Lesesucht und Lesewut," in *Buch und Leser,* ed. Herbert G. Göpfert (Hamburg, 1977), pp. 89–124.

115. See B. Fabian, "Die erste Bibliographie der englischen Literatur des achtzehnten Jahrhunderts: Jeremias David Reuss' *Gelehrtes England,*" in [Festschrift für Gerhard Liebers, vol. I], *Erlesenes aus der Welt des Buches: Gedanken, Betrachtungen, Forschungen,* ed. Bertram Haller (Wiesbaden, 1979), pp. 16–43.

116. See Ruprecht, op. cit.

117. See Götz von Selle, *Die Georg-August-Universität zu Göttingen, 1737–1937* (Göttingen, 1937), p. 186.

118. See Vinz, op. cit., pp. 155–156. On Walther's international business relations, see Martin Fontius, "Zur literarhistorischen Bedeutung der Messekataloge im 18. Jahrhundert," *Weimarer Beiträge* 7 (1961): 614–615.

119. My information comes from Paul Emanuel Richter's petition of 7 May 1781 (see note 60).

120. For a list, see Spieckermann, op. cit., pp. 26–30.

121. See *Der deutsche Merkur* 5 (1774): 368–369; and *Allgemeine deutsche Bibliothek* 26 (1775): 282.

122. See Johann Jacob Gradmann, *Das gelehrte Schwaben: oder Lexicon der jetzt lebenden schwäbischen Schriftsteller* ([Ravensburg], 1802), pp. 564 ff., and Balthasar Haug, *Das gelehrte Wirtemberg* (Stuttgart, 1790), pp. 162, 238.

123. For information on some of these publishers, see Rudolf Schmidt, *Deutsche Buchhändler, deutsche Buchdrucker: Beiträge zu einer Firmengeschichte des deutschen Buchgewerbes* (Berlin, 1902–1908; reprint Hildesheim, 1979).

124. The literature on this subject is extensive. The latest and most balanced account is presented by Reinhard Wittmann, "Der gerechtfertigte Nachdrucker? Nachdrucker und literarisches Leben im achtzehnten Jahrhundert," in *Buch und Buchhandel in Europa im achtzehnten Jahrhundert*, Wolfenbüttler Schriften zur Geschichte des Buchwesens 7 (Hamburg, 1981): 293–320.

125. See B. Fabian, "Die Messkataloge des achtzehnten Jahrhunderts," in ibid., pp. 321–342.

126. See Pütter, *Der Büchernachdruck nach ächten Grundsätzen des Rechts* (Göttingen, 1774).

127. See Ernst Vollert, *Die Weidmannsche Buchhandlung in Berlin, 1680 bis 1930* (Berlin, 1930). Most of the eighteenth-century catalogs issued by Weidmann are lost; see Karl Baerent, "Kataloge der Weidmannschen Buchhandlung aus der ersten Hälfte des XVIII. Jahrhunderts," *Zeitschrift für Bücherfreunde*, N.S. 5 (1914): 236–241. Those issued in Stockholm in 1721 have survived in the Kungliga Biblioteket in Stockholm. I am grateful to Dr. Sten G. Lindberg for drawing my attention to them.

128. The first of the Leipzig booksellers to import a variety of English books appears to have been Johann Wendler; see his advertisement in the autumn fair catalog of 1755 (p. 639). Individual titles sold by various booksellers were regularly announced, so that at least a rudimentary list of the imports of English books can be extracted from the fair catalogs.

129. The pioneer study was conducted by Giles Barber, "Books from the Old World and for the New: The British International Trade in Books in the Eighteenth Century," *Studies on Voltaire and the Eighteenth Century* 151 (1976): 185–224.

130. See Albrecht Kirchhoff, "Der ausländische Buchhandel in Leipzig im 18. Jahrhundert," *Archiv für Geschichte des deutschen Buchhandels* 14 (1891): 155–182; and "Der Zeitpunkt des Wegbleibens der Holländer von der Leipziger Messe," ibid. 17 (1894): 363–365.

131. An interesting memorandum on the structure of the German book trade around 1751 was published by Wilhelm Ruprecht, "Göttinger gelehrten Buchhandlungen: Pläne aus der Frühzeit der Georg August-Universität," *Archiv für Geschichte des deutschen Buchhandels* 21 (1930): 212–213.

132. See B. Fabian, "Die erste englische Buchhandlung auf dem Kontinent," in *Festschrift für Rainer Gruenter* (Heidelberg, 1978), pp. 125–145.

133. For details see "English Books and Their Eighteenth-Century German Readers," in *The Widening Circle: Essays on the Circulation of Literature in Eighteenth-Century Europe,* ed. Paul J. Korshin (Philadelphia, 1976), pp. 138–139.

134. A good example is Friedrich Heinrich Jacobi. See J. Th. de Booy and Roland Mortier, "Les années de formation de F. H. Jacobi, d'après ses lettres inédites à M. M. Rey (1763–1771). . . ," *Studies on Voltaire and the Eighteenth Century* 45 (1966): 5–204.

135. Friedrich Nicolai printed 800 copies of Reuss's *Alphabetical Register,* intended for general use as a bibliographical reference work on contemporary English literature; a fairly large number of them apparently remained unsold. See Fabian, "Die erste Bibliographie der englischen Literatur," op. cit.

136. Henry Pettit, ed., *The Correspondence of Edward Young, 1683–1765* (Oxford, 1971), p. 534.

137. See Fabian, "Die erste Bibliographie . . . , " op. cit., p. 34.

138. The announcement was made in the *Göttingisches Magazin der Wissenschaften und Litteratur* for 1783. My information comes from the original wrappers preserved in the copy of the municipal library of Trier. See also Friedrich Lauchert, *G. Chr. Lichtenberg's schriftstellerische Thätigkeit in chronologischer Uebersicht dargestellt* (Göttingen, 1893), pp. 84 ff.

139. *The British Mercury* (published in Hamburg) 9, no. 18 (2 May 1789): 160.

140. Erich Hintzsche, ed., *Albrecht Hallers Tagebücher seiner Reisen nach Deutschland, Holland und England, 1723–1727,* Berner Beiträge zur Geschichte der Medizin und der Naturwissenschaften, N.S. 4 (Bern, 1971), p. 93.

141. See Marie-Luise Spieckermann, in *Factotum: Newsletter of the XVIIIth Century STC,* no. 4 (1978): 20.

142. See Roger Bauer, "Die österreichische Literatur des Josephinischen Zeitalters: Eine werdende Literatur auf der Suche nach neuen Ausdrucksformen," *Studien zum achtzehnten Jahrhundert* 1 (Nendeln, 1978): 25–37.

143. *Kurzgefasste englische Sprachlehre den Deutschen zur erleichterten und gründlichen Erlernung dieser Sprache* (Wien: Sonnleithner, 1783). See Alston, II, no. 432 (note 25).

144. Vienna: Printed for R. Sammer, bookseller, 1798. The collection consisted of *Tristam Shandy* (Vols. 1–4), *A Sentimental Journey* (Vol. 5), and the continuation by John Hall-Stevenson (Vol 6), *Letters of the late Rev. Mr. Laurence Sterne* (Vols. 7–8), and the spurious *Koran* (Vol. 9). Each title was published separately in 1797 and 1798.

145. Attention was first drawn to Thurneysen by Giles Barber, "J. J. Tourneisen of Basle and the Publication of English Books on the Continent c. 1800," *Library,* 5th ser., 15 (1960): 193–200. So far the most extensive account of Thurneysen is given by Martin Germann, *Johann Jakob Thurneysen der Jüngere, 1754–1803: Verleger, Buchdrucker und Buchhändler in Basel,* Basler Beiträge zur Geschichtswissenschaft 128 (Basel and Stuttgart, 1973).

146. See *Gothaische gelehrte Zeitungen,* 10 October 1787, p. 664.

147. Volumes 1–2 use the words "printed for J. J. Tourneisen," while volumes 3–12 and the index volume state "printed by J. J. Tourneisen."

148. See J. E. Norton, *A Bibliography of the Works of Edward Gibbon* (Oxford, 1940), pp. 96–97.

149. Barber and Germann (note 145) provide lists of the reprints.

150. Bolingbroke, 1788; second edition 1791; according to Germann (note 145) there was also a third edition dated 1791 but presumably printed in 1799 (see p. 137). Robertson, 1788; second edition 1793. Blair, 1788. Ferguson, 1789. Hume, 1789. Gillies, 1790. Middleton, 1790. Smith, 1791.

151. See *Gothaische gelehrte Zeitungen,* 16 July 1791, p. 545.

152. In his advertisement (note 151) Thurneysen referred to Shakespeare and Pope as "die beyden Lieblingsdichter der Engelländer."

153. Catalog for June 1789, appended to *The British Mercury.*

154. See *Carl Wilhelm Ettingers Verzeichniss seiner sämmtlichen Verlagsbücher* (Gotha, 1792 and 1796).

155. Shelfmark: C.134.dd.i.

156. Unpublished letter to J. J. Eschenburg, 15 May 1795 (Herzog August Bibliothek, Wolfenbüttel).

157. For Levrault see Frédéric Barbier, *Trois cent ans de librairie et d'imprimerie: Berger-Levrault, 1676–1830,* Histoire et civilisation du livre 2 (Geneva, 1979).

158. British Library, shelfmarks 10863.b.37 and 10026.ccc.12.

159. See Remnant's catalogs for October 1788 and June 1789.

160. 1793, II (26 August), p. 1368.

[5]　Book Production and Censorship in France, 1700–1715

Raymond Birn

ALTHOUGH HARDLY TWO decades old, *histoire du livre* has become in France a sturdy, confident companion to its more venerable relations—political, social, and intellectual history. Long neglected by historians of literature for whom the masterpieces were what counted, the field burgeoned in the 1960s, when scholars trained in the "Annales" school of social history looked to book collecting and reading habits for their reconstruction of the culture of elites, particularly during the premodern era.[1] For the social historian the books that Frenchmen owned in the seventeenth and eighteenth centuries assumed nearly as much importance as the objects they sold, the persons they married, the regions in which they resided, and the length of their lives.

Historians connected with the well-endowed École des hautes études en sciences sociales, located in the Maison des sciences de l'homme, in Paris, and students at the prestigious training center for archivists and librarians, the École nationale des chartes, turned out an impressive number of monographs, articles, and theses. Book production and distribution rates, documented with impressive graphs and charts, were drawn up with such vigor, and even passion, that it has become nearly unthinkable today to write a social history of early modern French elites without first snooping about for a private library, a death inventory of books owned, or at least reference to reading materials in correspondence. In the 1960s and 1970s a few path-breaking syntheses concerned with production and dissemination appeared, chief among which remains Henri-Jean Martin's magisterial *Livre, société et pouvoirs à Paris 1598–1701,* 2 vols. (Geneva: Droz, 1969). Within the past half-dozen years the French techniques of scholarship have become highly sophisticated, elegant, and in large measure quantitatively based.[2]

On this side of the Atlantic, however, the tendency appears to be towards a humanistic approach. Social histories of publishing by North Americans, at least when dealing with European subjects, are remarkably free from the many-tiered staircases, cardiographs, inverted parabolas, and other varieties of squiggly lines that dominate the social scientific orientation of their French colleagues. Whether the differences have more to do with distance from the archives than with declarations of independence from methodological orthodoxies I cannot say. My purpose here, however, is not to compare the work of "Annales" historians with very recent studies by Americans.[3] My aim, rather, is to examine a relatively limited, although quite distinct, period in French history and indicate the ways in which the history of the book traverses intersections marked by the history of politics, society, religion, and culture. I hope to illustrate how awareness of one aspect of *histoire du livre,* namely, state-sponsored censorship, can enrich our understanding of the last fifteen years of Louis XIV's reign. What is important about the years 1700–1715 is precisely what the regime tried to silence: religious controversy, a loss of faith in absolutist political institutions, a search for alternatives to an economic system built upon corporate privilege. For the first time since the Protestant Reformation a significant cross section of writers risked reputation and physical safety by challenging royally sanctioned orthodoxies. Thus, the story of books and censorship during this period informs us, *à rebours,* of the origins of the Enlightenment.

I

Historians obsessed with sunsets, twilights, and crises of national conscience have discovered in the last decade and a half of Louis XIV's reign an especially fruitful period. "The government of old age" and "the effacement of Versailles" are Robert Mandrou's chapter titles for this period in his recent history of Europe from 1661 to 1715.[4] A superannuated king fighting an unwinnable war, deluding himself with untenable symbols of royal power; a country at the brink of economic collapse, awaiting outdated mercantilist and monopolistic ideas to perish with the crowned fool; intellectuals and social critics groping for administrative and theoretical alternatives to a system that was leading France to national disaster and possible dismemberment—such are the apocalyptic images derived from the years 1700 to 1715.

Nearly all the important books of the period reflect disenchantment and the quest for change, and nearly all their authors ran into trouble over them: Archbishop Fénelon, first for religious heterodoxy, the Quietism of the *Explication des maximes des saints sur la vie intérieure* (1697) and later for allegorical satire, the *Aventures de Télémaque, fils d'Ulysse* (1699); Richard Simon for his path-breaking critical translation of the New Testament (1702); Marshal Vauban for his treatise on tax reform and tax privilege, the *Projet d'une dîme royale* (1707); Abbé de Saint-Pierre for his pacifist response to the tarnished conception of *gloire nationale,* the *Projet pour rendre la paix perpétuelle en Europe* (1712); and Nicolas Fréret for his shocking Germanophile interpretation of the origins of the French nation (1714). Certain critics of the system like Fontenelle remained protected by court and academy. Others, like Bayle or Michel Le Vassor, survived by working in exile. Condemnation, of course, guaranteed commercial success, and all of these writers were influential in their lifetime. None, however, provoked greater ripples of controversy than a tired septuagenarian priest of the Oratory, Pasquier Quesnel. Although once possessed of a censor's approval, his subsequent editions of the doctrinal handbook, *Réflexions morales sur le Nouveau Testament,* became, along with the monastery Port-Royal-des-Champs, the chief scapegoat of Louis XIV's struggle with Jansenism. The condemnation of the book and the destruction of the abbey reopened a bitter religious-political struggle that runs like a thread through much of eighteenth-century history.[5]

For all their notoriety, these books far from monopolized government attention. For every folio edition of Bayle's *Dictionnaire historique et critique* that found its way into France from 1700 to 1715, hundreds of potboilers *en blanc* circulated in octavo or duodecimo; many were no more than pamphlets, yet all contributed to the collective mentality of elites who were rejecting ingrained orthodoxies. For bibliographic confirmation of the existence of these books and pamphlets the historian eschews the great literary and cultural histories of Gustave Lanson and Paul Hazard and heads instead for Antoine Barbier's *Dictionnaire des ouvrages anonymes,* Jacques-Charles Brunet's *Manuel du libraire et de l'amateur de livres,* Gustave Brunet's *Imprimeurs imaginaires et libraires supposés,* contemporary police reports, or the great registers of the Paris Booksellers' and Printers' Guild.[6] Here, for example, is a typical report of a raid, conducted at the expense of the Paris bookseller Christophe Remy in January 1702:

> At Remy's we found several old Jansenist and Quietist books, the *Mémoires de la Paix de Riswick,* the *Histoire amoureuse des Gaules,* the *Demêlés de la Chine,* the *Pensées philosophiques* and a single small book entitled *Réflexions sur les affaires présentes de la couronne d'Espagne.* I have had everything seized and brought over to the guild-hall of the booksellers. . . . [7]

The haul represented quite accurately the regime's perception of what ought to be silenced and the bookseller's perception of what the market wanted: illicit books about religious controversy and heresy, satires of the royal court veiled as fables, critiques of Louis XIV's intervention in the Spanish Succession issue, accounts of the Jesuits and their subsequent humiliation over the issue of the Chinese rites.

Recently I have attempted to identify regions in and around early eighteenth-century Paris where commerce in prohibited and pirated books seemed to flourish. The first locale was the university quarter. Among tutors and their pupils in several colleges around the Sorbonne, I have located sellers and authors alike who defied the regime both by their trade and by the contents of their writings. For example, in the room of the tutor Lejeune at the Collège de Cambrai the police discovered, in July 1701, 301 prohibited and pirated books, a ream and a half of printed sheets, and two indecent oil paintings. The overwhelming majority of Lejeune's books comprised two titles: 161 Jansenist-inspired letters to the Jesuits commenting upon a thesis defended at their Collège Louis-le-Grand and 100 satires directed against Archbishop Fénelon entitled *Télémaque spirituelle*.[8] Later the same year the police discovered a veritable academic counterculture at the Collèges de Navarre, du Plessis, and d'Harcourt.[9] The band of pornographers there included tutors (priests without parishes), an unlicensed physician, and precocious tutees who were, for the most part, rebellious teenaged sons of provincial merchants, robe officials, and farmers-general. The books with which the group was caught included both classic and modern pornography: the positions of Aretino, an *Aloysia* with illustrations, and *L'École des filles*; sexually inspired insults of public figures—*Les amours de madame de Maintenon, Les amours de Messaline reine d'Angleterre avec le roi de France, Le tombeau des amours de Louis le Grand*; political and religious scandal—*Le salut de France dédié à monsieur le dauphin pour raser son père, Le capucin démasqué*, and *Le cochon mitré*.[10] Tutors and tutees alike were composing similar trash for future clandestine publication. Among the manuscripts uncovered by the police were licentious biographies of Henry IV, Louis XIII, and Louis XIV; sexual fantasies dealing with the scandals of monastic life; and pornographic exposés of *les grands*. As though all this were not enough, subsequent investigation proved that the tutors' rooms were not merely warehouses for illicit books and manuscripts. They were dens of homosexual activity as well.

A second set of locales, somewhat less seamy, took in the Palais on the Île de la Cité, home of the Parlement of Paris, and various suburban châteaus, including that of Versailles itself. Favored book peddlers, protected by the governance of the Palais and Parlement, established stalls for their wares in the hallways of the sovereign courts; and both great nobles and royal ministers were able to build private libraries relatively immune from the restrictions of censorship and inspection.[11]

Concerning unapproved suppliers of this clientele, we have been somewhat in the dark. One such distributor, however, was arrested on 6 June 1705. He was Joseph Huchet, "bourgeois de Paris," erstwhile private secretary to several parlementary officers and former reader for Honoré Courtin, late dean of the king's Council of State. Huchet was accused "of trafficking in prohibited books that he obtains from several sellers and correspondents in Liège, Tournai, and other places, among which are books against the king and against religion."[12] Unlike the tutors at the colleges, Huchet was experienced, well connected, and highly organized. He had suppliers in Angers, Alençon, Valenciennes, Rouen, Reims, Metz, Châlons-sur-Marne, and Verdun. He stored his merchandise at the *hôtels* de Sully and de Condé in Paris, in the château de St. Maur, and in other elegant suburban country houses of the aristocracy. His customers included Paris booksellers as well as the elites of robe and court. During a smuggling career that lasted from 1699 until 1705, Huchet handled more than five hundred titles and several thousand books. Most assuredly he was the leading Paris source for pirated and prohibited books during the first years of the new century.

Among Huchet's wares were pirated folio editions of Le Maistre de Sacy's translation of the Bible, as well as the great dictionaries of Furetière, Moréri, and Bayle—appropriate luxury items for an aristocratic clientele. However, Huchet was not above importing Dutch news gazettes, Jansenist and Protestant books, political commentaries, *histoires galantes,* and trash—works that included *L'Histoire du Palais royal, Le Rasibus ou le procez fait à la barbe des Capucins par un moine défroqué, Vénus dans le cloître,* and *Les Jésuites sur l'échaffaud.*

Huchet's customers were insatiable. In December 1703, when Paris booksellers complained that the war economy had undermined their market, he was pleading with his leading supplier, the Liégeois printer J. F. Broncart, to send him all the *Théâtres italiens*— ". . . Théophrastes, Corneille, Mézeray, Boileau, Rabelais, Horace by Dacier and *Les Annales de la Cour*—that Broncart could obtain. The price Huchet paid was customarily 25 to 50 percent lower than what Paris booksellers charged, and he passed on his discounts to his customers.

A third area of interest were the shops of the Parisian master printers and booksellers, ghettoized in the rue St. Jacques and the crooked, narrow paths of the Latin Quarter, as well as on the quai des Augustins and round the Palais. A late seventeenth-century creation of Colbert's, the guild ostensibly served as auxiliary to the police; its officers prepared to raid its own membership and report assiduously to the chancellor of France and his delegated director of the book trade. The syndic of the guild collected a blacklist of names and infractions that he shared with the police, and occasional descents upon the shops did take place.[13] Well might they. I have discovered that from 1700 to 1707, for example, nearly one-fourth of the master sellers and printers of Paris were caught with illegal books either imported from Holland or else manufactured on underground presses in the capital. And those caught were not necessarily the most impecunious of the masters. They often bore the names of the oldest and most elite families: an Émery caught with prohibited books hidden in a case of jam sent from Rouen; various Brunets caught with the *Mémoires du chevalier du Rochefort, Vie de Turenne, Cérémonies chinoises, Clef du cabinet des princes de l'Europe,* and *Intrigues secrètes du duc de Savoie;* a Charles Bessin caught with a *Comte de Gabalis, Mémoires de Danemark,* and *Journal amoureux de la cour de Vienne;* a du Bourg caught with the apocryphal "testaments" of both Colbert and Louvois, Pascal's *Lettres provinciales,* La Fontaine's *Contes, Télémaque,* the *Tableau de l'amour considéré dans l'état du mariage,* and *Vénus dans le cloître.* The seizures had little effect upon the subsequent professional standing of those caught. While those embarrassed by the police included a former official of the guild and a director of the Imprimerie royale, 14 other offenders were to cherish guild officerships later in their lives.[14]

Finally, scattered throughout the capital and its suburbs were the authors. Beyond the famous and high-minded—Fénelon, Boulainvilliers, Vauban, the Abbé de St. Pierre—stood shadowy battalions of obscure Jansenists, Molinists, anti-absolutists, or just plain Grub Streeters: from the saintly Thierry de Viaxnes, whose cell at the Benedictine abbey of Hautvilliers on the Marne was a clearinghouse for Jansenist manuscripts, and the martyred octogenarian Gabriel Gerberon, rotting away in Vincennes prison for his lifelong theological independence,[15] to Gatien Courtilz de Sandras, the most prolific author of the time and likely the most widely read.[16] Courtilz's police dossier of 1702 best sums up his contemporary reputation:

> . . . Noble of the sword, 55 years of age, who bears himself well and earns plenty every day by distributing pernicious books in Paris. . . . He is a composer. He has composed the so-called testaments of the late Monsieur de Louvois and Monsieur Colbert, and the life of Monsieur de Turenne. . . . He often goes to Holland to have his works printed. He possesses the secret of having them enter Paris by virtue of his secret contacts. He has distributed an extraordinary number of them, he sells them unbound. . . . He says that a police commissioner protects him, and his wife boasts of it. It is Commissioner de la Mare.[17]

Protected by a high Paris police official, who very likely preferred to work out private arrangements with Courtilz rather than have his books scattered haphazardly among itinerant peddlers, this aristocratic author-salesman enjoyed a kind of tacit permission for nearly twenty years. His major books—the *Annales de la cour et de Paris pour les années 1697 et 1698, Mémoires de mme la marquise de Fresne, Mémoires de M.L.C.D.R.,* apocryphal political testaments of Colbert and Louvois, and a *Vie du vicomte de Turenne*—titillated scandal-thirsty Frenchmen. Courtilz de Sandras filled a need for satire that escaped state censors, and his métier cost him an occasional stay in the Bastille. Once out, however, he returned to his pen and his sales. Until his death in 1712, he wrote and peddled continuously. During the final year of his life he even contracted a morganatic marriage that served as ironic capstone to his career: The sword nobleman Courtilz de Sandras, sieur du Verger, married the bourgeoise Marguerite Auroy, widow of a master bookseller of Paris.[18]

II

Enjoyable though the chore would be, the purpose of this chapter is not to explore the territory of Grub Street in the early eighteenth century. However, from what I have observed so far, its sociology—disenchanted clerics who either had lost their faith or else were hostile to the regime's narrow views of orthodoxy, professionals who were prevented from practicing because of monopolistic corporate restrictions, guildsmen who resisted Colbertine economic policies, opportunistic parasites who pandered to the powerful, the occasional nobleman who found pen more profitable than sword, college students who harbored a resentment against the old authoritarian structures—does not vary significantly from the sociology of Grub Street half a century later, as unearthed by Robert Darnton.[19] The literary underground of the early eighteenth century seemed to be quite divided between ideological commitment and the quest for profits, and at least certain segments of it were the spiritual ancestors of Darnton's prerevolutionary low-lifers. The main thrust of this chapter, however, will be an attempt to examine "the other side"—that is, the perspective of those who defined the boundaries of the permissible, from Chancellor Pontchartrain through his delegated executors of the royal will: the first state-appointed director of the book trade in France, Pontchartrain's nephew, Abbé Jean-Paul Bignon; the police; and, most notably, the royal censors.[20] From the moment Louis II Phélypeaux de Pontchartrain assumed the chancellorship of France in 1699, he tried to push aside competing claimants to censorship authority—the university, episcopacy, Parlement—and developed the secular institutions that were to assume unique responsibility over what books could be sold and distributed in the country. A year in office, he expressed his will to Christophe Ballard, syndic of the sellers' and printers' guild of Paris: "The intention I have for comprehending in-depth matters of the book trade, in order to bring it to perfection more than is presently the case, has me search with care for the pieces that can provide knowledge of it. And the attention and care that Monsieur l'abbé Bignon wishes to devote to this matter leave me no doubt that we shall succeed in our efforts."[21]

To be sure, Pontchartrain was a man of faith. Although he underestimated the depth of resistance at a time when the authoritarian structures of the past generation were being called into question, he was obsessed with strengthening their institutional base. And that base comprised the offices at his disposal. As far as the older structures were concerned, he tried to accelerate their demolition. Concerning the university, for example, whatever stock the doctors of the Sorbonne once possessed over independent censorship judgments was rendered worthless in 1702 during the so-called *cas de conscience* affair.[22] In elemental terms the matter involved the theological entrapment of 40 professors who, by implication, were caught denying that Cornelius Jansen had held heretical opinions. Nearly all retracted, but the damage was done. Tainted with heresy, the doctors now had to submit to the suspicion, if not contempt, of state officials.

In the same year Pontchartrain undermined nearly all the pretensions French bishops held over censorship authority in their dioceses. In a showdown over authority with the archbishop of Paris, Louis-Gaston de Noailles, and Louis XIV's favorite political theorist, Bishop Jacques Bénigne Bossuet, Pontchartrain prohibited the award of publishing permits, a right heretofore exercised by bishops. Moreover, the chancellor required the bishops either to submit their own writings to state-appointed censors or to apply directly to his office for individual exemptions. Pontchartrain even reserved the right to award approval for missals and prayer books required in the dioceses.[23]

The less pliant Parlement of Paris, the great administrative law court, would reassert in the course of the eighteenth century its title to repressive censorship.[24] Under Pontchartrain's pressure, however, during the final years of Louis XIV's reign the Parlement relinquished whatever claims it still possessed over the judgment of manuscripts. Whenever he was able, Pontchartrain maneuvered the Parlement into furthering his aims and extending his policies. Faced, for example, in 1705 with a widely circulating Jansenist pamphlet called the *Correction fraternelle*, the chancellor requested and obtained a parlementary condemnation, because, in his view, "A parlementary order will seem more solid and be better received by everyone" than would a heavy-handed *arrêt* issued by the Royal Council.[25]

The aforementioned floodtide of unapproved literary production illustrates what tasks in the cause of repressive censorship the chancellor faced. Pontchartrain understood that Paris was the destination rather than the source of unlicensed, unapproved books. After 1699 he emphasized an aggressive bureaucratic struggle against printers and sellers throughout France. In the *généralités* of the kingdom intendants and police officials were deluged with warnings and threats. Rightly suspecting Rouen to be one of the two major sources and entrepôts of illegal books in the northern part of the kingdom, Pontchartrain bluntly informed Intendant d'Herbigny in October 1701 that under no circumstance was commercial advantage to assume higher priority than the policing of ideas.[26] A year and a half later, again addressing d'Herbigny, Pontchartrain fulminated over a veritable conspiracy in the great Norman town: ". . . There is no place in the entire kingdom where forbidden writings are printed with more license than in Rouen. It appears that the reason for such license is the police ruling in this city that the freedom of commerce must be protected against all else, in order to favor the ways of attracting money."[27] The chancellor demanded an end to this policy.

Rouen was a particularly difficult case. Not only was it an important port for English and Dutch commerce but its police lieutenant was Pierre Le Pesant de Boisguillebert, a tax and agrarian reformer who in 1695 had himself authored one of the period's most notoriously illegal books, the *Détail de la France*. Unable to dismiss Boisguillebert, who had his own protectors at Versailles, Pontchartrain was reduced to upbraiding him unmercifully.[28] Rouen was not the only town to feel the pressure of Pontchartrain's crusade and the sting of his sarcasm. Intendants, parlementaires, bishops, and authors alike—from Toulouse and Lyon in the south to Lille and Valenciennes in the north—were bombarded.[29] Angered by the laxity of local police judges who were tolerating the publication and circulation of pamphlets he deemed unacceptable, Pontchartrain ordered in 1707 that the manuscripts of such *brochures* be read not only by local authorities but also by the royal censors at Versailles.[30]

Unenforceable as this last order was, it represents only the most extreme example of the censorship by decree that was Pontchartrain's hallmark. He preferred action. For example, the second most important series of hideouts for illegal books that were printed in the Low Countries and headed for Paris was the string of towns along the plain of Champagne: Reims, Châlons-sur-Marne, Ste. Menehould, Troyes, Vitry-le-François. Printers and sellers alike had established a successful smuggling network and, in Pontchartrain's view at least, for decades the local police had been looking the other way. Barely two months in office, the new chancellor inspired book guild, police, and judicial officials in Paris to embark upon a veritable invasion of Champagne to uncover and root out the traffic. In an effort coordinated by a parlementary lawyer named Cousin, printshops, sales shops, cafés, inns, stables, warehouses, barges on the Marne, and even the episcopal residence at Châlons were inspected. The investigation lasted six months and implicated all the major booksellers in Champagne.[31]

Lyon had its great raid, too,[32] and in 1701 the chancellor coordinated tactics to impose censorial authority upon the trade. First a great national inquest of printshops of the realm was made, followed in 1704 by a regulatory decree that established new limits on the number of master printers to be tolerated in France.[33] The intention was clear—to drive the poorest, those most suspect of illegal activity—out of business. As Pontchartrain wrote to Boisguillebert: "There already are too many printers and booksellers in Rouen. Their number renders them so poor, and their poverty is for them such a dangerous temptation to break the rules that, far from increasing their number, we must reduce it."[34]

Pontchartrain embarked upon three additional bureaucratic measures. First he redefined the privilege-award system so that all books legally printed in France had to secure a permit affixed with the royal seal.[35] Next he created for his nephew, Jean-Paul Bignon, the Bureau pour les affaires de chancellerie et librairie, the department that would supervise the eighteenth-century apparatus of privilege management over books. Finally, Pontchartrain both expanded and centralized the royal censorship bureau, the regulatory agency of subject specialists that was entrusted with defining the limits of ideas fit for public consumption.

III

Since the mid-sixteenth century the state had used patent letters and privileges as one means of surveillance over book production. However, it was not until the 1620s that the chancellor began appointing royal censors on a regular basis. Sorbonne theologians were to consider religious books, royal secretaries profane ones. The disappearance of the Archives de la chancellerie makes it virtually impossible to reconstruct the evolution of the system of state censorship in the second half of the seventeenth century. After 1699, however, the precious registers of approvals and rejections assume significance, and the final 15 years of Louis XIV's reign are highly informative.[36]

First of all, the registers identify the royal censors. For the period from 1699 to 1704, 56 different individuals evaluated both manuscripts and books seeking permission renewals. For the next five-year period 82 individuals rendered judgments. And from 1710 through 1715 at least 117 different examiners were at work. Most royal censors received pensions and were specialists. Indeed, many belonged to one or more of the great official academies. In profane areas they were highly competent, well-respected, and even original minds—all of which suggests that they were not selected chiefly to confirm the pedestrian and eliminate the novel. Among them were the philologist André Dacier, the genealogist Pierre de la Garde d'Hozier, the archivist Pierre de Clairambault, the botanist Joseph Pitton de Tournefort, the historian Michel Félibien, and the polymath Bernard de Fontenelle. The censors of religious books were another matter. First and foremost, they had to be free of any taint of either heresy or controversy. Independence of thought and originality of mind were, in these instances, liabilities. Nearly all came from the Sorbonne's faculty of theology or the Collège de Navarre. Jacques Le Brun has identified the majority of them, summed up their careers, and concluded that "the relative lack of originality, the retractions that determine the careers of these men, well illustrate that they were tightly beneath the thumb of ecclesiastical or political authorities."[37] Representative of this group were Edme Pirot, Pierre Courcier, and Jean-Antoine Pastel—Sorbonne regulars, Gallicans, creatures of the powerful who were sensitive to the currents of orthodoxy and ever ready to beat a hasty retreat.

From 1700 through 1715 the royal censors dealt with 6,017 publication requests. For the most part the requests were for permission to print in France, although an occasional one might be for permission to import a book from the Low Countries or the principality of Liège. The party desiring the permit, customarily either an author, seller, or printer, was identified, as was the royal censor of an approved manuscript. Anonymity was preserved for the examiner of a rejected title, however. When it was a question of a new edition or even a reprinted one, the register incorporated the book's publishing history. If the censor approved a manuscript treating a nonreligious topic, one of several formulas might be employed, ranging from a noncommittal "I have found nothing that should prevent impression," through a slightly more elegiac "It seems to me that reading of this will be useful and agreeable to the public," to the much rarer case of individualized adulation of an author's genius. For profane books the favorite words of approval were "useful," "exact," "instructive." For religious books approvals generally were curt and unenlightening. Indeed, they were customarily couched in a negative formula: "I have found nothing contrary to the purity of the faith and morals."

When rejecting manuscripts, the censor might set down quite specific reasons for disapproval or else remain tantalizingly vague. There were occasions where a censor's approval was overruled by higher authority.[38] For the most part, however, it appears that censors, especially of religious books, were circumspect and must have inquired directly among the powerful before rendering potentially controversial decisions. For the historian their disapprovals are particularly interesting. These determinations establish the cultural bases for Pontchartrain's reorganization of the book trade and set the tone for the limits imposed on intellectual orthodoxy in France at the dawn of the Enlightenment.

Before we consider the qualitative aspects of the reports, it is useful to make a few quantitative observations. By far the largest category of books examined dealt with religious subjects: 48.4 percent of the total. The category of belles-lettres dominated the profane books, followed by other categories encompassing history, geography, politics, and law, considerably behind, and science and medicine taking up the rear. Of the 6,017 requests, 692 (11.5 percent of the total) were explicitly disapproved. For each year between 1700 and 1707, the annual rate of disapprovals exceeded the 11. percent average. On the other hand, between 1707 and 1716, only in one year did the annual disapproval rate exceed the average (12.1 percent in 1709).

As the habits of the system became entrenched, it appears clear that degrees of tolerance (or laxity) widened. Compared to their standards for profane books, examiners were more rigorous in their treatment of religious subjects. Disapprovals of religious books averaged 13 percent per year, whereas disapprovals of profane books averaged 10 percent. Moreover, a considerable number of secular books were reproved because of allegedly disrespectful remarks about religion. It is possible, of course, to refine statistics almost indefinitely. Rather than succumb to the temptation of experimenting with my pocket calculator, I would conclude that the repressive aspects of Chancellor Pontchartrain's furious letters and bureaucratic apparatus proved less severe than one might reasonably have expected. Nearly nine of every ten books brought before a state examiner passed muster the first time around. Was this the consequence of ingrained *self*-censorship existing in the minds of would-be authors? Or were significant numbers of authors and sellers already evading the censorship process altogether by printing in the Low Countries and employing smuggling tactics or other evasive devices to distribute their books in France? Establishment of the *permission tacite* register in 1718 may well have legitimized a fait accompli.[39] It also legitimized the fact that the French reading public, a full generation before the *philosophes,* had gone beyond the canons of taste established even by relatively tolerant censors.

Why did a censor reject a religious book? The years 1700 to 1715 found France plunged in several varieties of theological controversy. In the wake of Archbishop Fénelon's humiliation over Quietism, examiners looked askance at works that stressed the mystical side of Catholicism at the expense of its formalistic, rational one. *La vie et les rares vertus de s^{te}. Marie Madeleine de Pazzi* was disapproved because "the work is filled with Quietism and revelations."[40] In 1708 an *Abrégé de la perfection chrétienne* was rejected as "for reopening the questions of the book *Des maximes de Saints.*"[41] In 1709 an *Occupation intérieure des mourants* was reproved for being filled with the tenets of Quietism,[42] and as late as 1713 *Diverse aspirations pour élever son coeur à Dieu* was turned down for being "infected with Quietism."[43]

A fear of Quietism rendered suspect all aspects of Catholicism that emphasized particularly intense forms of popular piety and exaggerated miracle working. Reflecting the position of the post-Tridentine Church, censors believed that religious inspiration had to derive from proper instruction and not spontaneously from the hearts of the masses. Therefore, C. Fournier's *Histoire de Saint Gauderic, confesseur* was disapproved because its lack of common sense led it to accept miracles authorized solely "by virtue of witness made by village peasants."[44] The Oratorian Father Mauduit's translation of the *Traité des voies de Dieu* by St. Elizabeth of Schönau failed to secure approval because the miracles ostensibly witnessed by an angel were in reality the "unsupportable visions of an obscure monk."[45] Further reason for discounting popular miracle, mystery, and unverified saints' lives was the censors' fear of incurring the ridicule of Protestants. Father Bertholde of Toulouse saw his *Vie de Cathérine de Cardone soeur du Tiers Ordre de Notre Dame du Mont Carmel* rejected as "hardly more than a collection of unverified, fabulous miracles, altogether shameful to religion, prejudiciable to the instruction of the people whose simplicity is abused, and subject to the mockery of heretics."[46] A history of the notorious devils of Loudun, proposed in 1705 by the Jesuit Surin, was turned down for these reasons: "1. because it contains Quietist maxims; 2. because it fails to conform to the rulings of the Church on exorcisms; 3. the author accepts as truths all responses of the devil; 4. he treats the entire matter too feebly, in comparison to the way Protestants have treated it."[47] The rejection for entry into France of an abridgment of the life of St. Anthony of Padua, printed in Mons in 1692, and ostensibly circulating in France, aptly summarizes the values of the examiners: "This little book is filled with unverifiable facts, insufficiently authorized miracles, superstitious devotional practices, outrageous worship of the saint, and, besides, the style is pitiful."[48]

More than Quietism, popular piety, or even Protestantism, it was the renewal of Jansenist controversy that particularly obsessed the state's defenders of religious orthodoxy in the early eighteenth century. In 1703 a royal order prohibited the composition, printing, and distribution of books dealing with "the old arguments concerning the doctrine of Jansenius."[49] Of course, such a ruling simply encouraged printers and sellers alike to dig underground and raise and sell the forbidden fruit at inflationary prices. The *cas de conscience* affair, the destruction of Port-Royal, the publication of the papal Bull Unigenitus, and the publicized imprisonment of Jansenist martyrs converted a theological controversy into a grave domestic crisis that included book seizures and burnings.[50] Most Jansenist authors went underground, but a few hazarded the risks of working through the channels of censorship. Jacques Le Brun notes that a work such as Opstraet's *Theologus Christianus,* which went through printings at Louvain in 1692, 1697, and 1698, found itself lately rejected, in the censor's words, "for good reasons."[51] More frequently, however, it was well-meaning anti-Jansenist works such as Hilaire Dumas's history of the five propositions that paid the price for the regime's law of silence.[52] Censors were ardent Gallicans who defended the liberties of the national church and rejected volumes that upheld "too vigorously the infallibility of the Pope"[53] or that were "injurious to the bishops and contrary to our freedoms."[54] Prudence—a fear of falling into error, be it crypto-Protestant or theologically inexact—further dictated judgments. For the censors theology clearly remained a science that was on the one hand to be defended from heresy and on the other to be protected from enthusiasm.

In the area of profane books, the examiners' approach to belles-lettres paralleled their approach to religion. They displayed an overarching concern with "popular" literature and condemned its superstitious themes, naiveté, and disorderly, unclassical style. In 1710, for example, the Rouen printer Besongne fell victim to a blanket disapproval of stories that had formed the basis of printed folk literature for the past two centuries—*Jean de Paris, Pierre de Provence, Richard sans peur, Robert le diable, L'Espiègle, Civilité puérile,* and *Quatrains de Pybrac.* "Filled with liberties that are too great," wrote the censor in a manner reminiscent of his colleagues' attitudes toward saints' lives.[55] *L'Homme détrompé, ou le criticon de Baltazar Gracian,* published in The Hague, was turned away for its thematic "extravagances."[56] *Daniel, tragédie,* by a certain Dieusat, was rejected for being "filled with faults against common sense, language, and poetry."[57] Montfaucon de Villars's *Le comte de Gabalis,* the widely popular compendium that ridiculed the Rosicrucians, Cabalists, and other devotees of esoterica, found itself reproved in 1706 because of its "absurdities" and again in 1714 for "its bizarre systems"— this despite the fact that it had gone through at least nine editions since its first publication in 1670.[58] The popular and didactic adaptations of classics, such as *Les amours de Didon, ou traduction françoise du quatrième livre de l'Enéide de Virgile, avec des réflexions morales et critiques,* were considered a perversion of the pristine originals and rejected for their "poor diction, lack of order, and ill-founded reasoning."[59]

In particular, popular almanacs suffered. In 1700 the *Almanach du berger,* which had helped make the fortune of its printer Jacques Oudot of Troyes, was silenced.[60] Four years later an *Almanach journalier pour les années 1705 et suivantes* was rejected not merely because it lifted the lists of public offices from Laurent d'Houry's officially approved *Almanach royale* but also because it was "filled with calculations and vain astrological predictions; because for each day of the year the author predicts different temperatures of the air and marks as assured both happy and unhappy days, both good ￢nd bad, for the different activities of life . . . which only serve to encourage superstition in the minds of the people."[61] Pithy as they are, the rejections illustrate a pattern of reasoning: "The erudition is too trivial"; "the adventures are childish, lacking genius and spirit"; "too non-instructive, too subject to error, too vague, too confused, too disagreeable to warrant publication"; ". . . it is better for letters to halt the course of this inundation of little stories and fairy tales that only bore people of good taste and ruin the minds of others. . . ."[62] The examiners launched an aggressive campaign against enthusiasm, credulity, the fantastic, and the vulgar. Their weapons were those of proper classical accuracy and good taste. They denigrated the values of popular culture without necessarily extending the virtues of the elite to the people.

In their pursuit of quality control the censors did not neglect satire and libertinage. A time of disillusion and defeat, the last years of Louis XIV's reign had more than their share of poets, novelists, and short-story writers who veiled social and political criticism behind extravagant and licentious fiction. Although the mature "philosophic" tale, accounts of voyage, and dictionary remained a generation away, Courtilz de Sandras, Eustache Le Noble, François Gacon, and Robert Chasles set the literary tone of the regency. All of these writers published abroad; their works were smuggled into France or else obtained preferential treatment. Courtilz de Sandras was persistent in maintaining his sales; Gacon forged privileges to keep up his commerce;[63] and Le Noble was the most ingenious of all—back in the 1690s he had established a distribution service while imprisoned in the Châtelet. He smuggled out manuscripts of *L'École des sages* to visiting peddlers, and editions of the work subsequently surfaced in Lyon, Toulouse, Bordeaux, and elsewhere.[64] Pontchartrain cracked down. He had censors turn down permission for entry into France of a memorial edition of St. Évremond's works, stating as his reason that "there are several entire pieces in these two volumes that cannot be approved, and too much labor would be involved if one wished to throw out what was objectionable."[65] A collection of Le Noble's poems was rejected for containing "satirical sections that would offend individuals who might recognize themselves there."[66] Gacon's *Traduction nouvelle des oeuvres d'Anacréon avec des remarques et une satire contre l'amour propre* was disapproved for its preface and notes, which were termed "too lively and too dishonest."[67] Pierre Richelet's controversial *Dictionnaire françoise,* although published already in Holland, Geneva, and (in a pirated edition) Lyon, was denied an entry permit for being a "bad book, injurious to several persons, and contrary to proper morals."[68] Giving offense to living persons was a scandal the censors particularly wished to avoid; on the other hand, it also ensured the editions would sell out. Examiners therefore struck down at *romans à clef* imitative of *Télémaque,* or else erotic tales with contemporaneous inferences.[69]

Finally, there was the issue of unacceptable themes. Surprisingly, only a small number of reprobations cited inappropriateness of subject matter as the reason for disapproval. Pardou's *Prince Doria, histoire galante* was considered scandalous for relating the love affair between a brother and sister.[70] A *Mille et un bons mots, contes à rire et gasonades nouvelles* was considered "overly bold little stories, and partially scandalous besides."[71] Subligny's *La fausse Clélie, histoire françoise galante et comique,* which circulated without difficulty forty years earlier, failed twice to secure a permit renewal. In 1709 the novel was considered "too free"; in 1711 it was rejected for being a work "that is too liberal for these times."[72]

Moving from literature to history, geography, accounts of voyages, and current events, the censors expressed much more sensitivity toward subject matter than toward style. They also revealed critical preconceptions about the nature of historical writing that set their views apart from the "philosophic" history of the succeeding generation. Concerning the relatively distant past, accuracy and dispassionate objectivity marked the censors' standard. Controversy, didacticism, even interpretation, were to be avoided. Therefore, Le Noble's translation of some Italian-inspired "political reflections" upon aristocratic conspiracies against Julius Caesar, Nero, and the Medici was rejected because the material he treated was both "delicate and dangerous."[73] An anonymous history of England, published in Holland in 1695, was denied entry eleven years later because its author was "neither sufficiently disinterested nor sufficiently equitable" in his evaluations.[74] The Abbé de Bellegarde's catechistic history of France was turned down for "containing matters contrary to good morals and to the interests of the Royal House";[75] and a biography of England's Margaret of Anjou was disapproved for combining the "disagreeableness of history with the insipidness of a novel."[76]

With respect to recent times, however, objective criteria had to yield to the regime's current political line. Although dead for two generations, Cardinal Richelieu was still an insufficiently historical personage to warrant dispassionate treatment. Evaluation had to assume the form of eulogy. An account of the cardinal's ministry thus was rejected in 1702 for what a censor considered to be too harsh a treatment, and a comparison between Richelieu and Ximenes submitted two years later was turned down because the Frenchman's memory was either "stained in several places" or else recalled at the expense of his sovereign, Louis XIII.[77] Authors had to treat living figures with immense care, for the attitude of censors was quite unpredictable. In 1712 the author of an anonymous *Miroir magique de Pasquin* was understandably reprimanded for injuring the character of the French Commander de Villars, but he was taken to task equally for poking fun at Villars's adversary, Prince Eugene.[78] And a commentary upon the terrible famine year 1709 was disapproved not only for its "overly vivid portraits of misery" but also for its "overly strong invectives against the allies"—namely, France's enemies Holland, England, and Austria.[79] From the standpoint of the censors, among the most common errors of political authors were a predilection for ultramontanism and an insufficiently vigorous defense of Bourbon claims to Spain.[80] As Joseph Klaits has shown, the

French foreign minister Colbert de Torcy wanted to limit political propaganda to the sort produced by his paid agents.[81] Therefore, those who maintained independence and submitted their writings to normal censorship understandably found the going difficult.

While works on geography were disapproved generally for reasons of inexactitude, voyage literature was suspect for veiling impious or politically dangerous ideas. To those familiar with the propaganda value of both the genuine and fictitious extraordinary voyage in the literature of the Enlightenment, the suspicions of the censors were well founded.[82] Jean Dumont's *Voyage en France, en Italie, en Allemagne, à Malte et en Turquie*, originally published in Holland in 1699, was denied entry to France seven years later as a consequence of the book's "mockery of the Catholic religion."[83] Dampier's *Nouveau voyage autour du monde* was turned down because "there exist in this work matters that are too freely stated with respect to morals and religion."[84] A collection of *Entretiens des voyages sur mer* was rejected for containing scornful remarks and satire against the government and clergy.[85] A *Voyage d'Alep à Jérusalem* was disapproved because "there are places in this book where the ceremonies of the Church are turned to ridicule."[86] "Satirical," "injurious to the Royal Council and dangerous for religion," "a pure and vain idea where the author has taken pains to add several rather violent satirical traits, particularly against the clergy"—such phrases unflatteringly described this genre.[87] Curiously enough, the censors made no reference to the authenticity of the accounts of the voyages. Nevertheless, during the first decade and a half of the century travel literature already was well developed as a vehicle for social and institutional critique.

Disapprovals of manuscripts dealing with medical subjects were proportionally rarer than those concerned with history or current events. Customarily the stated causes for rejection were similar to those given for disapprovals of religious books: inexactitude, the tendency to dwell upon superstition, an inelegant style. From the vantage point of Paris, physicians in the provinces seemed like bunglers who totally lacked the proper theoretical underpinning. A well-intentioned *Critique de la médecine ancienne et moderne et du chirurgien des riches et des pauvres* by a Dr. Dufour was treated as "the work of an old provincial physician who, knowing barely any anatomy and no chemistry whatsoever, produces rhapsodies and nothing else that cannot be derived from the most contemptible authors."[88] Jean Bernanos's *Recueil de rémèdes pour les maladies du corps humain* was disapproved for listing a large number of cures that either were well known or else found elsewhere. Furthermore, the cures went "beyond the possible," even if the censor ignored those "that are simply superstitious."[89] The censors clearly conceived of publications on medicine as works intended for use by learned specialists and not as handbooks for the public, however cultivated the public might be.

Thus disapprovals sing a familiar refrain of condescension and corporate-mindedness: "There is nothing in this work that isn't well-known, and the style is barbarous"; "style less than mediocre, matters that are found everywhere"; "nothing new, and the work is badly written"; "uninformed work of an unlettered individual."[90]

Among the miscellany of books that defy precise categorization, what were once euphemistically called marriage manuals offended the censors. Although these works were, in explicitness and sense of purpose, light-years away from present-day "joy of sex" introductions to sexual fulfillment, several were either sufficiently detailed or else lacking in Christian foundation to merit condemnation. Manuals written in Latin did not fare better. One may wonder, of course, just what motivated the anonymous author to propose his *Polygamia Triumphantia* in the first place, but the censor's rejection was predictable: "This work contains a doctrine contrary to good morals and the true religion."[91] A manual more sober in purpose was *Réflexions critiques touchant l'humeur, les moeurs et les inclinations du sexe, avec quelques portraits & une formulaire pour les hommes qui veulent se marier et passer doucement leur vie dans l'état du mariage,* which was rejected for "containing reflections that are too childish" as well as remarks contrary to "proper morals."[92] "Matters that are known [and] treated much better in other books" was the reason cited for the initial disapproval of a *Manuel de ceux qui veulent s'engager dans le mariage et de ceux qui s'y trouvent engagés,* while several months later an ostensibly revised manuscript was newly rejected because "the author treats marriage in the manner of the pagans."[93]

Views on women, children, and education that departed from collective norms of orthodoxy also proved to be unacceptable. Louise de Bazin's essay *De l'injustice des hommes envers les femmes dédié à Mme de Maintenon* was rejected "because the truth is not treated with sufficient tact," although a revision was subsequently approved.[94] A belief that morality ought to be treated with more gravity was the reason given for disapproval of a *Morale critique contre la vanité des femmes.*[95] "Ideas that could prejudice children against healthy and exact philosophy" were rejected by the censors in *Le livre des enfans où sont contenuës les idées premières et générales de toutes les choses dont les enfans peuvent avoir connoissance.*[96] "A work filled with ineptitude and very useless besides" was the judgment rendered concerning *Nouvelle méthode par demandes et par réponses pour l'instruction de la jeunesse qui commence à apprendre la langue latine.*[97]

Finally, an occasional foreign author of notoriety fell victim to the censor's quill. Chief among these was Locke, whose Amsterdam edition, in French, of the *Essay Concerning Human Understanding,* was forbidden entrance into France because "the metaphysics of this author has dangerous consequences."[98]

To do justice to the censors their positive as well as negative decisions should be analyzed. Approvals customarily were given without comment, were accompanied by a noncommittal "bon," or else were composed according to a hierarchy of praiseworthy phrases. Moreover, since a book's title often yields as little useful information as does its cover, any analysis of the some 5,500 approvals is unlikely to offer much qualitative information. Short of locating and reading a large number of the books, the historian is limited to counting and categorizing titles. On the other hand, as I hope I have suggested, the censors' disapprovals contribute to our understanding of the then official canons of taste. Painfully brief as most of the judgments were, we can see that stylistic gracefulness, exactitude, reason, and empirical validity weighed at least as heavily in determining the censors' values as did tradition and authority. Louis XIV's censors were certainly in the forefront of the struggle against religious or moral innovation. However, it was not innovation as such that they opposed. Rather it was what they deemed to be insufficiently based novelty, unproven according to standards of sound judgment and common sense—therefore either dangerous or worthless. Although the encyclopedists might surely consider the royal censors of the previous generation to have contributed to public ignorance and intellectual stagnation[99] and at least two contemporaneous in-house memoranda suggest the same—[100] the fact remains that the theoretical bases for decision making among the censors themselves were rarely at variance with the criteria for truth with which we associate the French Enlightenment. The parting of the ways had nothing to do with a denial of critical liberty, but rather with disagreement over its permissible range.[101]

NOTES

1. A partial reference list would include the following: François Bluche, *Les magistrats du Parlement de Paris au XVIIIe siècle, 1715–1771* (Paris: Les Belles Lettres, 1960), pp. 291–296; Jean Meyer, *La noblesse bretonne au XVIIIe siècle* (Paris: Imprimerie nationale, 1966); Pierre Deyon, *Amiens, capitale provinciale: Étude sur la société urbaine au XVIIe siècle* (Paris and The Hague: Mouton, 1967), pp. 286–288; Maurice Garden, *Lyon et les lyonnais au XVIIIe siècle* (Paris: Les Belles Lettres, 1970), pp. 457–471; and Yves Durand, *Les Fermiers généraux au XVIIIe siècle* (Paris: Presses Universitaires de France, 1971), pp. 561–573. Although a cultural historian more influenced by Daniel Mornet than by the "Annales" school, Louis Trénard provided an important impetus to analysis of private libraries and book collections in the field he baptized "social history of ideas." See, for example, Trénard's thesis, *Histoire sociale des idées: Lyon de l'Encyclopédie au préromantisme* (Paris: Presses Universitaires de France, 1958), Vol. I, pp. 129–148.

2. I can only give a brief sampling here. It is acknowledged that the two volumes of essays called *Livre et société dans la France au XVIIIe siècle* under the direction of François Furet of the École des hautes études en sciences sociales (Paris and The

Hague: Mouton, 1965, 1970) inspired the trends of subsequent research; and the revived *Revue française d'histoire du livre* offers a regular periodical outlet. After Martin's study, the most significant recent monographs dealing directly with the early-modern French book trade are Jean Quéniart, *L'Imprimerie et la librairie à Rouen au XVIIIe siècle* (Paris: Klincksieck, 1969); René Moulinas, *L'Imprimerie, la librairie et la presse à Avignon au XVIIIe siècle* (Grenoble: Presses Universitaires de Grenoble, 1974); and Suzanne Tucoo-Chala, *Charles-Joseph Panckoucke et la librairie française 1736–1798* (Pau: Marrimpouey Jeune; Paris: Jean Touzot, 1977). The most original and recent attempts to connect the influence of books to particular social milieux are Daniel Roche, *Le siècle des lumières en province: Académies et académiciens provinciaux, 1680–1789* (Paris and The Hague: Mouton, 1978), 2 vols.; and Jean Quéniart, *Culture et société urbaines dans la France de l'ouest au 18e siècle* (Rennes: Université de Haute Bretagne, 1979). For an analytic survey of the literature, see my article *"Livre et société* after Ten Years: Formation of a Discipline," *Studies on Voltaire and the Eighteenth Century* 151 (1976): 287–312.

3. Elizabeth L. Eisenstein, *The Printing Press as an Agent of Change: Communications and Cultural Transformations in Early Modern Europe* (Cambridge and New York: Cambridge University Press, 1979), 2 vols.; Robert Darnton, *The Business of Enlightenment: A Publishing History of the Encyclopédie, 1775–1800* (Cambridge, Mass.: Harvard University Press, 1979).

4. Robert Mandrou, *Louis XIV et son temps,* Peuples et civilisations, 10 (Paris: PUF, 1973), pp. 293–347.

5. For some, but by no means all, of these books, an official condemnation exists in print. Fénelon's humiliation, for example, was recorded by the Déclaration du Roy, qui ordonne l'exécution de la constitution de N.S.P. le Pape en Forme de Bref du 12 mars 1699, portant condamnation d'un livre intitulé Explication des maximes des saints sur la vie intérieure composé par M^r. l'archevêque de Cambray (Bibliothèque nationale, Fonds français. Ms. 22088, no. 45. Versailles, 4 August 1699). A state-inspired ordinance of Louis-Gaston de Noailles, archbishop of Paris (F. F. 22088, no. 51. Paris, 15 September 1702), was employed to suppress Simon's translation of the New Testament. An order in council had the Paris police lieutenant René Le Voyer d'Argenson take after the *Project d'une dîme royale* (F. F. 22088, no. 78. Versailles, 14 March 1707). The condemnations of the *Réflexions morales* were the most grandiose of all: first an order in council (F. F. 21739, fols. 142–43. Marly, 11 November 1711), followed by a papal Bull, *Unigenitus Dei Filius,* which Louis XIV pressured Clement XI into issuing (F. F. 22088, no. 106. 8 September 1713).

6. Antoine Barbier, *Dictionnaire des ouvrages anonymes,* 3rd ed. (Paris: P. Daffis, 1872–1879), 4 vols.; Jacques-Charles Brunet, *Manuel du libraire et de l'amateur de livres,* 5th ed. (Paris: Firmin-Didot, 1865), 6 vols; and Gustave Brunet, *Imprimeurs imaginaires et libraires supposés* (New York: Burt Franklin Reprint, n.d.). The great folio registers of the Paris Booksellers' and Printers' Guild are located in the manuscripts room of the Bibliothèque nationale and are complemented by the Collection Anisson-Duperron. The major collections of Paris police reports are in the uncataloged cartons of the Archives de la Bastille in the Bibliothèque de l'Arsenal. From 1866 to 1904, François Ravaisson-Mollien published selections of these reports in

his convoy of volumes, the *Archives de la Bastille* (Paris: A. Durand and Pedone-Lauriel, 1866–1904), 19 vols.

7. Ravaisson, op.cit., Vol. 10, p. 408.

8. Anne Sauvy, *Livres saisis à Paris entre 1678 et 1701* (The Hague: Martinus Nijhoff, 1972), pp. 67–68, 315, 319.

9. Bibliothèque de l'Arsenal, Archives de la Bastille. Ms. 10539.

10. See my article "Les colporteurs de livres et leur culture à l'aube du siècle des lumières: les pornographes du Collège d'Harcourt," *Revue française d'histoire du livre*, no. 33 (1981): pp. 593–623. An appendix to the article identifies most of the books seized. Besides the reference works listed above, the most useful bibliographical sources are Émile Bourgeois and Louis André, *Les sources de l'histoire de France. XVIIe siècle (1610–1715)* (Paris: A. Picard, 1913–1935), 8 vols.; Pierre M. Conlon, *Prélude au siècle des lumières en France, 1680–1715* (Geneva: Droz, 1970–1976), 6 vols; Léonce Janmart de Brouillant, *La liberté de la presse en France aux XVIIe et XVIIIe siècles, histoire de Pierre de Marteau, imprimeur à Cologne (XVIIe et XVIIIe siècles)* (Paris: Quantin, 1888); Jacques Le Long, *Bibliothèque historique de la France contenant le catalogue des ouvrages imprimés et manuscrits qui traitent de l'histoire de ce royaume . . .* (new edition by Fevret de Fontette, Paris: Hérissant, 1768–1778), 5 vols.; Gabriel Peignot, *Dictionnaire critique, littéraire et bibliographique des principaux livres condamnés au feu, supprimés ou censurés* (Bologna: Forni, 1966); and Carlos Sommervogel, ed., *Bibliothèque de la Compagnie de Jésus* (Brussels: O. Schepens, 1890–1930), 12 vols.

11. Eight master or journeyman printers, sellers, or binders, who were either too old or too feeble to labor in shops, were customarily allowed to man bookstalls in the Palais under the protection of the Parlement of Paris. Their wares were supposed to be government documents, almanacs, and booklets of no more than eight sheets printed with privilege in the capital. However, they were the source of all sorts of illicit merchandise and used the Palais as a kind of privileged sanctuary immune from police activity. See, for example, the official report of 27 November 1699 (F. F. 21749, fols. 43^r–45^r). Abbé Jean-Paul Bignon, the first delegated director of the book trade, established lines of communication with agents in Holland for books that would bypass normal inspection points for entry into France. The French Huguenot émigré J.-F. Delorme was Bignon's chief supplier of books intended for Bignon and Bignon's high-placed friends. As an example of the kind of correspondence Delorme addressed to Bignon, here is a letter from Amsterdam dated 11 August 1707: "I very humbly request permission from your eminence to ship to Paris some copies [of Jansenist books] under the [customary] cover. Madame the marquise de l'Hôpital has sent me an order requesting several books, but as I believe that some of them would never pass the booksellers' guildhall [in Paris], I deem it appropriate to send your eminence a copy of the aforementioned order, so that y.e. will be so kind as to permit me to ship her the books." Isabella-Henrietta van Eeghen, *De Amsterdamse Boekhandel 1680–1725* (Amsterdam: Scheltma and Holkema, 1960–1967), Vol. 1, p. 126. The Paris bookseller Jean-Baptiste Musier was Bignon's favorite agent in the capital.

12. Unlike Musier, Huchet worked on his own, employing convenient protections whenever the occasion arose. His dossier is located in the Bibliothèque de l'Arsenal Archives de la Bastille. Ms. 10561.

13. The most complete blacklist is for the year 1706 (F. F. 21748, fols. 105ʳ–106ᵛ Infractions des statuts & ordonnances du Roy données aux imprimeurs et libraires de la ville de Paris en 1706). A good example of descents led by guild officers is that of 26–27 April 1702 (F. F. 22081, no. 64, Procès verbal de visite faite dans les imprimeries de Paris par les sieurs Pierre Trabouillet syndic, Louis Sevestre, Pierre Émery, Jean-Baptiste Coignard et Pierre Delaunay adjoints).

14. For a complete analysis, see my article "La contrabande et la saisie de livres à Paris à l'aube du siècle des lumières," *Revue d'histoire moderne et contemporaine* 28 (1981): 158–173.

15. Ravaisson, op. cit., Vol. 12, pp. 126–127 (F. F. 15789, fols. 87ʳ–88ᵛ, Retractation et soumission du père Gerberon religieux benedictin, May 1710).

16. Benjamin Mather Woodbridge, *Gatien de Courtilz, sieur du Verger: Étude sur un précurseur du roman réaliste en France,* The Johns Hopkins Studies in Romance Literature and Languages, 6 (Baltimore: Johns Hopkins; Paris: PUF, 1925).

17. Ravaisson, op. cit., Vol. 10, pp. 9–10.

18. Woodbridge, op. cit., pp. 1–17.

19. Robert Darnton, "The High Enlightenment and the Low-Life of Literature in Prerevolutionary France," *Past and Present* 51 (1971): 81–115.

20. An École des chartes thesis describing the administrative machinery of censorship in the first half of the eighteenth century is H. de Beaumont, "L'Administration de la librairie et la censure des livres de 1700 à 1750," *Positions des thèses soutenues par les élèves de la promotion de 1966 pour obtenir le diplôme d'archiviste-paléographe* (Paris, 1966), pp. 72–78.

21. F. F. 21111, fol. 530, 5 November 1700.

22. *Histoire du cas de conscience signé par quarante docteurs de Sorbonne, contenant les brefs du pape, les ordonnances épiscopales, censures, lettres et autres pièces pour et contre le cas, avec des réflexions sur plusieurs des ordonnances* (Nancy: Jos. Nicolai, 1705–1711), 8 vols.

23. John D. Woodbridge, "Censure royale et censure épiscopale: Le conflit de 1702," *Dix-huitième siècle* 8 (1976): 333–355.

24. F. F. 22088, no. 99, Arrest de la Cour de Parlement sur un imprimé portant titre *Réponse du cardinal de Noailles au mémoire que le Roy luy a fait l'honneur de luy donner,* 15 June 1712; F. F. 22088, no. 101, Arrest de la Cour de Parlement, portant condamnation & suppression d'un livre qui a pour titre *Historiae Societatis Jesu Pars Quinta. Tomas Posterior ab Anno Christi 1591 ad 1616 Authore Josepha Juvencio Societatis Ejusdem Sacerdote,* Romae 1710 (24 March 1713).

25. F. F. 15798, fol. 3, Pontchartrain to Achille de Harlay, first president of the Parlement of Paris, 24 November [1705].

26. Pontchartrain to Herbigny, 19 October 1701, in G. B. Depping, ed., *Correspondance administrative sous le règne de Louis XIV* (Paris: Imprimerie impériale, 1850–1855), Vol. 2, p. 706.

27. Ibid., 4 April 1703, p. 707.

28. Ibid., Pontchartrain to Boisguillebert, 18 October 1701, p. 778.

29. Bibliothèque nationale, F. F. 22140, fols. 109^r–110^r; F. F. 22141, fol. 47^r; F. F. 22142, fol. 152^v. See Depping, op. cit., Vol. 2, pp. 336–337, 383–384, 776–778, 781–782, 783–784, 791, 805–807, 857–858, 861–862, 865.

30. Bibliothèque nationale, Collection Joly de Fleury. Ms. 1682, fols. 49–50. Pontchartrain to Henri-François d'Aguesseau, procurer-general of the Parlement of Paris, 20 October 1707.

31. F. F. 21749, fols. 206^r–210^v [1699].

32. F. F. 22131, fols. 178^v–181^r, 13 October 1704.

33. F. F. 22062, no. 48, Extrait des registres du Conseil d'Estat privé du Roy, 6 December 1700; Claude Saugrain, *Code de la librairie et imprimerie de Paris* (Paris: Aux dépens de la Communauté, 1744), p. 201; Arrêt du Conseil, 21 July 1704.

34. Pontchartrain to Boisguillebert, 6 December 1701, in Depping, op. cit., Vol. 2, pp. 358–359.

35. François-A. Isambert, Alphonse-H. Taillandier, and Decrusy, eds., *Recueil général des anciennes lois françaises depuis l'an 420 jusqu'à la Révolution de 1789* (Paris: Belin-Le Prieur, 1821–1833), Vol. 20, pp. 393–394; Lettres patentes portant règlement sur la librairie, 2 October 1701.

36. F. F. 21939–21942, Registre de monsieur l'abbé Bignon contenant les ouvrages présentés à Mgr. le Chancelier Phélypeaux [de Pontchartrain] par les auteurs ou les libraires, la distribution desd. ouvrages à m^{rs}. les examinateurs, avec les approbations ou motifs de reprobation, etc.

37. Jacques Le Brun, "Censure préventive et littérature religieuse en France au début du XVIIIe siècle," *Revue d'histoire de l'église de France* 2 (1975): 212.

38. As, for example, de Mongazon's *Dialogue de la raison et de l'imagination* (F. F. 21939, fol. 101^v, no. 1422, 13 March 1704).

39. F. F. 21990–21994, Registres des livres d'impression étrangère présentés pour a permission de débiter, 1718–1774. See also F. F. 21981, 21983–21988, 21989, all of which deal with books awarded the *permission tacite*. For a description of the *permissions tacites,* see David T. Pottinger, *The French Book Trade in the Ancien Regime (1500–1789)* (Cambridge, Mass.: Harvard University Press, 1958), p. 67.

40. F. F. 21939, fol. 76, no. 1149, 14 July 1704.

41. F. F. 21941, fol. 44^r, no. 455, 1 March 1708.

42. F. F. 21941, fol. 100^v, no. 1051, 5 September 1709.

43. F. F. 21942, fol. 143, no. 825, 16 February 1713.

44. F. F. 21939, fol. 76^v, no. 1158, 10 August 1703.

45. F. F. 21939, fol. 77^v, no. 1170, 6 December 1703.

46. F. F. 21939, fol. 93^v, no. 1337, 13 December 1703.

47. F. F. 21940, fol. 30^v, no. 301, 26 February 1705. *Abrégé de la véritable histoire de la possession des religieuses ursulines de la ville de Loudun du diocèse de Poitiers, arrivée en 1632.* In 1828, the Association catholique du Sacré-Coeur published Surin's manuscript as *L'Histoire abrégée de la possession des ursulines de Loudun et des peines du P* Surin. See Bibliothèque nationale, *Catalogue général des livres imprimés. Auteurs*, Vol. 180, p. 712.

48. F. F. 21939, fol. 77^v, no. 1174, 2 August 1703.

49. F. F. 22088, no. 54, Arrest du Conseil d'Estat . . . portant deffenses de composer, imprimer ni débiter aucuns libelles sur les anciennes contestations concernant la doctrine de Jansenius. Versailles, 5 March 1703.

50. Dramatic documentary evidence of the condemnation and seizure of largely Jansenist books can be found in F. F. 22087, no. 166, passim, for the late seventeenth century; and F. F. 22088, no. 47, passim, for the early eighteenth century.

51. Le Brun, op. cit., pp. 214–215.

52. Hilaire Dumas, *Histoire des V propositions de Jansenius, revue, corrigée et augmentée* (Liège: Moumal, 1699), is the most celebrated case in question. Even before the law of silence over Jansenism it was refused entry into France. F. F. 21939, fol. 52^r, no. 816, 17 August 1702.

53. F. F. 21939, fol. 33^r, no. 518, 31 July 1701. *Jacobi Platelii Soc. Jesu Synopsis Totius Cursus Theologici* (Cologne, 1698), 5 vols.

54. F. F. 21942, fol. 340, Registre E. no. 492, 3 October 1715. *Le manuel des evêques* See also Le Brun, op. cit., p. 216.

55. F. F. 21941, fol. 113^v, no. 1190, 1 March 1710. See also Robert Mandrou, *De la culture populaire aux 17e et 18e siècles: La Bibliothèque bleue de Troyes* (Paris: Stock 1964); and Geneviève Bollème, *La Bible bleue: Anthologie d'une littérature "populaire"* (Paris: Flammarion, 1975).

56. F. F. 21941, fol. 63^v, no. 652, 30 August 1708. See also Geoffrey Atkinson, *The Extraordinary Voyage in French Literature Before 1700* (New York: AMS Reprint 1966), pp. 141–143.

57. F. F. 21942, fol. 282, Registre E. no. 214, 15 May 1715.

58. F. F. 21940, fol. 87^v, no. 885, 29 April 1708; F. F. 21942, fol. 311, Registre E. no 348, 22 May 1715; See also Sauvy, op. cit., pp. 325–326.

59. F. F. 21942, fol. 338, Registre E. no. 482, 27 August 1715.

60. F. F. 21939, fol. 22^r, no. 325, 18 November 1700. The almanac obtained approval, however, in 1712: F. F. 21942, fol. 134, no. 768, 8 December 1712.

61. F. F. 21939, fol. 119^r, no. 1638, 18 September 1704.

62. F. F. 21939, fol. 29^r, no. 454, 7 June 1701. Pompard's *Mélange d'érudition et de galanterie;* F. F. 21939, fol. 47^r, no. 743, 17 May 1702. Maunory's *Erreurs du monde sous les aventures du roy coq et de la sage fourmi;* F. F. 21939, fol. 59^v, no. 927, 26 November 1702. De Lyonnière's *Le sort de la langue françoise;* F. F. 21939, fol. 66^v, no. 1013, 13 February 1703. The Countess d'Auneuil's *La forest de Marli, nouvelles du tems.* De Lyonnière eventually obtained approval, and his book appeared in 1703. See Barbier, op. cit., Vol. 4, p. 533.

63. F. F. 21744, fols. 166^{r-v}, Extrait des registres du Conseil d'Estat, 26 March 698.

64. F. F. 21744, fol. 85, Extrait des registres du Conseil d'Estat, 5 May 1692.

65. F. F. 21940, fol. 51^v, no. 515, 6 August 1705.

66. F. F. 21939, fol. 98^v, no. 1387, 15 January 1704. *L'Allée de la seringue, ou les noyers et la fradine ou les ongles rognés, poëmes.* A clandestine version of this collection was published in 1690 "À Francheville, chez Eugène Aléthophile," Bibliothèque nationale, *Catalogue général,* Vol. 94, pp. 885–886.

67. F. F. 21940, fol. 67^v, no. 670, 29 November 1705. A translation by Gacon of the odes of Anacreon and Sappho was published in Rotterdam in 1712. Bibliothèque nationale, *Catalogue général,* Vol. 56, p. 361.

68. F. F. 21939, fol. 80^r, no. 1202, 6 September 1703.

69. F. F. 21939, fol. 96^v, no. 876, 15 July 1706. *Commencement de l'histoire de Télémaque ou de l'Odyssée d'Homère;* F. F. 21942, fol. 286, Registre E no. 232, 13 May 715. *Les amours du comte de Soissons, nouvelle galante.*

70. F. F. 21939, fol. 33^v, no. 535, 28 August 1701.

71. F. F. 21942, fol. 212, no. 1224, 22 April 1714.

72. F. F. 21941, fol. 94^r, no. 994, 12 November 1709; F. F. 21942, fol. 51, no. 292, 3 September 1711. See also Barbier, op. cit., Vol. 2, p. 437.

73. F. F. 21939, fol. 46^v, no. 730, 21 July 1702. *Réflexions politiques sur les conspirations de Brutus, contre César, de Pison contre Néron, et des Pazzi contre les Médicis, mêlées de traits curieux d'histoire . . .*

74. F. F. 21940, fol. 77^r, no. 770, 14 January 1706. *Abrégé de l'histoire d'Angleterre écrite sur les mémoires des plus fidelles autheurs anglois . . .* (The Hague: E. Foulque, 695). Conlon, op. cit., Vol. 2, no. 6956.

75. F. F. 21941, fol. 39^r, no. 398, 26 January 1708. *Abrégé de l'histoire de France par demandes et par reponses.*

76. F. F. 21942, fol. 154, no. 887, 20 May 1713. *Histoire de Marguerite d'Anjou, rein* *d'Angleterre.*

77. F. F. 21939, fol. 53ʳ, no. 826, 10 August 1702. *La politique universelle, ou entre* *tiens curieux sur le ministère du cardinal de Richelieu, sur l'histoire & sur la morale* F. F. 21939, fol. 104ᵛ, no. 1463, 8 April 1704. *Parallèle du cardinal Ximenes ministr* *d'Espagne & du cardinal de Richelieu, ministre de France, contenant l'histoire du gou* *vernement de ces 2 monarchies sous le ministère de ces cardinaux.*

78. F. F. 21942, fol. 131, no. 748, 9 February 1713.

79. F. F. 21941, fol. 103ʳ, no. 1083, 13 February 1710. *Lettre de consolation écrite pa* *un seculier à un de ses amis sur les calamités publiques.*

80. F. F. 21940, fol. 97ᵛ, no. 1003, 21 April 1706. *Deffense de Philippe 5 roy d'Espagne* *contre le prince Charles archiduc d'Autriche pretendu roy d'Espagne sous le nom a* *Charles.*

81. Joseph Klaits, *Printed Propaganda under Louis XIV: Absolute Monarchy an* *Public Opinion* (Princeton, N.J.: Princeton University Press, 1976). Klaits has illumi nating information on newsletter propaganda in France and Colbert de Torcy' efforts to control it. See especially Chapters 1–4.

82. Geoffrey Atkinson's volumes remain the standard. See note 56 and *The Extra* *ordinary Voyage in French Literature from 1700 to 1720* (New York: Burt Frankli Reprint, n.d.).

83. F. F. 21940, fol. 76ᵛ, no. 762, 14 January 1706 (The Hague: E. Foulque an François L'Honoré, 1699), 4 vols. Conlon, op. cit., Vol. 2, no. 9324.

84. F. F. 21940, fol. 77ʳ, no. 765, 14 January 1706. The French translation ha already gone through at least three editions. Bibliothèque nationale, *Catalogu* *général,* Vol. 35, pp. 466–467.

85. F. F. 21940, fol. 77ʳ, no. 766, 14 January 1706.

86. F. F. 21940, fol. 77ʳ, no. 768, 14 January 1706.

87. F. F. 21942, fol. 181, no. 1049, 14 November 1713. *Voyage d'Angleterre par m. [A* *F. Bourreau] Deslandes* (Villefranche, 1717). Bibliothèque nationale, *Catalogu* *général,* Vol. 17, p. 892; F. F. 21942, fol. 204, no. 1176, 1 February 1714. *Nouvel* *relation concernant les voyages de Thomas Gage, dans la Nouvelle Espagne . . .* (Pari C. Clouzier, 1676), 2 vols. Bibliothèque nationale, *Catalogue général,* Vol. 56, p. 45 F. F. 21939, fol. 126ʳ, no. 1725, 8 December 1704. *Idée d'un règne doux et heureux, c* *relation du voyage du prince de Montberand dans l'ile de Naudely.*

88. F. F. 21939, fol. 50ᵛ, no. 797, 1 March 1703.

89. F. F. 21939, fol. 53ʳ, no. 827, 25 October 1702.

90. F. F. 21940, fol. 40ʳ, no. 392, 26 May 1705. *Recherche méthodique de la caus* *symptômes et guérison de chaq'une des fièvres, tant intermittentes que continues, simples* *malignes* by Dr. Vivien; F. F. 21940, fol. 52ᵛ, no. 524, 23 July 1705. *De Nobilita* *Medicinae* by Sr. Alphugius; F. F. 21941, fol. 118ʳ, no. 1233, 7 August 1710. *Dissertatic*

sur la constitution du sang pendant le tems de la fièvre by P. Flotte, Augustinian; F. F. 21942, fol. 308. Registre E., no. 334, 8 May 1715. *Traitté de la santé, et de la prologation de la vie.*

91. F. F. 21940, fol. 77ʳ, no. 767, 14 January 1706.

92. F. F. 21939, fol. 38ᵛ, no. 616, 5 January 1704.

93. F. F. 21941, fol. 128ʳ, no. 1347, 28 August 1710; F. F. 21941, fol. 132ᵛ, no. 1399, 18 September 1710.

94. F. F. 21942, fol. 196, no. 1132, 4 January 1714; F. F. 21942, fol. 297; Registre E., no. 282, 4 March 1715.

95. F. F. 21940, fol. 97ʳ, no. 999, 18 November 1708.

96. F. F. 21940, fol. 72ʳ, no. 717, 10 February 1706. Approved, F. F. 21940, fol. 90ᵛ, no. 920, 20 May 1706. Conlon, op. cit, Vol. 3, no. 13085 notes *Le livre des enfans ou idées générales & définitions des choses dont les enfans doivent être instruits* (Paris: Charles Osmont, 1706).

97. F. F. 21942, fol. 134, no. 767, 4 May 1713.

98. F. F. 21940, fol. 77ᵛ, no. 775, 24 January 1706.

99. Understandably, the article "Censeurs de livres" in the *Encyclopédie* largely confined itself to an historical narrative. The most severe criticism of the institution of censorship concerned the delays endured by authors or publishers awaiting results of an examination: "It sometimes occurs that the great number of books for which [royal censors] are responsible, or other reasons, place them in the disagreeable necessity of reducing authors or publishers who await their judgment to the state of those poor wandering souls on the banks of the Styx who implore Charon to ferry them across." *Encyclopédie, ou dictionnaire raisonné des sciences, des arts et des métiers* (Paris: Briasson, David the Elder, Durand, 1751), Vol. 2, p. 819.

100. Bibliothèque nationale, Nouvelles acquisitions françaises. Ms. 3546, fols. 53ʳ–56ʳ. Mémoire touchant la déclaration du 5 septembre 1711 [1711.] Collection Joly de Fleury. Ms. 1682, fols. 51ʳ–52ᵛ. Projet. Raisons de l'établissement d'un Conseil de Littérature, pour faire fleurir la littérature & encourager les sçavans à donner leurs ouvrages au public avec quelques résolutions . . . [1715].

101. In his discussion of religious censorship, Jacques Le Brun places emphasis upon the ambiguities between the censors' "enlightened" judgments and their refusal to acknowledge a critical spirit. See op. cit., p. 225.

[6]   From Censorship to Copyright: Aspects of the Government's Role in the English Book Trade 1695–1775

John P. Feather

IN EIGHTEENTH-CENTURY England there was a good deal of national self-congratulation, and not a little national complacency, underlying comparisons of Gallic tyranny with English liberty. Yet the press in England was subject to political pressures and commercial constraints that were in some ways more insidious than the open and clearly defined censorship operated by the Directoire de la Librairie. It is now over forty years since Laurence Hanson wrote the classic study of this subject,[1] but not only the lapse of time makes it worthwhile to reconsider the matter. As he himself wrote, Hanson "dealt almost exclusively with the newspaper press,"[2] and that, as we shall see, gives an incomplete picture both of the power of the printed word and of the limitations on that power. Furthermore, two generations of historians have redrawn our picture of eighteenth-century English government and administration, and we now have a wholly different image of the nature and working of that political system.

The questions I shall ask are three. First, what were the limits on freedom, and how and by whom were they defined? Second, how did the control of the press work in day-to-day terms of organisation and personnel? And, finally, what was the reaction of the book trade to the existence of controls, and how far did it continue its traditional attitude of cooperation with the authorities? All of these are large and complex issues, and I can do no more than skim the surface of them. Indeed, I offer this paper as an interim report that sketches the outlines of answers to these questions and fills in some of the outlines with a little more detail.

The documentary sources that could be tapped are vast, but in preparing this paper I have concentrated on the official records: the State Papers and the papers of the Treasury Solicitor, the government's chief permanent legal adviser. There was, however, no clear distinction between public and private records in the eighteenth century, and the papers of Harley, Walpole, and Newcastle, to name but three, all contain documents of a class that are also found in official records; these and other archives will be the subject of further investigation.

> To be free, is to live under a government by law. The *liberty of the press* consists in printing without any previous license, subject to the consequences of law. The *licentiousness* of the press is *Pandora's* box, the source of every evil. Miserable is the condition of individuals, dangerous is the condition of the state, if there is no certain administration of law to protect individuals, or to guard the state.[3]

Lord Chief Justice Mansfield spoke these famous words in 1783, while summing up in the trial of William Davies Shipley, dean of St. Asaph, for seditious libel. Like other familiar quotations, however, it deserves to be restored to its context. Mansfield's summing up addressed a particular problem arising from a lower court verdict that Shipley was "Guilty of publishing only" and, as defence counsel explained to Mr. Justice Buller, "that they mean to find that there was no sedition."[4] Mansfield upheld Buller's objection to this verdict, although in fact Shipley was acquitted on a technical fault in the indictment.[5] In making his judgment, however, Mansfield provided us with a vivid insight into the problem of censorship in an open society governed by the rule of law.

Mansfield admitted that he could not cite accurate precedents because they were not properly recorded, and he was, consequently, obliged to rely on his own memory. This took him back to 1731, when he was a Junior in the trial of the publishers of *The Craftsman* for the same offence. In that trial, Lord Chief Justice Raymond had taken the view, also adopted by Buller and now upheld by Mansfield, that the jury could decide only whether the accused had written, printed, or published the passage cited in the indictment; whether or not it was a libel was a point of law and fell in the province of the judge, not the jury. Mansfield reminded the court that Raymond had been called to the bar in Anne's reign, that he had been Solicitor-General and Attorney-General under George I, and that he was furthermore a close friend of Sir Edward Northey, another attorney-general during the same reign.[6] Mansfield argued, in effect, that Raymond knew what were called the "ancient proceedures" because the latter had helped to develop them during his time at the bar and on the bench. By the standards of English law this was remarkably recent antiquity, but Mansfield's judgment, pervaded by the need to demonstrate the practice since the abolition of pre-publication censorship in 1695, was, in fact, an account of the evolution of the law's attitude to the press since the end of the seventeenth century and of the slow acceptance of ground rules for freedom and restraint. The problem had been, and remained, very difficult. In a society with an elective, if oligarchic, constitution, in which the elected body, the House of Commons, was continually increasing its power, political quarrels inevitably took a printed form; there was no other medium through which the parties could address their ultimate master, the electorate.

One subject was, however, too delicate to be discussed: the succession to Queen Anne, and, after 1714, the possibility of a Stuart restoration aided by the Jacobites. The Protestant succession, and Parliament's power to regulate it, were so fundamental to the constitution of post-revolutionary Britain that denial of them was made High Treason in 1707. In fact, the only prosecution to take place under this statute was that of John Matthews, who in 1719 was hanged for allegedly having printed the notorious *Vox Populi, Vox Dei.*[7] The problem was whether everything else could be freely discussed, and, if not, where the boundary lines were to be drawn; these boundaries would have to be delimited by the courts, since there was no other statute law on the subject or any realistic hope of new legislation. In other words, although the book and newspaper trades had to take risks, so too did the government for fear that its opponents would be acquitted if they were brought to trial.

In practice, by 1714, politicians of all parties accepted that licensing would never be revived. Even Queen Anne's last two parliaments, elected in 1710 and 1713, and dominated by the High Tories, failed to pass licensing bills on four occasions, mainly because moderate Tories, including Joseph Addison, joined the Whigs in objecting in principle to this form of censorship.[8] After the virtual destruction of the Tory party in 1714 there was no serious possibility of a new licensing act. By 1723, even the High Tory Duke of Wharton could write of the freedom of the press as a "Bulwark of our Liberty,"[9] and Sir Robert Walpole, probably in about 1730, endorsed this sentiment:

'Tis therefore to be hoped . . . that these Gentlemen's [the authors' and publishers'] Eyes will be opened—before it be too
late, and that they will readily concurr in any reasonable &
gentle methods for preserving the Liberty of The Press, and at
the same time rendring the exercise of that Liberty compatible
wth the enjoyment of all our other Rights and Liberties; wch is
the most that I contend for, and the least that can be done in a
free and well-govern'd nation.[10]

This statement, like Mansfield's fifty years later, assumes that the first
consideration must always be the security of the state, but also that, provided there is no serious danger to security, freedom of the press is both
permissible, and even desirable, in a "free and well-govern'd nation."

The Limits on Freedom

What were the limits on freedom? One, the law against Jacobite propaganda, has already been mentioned; since this law was never actually applied, except in the case of the unfortunate Matthews, it was no more than
an ultimate deterrent. Continuous pressure on the Jacobites was exerted by
the law of seditious libel.

Mansfield clearly believed that the reign of George I was the crucial
period in the development of the law of seditious libel. In the first decade
after 1714 there was widespread sympathy for the Stuarts, which increased
due to the unpopularity of the German-speaking monarch and his German-
speaking mistresses, all of whom manifestly preferred Hanover to St.
James's. This sympathy was clearly reflected in print, especially in one of
the most important and neglected of the propaganda media: the ballad. The
government was virtually obliged to mount a compaign against the Jacobite writers and printers.

Among the State Papers are many Jacobite ballads that were either prosecuted or considered for prosecution between 1714 and 1727. Most of these
unrecorded broadsides[11] came from the press of one printer, Francis Clifton.
Clifton was, as a consequence, deeply unpopular with many of his contemporaries: Thomas Gent, the York printer, knew Clifton during his own
apprenticeship in London and called him a "Wretch";[12] an Under-Secretary
of State was told in 1720 that Clifton was a "Papist & Jacobite";[13] and a judge
described Clifton as "an Notorious Catholic Printer."[14] Yet Clifton was by
no means the only Jacobite, or the only Catholic, to own a printing press.
Clifton's troubles arose from the fact that he was too good at his job. At least

one of his ballads was printed in an edition of 10,000 copies,[15] and he was extraordinarily efficient in arranging for their distribution.

Ballads were sold and sung in the streets, usually by women who were known as "hawkers" or "mercuries." Although the ballad is a phenomenon normally associated with the sixteenth and seventeenth centuries, it continued long after 1700, even in London,[16] and was more important than has been generally recognised. Although the pamphlet and the newspaper gradually supplanted the ballad as the chief instrument of propaganda, the ballad remained the cheapest, quickest, and most effective way of reaching a mass urban audience.[17] This was certainly true of Jacobite literature until about 1730.

Closely related to the Jacobite question was the problem of attacks on the Church of England, not only by Roman Catholics but also by High Churchmen. In a sense, the attacks of the High Churchmen, while just as political as those of the Catholics, were even more dangerous because they came from persons who professed to be loyal to the new dynasty. Not until the condemnation of Bishop Atterbury of Rochester for Jacobitism in 1723 was the general equation of High Churchmanship, High Toryism, and High Treason finally confirmed.[18]

By implication and association all High Churchmen were suspect, as publisher Richard Welton discovered in the year after Atterbury's exile. Welton was probably innocent, a sincere fool with no instinct for self-preservation.[19] He published *The Substance of Christian Faith and Practice: Represented in Eighteen Practical Discourses,* apparently at his own expense, in 1724.[20] The book had, however, a rather longer history, for as early as February 1723 the authorities were taking an interest in it. On 8 February, a manuscript list of subscribers was confiscated from the house of John Hook, a bookseller in Fleet Street,[21] who was arrested along with George James, the printer, and three other booksellers on the same day.[22] They were released three days later when they had supplied the information the government wanted: the name of the author. Welton was in custody by 25 February and released between 11 and 18 March;[23] he and his book trade associates were released from their recognizanses in May 1723.[24]

When the book was finally published, some six or more months after these events, it bore many signs of its troubled history. To the bibliographer it presents a baffling complexity of cancelled leaves.[25] All the cancellations occur in passages dealing with contentious subjects on which the High Churchmen veered toward support of Divine Right and strict hereditary succession; most notable among these passages is a sermon with the seemingly innocuous title of "The Efficacy of the Prayers of Good Men," which deals with pious princes, arbitrary government, and the "throne of righteousness," that is, at least by implication, contrasted with the monarchy of the United Kingdom (L6-7, M1; pp. 155–158, 161). The other offensive passage was in a sermon on "The Shipwreck of Faith," which attacked the "comprehension" of the Church of England and the attempt to modify its doctrines to attract the dissenters; this is contrasted with the High Church ascendancy under good Queen Anne (S2-4; pp. 259–293).

All of this was little more than harmless eccentricity. Even in its final form, with the offending passages toned down in the cancellations, the general tenour was still strongly Tory and High Church, but the government did not want to make unnecessary trouble for itself by drawing public attention to this sort of minor irritant. Welton was allowed to hold his views, and even to publish them, as long as he avoided direct reference to the Stuart succession.

Jacobite views were investigated wherever they appeared, whether in ballads, newspapers, or books. One book that caused its author and printer a great deal of difficulty was *An Historical Account of the Advantages That Have Accru'd to England by the Succession of the House of Hanover*, written by Mathias Earbery, printed in the shop of Stephen Gilbert[26] in 1721, and published in 1722 in two parts. The title was ironic, for Earbery argued that William III had involved England in Continental broils for the benefit of Holland, and that George I had continued the tradition with Hanover as the beneficiary. Within this general argument, however, there were specific passages that infuriated the government. Walpole and Townshend, wrote Earbery, were out of power between 1714 and 1717 because "They had at that time some remaining bowels of compassion for their country" (Pt. 1, p. 27),[27] "But upon cooler Thoughts, when they afterward saw that their Country must be ruin'd . . . they have since fortifyed themselves with new Resolutions, and on recollection found it convenient to be sharers in the publick booty" (Pt. 1, pp. 27–28). In other words, they returned to office. Turning to the House of Hanover itself, Earbery informed his readers that William III bought the allegiance of Brunswick with "English gold (which they have had a particular Veneration for ever since)" (Pt. 2, pp. 3–8). He further described George I's mother, the Electress Sophia, as "very Amourously inclined," and, in passing, added that it was generally noted that none of her children bore much resemblance to her husband (Pt. 2, pp. 9–10). Finally, after some twenty pages of personal abuse, Earbery turned to politics, but not before he had edified his readers with the information that George I sleeps with his mistress's daughters (Pt. 2, pp. 11–34). He ended by challenging the ministry to prosecute him so that he could produce the evidence that supported his claims (Pt. 2, p. 55).

The government could not ignore such a challenge, but its position was undoubtedly exacerbated by the popularity of Earbery's book. In 1721 and 1722 there were at least seven editions of Part One and six of Part Two.[28] The combination of libel and popularity was not to be tolerated, and, despite Earbery's protestation that he had written for financial rather than political motives,[29] everyone involved was examined at the Secretary of State's Office, although not without considerable difficulty.[30]

No historian, even if less abusive than Earbery, was wholly safe in dealing with the last 25 years of Stuart England. Thomas Salmon's *A Review of the History of England* was reported to Cartaret in January 1724 by that strange character "Orator" Henley.[31] In the first volume nearly a quarter of the 466 pages of text were concerned with the reign of James II, about which Salmon challenged two conventional views: first, that James had abdicated, and, second, that Parliament had never declared the crown to be elective (pp. 464–465). The second volume, published in the same year, dealt only with the reigns of James II, William III, and Anne. Although the latter volume was not overtly Jacobite, Salmon did attack party politics of the period since the Glorious Revolution. It seems that he was not, in fact, prosecuted; certainly, there is nothing to indicate that Henley's complaints were ever fully investigated.

Bevil Higgons was not so lucky, but neither was he so cautious. In *A Short View of the English History,* published in 1724, he wrote of the Stuarts as having "a clearer Title to the Crown than any Soverain House in *Europe* can boast" (p. 288). This was, admittedly, in the context of the succession to Elizabeth I in 1603, but the implication was unmistakable. There was even perhaps a certain disingenuous ambiguity in arguing that the reign of James II ended "inauspiciously" (p. 43); however, one passage was unforgivable, for it cast doubt on the motives, and even on the religion, of the heroes of Protestant England, the men who made the Revolution:

> It is certain, the first design of mining King *James,* tho' form'd in the Stone Gallery at *Whitehall,* was afterwards chiefly manag'd at the Courts of *Madrid,* and *Vienna,* and at last brought to Perfection in the Consistory at *Rome,* being the first and only Popish Plot that ever succeeded in *England* (p. 418).

All this appeared in the version that was finally published in 1724. William Lewis, a bookseller in Covent Garden, was arrested as early as 12 December 1722 for his part in the publication.[32] Lewis claimed that he had objected to some passages, but that, although Higgons agreed to make some alterations, three or four sheets of the original version were printed while Lewis was out of town.[33] The Under-Secretary of State did not believe him and had Lewis committed for trial,[34] although the real concern was to find the author. On the same day, the government arrested the printer, Thomas Edlin, who also claimed to have insisted on alterations in the book. Higgons had refused to make them, the printer alleged, and Edlin was forced for commercial reasons to print the book, of which he had distributed 100 of the 500 copies.[35] The books were confiscated, and

Higgons himself was arrested on 22 March 1723, but released on bail in May.[36] Finally, in September 1724, Higgons asked for the confiscated books to be released to "satisfie the demands of the subscribers."[37] It seems that this is what happened, and that the book was then published. It was reprinted three years later by Thomas Johnston at The Hague,[38] and again in 1748,[39] significantly, by the well-known Catholic printer Thomas Meighan.[40] It was reprinted once more in 1748 "by the Booksellers of London and Westminster."[41]

The Jacobite publications of George I's reign are significant not only because they are the largest single group of prosecutions for seditious libel in the whole period from 1695 to 1775, but also because Mansfield had these cases in mind when he referred to the "ancient proceedures." We can draw two important conclusions from this study. First, it seems clear that the government was only concerned with books that were seriously and fundamentally seditious. Mild aspersions on the Revolution or the eccentric ramblings of overzealous High Churchmen were ignored. Second, it is impossible to avoid the conclusion that a book's popularity was a factor in the decision to prosecute in marginal cases. Clifton's ballads in editions of 10,000 copies, or Earbery's much reprinted attack on the dynasty, could not safely be ignored. Salmon, on the other hand, could be, and was, forgotten, since no attention was drawn to his indigestible prose by the publicity of a trial in King's Bench. Censorship there certainly was, and a constant wariness about the products of the press, but it was neither universal nor oppressive; it was, on the contrary, eclectic and pragmatic.

Two other subjects regularly attracted the attention of the authorities, and they were closely connected. One of the most important causes of the unpopularity of the first two Georges, as we have already seen, was the not entirely unfounded belief that the Hanoverian connection dragged England into Continental wars and alliances that were not in her own best interest, and that cost a great deal of English money.[42] Conversely, both George I and George II expected to have the last word on foreign policy and were deeply sensitive to criticism of it. In 1724, when England and Spain were in dispute about English trading rights in the Spanish colonies in central America, the *Evening Post* was investigated for even discussing the matter, and the alleged author of the paragraph was arrested.[43] In 1724, both the *Daily Post* and the *Post Boy* were investigated in connection with an article on the related, and equally contentious, subject of English trading rights at Ostend in the Spanish Netherlands.[44] Not only the newspapers were in danger; the caricature print, which by the 1730s was displacing the ballad as the propaganda of the streets, was also suspect. In 1731, the publishers of a print called *Robin's Game,* which severely criticised Walpole's foreign policy, were indicted by the Middlesex Grand Jury for seditious libel.[45]

Even more than attacks on foreign policy, attacks on the monarch himself were pursued with the utmost vigour. When the *Freeholder's Journal* insulted not only Walpole and Townshend but also George I and his mistress, the Duchess of Kendal, at the height of the South Sea Bubble crisis, the author, printer, and publisher cannot have expected to avoid punishment.[46] The sensitivity of royalty, however, was more strikingly demonstrated by the investigation of both the *Daily Post* and the *Weekly Journal* in 1727 for carrying a seemingly innocuous report that there was to be a new "Imperial Crown of this Kingdom."[47] Less surprising was the government's interest in a letter from John Halden to one Allan at the Old Man's Coffee-House at Charing Cross, which was intercepted at the post office in 1723. Halden asked Allan to arrange for a reprint of *A Manifesto, or the Standard of the Church of Scotland,* in the hope that it would help "to Deliaver us from the Heavy Yoke of Monarchy."[48]

It is, however, important to realise that these and other ballads, books, newspapers, and prints that were investigated or prosecuted constituted a tiny minority of the output of the press. Even opposition papers like the *Weekly Journal* or the *Craftsman* for the most part went along their way undisturbed, until they overstepped the rather nebulous bounds of the permissible.[49] Politicians were certainly aware of the power of the press, and every successful minister after Harley exploited it, but they had neither the time nor the energy to control it in detail. The Stamp Act of 1712 was perhaps intended as a measure of censorship. If so, however, it failed in the long term,[50] and Walpole rightly ignored a rather foolish proposal for replacing all existing newspapers by one favourable to the government. The idea was to attract all advertising away from the former to the new paper, but the proposer of this scheme, Thomas Rose, failed to explain how this was to be achieved.[51] More practical was the exploitation of the comparative freedom of the press by planting favourable stories and publishing pro-government pamphlets and ballads. Even the representatives of foreign governments in London took advantage of the English eccentricity of a free press.[52] It was all part of the hard lesson of learning to live with the press.[53]

The Machinery of Control

The laxity in exercising censorship was, however, also a reflection of the extreme difficulty of instituting prosecutions and ensuring their success. The first problem was to discover the libels and their authors, printers, and publishers. Finding the libels themselves was all too easy: they were to be had in every coffeehouse and on every street corner in London. But finding those responsible for the libels was another matter. In 1704, Daniel Defoe proposed, on behalf of Harley, a scheme for compulsory imprints;[54] this idea was revived in 1712[55] and was still in the air in 1730.[56] It was enacted, however, only at the height of the anti-radical fervour of the 1790s, in the Seditious Societies Act of 1799.[57] In the absence of such a law, the pursuit of offenders was often so difficult that it was barely worthwhile.

We now come to the central paradox and the central problem of the whole issue, both for its participants and for its historian. How was it decided to pursue or to ignore a particular publication? The civil servants responsible for investigating alleged libels had to turn for advice to the law officers, usually the Attorney-General or the Treasury Solicitor. In 1717, Edward Northey was consulted about two Jacobite ballads, and he confirmed that they were indeed libellous and "the crying of [them] criminal."[58] Fifty years later the procedure was the same when the Earl of Rochford, the Secretary of State, constantly worried William de Grey, the Attorney-General, with possible libels.[59] But de Grey was cautious. In August 1770, he was sent a copy of an alleged libel and wrote to Rochford that:

> There is no doubt, but that it is Criminal by our Laws, to
> offer such Insults to Princes in Alliance with His Majesty as
> may tend to disturb the Publick Peace, or break the Friendship
> subsisting between His Majesty and his Allies.

This, however, was only de Grey's formal opinion; he enclosed with it an informal note, which suggested that Rochford abandon any idea of a prosecution. Instead, Rochford should content himself with sending a man to the offending printer to warn against repeating his folly and to threaten him with prosecution if he does so.[60]

Since prosecutions were costly, time-consuming, and unpredictable, de Grey's hesitation had parallels throughout the period, and the politicians must often have felt frustrated by the caution of the lawyers. In 1714, Northey was asked for an opinion on the prosecution of the author, printer, and publisher of the *Flying Post*, which had offended in a recent issue.[61] The author was believed to be Daniel Defoe,[62] but Northey concluded that "there is no evidence against him" except that of the printer, William Hurt, who was unreliable. Hurt himself had been in the pillory in 1713 for printing *The British Embassadress's Speech to the French King*, a libel on Queen Anne.[63] Northey doubted whether there was any point in taking further action against Defoe: "I submit whether it will be worth the charge to prosecute him." Only the publisher, one Baker,[64] could easily be prosecuted; he could be charged with selling the paper on the evidence of the messenger who had bought a copy from him. The case was dropped.

The law officers were, therefore, crucial to the whole system of censorship by vigilance, and many investigations were abandoned for want of adequate evidence. In effect, this resulted in a vital, although largely unintentional, safeguard of the liberty of the press. Juries expected to be presented with reasonable evidence of guilt, and the judges were, for all practical purposes, incorruptible. This made the government lawyers even more circumspect than lawyers are constitutionally inclined to be. It was freedom by default, but it was unquestionably freedom.

The law officers, therefore, helped to define the law itself, as they understood it, by giving advice on which cases should be taken into court. In 1718, Anthony Cracherode, the Treasury Solicitor, considered the whole question of the law of libel. It was to such definitions as Cracherode's that Mansfield was referring in 1783, since the policy developed and recommended by Cracherode, Northey, and Raymond was based on such principles. Cracherode recommended the use of the common law, rather than statutes old or new, partly because the judge had wide discretionary powers about punishment. Accepting that juries could only decide on the fact of publication, he merely added that false news, the dissemination of which was an offence, had to be proved to be false.[65]

This left the civil servants with the task of gathering evidence. The officers principally involved in this, the Under-Secretaries of State, were the chief permanent officials at the Secretary of State's office, and had many other duties and inadequate assistance.[66] They relied on three sources of information: the King's Messengers, paid informers, and crown officials.

There were never enough messengers for all the work that had to be done. In 1722, this problem exercised the mind of Charles Delafaye, the long-serving Under-Secretary who dealt with libels. The establishment was of forty messengers, but two had retired, six "seldom or never attend," two were "Chamber Keepers," that is, in charge of prisoners, and one was *hors de combat* after an accident while on official business abroad.[67] In practice, therefore, Delafaye had about thirty messengers. In the same year, in "A Proposal for Suppressing of Libels,"[68] Delafaye suggested that a new officer should be appointed who was "skill'd in the Law," and that a messenger should obtain a copy of every new publication and take it to this officer to check for possible libels.[69] At about the same time, Cracherode wrote to Townshend, the Secretary of State, suggesting that one Mr. Paxton should be appointed at a salary of £200 per annum to assist himself and the messengers in the pursuit of libels.[70] A few years earlier it had been suggested that Cracherode himself should read all the newspapers and refer libels to the Attorney-General.[71] Townshend did nothing, despite the added incentive of Cracherode's promise that the Treasury would pay the salary of the new officer. Delafaye was cynical enough to point out that the salary, whatever its source, needed to be paid regularly.[72]

Schemes to suppress libels, whether by new legislation or by increasing the establishment of law enforcement officers, were made from time to time throughout the period, but none was ever adopted. Occasional attempts were made to reinterpret existing laws; in 1740 an opinion was obtained on the possibility of suppressing the mercuries by using the laws requiring hawkers to be licensed,[73] or by prosecuting them under the Stamp Act for selling unstamped material. The Stamp Commissioners, however, had already tried the latter and failed, while the lawyers produced a whole series of objections to the rest of the plan. They asked whether the mercuries were covered by the legal definition of peddlers, and pointed out that the act of William III's reign, which required peddlers to be licensed, specifically excluded the sellers of printed matter. The complications were too great, and no more was heard of this plan.[74] Another suggestion, which was occasionally acted upon, was to prosecute the coffeehouses where libellous newspapers were sold or made available to customers.[75]

Walpole, like Harley before him, was content to prosecute the more outrageous publications and to counteract milder attacks by subsidising government newspapers and employing pamphleteers. As a consequence, the harassed Under-Secretaries had to do the best they could with the material at hand—handicapped, as they saw it, not only by the lack of money and personnel, but also by the intricacies, delays, and niceties of the law. The consequence was to throw them into the arms of the informers.

Delafaye had a wide circle of agents, some of them inherited from Harley and Defoe. He was always, however, willing to consider new recruits. In 1723, one William Wood offered himself as an informer; Delafaye immediately accepted the offer and sent back a list of printers against whom he wanted evidence, especially those involved in the *Freeholder's Journal*.[76] It was always difficult to deal with informers. Although they all protested their loyalty and devotion, most were working for money or for personal advantage of some other kind. Richard Shaw, Delafaye's chief provider of information against Clifton, was in Newgate for several years and fed information to the Under-Secretary in the hope of gaining his freedom. On one typical occasion Shaw reported that Clifton was printing "a sad thing," and ended his letter with "My Liberty I pray if possible in 3 months."[77] In the previous year, Shaw, who had been sentenced to transportation, begged to be sent to Bedlam rather than America in recognition of his services.[78] Even Francis Clifton, when he was in deeper trouble than usual, once offered himself as an agent. Protesting, albeit unconvincingly, that he had "no Interest but Serving the Governmᵗ.," he approached Townshend through intermediaries with a proposal to act as an informer on clandestine printers, in exchange for bail, adding that "none can find them out better than they that are in the Secret."[79]

Informers often found themselves in difficulties, or even danger. Samuel Negus, the compiler of the famous list of printers published by John Nichols in his *Literary Anecdotes* some seventy-five years later,[80] was ruined when his work for the government became known. The booksellers no longer sent him printing work, and he was obliged to ask Delafaye for a place at the post office as compensation.[81] In the late 1720s, an anonymous informer reported to Delafaye that there were in circulation thousands of copies of a Jacobite broadside called *A Letter Wrote . . . from Rome by a Noble Traveller to His Father in England;* he considered it his duty to report this, even though he had "suffer'd by my Secrett Service for the Present Government."[82]

Not all informers, however, were covert agents; government officials of all kinds were expected to provide information on a wide range of topics, including anti-government propaganda. The post office intercepted letters and opposition newspapers and pamphlets; the officers of the Customs House were charged with the duty of enforcing the laws against the import of books; justices of the peace and other local officials were expected to keep an eye on activities in their own localities; and the bishops had a special duty to watch theological and ecclesiastical publications. In 1719, for example, George Thorold, the Lord Mayor of London, assured Delafaye that all City officers would be instructed to arrest the hawkers and singers of Jacobite ballads.[83] Such actions were not confined to the capital. In 1722, the collector of customs at Chester seized a parcel of Jacobite prints that had arrived from Dublin for distribution in England and sent them to his superior officer in London.[84] In 1724, the mayor of Stafford reported that the head master of the school there had been distributing Jacobite propaganda, but this turned out to be a malicious accusation arising out of local squabbles.[85] Both the justices and the clergy of Staffordshire were instrumental in the prosecution of Edward Elwall, a Unitarian minister, in 1724,[86] and their complaint was supported by William Wake, the Archbishop of Canterbury.[87] By far the most enthusiastic of the bishops, however, was Edmund Gibson, whom Walpole moved from the comparative obscurity of Lincoln to the opulent and powerful see of London in 1723, precisely because of his unswerving devotion to the Whig and Hanoverian cause.[88] Indeed, Gibson became the main channel through which the clergy brought seditious literature to the government's attention;[89] since he was also Walpole's chief adviser on ecclesiastical patronage, the potential advantages to his informants were obvious.

Gathering the information, however, was only the first stage; it had to be assessed, and some of it proved to be unreliable or, as in the case of Elwall, simply malicious. The next step was to examine the accused and the witnesses in the hope of finding evidence that would hold up in court. The examinations were held at the Secretary of State's Office and were usually conducted by the under-secretary. Occasionally, however, the secretary himself was the examiner, as Harley was in the case of *The Memorial of the Church of England* in 1704.[90] More than 100 years later, Thomas Barnes, editor of *The Times,* was examined by no fewer than eight ministers, including the Prime Minister, the Home Secretary, and the Duke of Wellington, as well as the Attorney-General, about an article on the Peterloo massacre.[91] This was exceptional, but in the absence of an adequate police force or a professional magistracy, it was inevitable that high-ranking officials should have to do the job themselves. Occasionally, the Treasury Solicitor conducted the examination, but this seems to have been uncommon.[92]

The examiners, whoever they were, had to cope with a multitude of problems that can be summarised in one word: perjury. Reading through the examinations, one is truly astonished to discover how many printers were out of London when their presses were surreptitiously used by their sons and apprentices for printing seditious books, as William Lewis was when Higgons's book was in the press. The real problem, however, came in assigning responsibility for the publication.[93] Richard Nutt presumably knew that he was playing a long shot when he denied that he was the printer or publisher of the *Daily Post,* which had his name in the imprint. He did at least admit that he knew of no other Richard Nutt in the trade whose name it might be.[94] Indeed the investigation of one particular issue of the *Daily Post* in July 1729 exemplified a whole range of problems faced by the authorities. Nutt denied his connection with it altogether; Catherine Nutt, his daughter-in-law, admitted that she sometimes sold the *Daily Post,* but could not be certain that she had sold copies of that issue. John Peele, the publisher, from whom she had obtained her copies, had been in Wiltshire for ten days when this issue appeared and so could not say whether it had been sold from his shop. And, as the final blow, it was claimed that the offending passage was merely copied from another newspaper.[95]

Copying from another newspaper was a stock excuse; consequently, several papers sometimes had to be investigated to trace the source of a single story. An interesting, if improbable, variant was John de Fonseca's claim that, far from having written an offending paragraph of which the government had a manuscript in his hand, he had merely copied it from the newspaper "out of Curiosity."[96] Examples of evasion and outright lies could be almost endlessly multiplied. The examinees were, of course, trying to save themselves from Newgate, or fines, or the pillory, or all three, but their instinct and talent for deception and self-preservation put yet another obstacle in the way of the would-be censors. Whatever their motives, they too made a real contribution to the development of a free press.

The Book Trade and the Censors

I have already pointed out that the ballads, newspapers, and books that attracted official attention in this period represented a tiny proportion of those published, far less than one per cent. As we have seen, by no means all of those that were investigated were prosecuted, and not all prosecutions were successful. Although it is true, in strictly legal terms, that only pre-publication censorship was abolished in 1695, it is a gross oversimplification to suppose that nothing else changed. As long as there was a licensor, the government could prevent the publication of any unwelcome fact or opinion and had clear grounds for prosecution if an unlicensed book were published. A completely different situation was created by the lapse of the Licensing Act, for even the Messenger of the Press, Robert Stephens, could not keep track of all publications, especially when the multiplication of newspapers increased the flow to a flood.[97] The other preoccupations, most of them far more important, of the officials at the Secretary of State's Office, did not permit them to concentrate for long on the problems of the press. Their masters, the politicians, also changed their attitudes; Harley pioneered the use of government propaganda, and the tradition was revived by Walpole and continued, when necessary, by his successors.[98]

There was, however, another party involved: the men who printed, published, and above all financed these publications, the book trade. Traditionally the trade had collaborated with the government in controlling the press, and until 1640 had virtually administered the censorship system itself through the Stationers' Company. After the Restoration it had continued to cooperate with the messenger and the licensor. There was, however, a large measure of self-interest in this cooperation. By the end of the sixteenth century, the register of licenses was being used by the trade as a register of copy ownership and was still treated as such in 1695. Consequently, for the trade, the lapse of the Licensing Act meant above all the lapse of the legal basis for compulsory registration of copies. The booksellers' collective clamour for the restoration of licensing in the decade after 1695 has to be seen not as a sign of their devotion to censorship, but rather of their desire to restore legislative order to the trade by a law to protect copy owners. When Harley, a known opponent of licensing, consolidated his power in 1704, the trade changed its tack, and in 1707 petitioned for a Copyright Act, which was achieved in 1710.[99]

In fact, the trade was no more anxious than the politicians to have a completely free press, but its reason was different: not the protection of the state, but the protection of investments, especially investments in copies. In this context, it is important to recognise how greatly the economic structure of the English book trade changed between about 1690 and about 1730. Printing houses grew in size; the wholesaling congers came to dominate the distribution system, not only in London but also in the rapidly expanding provincial market; and, most significantly, the small, tightly knit, and self-elective group of copy owners came to depend on their collective monopoly of the most profitable books. Admission to these inner circles of the trade was difficult because it was expensive, and those who had achieved it had every reason to wish to protect their positions. These circumstances led to the futile and costly struggle over perpetual and common law copyrights in the 1770s.[100]

The same protectiveness, however, together with the changing economics of the book trade, also ensured a *de facto* continuation of the old tradition of cooperation with authority, but it was in a modified form. The trade now expected more of a *quid pro quo* from the government. This was clearly demonstrated in the 1730s, when the copyrights guaranteed by the 1710 act began to come into public domain. In 1731, the Court of Assistants of the Stationers' Company discussed the problem of the import of foreign reprints of English books in breach of the law and decided to seek the Attorney-General's opinion on the powers of the customs officers to confiscate all English books at the ports.[101] The government, as we have seen, already delegated to the Customs House responsibility for preventing the entry of seditious or libellous foreign books, and the trade seized on this opportunity to extend the customs functions for its own commercial advantage.

By 1735, the copyright issue was urgent, and the trade twice petitioned the House of Commons for new legislation,[102] emphasising in both cases the value of their copyright investments amounting in all, they claimed, to £150,000. The House of Commons appointed a committee to discuss the petitions, and the trade produced much evidence both of the high costs of publishing new books and of the undermining of their investments by the importation of Irish, Scottish, and Continental reprints.[103] A bill was brought in, and although it passed all its stages in the Commons, it was still in committee in the House of Lords at the end of the session.[104] The pressure did, however, have some effect, for in August 1735 the Master of the Stationers' Company was able to tell the Court of Assistants that the clerk had received a letter from the secretary of the Customs House informing him that several hundred Irish piracies had been seized at Carlisle.[105]

Parliament had more important concerns than copyright, and another attempt to amend the 1710 act failed for lack of time in the 1737 session.[106] In the next session, however, the publishers and the politicians began to find some common ground: a shared desire to ban the import of books. A bill was brought into the House of Commons in April 1738, only to fail in the House of Lords on its third and final reading.[107] The same bill was revived in 1739, however, and received the Royal Assent on 14 June.[108] The trade did all that it could to ensure that this act was enforced and in 1759 went to the extent of sending what amounted to threatening letters to the provincial booksellers to remind them that all imported English books were *ipso facto* piracies.[109]

In other words, the trade did all that it could to secure a legal framework within which its copyrights could be protected. This in itself represented a form of control that prevented the unrestricted circulation of printed matter. There were, however, other, less tangible factors at work. It has already been suggested that the ballad was an important medium of propaganda in the early eighteenth century, and that it was to some extent succeeded by the caricature print; but both were slowly displaced by the newspaper. Producing a newspaper could be profitable, but it was very expensive, requiring heavy investment in presses and type, high labour costs, and the purchase of large stocks of stamped paper. These considerations alone made the newspaper trade circumspect. The government could and did confiscate presses, interfere with circulation through the post office, and subsidise rival newspapers either directly or through the placing of profitable official advertisements. The newspaper printers were too committed to their businesses to risk any or all of these fates, with the result that opposition papers were as heavily subsidised by their supporters as government papers were by theirs.[110] The balance advocated by Swift, Addison, and others in the last years of Anne's reign was thus achieved and enabled all reasonable political debate to be conducted freely and publicly.

The relationship between the politicians and the publishers was complex and subtle, as it must always be in an open society. There was a growing philosophical commitment to a free press, but equally a feeling that the press could not be wholly unrestricted. In practice, the press restricted itself in the middle of the eighteenth century, partly because of internal economic pressures and partly because of a general observance of the guidelines that had been so painfully evolved by Northey, Delafaye, Cracherode, and other, more anonymous, public servants in the first dangerous decade of Hanoverian England. By 1775, England had a press whose freedom could be subverted only by the sort of arbitrary government that at that time seemed inconceivable, but that was to emerge in the panic-stricken reaction to the French Revolution twenty years later. This freedom of the press was hedged by many subtle restraints: the book trade defending its copyrights, the economics of printing and publishing, and the recent memory of the government's campaign against seditious libel in George I's reign. The boundaries of freedom even widened a little; in 1771, the House of Commons at last permitted, by default, the reporting of its debates, although still with some restrictions.[111]

The year 1775 marked a point of equilibrium in the history of the development of a free press in England. Publishers had learned the limits of freedom and generally observed them; politicians had learned both to tolerate and to exploit a free press. But the equilibrium was not to last. In 1774, when the House of Lords finally dismissed the chimerical notion of perpetual common law copyrights, and a bill to reverse its decision was rejected, the politicians had, in one stroke, destroyed the carefully constructed walls of protection around the English book trade. In 1776, Britain's complacency was shattered in Boston, the first of a series of political and economic shocks that transformed English society. The freedom of the press, defined with so much difficulty in the eighty years since the lapse of licensing, was now challenged again. It was not until the 1830s that the British press recovered, this time permanently, the liberty it had enjoyed during the quiet years of the mid-eighteenth century.

Acknowledgments

Documents in the Cholmondeley (Houghton) collection in Cambridge University Library are quoted by kind permission of the Most Hon. the Marquess of Cholmondeley. Documents in the Public Record Office are Crown Copyright.

NOTES

The following abbreviations are used in the notes:

B.L.	British Library, London
CJ	*Journal of the House of Commons*
C.U.L.	Cambridge University Library
DNB	*Dictionary of National Biography*
HMC	Historical Manuscripts Commission
LJ	*Journals of the House of Lords*
Plomer	*1668–1725* Henry R. Plomer, *A Dictionary of the Printers and Booksellers Who Were at Work in England, Scotland and Ireland from 1668 to 1725* (London, 1922).
Plomer	*1726–1775* H. R. Plomer, G. H. Bushnell, and E. R. McC. Dix, *A Dictionary of the Printers and Booksellers Who Were at Work in England, Scotland and Ireland from 1726 to 1775* (London, 1932).
P.R.O.	Public Record Office, London

1. Laurence Hanson, *Government and the Press 1695–1763* (Oxford, 1936).

2. Ibid., p. vii.

3. William Cobbett, *A Complete Collection of State Trials,* 33 vols. (London, 1809–1826), Vol. 21, col. 1042.

4. Donald Thomas, *A Long Time Burning* (London, 1969), pp. 109–112.

5. Cobbett, loc. cit.

6. Raymond was Attorney-General from 1720 to 1724, and Chief Justice of King's Bench from 1725 to 1733; Northey was Attorney-General from 1710 to 1718. See Basil Williams, *The Whig Supremacy 1714–1760,* 2nd ed. (Oxford, 1962), p. 474.

7. The statute is 6 Anne c. 7. For Matthews, see R. J. Goulden, *"Vox Populi, Vox Dei.* Charles Delafaye's Paperchase," *The Book Collector* 28 (1979): 368–390.

8. John Feather, "The Book Trade in Politics: The Making of the Copyright Act of 1710," *Publishing History* 8 (1980): 19–44.

9. Lewis Melville, *The Life and Writings of Philip Duke of Wharton* (London, 1913), p. 138.

10. C.U.L., MS. Cholmondeley (Houghton) 73/48/1,2 fol. 3. This is an anonymous "Essay upon the Liberty of the Press," carefully annotated and corrected by Walpole. The passage quoted is by the original writer, but Walpole has not altered it, and we can, therefore, take it to represent his views.

11. Of twenty-six that I have noted, only one is certainly in D. F. Foxon, *English Verse 1700–1750,* 2 vols. (Cambridge, 1975), (O 127), and two others may be (either D 121 or D 122 and what appears to be a reprint under another title of O 270). For a very cursory survey of the Jacobite material, see R. J. Goulden, "Jacobite Pamphlets in the Public Record Office," *Antiquarian Book Monthly Review* 3 (1976): 274–281.

12. P.R.O., SP35/33/198, Gent to Charles Delafaye, Under-Secretary of state, 30 October 1722.

13. P.R.O., SP35/22, fol. 183, Richard Burridge to Delafaye, 15 September 1720.

14. P.R.O., SP35/31, fol. 102^v, Mr. Justice Dewe to (Delafaye?), 27 April 1722.

15. P.R.O., SP35/22, fols. 172–173, "C.D." (an informer) to James Craggs, Secretary of State, 8 August 1720. The ballad may have been *The Sheppards Holiday,* P.R.O., SP35/22, fol. 176, endorsed with Clifton's mark as having been printed by him.

16. See, for example, Leslie Shepard, *The History of Street Literature* (Newton Abbot, 1973), pp. 80–81, concentrating on the period before the Great Fire of London in 1666. The mercuries also sold newspapers and pamphlets and are sometimes referred to as "pamphlet-sellers." They still existed in the second half of the century; see Thomas R. Adams, "The British Pamphlet Press and the American Controversy, 1764–1783," *Proceedings of the American Antiquarian Society* 89 (1979): 33–88, esp. pp. 51–52.

17. Victor E. Neuburg, *Popular Literature. A History and a Guide* (Harmondsworth, 1977), pp. 177–178, seriously underestimates the continuing political importance of the ballads. The range of ballads can be seen from Milton Perceval, ed., *Political Ballads Illustrating the Administration of Sir Robert Walpole* (Oxford, 1916); street singing is dealt with on p. xxx, and its influence in relation to that of the newspapers on pp. xxxv–xxxvi.

18. For the "trial" of Atterbury, see J. H. Plumb, *Sir Robert Walpole, the King's Minister* (London, 1960), pp. 44–49. I have not considered here two other issues: the purely theological question of blasphemy or the closely related offence of obscene libel. For the former, see Thomas, op. cit., pp. 63–73; and for the latter, David Foxon, *Libertine Literature in England 1660–1745* (London, 1964).

19. For Welton, see *DNB*.

20. The imprint reads "London: Printed for the Author. MDCCXXIV," but there is no list of subscribers, and I have not found a prospectus.

21. In Plomer *1668–1725*, p. 160, as J. Hooke.

22. P.R.O., SP35/41, fols. 167^v–168^r, 171. George James was a High Tory according to Samuel Negus (see John Nichols, *Literary Anecdotes of the Eighteenth Century*, 9 vols. (London, 1812–1815), Vol. 1, p. 289, n. +). The other three were John Norcott, John Tilly, and Motteram Newstat, none of whom is recorded by Plomer.

23. He wrote to Delafaye from prison on 24 February 1723 (P.R.O., SP35/41, fol. 233), and on 9 March (P.R.O., SP35/42, fol. 64). He appears in a list of prisoners held by the King's Messengers on 25 February (P.R.O., SP35/42, fol. 26) and on 11 March (P.R.O., SP35/42, fol. 70), but not in that of 18 March (P.R.O., SP35/42, fol. 130).

24. P.R.O., SP35/43, fol. 158.

25. Of the three copies I have seen, no two are identical, as can be seen from these collations:
B.L. (4453. d. 18.):
$8°$: πι A–M^8(±M2) N–X^8(±X1–3) Y–2H^8
Bodleian Library, Oxford (Vet. A4 e. 1493):
$8°$:A–L^8(±L6,7) M^8(±M8) N^8(±N4) O–S^8(±S3,4) T–X^8(±X1–3) Y–2H^8
C.U.L. (6.30.13):
$8°$:πι A–N^8(±N4) O–S^8(±S2,4) T–2H^8

26. Like so many of these semi-clandestine printers, Gilbert is not recorded by Plomer.

27. The quotations are from, and the references to, editions A(2) and B(3) in the list in note 28.

28. The bibliography is complicated, and there may be other editions that I have not found or that have not survived:

A Part 1

(1) "Printed in the YEAR M,DCC,XXII."
$8°$: [2], 26 pp.
(Beinecke Library, Yale University: Nz 722hi)

(2) "Printed in the year, 1722"
$8°$: [2] pp.
(B.L.: 1137. g. 1.(3.); Bodleian Library, Oxford: Pamph. 370(16); C.U.L.: Syn. 5. 72. 11^6)

(3) "Printed in the YEAR, 1722."
$8°$: 32 pp.
(B.L.: 101. f. 18.; Bodleian Library, Oxford: Mason AA 371(1))

(4) "Printed in the YEAR, 1722."
   8°: 56, [2] pp.
   (B.L.: T. 2228.(3.); Bodleian Library, Oxford: 2262 e. 51(2))

(5) "Printed in the Year, 1722."
   8°: [2], 32 pp.
   (C.U.L.: 7540. d. 71¹)

B Part 2

(1) "Printed in the Year MDCCXXI."
   8°: [ii], 44 pp.
   (Bodleian Library, Oxford: Mason AA 371(2); C.U.L.: Syn. 5. 72.
   11⁷)

(2) "Printed in the Year MDCCXXI."
   8°: [2], 38 pp.
   (C.U.L.: 7540. d. 71²)

(3) "Printed in the Year MDCCXXII."
   8°: [2], 55 pp.
   (B.L.: 1137. g. 1.(4.))

(4) "Printed in the YEAR M,DCC,XXII."
   8°: [2], 35 pp.
   (Beinecke Library, Yale University: College Pamphlets 818(3b))

C Both parts

(1) "Printed in the Year MDCCXXII."
   8°: 44 pp.
   (B.L.: 8133. a. 36.; Beinecke Library, Yale University: Bz 25.22)

(2) "Printed in the Year M,DCC,XXII."
   8°: 32 pp.
   (Beinecke Library, Yale University: Nz 722hi)

29. P.R.O., SP35/54, fol. 223, Earbery to Lord Townshend, Secretary of State, 26 December 1724.

30. P.R.O., SP35/30, fols. 203, examination of Richard Wood, 31 March 1722; 205, examination of William Garrot, 31 March 1722; 207, examination of Sarah Phillips, 31 March 1722; 209, examination of Richard Phillips, 31 March 1722; 211, examination of Mary Offley, 31 March 1722; SP35/31, fols. 13, examination of Richard Phillips, 4 April 1722; 21, examination of Samuel Redmayne, 5 April 1722; 23, examination of Hannah Mayo, n.d., but 5 or 6 April 1722; 30, examination of George Lee, n.d., but 5 or 6 April 1722; 32, examination of Richard Heathcote, 6 April 1722; 34, examination of Henry Lloyd, 6 April 1722. The problem was the identification of Earbery. Everyone knew who had written the book, but it had to be proved. The witnesses, most of the Gilberts' employees and members of their families, all followed Sarah Phillips's lead in saying that "a tall man in Black," "whose name she knows not,"

brought the copy to the printing house. Richard Phillips described the same man, adding that he was "lusty"; Mary Offley, their servant, complicated the issue further by describing him as a "tall black man" (who would certainly not have been inconspicuous in the streets of early Hanoverian London!), and added a vivid description of his "long black perwigg and black Clothes." Hannah Mayo was less eloquent; she thought he was only "Middle sized." Other papers relating to this case are P.R.O., SP35/31, fols. 39, 63, 69, 123, 148, 150; SP35/40, fols. 106–183, 222–223, 226; SP35/52, fols. 125–126, 127; SP35/53, fols. 144; and SP35/54, fols. 223.

31. See Graham Midgley, *The Life of Orator Henley* (Oxford, 1973). Midgley deals with Henley's employment by the government as a propagandist (pp. 216–218), but does not mention his work as an informer. Henley's reports on Salmon are P.R.O., SP35/48, fols. 85, 90, 92, 101, all Henley to Lord Cartaret, Secretary of State, 28 January, 30 January, 31 January, and 4 February 1724; and fol. 206, a list of offending passages in Henley's hand, February 1724.

32. P.R.O., SP35/34/105, Lewis to Samuel Buckley, Under-Secretary of State, 13 December 1722.

33. P.R.O., SP35/34, fols. 227–228, examination of Lewis, 13 December 1722.

34. P.R.O., SP35/34, fols. 229–231, Buckley to Delafaye, 13 December 1722, enclosing Lewis's petition for bail.

35. P.R.O., SP35/34, fols. 243–245, examination of Edlin, 13 December 1722.

36. P.R.O., SP35/43, fols. 162, list of prisoners in the custody of the King's Messengers; 223, ibid., with a note by Higgons's name, "to be bailed."

37. P.R.O., SP35/52, fols. 25–26, Higgons to (the Secretary of State's office), 5 September 1724.

38. Bodleian Library, Oxford: Vet. B4 e. 59; C.U.L.: 7540. d. 135.

39. C.U.L.: Acton. d. 25. 15.

40. For whom see Plomer *1726–1775*, pp. 167–168.

41. Bodleian Library, Oxford: 8° Rawl. 90.

42. Plumb, op. cit., pp. 26–29.

43. *Evening Post* 2347 (8–16 Aug. 1724); P.R.O., SP35/51, fols. 41, 42–43, 44–45, 124; SP35/52, fols. 11, 13–15.

44. P.R.O., SP35/62, fols. 77, 79–80, 81–82, 88–89. For both these issues, see Williams, op. cit., pp. 196–202.

45. This print was one of a series that illustrated the *Craftsman*; see M. Dorothy George, *English Political Caricature to 1792* (Oxford, 1959), pp. 80–81.

46. P.R.O., SP35/30, fol. 197; SP35/31, fols. 85, 156. See Thomas, op. cit., p. 53.

47. *Daily Post* 2404 (7 June 1727); *Weekly Journal* 112 (10 June 1727); P.R.O., SP35/64, fols. 377–378, 392. It is tempting to see this as a comment on the ill-health

of George I (a topic that would have been unacceptable), who died at Osnabrück on 11 June, but his death was sudden and unexpected (Plumb, op. cit., p. 154).

48. P.R.O., SP35/47, fols. 291, n.d., but 1723. *A Manifesto*, with the imprint "Printed in the Year MDCCXXIII," is a quarto pamphlet of eight pages, possibly Scottish, but more probably Dutch, in origin. There is a copy in P.R.O., SP35/47, fols. 91–94.

49. For the opposition press, see, for example, Michael Harris, "The Structure, Ownership and Control of the Press, 1620–1780," in George Boyce, James Curran, and Pauline Wingate, *Newspaper History from the Seventeenth Century to the Present Day* (London, 1978), p. 95. For a vast survey of newspaper finance, see the same author's "The London Newspaper Press, ca. 1725–1746," (Ph.D. diss., London Univ., 1973), pp. 64–130.

50. See J. A. Downie, *Robert Harley and the Press* (Cambridge, 1979), pp. 148–161. For the initial success of the Stamp Act, see Henry L. Snyder, "The Circulation of Newspapers in the Reign of Queen Anne," *The Library*, 5th ser., 23 (1968): 206–235. The 1725 Stamp Act was perhaps a little more successful as a control measure, and the increases in duty during and after the Napoleonic Wars certainly had this intention.

51. C.U.L., MS. Cholmondeley (Houghton) 74/1a/1,2.

52. A notorious example was a story planted by the Spanish ambassador in 1734; see William Coxe, *Memoirs of the Life and Administration of Sir Robert Walpole*, 3 vols. (London, 1798), Vol. 3, pp. 170–173. The Spanish ambassador had tried the same trick in 1726: P.R.O., SP35/62, fols. 77, 79–82, 88–89.

53. By the 1730s, at the latest, it was accepted that *de facto* the newspapers were the best way of obtaining information about current events. A few random examples of correspondents referring their addressees to newspapers are Sir Charles Wager, M.P., to Horace Walpole in 1734 (Coxe, op. cit., vol. 3, pp. 167–168); one "R.Y." to George Kenyon, about the Battle of Fontenoy, in 1745 (HMC Kenyon, p. 472); and the Earl of Hardwick to the Duke of Newcastle, about elections in Huntingdonshire, in 1752 (B.L., MS. Addl. 32,730, fol. 47ᵛ).

54. Daniel Defoe, *An Essay for the Regulation of the Press* (London, 1704), pp. 14–18.

55. Feather, op. cit., p. 38.

56. C.U.L., MS. Cholmondeley (Houghton) 73/48/1,2, the "Essay" quoted above, note 10.

57. Thomas, op. cit., p. 142.

58. P.R.O., SP35/8, fols. 48–50, Northey to Delafaye, 1 February 1717.

59. See, for example, P.R.O., SP37/7, fols. 19, de Grey to Rochford, 3 March 1769; 160, de Grey to Rochford, 13 March 1770.

60. P.R.O., SP37/7, fol. 204, de Grey to Rochford, 16 August 1770.

61. *Flying Post* 11 (10 August 1714); P.R.O., SP35/1, fol. 98, opinion of Northey, 29 August 1714.

62. J. R. Sutherland, *Defoe* (London, 1937), p. 205; John Robert Moore, *A Checklist of the Works of Daniel Defoe,* 2nd ed. (Hampden, Conn., 1971), no. 531.

63. On this episode, see Downie, op. cit., pp. 176–177.

64. There are several Bakers in Plomer *1668–1725;* this may be the John Baker on pp. 14–15.

65. P.R.O., SP35/13, fol. 12, Cracherode to Buckley, 2 October 1718.

66. See Mark A. Thomson, *The Secretaries of State 1681–1782* (Oxford, 1932), pp. 130–141.

67. P.R.O., SP35/24, fol. 151, a list of messengers, 1722.

68. P.R.O., SP35/40, fol. 228.

69. No action was taken.

70. P.R.O., SP35/31, fols. 36–37, Cracherode to Townshend, 7 August 1722.

71. P.R.O. SP35/13, fol. 79^v, a memorial on the *Weekly Journal,* to which is added "A Method for Suppressing News Papers of the Nature," n.d., but 1718.

72. Ibid.

73. 9 & 10 William III c. 27; 3 & 4 Anne c. 4; 4 George I c. 11; 11 George I c. 8.

74. C.U.L., MS. Cholmondeley (Houghton) 75/28/1.

75. P.R.O., SP35/13, fol. 79^v; see note 71.

76. P.R.O., SP35/41, fol. 159, Wood to Delafaye, 7 February 1723, and Delafaye's draft reply.

77. P.R.O., SP35/30, fol. 4, Shaw to Delafaye, 3 January 1722.

78. P.R.O., SP35/26, fols. 209–210, Shaw to Delafaye, 30 May 1721.

79. P.R.O., SP35/27, fol. 85, John Clarke to Buckley, 22 June 1721.

80. See note 22.

81. P.R.O., SP 35/48, fol. 71, "The Case of Samuel Negus Printer," 23 January 1724.

82. P.R.O., SP35/66, fol. 217, "W.M." to Delafaye, n.d.

83. P.R.O., SP35/18, fols. 198, Delafaye to Thorold, 12 November 1719; 200, Thorold to Delafaye, 13 Nov. 1719.

84. P.R.O., SP35/34, fol. 174, Charles Catherne, Collector of Customs, to Delafaye, 6 December 1722.

85. P.R.O., SP35/25, fols. 121, 123–125, William Abnet, mayor of Stafford, to Lord Chetwynd, 6 February 1721, enclosing two examinations of witnesses; 81, Joseph

Walford to William Levinson-Gower, M.P., 6 February 1721; 156–158, Levinson-Gower to (Walford?), 14 February 1721.

86. See Elwall's own account in *Memoirs of Edward Elwall* (Birmingham, 1817), pp. 5–9. This was another malicious prosecution; see the account of Elwall in *DNB.*

87. P.R.O., SP35/52, fols. 43–44, Wake to Townshend, 14 August 1724.

88. Plumb, op. cit., p. 95; Norman Sykes, *Edmund Gibson, Bishop of London 1669–1748* (London, 1926), pp. 83–122.

89. For example, P.R.O., SP35/43, fol. 352, with which Gibson enclosed two pamphlets (now missing) that had been sent to him by the bishop of Exeter's chaplain, 20 December 1723.

90. Downie, op. cit., pp. 80–100.

91. Derek Hudson, *Thomas Barnes of The Times* (Cambridge, 1944), pp. 37–38.

92. One example is the investigation of a pamphlet on the Gin Act of 1736 in P.R.O., TS11/1027. But the documents in TS11 were unavailable when this paper was in preparation, and I have had to rely on the typescript calendar in P.R.O. There may be more examples of this practice than I have so far discovered.

93. The Earbery case is an excellent example (see note 30) and is paralleled by the "woman in white" who delivered the manuscript of *A True Memorial* in 1704 (see note 90).

94. P.R.O., SP36/13, fol. 101, examination of Richard Nutt, 19 July 1729.

95. P.R.O., SP36/13, fols. 108, examination of Catherine Nutt, 19 July 1729; 118, examination of John Peele, 21 July 1729.

96. P.R.O., SP35/52, fol. 11, examination of de Fonseca, 2 September 1724.

97. For Stephens, see John Robert Moore, " 'Robin Hog' Stephens: Messenger of the Press," *Papers of the Bibliographical Society of America* 50 (1956): pp. 381–387.

98. For the government press, generally, see Hanson, op. cit., pp. 84–122; and, for Harley, see Downie, op. cit., passim.

99. For a more detailed account, see Feather, op. cit.

100. The best general account is still that of A. S. Collins, *Authorship in the Days of Johnson* (London, 1927), pp. 82–113; but see also Gwyn Walters, "The Booksellers in 1759 and 1775: The Battle for Literary Property," *The Library*, 5th ser., 29 (1974): 287–311.

101. Stationers' Company, Court Book H, pp. 428, 430, 431, 435, 437, meetings of 6 July, 3 August, 7 September, 2 November, and 7 December 1731, and 7 February 1722.

102. *Reasons humbly Offered to the Consideration of the Honourable House of Commons, in Support of a Bill for Making More Effectual an Act Passed in the Eighth Year of Her Late Majesty Queen Anne, Intitled, An Act for the Encouragement of Learning;* and,

Further reasons humbly offered. . . . Both in the Bodleian Library, Oxford, John Johnson Collection.

103. *CJ*, Vol. 22, pp. 411–412.

104. Ibid., p. 482; *LJ*, Vol. 24, pp. 543–544, 548, 550.

105. Stationers' Company, Court Book I, pp. 69–70.

106. *CJ*, Vol. 22, pp. 741, 764, 800; *LJ*, Vol. 25, pp. 73, 81, 91, 99, 106, 111–112.

107. *CJ*, Vol. 23, p. 157; *LJ*, Vol. 25, pp. 242, 244, 251, 254, 255–256, 259.

108. *CJ*, Vol. 27, p. 320; *LJ*, Vol. 25, pp. 362, 363, 368, 370, 372, 374, 395, 418–419. The statute is 12 George II c. 36.

109. They were printed by Alexander Donaldson, *Some Thoughts on the State of Literary Property* (London, 1764); see also Walters, op. cit.

110. See note 49.

111. See Frederick Seaton Siebert, *Freedom of the Press in England 1476–1776* (Urbana, Ill., 1965), pp. 346–363. An important corrective to the traditional view is A. Aspinall, "The Reporting and Publishing of the House of Commons' Debates 1771–1834," in Richard Pares and A. J. P. Taylor, eds., *Essays Presented to Sir Lewis Namier* (London, 1956), pp. 227–257.

[7] The Publishing Industry and Printed Output in Nineteenth-Century France

Frédéric Barbier

IN RECENT YEARS, French as well as foreign scholars[1] have cast light on the profound changes in the economics of publishing that occurred in the nineteenth century. Nearly four centuries after the Gutenberg revolution, there took place what can be called the "second revolution of the book." It was characterized, first of all, by an enormous jump in the bulk of printed output, in which the periodical press played an ever increasing role. Simultaneously, production and distribution were radically altered. Yet, despite this transformation, which is at the basis of the publishing industry as we know it today, only a few monographs have dealt with the subject. Indeed, one must concede, a synthesis is to a large extent beyond the present state of our knowledge.[2]

The goal of this chapter is to gather into a coherent picture all the information we possess on the evolution of printed output in nineteenth-century France[3] and to show how it was affected by the economic and social changes of the Industrial Revolution. We will conclude by looking more closely into two particular aspects of this evolution—namely, the appearance on stage of a newcomer, the publisher, and the transformation of marketing techniques and structures.

This chapter was originally presented in French at the symposium and was translated for this volume.

Social Underpinnings: French Society and the Printed Book, 1811–1914

Historians have coined the expression "blocked society"[4] to characterize the economic and social history of sixteenth- and seventeenth-century France. A traditional demography, an economy still largely rooted in auto-consumption, archaic financial structures—these were all regulating factors that prevented for the most part major change in social and economic structures. At the dawn of the Industrial Revolution, and first of all in England, the eighteenth century witnessed indexes of changes to come, particularly in the economic realm. From 1780 to 1820 the effects of these changes[5] were strong enough for the society as a whole to be progressively affected, and expansion replaced blocked economic and social structures. For the first four centuries of its existence the book trade in France fit perfectly within this larger economic and social pattern. Our first goal, then, is to outline the major changes in both eighteenth- and nineteenth-century French society, which more or less directly influenced the book market.

First and foremost, demographic growth opened a new potential market for the book trade. The French population increased from 27,350,000 in 1801 to 34,230,000 in 1841 and to 37,672,000 in 1881. It is important to note, however, that in spite of this increase, France lost its place as the most populous European country[6] and that the rate of increase was progressively declining. This may be one of the reasons why the Industrial Revolution affected relatively slowly the printing industry in France. The rate of population growth was 18 percent between 1750 and 1800 and 24 percent between 1800 and 1850, as opposed to 50 percent and 92 percent, respectively, in the British Isles.

Yet a twofold phenomenon, already begun under the ancien régime, accentuated the effects of population increase in France. First was the development and acceleration of urbanization in general. The percentage of the rural population decreased from 75 percent in 1850 to 69 percent in 1870 and to 56 percent in 1910. Reading, which by definition is an urban phenomenon, was promoted by an increase in urban population from around 6 million in 1821 to 14 million in 1881. Second—and this is an essential factor in the formation of the French publishing industry as we know it today— "of the large cities . . . Paris increased the most."[7] The annexation of the small crown (1860), plus immigration from the provinces, increased the Parisian population from 945,000 in 1856 to 2.3 million in 1886. From the Second Empire on, the population of the suburban districts (Seine, Paris excluded, and Seine-et-Oise) also tended to increase at a rate unheard of until then. These factors, which compounded the ancien régime tradition in which significant publishing was centralized,[8] favored the growth of printed output, but also caused the geographical disequilibrium that to this day characterizes the book-related professions and activities in France.[9] Although the short- and medium-term effects of these changes were positive, the long-term results may prove ultimately to be negative.

Aside from demographic growth and urbanization, other factors contributed to the gradual formation of a more important, nationwide market for French publications. First and foremost among these were increased education and, at its most elementary level, the spread of literacy.[10] Chronologically, it is justifiable to distinguish between the part of France north of the "Maggiolo line,"[11] which for the most part was literate by the eighteenth century, and a "backward" France, which attained literacy only in the nineteenth century. From this point of view, the second half of the century was not only a period of catching up for the backward regions but also the realization in practice of the drive to universal literacy called for by the principle of equality. "The closing of the gap between north and south, between men and women, was not only the result of a normal compensatory process to be expected over time; it was characterized by an accelerated trend toward literacy in many of the backward departments at the end of the eighteenth century."[12] During the period 1880–1890, literacy reached the whole of French society, and for the first time access, or rather the possibility of access, to the written word became a mass phenomenon. Schooling completed this development at a higher level. According to the available statistics, the number of pupils increased from 1,120,000 in 1820 to 2,900,000 in 1840. Following the promulgation of the Falloux law of 1850, which encouraged the growth of Catholic education, and the decree of 1852, the number of pupils reached progressively 4,300,000 in 1863 and 4,700,000 in 1877, despite the loss of Alsace-Lorraine. With the law of 28 March 1882, which established compulsory education, the 5 million mark was reached; the percentage rate of enrollment in school rose from 47.5 percent in 1850 to 93.5 percent of the school-age population in 1894.[13]

The traditional economy of the book and periodical was now faced with a new public with new demands. The quantitative growth of the potential reading public was accompanied and compounded by other changes as well (some of these will be passed over rapidly, for even though they were instrumental in the formation of a national book market, they were not specifically French in nature): the extension of roads, the appearance and development of the railroad system (17,000 kilometers in 1870), and luggage and postal services, as well as the possibility of quick payments through money orders.

New needs for communication arose in nineteenth-century industrial society that explain the development of the media as characterized by MacLuhan.[14] Among these, printing was to play an essential role, as exemplified by a change in attitude toward the book by an ever-increasing segment of the population. Without question the 1789 revolution was a decisive element in the new debate concerning the role of literacy and the printed medium, as has been shown by François Furet and Jacques Ozouf: "On 4 November 1790, the *Feuille villageoise* which campaigned against ignorance in the countryside asked: 'Why were the rights of man known so late?' The answer was: 'Because the people could not read, they could not learn for themselves, and in consequence, let themselves be indoctrinated by others.' Schooling came to represent *par excellence* the unlimited power of society over the individual."[15] One should add that schooling and, beyond that, access to the printed word as the vehicle of all knowledge, were concepts well in keeping with the philosophy of the Enlightenment.

In addition to the pedagogical push of the revolutionary period, economic factors also stimulated educational efforts. The new bourgeois, industrial society needed workers capable of reading and writing (even though the correlation between literacy and industrialization is highly debatable).[16] Throughout the country an increasingly rapid and regular network of communications—whether of persons, goods, information, or ideas—progressively developed. As "there is no room for illiterate workers in modern industry,"[17] chances for upward mobility, or even of belonging to the social structure, were foreclosed for those who had no access to books or periodicals.

The foregoing briefly outlines the elements that explain and underlie this "second revolution of the book" in nineteenth-century France. From then on, the printed word became one of the primary objects of mass consumption. We will attempt in the following to outline the principal functions fulfilled by the French printing industry.

Possibly the most traditional but also the most important of all markets was that for religious works. The typology of religious books can be divided into three main categories. The first, comprising prayer books, Bibles, missals, and choir books, was a sure source of revenue for many provincial printers. (Although the output was massive, the demand could nevertheless be met by traditional printing establishments, and distribution was practically guaranteed.) The efforts of the major printing firms of the First Empire to obtain the *privilège* for *Cantiques* within a given diocese are well documented.[18]

Stimulated by the work of German historians and philologists, the resurgence of biblical studies between 1863 and 1881 accelerated the publication of translations of the Bible. There was, of course, a direct link between this renewal of interest and the publication of *La vie de Jésus* by Renan, itself influenced by the work of the German school of exegesis.

The second category of religious publications, works of popular devotion, was even more significant economically. A multitude of small reli-

gious texts and, above all, moralizing anecdotes were distributed by peddlers throughout rural areas. Some printing and publishing firms specialized in the massive production of such works, which had both relatively
low production costs and virtually guaranteed distribution. The firms of
Martial Ardant in Limoges, Mame in Tours, Popelin in Dijon, Vanackère
in Lille, and Berger-Levrault in Strasbourg were established along the
routes of the peddlers they supplied, from the Haute Garonne throughout
France.[19]

To these publications, which were produced in massive quantities, can be
added religious prints, pious images, "Mementos of my First Commu-
nion," and the like. All were put out for the most part by local printers, but
occasionally bore the trademark of specialized firms. The production of the
Pellerin firm in Epinal is well known, but as peddling opened a wider
market to this kind of imagery, the lithographic firm of Wentzel of Wis-
sembourg was also able to establish itself as a prime producer for this
market.[20]

The works of popular devotion were aimed at two segments of the
public at once, the pious and children. This is shown by the proliferation of
"bibliothèques": Bibliothèque religieuse, morale, littéraire from Ardant,
Bibliothèque morale de la jeunesse from Mégard (Rouen), Bibliothèque
chrétíenne de l'adolescence et du jeune âge, Bibliothèque pieuse des catho-
liques, and Bibliothèque de la jeunesse chrétienne from Mame—to name a
few. The extraordinary success of this type of publication is reflected in the
bibliography of its most famous author, Canon Johann Schmid. It records
no fewer than 2,666 works published up to 1890.[21] Even though modernized, the religious book remained, as it had been in the seventeenth century, the traditional output of the provinces[22] and, along with almanacs, the
most widely distributed of all works.[23]

The intensity of religious feelings and of religious controversy is evident
in the third category. The first best-sellers of modern French publishing
were in fact religious polemical works. Eugène Renduel, who opened his
establishment in 1828 on the quai des Grands Augustins, had his first major
success with *Soirées Walter Scott* by the bibliophile Jacob; then came a
triumph in 1834, with *Paroles d'un croyant* by Félicité de Lamennais. Renduel put out four editions in-8° and two in 18° within the same year. Three
additional editions were published by Daubrée & Cailleux in 1835, and there
were a good twenty more by the end of the Second Empire from various
publishers, among them Michel Lévy and Garnier frères. As early as 1834,
Aillaud in Paris and Gottlob Louis Schüler in Strasbourg published two
German translations, while English, Spanish, and Polish versions appeared
simultaneously.[24] Renduel's success—100,000 copies sold in the first year—
enabled him to launch himself in the literary field, a phenomenon we will

examine later on. The success of *Paroles d'un croyant,* in which Sainte-Beuve played a role, marked the beginning of the era of mass production made possible by stereotyping.

The second such success, also in the religious domain, followed basically the same pattern. In 1863, Michel Lévy frères published Book I of *L'Histoire des origines du christianisme, La vie de Jésus* by Renan. It was an immediate and overwhelming success. The text was reprinted ten times in 1863 and three times in 1864. The same year, Michel Lévy frères also published an abridged edition, which was reprinted fourteen times in 1864 and continued to be published on a regular basis until 1898. Again, in 1870, the publisher attempted to stimulate the market with a quarto edition illustrated with sixty drawings. *La vie de Jésus* was the single largest publishing success in nineteenth-century France. Within the first four years alone, 1.4 million copies were sold; in its German version, the work was also widely distributed from 1864 onward.[25]

The other mass market of the nineteenth-century French publishing industry was for children's books. Many of the major Parisian and provincial publishing firms owed their initial success to children's books. The most prestigious of them all was Louis Hachette, who took over the publishing house Brédif in August 1826 and started out with schoolbooks. From 1832 onward, and in association with the old firm of F. G. Levrault,[26] Hachette published the *Manuel général, ou Journal de l'instruction primaire.* After passage of the law of 18 January 1833, Hachette received most of his orders from the Ministère de l'instruction publique, even before taking over, in 1835, the Bibliothèque de l'enseignement primaire from the firm of P. Dupont.[27] In 1838, Victor Masson, an ex-clerk at Hachette, established his own publishing house, specializing in medicine and education. Following the same pattern, Armand Colin launched his firm by publishing the *Grammaire* of Larive and Fleury[28] in 1870. New means of advertising—in particular, distribution of examination copies to educators—allowed for a circulation of several million over a few years. The passage of the school laws introduced by Jules Ferry (1882) was directly responsible for the success of Fernand Nathan, who within a few years became one of the leading Parisian publishers. Soon he combined publishing, per se, with the manufacture of educational materials.

Textbooks, however, were only one among various types of educational works aimed at both adults and children. In the encyclopedic tradition of the eighteenth century, a quantity of dictionaries and collections, both specialized and general (such as the *Dictionnaire des sciences naturelles* from Levrault[29] and *L'Encyclopédie des gens du monde* from Treuttel and Würtz), were put on the market. In some cases, educators themselves played a direct role in the compilation of such works. Louis Hachette was an alumnus of the École normale. Pierre Larousse and Augustin Boyer, who were to establish the Librairie Larousse in 1852, were former educators; they began with educational and pedagogical treatises before launching, in 1865, the *Grand dictionnaire universel du XIXème siècle* (completed in 1876). Finally, parallel to Hachette, the bookseller-publisher Mame exploited the field of religious education and Catholic pedagogy, which we have already touched on.[30] The statistical figures at our disposal are scant but nonetheless reflect the massive proportions of the educational market. Educational works, which accounted for 80 titles in 1811,[31] increased to 275 in 1836 and reached 1,000 in 1890.[32] Linked to this phenomenon was the appearance on the market of "recreational" and gift books, the success of which has already been mentioned in connection with the small "bibliothèques" put out by publishers of religious works.

In nineteenth-century bourgeois society, the view of the child was fundamentally altered, and as a result, from 1810 onward the possibilities in the children's book market seemed unlimited.[33] Actually, the movement was begun as early as 1782 by the publication of *L'Ami des enfants* by Arnaud Berquin, soon followed by *L'Ami de l'adolescence* in 1785. These were republished throughout the nineteenth century by Didier, Garnier frères, and above all by Ardant and Thibaut, who alone brought out twenty-three printings of *L'Ami des enfants* between 1875 and 1895.[34] Women authors made their mark early in this field. Many of Madame Pauline Guizot's tales, and some of her stories "à l'usage de la jeunesse," were published in the collections of the Librairie Didier, the Bibliothèque universelle d'éducation and the Bibliothèque des enfants.[35] A renewal of the genre took place during the decade from 1850 to 1860. In 1858, the countess of Ségur[36] published in the Bibliothèque des chemins de fer *Les petites filles modèles,* which went through no fewer than twenty successive editions before 1900.[37] Then, with *Les malheurs de Sophie* in 1859 and *Les deux nigauds, L'Auberge de l'ange gardien* and *Le général Dourakine* in 1863, the Bibliothèque rose was launched. Publishing children's books became a well-established field (70,000 copies of *Les mémoires d'un âne* were distributed by 1874), and some publishing firms built most of their success on specialization in this sector. In 1862, Hetzel,[38] in collaboration with Jean Mace, started the *Magasin d'éducation et de récréation* and created the Collection Jules Verne, which, at the time of the takeover of Hetzel by Hachette in 1924, became the Bibliothèque verte.

The third and last mass market that we would like to mention here can be called the "literary trade." This sector of publishing was most affected by fads and fashions and had as its center Paris, which alone had a reading public capable of turning a literary venture into a best-seller. From the dawn of the century Paris was the scene of many speculative publishing ventures, as shown by the archives of printers, booksellers, and publishers. Most of these deals were struck in the shops of the quai Malaquais and around the Palais Royal. Balzac left us an invaluable description[39] of this "little world" and its practices, and some of its financial operations have been studied by modern historians.[40] The model of a successful literary venture was still a traditional one. With the occasional help of an advertising campaign (we will deal with this aspect later on), the publisher ran several parallel editions of 1,000 or 2,000 copies each, the bulk of which was distributed to the literary clubs.[41] The greatest commercial successes were *Corinne* by Madame de Staël and the *Méditations* of Chateaubriand. Both published by Nicolle in 1820, they had sales of 20,000 copies each within three years. Concurrently, the "complete works" format proved very successful and was an excellent source of regular income for publishers, since the editions were sold by subscription.

The concept of a classical literature, which it was deemed useful and above all in good taste to own, lay behind the new editions of Montesquieu, Voltaire, and Jean Jacques Rousseau, as well as the launching by Lefèvre in 1824 of his new Classiques français collection. A key figure in this feverish speculation was Ladvocat, the publisher of the "jeune littérature," who did not hesitate to pay as much as 300,000 francs to buy up the rights to the *Oeuvres* of Chateaubriand and who published Casimir Delavigne, Victor Hugo, Alfred de Vigny, and Sainte-Beuve, among others. Fashion, financial tightrope walking, and the need constantly to provide novelties to the literary clubs steadily raised the price of manuscripts of the Romantics. In 1830, Mame paid 6,000 francs for the first edition of *Hernani*[42] and barely broke even. In 1832, Victor Hugo received 15,000 francs from Gosselin and Renduel as an advance on *Quinquengrogne*, a work that was never completed. The widely used practice of borrowing money put the publisher at the mercy of even small delays in return of income. Thus, Ladvocat went bankrupt in 1832.[43]

The progressive reestablishment of the market was due initially to an aesthetic renewal that brought on the glorious era of illustrated works, with Tony Johannot, Gigout, and others as central figures; above all, however, the "Charpentier revolution" (1838) spurred the growth of the literary trade market. Gervais Charpentier, a former clerk of Ladvocat, strove for "more type to the page." His aim was to sell the first printing at cost and to realize a profit on the following printings by using stereotype. The Collection Charpentier, which started out with the publication of *La physiologie du goût* and *La physiologie du mariage*, sold for 3.50 francs per volume and had an unprecedented success. Competition soon arose. Established in 1836, Michel Lévy launched the Bibliothèque dramatique, followed by the Bibliothèque Michel Lévy and the Bibliothèque verte. In the latter, he republished *Madame Bovary* and also acquired Baudelaire's literary rights upon the author's death.

The Second Empire (1852–1870) witnessed a twofold development. First, as a direct consequence of literacy and of the greater ease and regularity with which distribution could be carried out, the periodical press made considerable advances. Polydore Millaud's *Petit journal,* which started in 1863 at a price of 5 centimes, sold 259,000 copies in 1865.[44] Part of its success came from serialization, a practice first used in 1836 by *La presse* and *Le siècle* and quickly adopted by the major periodicals. Concurrently with this boost in circulation for periodicals and with the popular success it brought to some authors, there was a break with literature per se. A popular literature, recognized as such, appeared. The "thunderbolt" of *Les Misérables* in 1857,[45] a genuine literary success, was the last of its kind. During the 1860s, it was Eugène Sue, Paul Faval, and Ponson du Terrail who dominated the literary scene. Their works, sold in parts at 10 centimes each, ensured the success of their publisher, Dentu.

The constant competition between the periodical press and the printed book, which reached its peak under the Third Republic (1875–1914), caused a ceaseless search for novelty, in a pattern similar to the one at the beginning of the century. In 1874, Calmann-Lévy published 1,724,000 volumes, while at the same time works in parts proliferated. In this context, the crisis of 1892 can be seen as one of genuine overproduction. The market was no longer capable of expansion, for literacy had been achieved and the economy had been restructured. The last decade of the nineteenth century marked the beginning of a recession for the French publishing industry.

The chief conclusion to be drawn from this brief outline is that the nineteenth century was the point of transition between the traditional civilization of the book and the post-Gutenbergian civilization described and analyzed by MacLuhan. Within a general context of growth, it was a period of collision. New tendencies, marked by the development of a mass reading public, met and battled traditional structures. Statistical analysis will help us refine this image.

Statistics of Nineteenth-Century French Publishing

To go beyond this somewhat qualitative description, we rely on the use of trustworthy statistical data to draw a more definitive picture. Although bibliographical lists do exist in the copyright deposit registers and in the archives of the Bibliothèque nationale,[46] no series of statistics have been drawn up from them, aside from a few limited attempts.[47] As fundamental as these sources are, they have to be put aside in favor of others that are more selective, such as the following retrospective bibliographies: *La*

France littéraire by Joseph Marie Quérard,[48] which records about two-thirds of the production between 1811 and 1838, and the *Catalogue général de la librairie française,*[49] the primary source for statistics on the second half of the century.[50] The *Bibliographie de la France,* published from 1811, was used by Robert Estivals in a first attempt to assess the printed output of nineteenth-century France.[51] The shortcomings and inaccuracies of these various publications, which had already been pointed out by contemporaries,[52] are such that it is not always possible to draw from them overall statistics concerning printed production, much less a number of series of statistics tracing the evolution of different types of books. The following will present some of the statistical information at our disposal.[53]

The only complete statistical series is that provided by the *Bibliographie de la France* from 1811 onward. Before turning to it, one should remember that "as far as publishing is concerned, the eighteenth century as a whole, and in particular the period from 1745 to 1775, was a time of expansion and even of great change."[54] The curve for the years 1810 to 1914 calls for two kinds of remarks (Figs. 1 and 2). First, in long-range terms, the nineteenth century was really the "century of growth," with 4,881 titles advertised in 1820, 11,882 in 1860, and 13,362 in 1900. An analysis of average movement shows that growth was rapid from 1810 to 1830, then slowed down until 1848–1850. From that point onward, the graphic depiction of growth shows a large bell-shaped curve that peaks around 1890 and reaches its low point after World War I. That decline had begun at the end of the nineteenth century and was compounded by the two world wars; French book production in 1939 barely rivaled that of the Second Empire, and the highest level of output, 14,849 titles in 1889, was not reached again until recently. Second, in the short run, the curve shows a succession of crises, which indicates how closely tied the fate of the publishing industry was to general conditions, whether economic or political. Apart from the expected crises of 1830, 1848, and 1870–1871, the curve reflects the index of economic activity of industrial France:[55] There are two periods of expansion, under the Restoration and the Second Empire, and two relatively difficult periods, under the July Monarchy and the Third Republic. In the latter case, the decline in book production reflected the progressive erosion of the climate of affluence.

Overall, the series thus obtained seems consistent with the other statistical series at our disposal. From 1770 to 1880–1890, the movement fits within phase A of a Sémiand cycle, whereas the correlation of our results with population data shows a linear ratio of about 62 percent (the ratio is markedly better with the exclusive use of urban population data, as opposed to data for the population as a whole). The series is also consistent with the export statistics of the French book trade, as established for the years 1815 through 1913, relative to a base index of 100 for 1913 (Fig. 3). It is

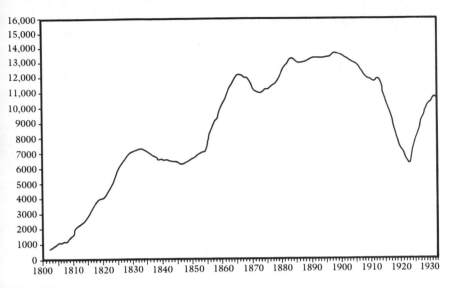

FIGURE 1

Statistics of titles announced in *Bibliographie de la France,* 1803–1940, 10-year moving average.

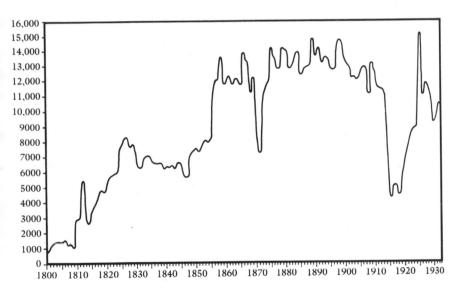

FIGURE 2

Statistics of titles announced in *Bibliographie de la France,* 1800–1940, number of titles per year. *Source:* Frédéric Barbier, "Le commerce international de la librairie française au XIXe siècle," *Revue d'histoire moderne et contemporaine* 28 (1981): 107.

also compatible with partial departmental statistics, such as those for the Bas-Rhin, whose printed output has been established for the years 1841 to 1869[56] (Fig. 4). Thus, even though it remains impossible to establish annual figures of production in absolute terms, it seems that the range and the general picture of the curve obtained from the *Bibliographie de la France* are in fact representative of the actual situation.

To complete these remarks, let us review the results, partial as they are, of the other documentary series mentioned above. For the second half of the nineteenth century, the *Catalogue* by Lorenz, Jordell, and Stein, even though less exhaustive, allows for a "much more precise [analysis] and a faster, more accurate tabulation than the disorderly presentation of the *Bibliographie de la France*."[57] This analysis enabled Christophe Charle to trace the main literary trends and to show a succession of cycles between 1840 and 1905. A period of growth, compounded by literary speculation that extended *grosso modo* from 1840 to 1890, was followed by a leveling-out period lasting a decade, followed in turn by a surge in the number of titles at the beginning of the twentieth century. This last increase is, in fact, the only element that jars with our results and can be explained probably by the fact that Charle's statistics are weighted toward literary works. Since these reflect the aggressive publishing policies of firms such as Fayard, more weight is given to re-editions and translations at the beginning of the twentieth century.

From a statistical point of view, Charle's tabulations allow us to follow the evolution of production in various literary genres during the second half of the nineteenth century; the figures are consistent with results obtained elsewhere. A quick overview reveals "the first characteristics of this evolution [as being] the rapid growth of the novel, which became the main genre, whereas under the July Monarchy, as far as the bulk of production is concerned, poetry and plays were predominant."[58] The number of novels published increased from some 300 in 1877 to about 750 in 1895, despite the fact that the overproduction mentioned previously had resulted in a drastic drop in overall output to the level of twenty years before. Publishers attempted to alleviate this structural crisis by traditional means, such as the "disastrous discount-price war," or by methods that bordered on swindling, such as putting new wrappers on old editions. Publishing output in poetry and especially drama was less sensitive to the general economic situation, but reflected it nevertheless.

The end of the Second Empire witnessed profound changes in reading habits. As mentioned by J. J. Darmon, the homogenization of the book market brought about the decline and then the disappearance of book peddling.[59] "The rural readers who could afford it, replaced the Bibliothèque bleue with new works distributed by the railroad, a phenomenon

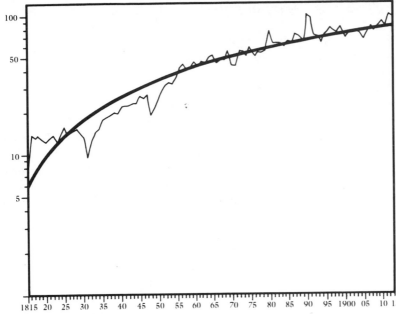

FIGURE 3

Exports of French books, 1815–1913. Relative values on a base of 100 in 1913. Bold line indicates trend.

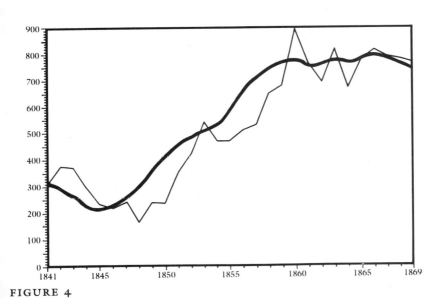

FIGURE 4

Statistics of copyright deposit for Bas-Rhin, 1841–1869. Bold line: number of titles published each year; angled line: 5-year moving average.

which accounted for the wide distribution of the novel. Others, less well-off, switched to the one sou press, which served as the literary support for the serialized novel."[60]

Statistical figures published on the occasion of the 1900 World Fair reflect the considerable growth of the provincial press. From 1868 to 1889, the number of nonperiodical publications decreased by 29 percent in Paris, but remained constant in the provinces. During the same period, the number of registered periodicals multiplied 2.5 times in Paris, and 12 times in the provinces. These figures, though not entirely definitive, do reflect the general trend. Circulation increased in the same proportions; for example, *Le Matin,* which sold 75,000 copies in 1889, reached 1 million copies in 1914, a year in which the combined circulation of 41 Parisian political dailies was 6 million copies.[61]

The following table shows both the stagnation of the Parisian trade in level of output of nonperiodical, copyrighted titles and the marked increase in the number of periodical titles. The pattern of evolution was similar, although more pronounced, in the departments. These figures enable us to estimate at about 40 percent the number of small editions and job printings, which do not show up in the *Bibliographie de la France* but which are taken into account in the statistics of the copyright deposit register.[62]

We shall complete this overview with a geographical survey of publishing and printing in nineteenth-century France. The French geography of the book differed radically, for example, from that of Germany during the same period because of the polarization between the capital, to which could be joined the main provincial centers, and the rest of France. The majority of printing firms were established in Paris, which alone had the market capable of creating and sustaining new structures of production such as "book factories" employing several hundred workers (Fig. 5). These, of course, differed radically in their organization from the traditional printing shops of the ancien régime.[63] Only a handful of provincial printing firms, such as Berger-Levrault in Nancy,[64] and above all, Mame in Tours, could be compared with the new Parisian establishments[65] (Fig. 6). The fact that the number of printing firms in the capital was officially limited to sixty must also have accelerated the process of concentration and modernization.

However, various samplings taken from the copyright deposit list reveal the darker side to the concentration of publishers in Paris. The crisis of the French publishing industry at the close of the nineteenth century was above all a Parisian crisis, with a drop in titles from 11,092 in 1845 to 10,009 in 1855, followed by 9,951 in 1865, 10,396 in 1875, 7,404 in 1885, and 4,618 in 1905. Provincial production, which was more directly tied to regional or local needs, was less affected by economic crises and fluctuations. In fact, it seems to have benefited from the process of expansion and integration that characterized the national market during the second half of the century.

PUBLISHING OUTPUT IN PARIS AND THE DEPARTMENTS, 1869 AND 1889
(INDEX BASE: 1869 = 100)

PARIS	1869	Index	1889	Index
Nonperiodicals	9,937	100	7,248	73
Periodicals	852	100	2,243	263
DEPARTMENTS				
Nonperiodicals	15,708	100	15,863	101
Periodicals	3,894	100	43,215	1,100

This is reflected in the tendency toward the multiplication of titles by provincial presses, even though circulation remained relatively low.

To a lesser degree, the same polarization can be observed among the departments themselves: in 1885, 16 departments (18.6 percent) yielded 7,292 titles (58.1 percent, Paris excluded); at the other end of the spectrum, 25 departments (29 percent) yielded only 702 titles (5.6 percent). Geographically, the dividing line is once again a variant of the "Maggiolo line" oriented on the axis Le Havre-Lyon. This disparity is attributable in part to the establishment of a number of large printing firms outside the capital, either in the provinces (as in the case of Mame) or in the communities surrounding Paris. These locations presented a threefold advantage: proximity to the largest of French markets, financial benefits (exemption from city taxation), and better control over the work force.[66] Between 1860 and 1914, the departments of Seine (Paris excluded), Seine-et-Oise, and Seine-et-Marne participated increasingly in the printed production in France, whereas the capital became the center of new "tertiary" activities revolving around the book trade. Paris was the favored location for the main offices of the great publishing firms and the first specialized distributors. The following section will be devoted to these various phenomena.

Demands and Strategies: Publishing and Distribution

The major changes in the economics of publishing in nineteenth-century France could not but cause significant modifications in the structures of production and distribution. We will not cover the problems of manufac-

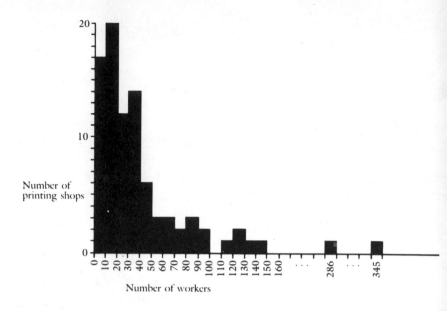

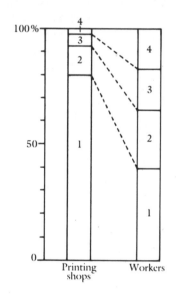

FIGURE 5

(Top) Parisian printing shops in relation to the number of their personnel, 1855.
(Bottom) Proportional distribution of workers and Parisian printing shops, 1855.
1 = printing shops with 1 to 50 workers; 2 = printing shops with 1 to 100 workers; 3 = printing shops with 1 to 150 workers; and 4 = printing shops with more than 150 workers.

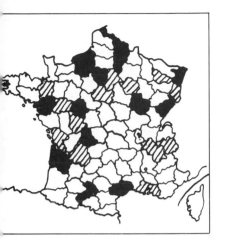
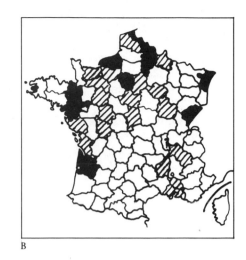

B

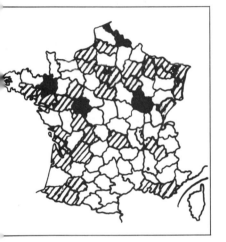
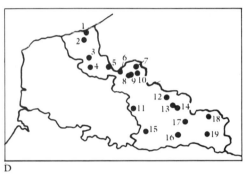

D

FIGURE 6

The industrial geography of the book in France, 1865. (Department of Rhône not included.)
(A) Number of book workers per department (black = 200+; grey = 100–199; white = <100).
(B) Number of steam engines used in printing shops (black = 20+; grey = 1–19; white = 0)
(C) Number of workers per printing shop (black = 100+; grey = 10–100; white = <10)
(D) Printing shops in the Departement du Nord 1855–1856. (1) Dunkerque; (2) Bergues; (3) Cassel; (4) Hazebrouck; (5) Bailleul; (6) Armentières; (7) Tourcoing; (8) Wazemmes; (9) Lille; (10) Roubaix; (11) Douai; (12) St. Amand-les-Eaux; (13) Anzin; (14) Valenciennes; (15) Cambrai; (16) Le Cateau; (17) Le Quesnoy; (18) Maubeuge; (19) Avesnes

ture per se, the evolution of printing establishments and the technologies having already been the subject of detailed studies.[67] Instead, we will begin with the publisher.

The profession of publisher in France developed from a set of new economic conditions and problems peculiar to the nineteenth century. Until the revolutionary period and the Restoration, a privileged few controlled the book market within a given area. From the sixteenth to the eighteenth century a few individuals, motivated by their speculative temperament, developed to the fullest the possibilities of publishing. Their success stemmed primarily from their monopoly of the ideology of the time. If we compare the success of Plantin with that of Petit, Cramoisy, or Panckoucke,[68] we see that it was not so much the means they used that varied, as it was their political leanings. The dates of the establishment of the great publishing firms under the Restoration and the Third Republic are a clear indication of a departure from the past: Dalloz (1824), Hachette (1826), Garnier (1833), Belin (1834), the Librairie générale de droit et de jurisprudence (1836), Calmann-Lévy (1836), Masson (1837), Privat (1839), Klincksieck (1842), Delmas (1848), Beauchesne (1851), Larousse (1852), Fayard (1855), Dunod (1858), Delagrave, Gauthier-Villars and Lethielleux (1864), Picard, Armand Colin and Tallandier (1870)—to mention only the firms that still exist today. On the other hand, after 1870, the establishment of new firms almost came to a stop, a sign of the quasi-saturation of the market and a presage of the crisis to come twenty years later.

Initially, most of these new firms were launched with school or university publications. This link between the publishing world and the school system, or more broadly the educational system, constituted a new type of privilege for the trade and was, above all, a new way of supporting the political power of the time. The control of a given market (or as we would say today, the occupation of a particular "slot") allowed for wide distribution at very low risk, a sufficient but necessary condition for the formation of new structures of production that affected both the manufacturing stage, with its twofold process of mechanization and integration, and the distribution stage. This principle was well understood by those provincial firms that based their development on specialization in a certain type of work, which in turn became their trademark in the public eye. Such was the case of F. G. Levrault, who for a while was the publisher of the *Dictionnaire des sciences naturelles,* authored by most of the professors at the Museum of Natural History in Paris before becoming, thanks to the *Annuaire militaire,* the foremost military publisher. Similarly, Mame was the foremost publisher of Catholic devotional works, and Hetzel specialized in children's books; some firms even specialized in a given distribution slot, as did Treuttel and Wurtz, the first importers of German books into France.

From the example of these firms, we can see that the problem for them was renewal in the face of change. In contrast to Charles Joseph Panckoucke,[69] the last great publisher of the ancien régime, a Louis Hachette was perfectly able to handle this challenge. As mentioned before, Hachette started his publishing firm in 1826. He took full advantage of the shift in political rule in 1830, and benefited from the passing of the law on elementary education in 1833. While specializing in textbooks, for which he obtained a quasi-exclusive privilege from the government, he also managed to launch the *Revue de l'instruction publique,* the *Manuel général de l'instruction primaire, L'Ami de l'enfance,* and others.[70] Once this basis was well established, he was able in 1852 to expand his activities in the direction of literary publications. Here the risks were greater, but the children's book market played a backup role. The concession, granted by the Compagnie des Chemins de fer du Nord, for the sale of publications in all the major stations of the system, and the launching of the Bibliothèque des chemins de fer ensured him a good start. Several years later, in collaboration with Charles Lahure, Louis Hachette started the *Journal pour tous,* which published illustrated novels at a circulation rate of 150,000 copies, followed by the *Semaine des enfants* in 1857.

Chronologically speaking, Hachette's third orientation was the publication of dictionaries, which soon became a major branch. This field had already ensured the fortune of his competitor, Larousse. As early as 1841, Louis Hachette had started the publication of the *Dictionnaire de la langue française* by E. Littré. He went on to publish the series of *Dictionnaires universels,* the *Dictionnaire d'histoire et de géographie,* the *Dictionnaire universel des contemporains* by Vapereau, the *Dictionnaire des sciences philosophiques* by A. Franck, the *Dictionnaire du commerce* by Joanne, and others.[71] Already at this time, the range of activities of the firm dictated the formation of a new type of organizational structure, one that is still in use in publishing firms. Beside the traditional departments, such as accounting and secretarial (which handled general correspondence, registration, and mailing of orders), new "departments" sprang up, such as the classics department, which was headed by René Vaubourdolle from 1924, and the general literature department.

Hachette's fourth orientation, dating back to the very end of the nineteenth century, completed in a logical fashion the structure of the firm. In 1897, he purchased the establishments of Périnet and Faivre and branched out into the new field of distribution. A rapid chronology of this new venture is as follows: When the Messageries Hachette were incorporated in 1918, the firm started to distribute for other publishing firms, notably Gallimard, from 1932 onward. On the foreign front, Hachette bought up in 1927 the shares of the Agence de librairie et de publication, which formed the nucleus of the new foreign department. The final and logical steps of this progressive buildup of the firm were the purchases in 1920 of the printing firm of Brodart and Gallois and in 1923 of the bindery firm of Joseph Taupin.

The sequence of this extraordinary success is clear. Every two or three decades, Hachette renewed itself by diversifying, and on each occasion monopolized to a large extent what proved to be a major field of the economy of the book. One can easily imagine how difficult it must have been to coordinate existing publishing activities with the task of opening a new market, particularly in the field of general literature. New legal structures[72] and technological developments permitted total control of the market for the distribution of a given work and brought about a new economy of publishing during the Second Empire. Two elements played a fundamental role here: first, the elimination of piracies, in particular Belgian ones, and second, a new policy regarding pressruns, which we will discuss shortly.[73]

David Bellos's study on the size of printings, based on statements of the printers themselves in the first half of the century, reflects the traditional character of the printing trade at the time.[74]

> In the course of the nineteenth century, very few works were issued in large numbers, on a regular basis. . . . Best sellers and some works in constant demand were stereotyped. This method, known since the end of the eighteenth century, was widely used during the Restoration for the reimpression of classical authors. From 1830 on, stereotyping permitted frequent reimpression, in small numbers, of works with a guaranteed distribution.[75]

The common practice, in Paris as well as in the provinces (Strasbourg in particular), was to run off a succession of small printings of no more than 1,000 or 2,000 copies each. Around 1860, the major publishers began to adopt another strategy that amounted to speculation on hypothetical bestsellers, whose sales would counterbalance the failures or financial shortcomings of other titles. Public opinion, and consequently advertising, became all the more important, while scandal itself was made to play its role. Michel Lévy launched his "Bibliothèque" with *Madame Bovary,* which had been turned down by Jacotet, and the 1857 trial of Flaubert's novel ensured the book's success. Lévy was to use the same strategy for *Les fleurs du mal* and *La vie de Jésus.* Since that period, successful literary publishing ventures called increasingly for large investments, both to withstand losses until best-sellers were found and to finance the serialized popular collections that stimulated the market. Thus, in 1878, Flammarion published Michelet, Hugo, and Zola at 0.10 francs an issue. Thematic collections multiplied, while *Pêcheurs d'Islande* (1886) went through 440 printings within a few years, and Zola's novels were regularly issued in printings of 100,000 and sometimes 180,000 copies. Fields as yet undeveloped stimulated the creation of new firms, which were of lesser importance, no doubt, but all the better rooted for being more specialized. The Librairie Champion is an interesting example of such a new firm.[76] These examples of speculation and the new publishing enterprises suggest, then, that the 1890 crisis was caused by overproduction in an already saturated market.

The new policy concerning edition sizes reached its logical conclusion in the practices of one of the main figures of the nineteenth-century French publishing world, Arthème Fayard. His father, originally from the Puy-de-Dôme, had opened a bookstore in Paris in 1857. Arthème followed in his father's steps in 1894, and launched his own collection, the Modern bibliothèque, in 1904. Texts of Maurice Barrès, Marcel Prévost, Paul Bourget, and many others were published in illustrated volumes that sold for 19 sous (95 centimes) and were regularly issued in runs of tens of thousands of copies. The immediate success of the first collection allowed Fayard to launch a second, Le Livre populaire, as early as 1905. In this collection, following the publication of *Chaste et flétrie* by Charles Mérouvel, he republished the best-sellers among the serialized novels[77] and sold a 700-page volume for 65 centimes. In the same vein, Fayard launched in 1913 the Meilleurs livres, a collection of classics priced at 0.10 francs per volume, and the Maîtres du roman populaire in 1914. Important as this phenomenon is for the history of publishing, it is equally so for literature. The widely circulated "popular novel," so dear to Fayard, received official recognition as a genre of its own with large printing runs. Yet publishers such as Gallimard competed against this new genre by publishing a "better brand of literature." In the aftermath of the World War I, Flammarion, the publisher of Jules Romains and Maurice Dekobra, issued 600,000 copies of Victor Marguerite's *La Garçonne*.[78] Thus, the "Arthème Fayard revolution" carried to its logical end an evolution initiated in the first half of the century.

Since the structures of distribution were necessarily linked to production, they were in their turn profoundly altered by new publishing policies. For example, advertising traditionally took three forms. One was the publication of catalogs, which were issued either periodically (hence the wealth of catalog collections at the Bibliothèque nationale),[79] or on the occasion of major events such as book fairs, whose catalogs form the basis of German bibliographical statistics. Similarly, the catalogs of some nineteenth-century firms were, in essence, current bibliographies of a specialized nature for that period. Such was the case for the Treuttel and Würtz catalogs of English and German works. Another traditional advertising element that was used to promote a particularly significant work was the prospectus. A small advertising tract, composed either by the author or, more likely, by a writer paid by the publisher, the prospectus recounted the general theme of the work and occasionally provided an outline; mainly, it specified the conditions of sale.[80] The third element, dating from the birth of professional book-trade periodicals, was the announcement of newly published titles, in particular in the *Bibliographie de la France*, and advertisements that recorded parts of the publisher's backlist. In addition, publishers sometimes distributed free copies of new publications to selected periodicals in the hope of getting reviews.

Overall, such advertising practices were aimed almost exclusively at professionals in the book trade. The exchange of catalogs and complimentary copies and the granting of commissions, whether reciprocal or not, were among the methods of a system perfectly adapted to the distribution of a few hundred or possibly a few thousand copies of a book among relatively small, geographically isolated, yet very well-defined groups. At its very best, this system could achieve distribution throughout Europe, as happened in the case of Panckoucke's 1817 edition of *Victoires et conquêtes . . . des français de 1792 à 1815,* which was distributed by means of a commission system in about one hundred French and foreign cities simultaneously.[81] Although such cases were rare exceptions, the example shows clearly how the success of an important edition was linked directly to the publisher's ability to secure exclusive rights to a given market through deals with his colleagues.[82]

With the advent of mass publication, which began with the "Charpentier revolution," the process was progressively reversed. The triumph of cheap popular editions and of the periodical press was accompanied by an actual reversal of advertising practices. Advertising was no longer geared to members of the book trade, but rather the general public. An advertising innovation, the poster, appeared at the end of the reign of Louis XVI and achieved unprecedented success under the Restoration. In Balzac's terms,

> the poster, the new and original creation of the famous Ladvo-
> cat, flourished for the first time on walls. In no time at all,
> Paris was full of the colorful imitations of this new form of
> advertisement. . . . To escape the tyranny of the journalists,
> Dauriat and Ladvocat were the first to invent the poster, and
> they caught the fancy of Parisians with their use of decorative
> types, bizarre colors, vignettes and later on lithographs; they
> turned the poster into a visual poem.[83]

As an immediate reaction to the appearance of the poster, announcements in journals became more refined; they began to vary in their choice of typeface and layout and then became illustrated in their own right. "In 1824, the *Bibliographie de la France* reverted to its weekly format, and the new typographical makeup of its two to four-page *feuilleton,* with no continuous pagination, was modified. Varied use of type of different size and body, eye-catching presentations, and blurbs transformed it from a mere notice of publication into a genuine advertisement. This major change was completed by 1834."[84] The last phase of this evolution, which, as David Bellos has pointed out, attests to the formation of a general reading public, was characterized by the appearance of distinctive wrappers that became the symbol of a firm and of its publications. Yellow covers were the mark of the Bibliothèque contemporaine of Calmann-Lévy, which published the fourth edition of *La vie littéraire* by Anatole France as early as 1889; the novels of Hector Malot were published in the Collection Charpentier, which later became Fasquelle's; and, at the turn of the century, the works of Edmond About were published by Hachette and printed on the presses of Paul Brodard in Coulommiers. A great deal of Fayard's success can be attributed to the distinctive appearance of his collection, which was displayed repeatedly in all the booksellers' windows.[85]

In addition to innovations in advertising, the organization of book distribution changed profoundly. As mentioned earlier, the traditional channels of distribution were twofold: book peddling in the rural areas and the bookstores in the cities.[86] The work of J. J. Darmon, supplemented in some cases by specialized monographs, shows that the nineteenth century as a whole, and in particular the period from 1820 to 1870, was the great era of book peddling.[87] Peddling actually enabled certain publishers, such as Wentzel, to launch and develop their firms to levels never before attained. Another well-known example is the Alsatian printer Le Roux of Strasbourg, who published 50,000 copies of *Le grand messager boîteux* in 1832 and another 100,000 copies in 1863. This particular work was issued "in a square octavo, illustrated with woodcuts and sold through peddling" in an almost entirely regional setting.[88] The book-peddling practice declined, however, as the remote and isolated regions increasingly came within reach of a national distribution network whose efficiency permitted the punctual distribution of periodicals even in rural areas. In itself quite significant, the progressive elimination of book peddling in the years after the fall of the empire coincided with the rapid expansion of the provincial press and the peak period of railroad development, which under the "Freycinet plan" called for the addition of 3,000 kilometers of local lines to complement the main system.

For this period, Claude Savart has drawn up statistics from various directories and statements that portray accurately the general evolution of bookstores between 1841 and 1901.[89] The fundamental issue confronting bookstores was raised in an article published in *Le Siècle* in 1869 and entitled, "Has the abolition of the licensing system, which prohibited sale outside of the cities, promoted a movement of decentralization in the points of sale?" Such decentralization was, in effect, one of the benefits the partisans of "freedom" expected from the 1870 amendment.[90] Overall, the

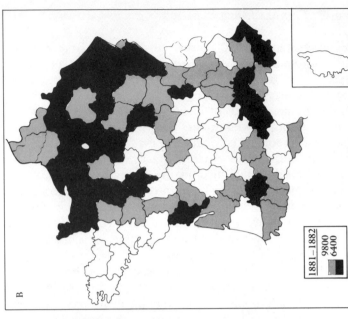

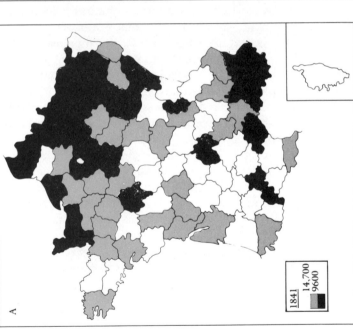

FIGURE 7

(A) Number of inhabitants per bookstore, 1841. (B) Number of inhabitants per bookstore, 1881–1882. *Source:* Claude Savart, "La liberté de la librairie (10 septembre 1870) et l'évolution du réseau des libraires," *Revue française d'histoire du livre*, no. 22 (1979): 9ff.

results of that legislation are clear: The number of booksellers increased along a curve consistent with the rise in printed output, with a marked acceleration under the Second Empire that culminated in the decade of liberalization from 1870 to 1880. That period was followed in turn by a deceleration in growth until the end of the century, a time when even the number of booksellers started to decrease. A geographical analysis (Fig. 7) reveals the permanence of the traditional structures, with the "Maggiolo line" once again as demarcation. The only significant evolution in book-selling took place at the very end of the century, which saw an acceleration in the number of booksellers in the departments of the southeast. Book-selling remained an urban phenomenon; and, what is more, in most large cities studied, the increase in the number of booksellers did not follow the curve of demographic growth. It is paradoxical that in a period that is rightly considered the height of printed production, the system of distribu-tion seems to have disintegrated, due to the disappearance of peddlers and the mediocrity of the network of booksellers.

Countering this twofold phenomenon, however, were newly formed channels and networks of distribution. In 1816, a first step was taken in a new direction when the bookseller-publisher Lefèvre sent his chief clerk, Hautecoeur, on rounds to the main provincial booksellers to obtain orders for his new publications. The appearance of this newcomer, the traveling salesman, clearly indicated the trend toward the formation of a national market for all major publications. It also marked the very begin-ning of specialized networks of distribution other than bookshops. The first such network dates back to 1839, the year in which Louis Hachette and Firmin Didot struck a deal to establish in the provinces an exclusive system of correspondents and booksellers to whom alone they would send their new publications. In practice, this first network was com-pleted with the establishment of railroad station bookshops, the contract for which was given to Napoléon Chaix, one of the founders of the aforementioned Messageries Hachette. It is noteworthy that, besides such independent and well-structured systems, which were soon backed up by a "sale or return" policy,[91] an important part of the market, in particular the international sector, was dominated by commission firms that sprang up as early as the July Monarchy.[92] Very little, however, is known about the relative importance of these various networks, and we are restricted for the most part to a qualitative description of the major trends of the century. The 1890s witnessed the official organization of the profession and the appearance of regulations. (The French national booksellers' association was created in 1891, and the first minimum-price list, an attempt to cope with a problem still very predominant today, dates back to 1892.)

Although the evolution of printed production in nineteenth-century France, in terms of structures of publication and distribution, seems particularly complex and sometimes contradictory, the century as a whole witnessed a twofold movement. First, the earlier period, which ended with the Second Empire, was a phase of expansion characterized by the entry of the general public into the age of the printed word. The book became the most important sociocultural means through which the cohesion of the new industrial society was ensured, particularly in terms of ideology. The second phase, though less uniform in appearance, consisted of a series of conflicting tendencies between 1870 and 1914. With the liberalization of the book professions and the law of 1881, the height of institutionalization was reached, but this was seemingly more a consequence of the preceding era than the result of tendencies specific to the end of the nineteenth century. Another quite important phenomenon, in our opinion, was the polarization of the reading audience that resulted from the new development, in distinct opposition to each other, of a "genuine" and a "popular" literature. Of the two, the latter was, of course, more important for both the printers and the publishers of the industrial age. Never before had such circulation figures been reached on a regular basis. Yet the "popular" market also presented certain risks, for its public was the more volatile of the two. Finally, the formation of a nationwide market, and above all the development of the periodical press, led to intense competition. For a while, growth was maintained through speculative means, no doubt artificial in nature; nonetheless, book production reached its peak around the years 1880–1890. Threatened by competition from other media in a market that saw no demographic growth and little economic growth in comparison with those in other European countries,[93] the French book industry began to decline at the end of the nineteenth century, on both the national and the international front.[94] The year 1880, the peak of the civilization of the printed book, also marked the end of the "Gutenberg galaxy" in France.

NOTES

1. Noteworthy are the works of Robert Escarpit (see the bibliography in *L'Écrit et la communication*, Paris, 1973) and Marshall MacLuhan, *La galaxie Gutenberg* (Montréal, 1967).

2. Most of the work has been carried out under the auspices of the École nationale des chartes, Paris: F. Barbier, *Nouvelles recherches sur l'imprimerie strasbourgeoise* (Paris, 1976); B. Vouillot, *Imprimeurs et libraires parisiens du Premier Empire* (Paris, 1979), etc. We also have available a number of studies of particular firms, such as Mame, Hetzel, Hachette, Fayard, and others.

3. We will not here go into the periodical press, which has been the subject of exhaustive studies, notably *Histoire générale de la presse française* (Paris, 1969–1976).

4. E. Le Roy Ladurie's inaugural lecture at the Collège de France, "L'Histoire immobile," *Annales; économies, sociétés, civilisations* 29 (1974): 673–692.

5. Two works are essential for this period and provide a very complete bibliography: E. Labrousse et al., *Histoire économique et sociale de la France*, Vols. 2 and 3 (Paris, 1970–1976); and P. Léon, *Histoire économique et sociale du monde*. Vol. 3: *Inerties et révolutions, 1730–1840* (Paris, 1978).

6. On these points, see the bibliographies in the works cited in note 5.

7. Labrousse, Vol. 2, p. 231.

8. J. Cain, R. Escarpit, and H.-J. Martin, *Le livre français, hier, aujourd'hui et demain* (Paris, 1972).

9. Only a small number of French publishers now have headquarters in the provinces, the main one being Privat in Toulouse. My own research on Strasbourg has shown that it was impossible for a provincial publisher to attain national importance in the nineteenth century without at least opening an "établissement" in Paris.

10. The bibliography is given in F. Furet and J. Ozouf, *Lire et écrire: L'alphabétisation des Français, de Calvin à Jules Ferry* (Paris, 1977).

11. M. Fleury and P. Valmary, "Les progrès de l'instruction élémentaire, de Louis XIV à Napoléon III," *Population* 12 (1957): 71–92; F. Furet and W. Sachs, "La croissance de l'alphabétisation en France," *Annales; économies, sociétés, civilisations* 29 (1974): 714–737. An overview is given by F. Furet and J. Ozouf, "Trois siècles de métissage culturel," *Annales; économies, sociétés, civilisations* 32 (1977): 488ff.

12. Furet and Ozouf, *Lire et écrire*, Vol. 1, p. 57.

13. A. Frost, *Histoire de l'enseignement en France, 1800–1967* (Paris, 1977).

14. MacLuhan, op. cit.

15. Furet and Ozouf, *Lire et écrire*, Vol. 1, p. 97.

16. Ibid., pp. 245ff.

17. R. Oberlé, "Étude sur l'analphabétisme à Mulhouse au siècle de l'industrialisation," *Bulletin du Musée historique de Mulhouse* 67 (1959): 99–110.

18. F. Barbier, *Trois cents ans de librairie et d'imprimerie, Berger-Levrault, 1676–1830* (Geneva, 1979).

19. J. J. Darmon, *Le colportage de librairie en France sous le Second Empire* (Paris, 1972).

20. The bibliography is given in my communication to the Congrès des sociétés savantes, Caen, 1980, "Le colportage bas-rhinois sous le Second Empire." In press.

21. According to Bibliothèque nationale, *Catalogue général des livres imprimés*.

22. *Livre et société dans la France du XVIIIème siècle,* 2 vols. (Paris and La Haye, 1965–1970).

23. G. Bollème, *La Bibliothèque bleue: Littérature populaire en France du XVIIIème au XIXème siècle* (Paris, 1971).

24. English edition (Paris, Belin, 1834); Spanish (Marseille, Barile and Boulouch, 1834; and Paris, Rosa, 1834); Polish (Paris, Pinard, 1834).

25. Ten editions, ranging from a "Billigste Volks-Ausgabe" to a "Pracht Ausgabe," came out in 1863 and 1864, and Kayser's *Vollständiges Bücher-Lexikon* records 23 impressions of those editions during those two years.

26. On this firm, see Barbier, op. cit.

27. The printer Paul Dupont published a number of pieces on the products that he displayed at the different world exhibitions, as well as a remarkable *Histoire de l'imprimerie,* 2 vols. (Paris, 1854). His enterprise is particularly well known, thanks to the *Notice historique* (Paris, 1849) and his own *Une imprimerie en 1867* (Paris, 1867).

28. *La première année de grammaire* . . . was published in 1871, and 201 successive editions came out up to 1917. The *Seconde année* and *Troisième année* were likewise published by Armand Colin: 78 editions of the *Seconde année* appeared up to 1893, 74 editions of the *Troisième année* up to 1925. Along parallel lines, A. Colin published in the same collection the "Livres du maître."

29. On this problem, see Barbier, op. cit., pp. 325–329.

30. The great printer-publisher in this field is Mame of Tours. For an account of this firm, see A^d *Mame et cie: Imprimerie, librairie, relivre* (Tours, 1862).

31. It should be noted that these figures are only for works announced in the *Bibliographie de la France.* The actual number of titles published was larger.

32. Note 31 applies here as well; it does seem, though, that the curve itself is representative of the actual situation.

33. We do not have for the nineteenth century a work comparable to Philippe Ariès' *L'Enfant et la vie familiale sous l'ancien régime* (Paris, 1960). A quick survey of French printed literature for children has, however, been made by Odile Limousin, *Recherches documentaires pour une histoire de la littérature de jeunesse française.* See certain chapters of this thesis in *Bibliographie de la France* (1971), no. 40, pp. 593ff. (Chronique).

34. Arnaud Berquin, poet from the Gironde, was a celebrated writer for children. He also helped to edit the *Feuille villageoise* and *Moniteur* at the start of the Revolution. For a checklist of his works, see *Dictionnaire des lettres françaises, XVIIIème siècle* (Paris, 1960), Vol. 1, pp. 182–183.

35. Pauline de Meulan (1773–1827) married Guizot in 1812. She devoted herself to a literary career at the beginning of the Revolution and participated in editing the *Publiciste* of Suard.

36. *Dictionnaire des lettres françaises, XVIIIème siècle* (Paris, 1960), Vol. 2, p. 391.

37. Thanks to the kindness of Henri-Jean Martin, figures are available on the number of copies printed of *Malheurs de Sophie* from 1864 to 1900:

Year	*Number*				
1864	5,516	1876	—	1888	11,000
1865	—	1877	11,000	1889	—
1866	5,511	1878	—	1890	11,000
1867	—	1879	11,000	1891	—
1868	5,488	1880	—	1892	11,000
1869	5,515	1881	13,200	1893	—
1870	5,977	1882	—	1894	—
1871	—	1883	11,000	1895	—
1872	5,500	1884	11,000	1896	11,000
1873	12,000	1885	—	1897	—
1874	—	1886	2,200	1898	11,000
1875	11,000	1887	11,000	1899	16,500
				1900	—

This table permits three observations about the policy of a large publishing firm in the second half of the nineteenth century: (1) Overall policy had been modified little and remained based on a succession of reprintings; (2) there are two periods of rupture, in 1872–1873 and 1898–1906 (a year in which the pressrun exceeded 22,000 copies); and (3) the crisis at the end of the century is clear—the number of copies published declined from 70,400 in the decade 1881–1890 to 49,500 in the decade 1891–1900.

38. On Hetzel, see *Magasin d'éducation et de récréation*, supplement to No. 511 of 15 June 1886; A. Parmenie and C. Bonnier, *Histoire d'un éditeur et de ses auteurs* (Paris, 1953); and *De Balzac à Jules Verne: Un grand éditeur du XIXème siècle, P. J. Hetzel* (Paris, 1966), which is the catalog of an exhibition.

39. An article by Françoise Parent, which is in preparation, (*Annales; économies, sociétés, civilisations*, 1979, p. 1037, note 16), is a study of the area around the Palais-Royal. See also the notes in B. Vouillot, *L'Imprimerie et la librairie à Paris sous le Consulat et l'Empire*, Ecole des chartes dissertation, 1979.

40. F. Barbier, "Quelques documents inédits sur l'abbé Delille," in *Studies on Voltaire and the Eighteenth Century* 189 (1980): 211–228.

41. F. Parent, "Les cabinets de lecture dans Paris; pratiques culturelles et espace social sour la Restauration," *Annales; économies, sociétés, civilisations* (1979): 1016–1038.

42. Victor Hugo, *Hernani, ou l'honneur castillan, drame* . . . (Paris, Mame and Delaunay-Vallée, 1838).

43. Ladvocat served as the model of the Romantic publisher depicted by Balzac in *Illusions perdues.*

44. *Histoire générale de la presse française* (Paris, 1969), Vol. 2, pp. 327–329.

45. Victor Hugo, *Les Misérables* (Paris, Pagnerre, 1862), 10 vols. in 5. The verso of the half titles bear the address: Bruxelles, chez A. Lacroix, Verboeckhoven et cie.

46. On these problems, see the remarks of David Bellos at the colloquium held at Oxford in 1977 on the theme of "Publishing and the Book Market in France and England in the Nineteenth Century," published as "Le marché du livre à l'époque romantique, recherches et problèmes," *Revue française d'histoire du livre*, no. 20 (1978): 647–660.

47. Ibid., p. 649.

48. One of the rare studies on French printed output written at the beginning of the twentieth century was by E. Morel in "Le livre français et la production mondiale," *Mercure de France*, 16 November 1912, pp. 760–774.

49. O. Lorenz, *Catalogue général de la librairie française* (Paris, 1867–   ).

50. See C. Charle, *La crise littéraire à l'époque du naturalisme: Roman, théâtre, politique* (Paris, 1979).

51. Estivals' statistics come from the table that appeared on the occasion of the centennial of the *Bibliographie de la France* in 1911, Vol. 100, 2nd series, no. 46 (17 November, 1911): 230–231.

52. G. Picot, "Le Dépôt légal et nos collections nationales," *Revue des deux mondes,* 1883, 3ème livr., pp. 622ff.

53. For some countries, considerably more information is available. In particular, Germany has the classic work of J. Goldfriedrich and F. Kapp, *Geschichte des deutschen Buchhandels,* 4 vols. (Leipzig, 1886–1913); and the more recent study of I. Rarisch, *Industrialisierung und Literatur: Buchproduktion, Verlagswesen und Buchhandel in Deutschland im 19. Jahrhundert* (Berlin, 1976).

54. H.-J. Martin, "La librairie française en 1777–1778," *Dix-huitième siècle* 2 (1979), pp. 87ff.

55. On this problem, see Labrousse et al., op. cit.

56. F. Barbier, "Le monde du livre à Strasbourg, de la fin de l'ancien régime à la chute de l'Alsace française" (Paris, 1980), unpublished thesis. See also F. Barbier, "Le commerce international de la librairie française au XIXe siècle (1815–1913)," *Revue d'histoire moderne et contemporaine* 27 (1981): 96–117.

57. Charle, op. cit.

58. Ibid.

59. Darmon, op. cit.

60. Charle, op. cit.

61. *Histoire générale de la presse française,* Vol. 2 (Paris, 1969).

62. My own research on the copyright deposit for ten-year intervals confirms this proportion, as does the general tendency of the curve obtained from the *Bibliographie de la France.*

63. Some studies have been carried out on this subject, based on concrete cases. They were reported on the occasion of a colloquium organized by the Institut d'étude du livre in Paris in 1979–1980 on the theme of "Espaces du livre." Analyses were given of traditional space of production based on the example of the Société typographique de Neuchâtel and industrial space of production on the basis of a factory constructed by Berger-Levrault in Nancy in 1878. See also F. Barbier "Les ouvriers du livre et la révolution industrielle en France au XIX^c siècle," *Revue du Nord, forthcoming.*

64. Ibid.

65. We have important information on a number of these firms: Berger-Levrault, Mame, the printing shop of Paul Dupont and l'Imprimerie nationale in Paris and Casterman in Tournai.

66. A N , F 18/2371.

67. M. Audin, *Histoire de l'imprimerie: Radioscopie d'une ère, de Gutenberg à l'informatique* (Paris, 1972).

68. P. Renouard, "Quelques documents sur les Petit, libraires parisiens et leur famille," *Bulletin de la Société de l'histoire de Paris et de l'Ile de France* 23 (1896): 133–153; H.-J. Martin, "Un grand éditeur parisien au XVIIème siècle, Sébastien Cramoisy," *Gutenberg Jahrbuch* (1957): 179–188; S. Tucoo-Chala, *Charles-Joseph Panckoucke et la librairie française, 1736–1798* (Pau and Paris, 1977).

69. Tucoo-Chala, op. cit.

70. J. Mistler, *La Librairie Hachette de 1826 à nos jours* (Paris, 1972).

71. Ibid. See also A. Rey, *Encyclopédies et dictionnaires* (Paris, 1982).

72. F. Barbier, "Le commerce international de la librairie française au XIXème siècle," op. cit.

73. F. Barbier, "Chiffres de tirage et devis d'édition: la politique d'une imprimerie librairie au début du XIXème siècle," *Bulletin d'histoire moderne et contemporaine,* no. 11 (Paris, 1978): 141–156.

74. Bellos, op. cit.

75. The case of the abbé Jacques Delille is an example of this preindustrial policy on the size of editions. The ample documentation provided by the archive of Berger-Levrault shows that this publishing model was dominant throughout the nineteenth century, so much so that the "industrial" model was quite marginal for most French printers of this period.

76. J. Monfrin, *Honoré Champion et sa librairie, 1874–1978* (Paris, 1978).

77. I owe thanks to Henri-Jean Martin for his kindness in supplying information from the very rich dossier of documents concerning the Librairie Fayard.

78. Some documentation concerning these editions (statistics concerning pressruns and sales) are now in the archive of Flammarion.

79. 8° Q 10 A and Q 10 B.

80. Some examples, notably a prospectus for *Dictionnaire des sciences naturelles*, are treated in Barbier, *Trois cents ans de librairie et d'imprimerie*. For the beginning of the nineteenth century, see also B. Vouillot, "Imprimeurs et libraires parisiens," op. cit.

81. *Victoires et conquetes . . . des français de 1792 à 1815*, 27 vols. (Paris, 1817) by General Beauvais, V. Parisot et al. Volume 1 includes the names of booksellers who agreed to take subscriptions, and the prospectus, according to which one paid 6.50 francs in advance, and for each successive volume upon receipt of the preceding.

82. Here, again, the example of Delille is highly informative.

83. *Illusions perdues*, pp. 173 and 313 of the edition of the Librairie générale française.

84. *Bibliographie de la France*, 150th anniversary number (1961), p. xvi.

85. Literary prizes provided another means of promotion, and the principal ones came into being precisely during this period.

86. Booksellers of this period recognized that there was a difference between an urban public, which could support a professional book trade, and a dispersed rural public, which one could hope to reach only by itinerant peddlars. One might be able to draw a parallel between the latter and the system of bookmobiles used today.

87. See notes 19 and 20.

88. Archives départementales du Bas-Rhin (Strasbourg), Vol. 18.

89. Claude Savart, "La liberté de la librairie (10 septembre 1870) et l'évolution du réseau des libraires," *Revue française d'histoire du livre*, no. 22 (1979): 91ff.

90. Ibid.

91. This practice was basically very simple. The publisher addressed directly "d'office" new publications to a certain number of booksellers and credited their account. At the end of a certain period, the booksellers had to return unsold books, and the accounts were then balanced.

92. In the case of Strasbourg, which we have studied, the phenomenon was particularly clear, for Eschenauer and Co., a commission house, occupied the first rank in the international book trade of that city in the nineteenth century.

93. See Léon, op. cit.

94. This is demonstrated by a progressive reversal in the direction of the French book trade's imports and exports. At the end of the nineteenth century, the export surplus is in large measure a result of the growing French-speaking colonial empire.

[8] Depression and Innovation in the British and American Book Trade, 1819–1939

James J. Barnes

TRADE DEPRESSIONS usually conjure up images of commercial contraction, unemployment, bankruptcy, and pessimism. For most booksellers and publishers in Great Britain and the United States, this has been all too true over the past two centuries. However, occasionally an individual or company has been able to weather the financial storm and turn the crisis to an advantage. These fortunate few comprise the subject of this chapter.

"Necessity is the mother of invention" could have been the motto for the book trade. For example, all three of the so-called "paperback revolutions" in American publishing history coincided with major crises in the economy.[1] Any number of other adverse conditions, both economic and social, can be cited for having either forced or enticed publishers and booksellers into new directions. Sometimes these turned into notable failures, but a surprising number resulted in spectacular successes.

In concentrating on economic impetuses to innovation, I do not mean to suggest that other kinds—political, social, legal, technological, and cultural—do not exist, for they clearly do. In this respect, one of my favorite passages, from James Lackington's memoirs, reflects the effects on the book trade of the turbulence of the French Revolution and the Napoleonic era.

> I have always found that bookselling is much affected by the
> political state of affairs. For as mankind are in search of amuse-
> ments, they often embrace the first that offers; so that if there
> is anything in the newspapers of consequence, that draws
> many to the coffee house, where they chat away the evenings,
> instead of visiting the shops of booksellers—or reading at
> home. The best time for bookselling is when there is no kind
> of news stirring; then many of those who for months would
> have done nothing but talk of war or peace, revolutions and
> counterrevolutions, etc. etc., for want of other amusement will
> have recourse to books; so that I have often experienced that
> the report of war, or the trial of a great man, or indeed any
> subject that attracts the public attention, has been some hun-
> dreds of pounds out of my pocket in a few weeks.[2]

Lackington argued aptly that for every political crisis that diverted people
from buying and reading books, there was probably a corresponding increase in the amount of time and money spent on newspapers, magazines,
and casual conversation; or, to put it another way, while booksellers lost
customers, the news vendors, coffeehouses, and pubs gained them.

Ever since I began to study the book trade I have been impressed by the
impact that economic conditions have had upon it. Dibdin aptly characterized the typical middle-class penchant for bargains when he described the
depressed London market in 1832: "Men wished to get for five what they
knew they could not formerly obtain for fifteen shillings."[3] John Murray's
comment to Gladstone in 1851 reveals the perennial predicament of many
booksellers and publishers each time the economy turned downward:[4]

> But it must be borne in mind that books are a *luxury;* when a
> time of distress comes the first expense to be curtailed is the
> purchase of books. That is done (without any outward display
> of economy) rather than laying down a carriage or dismissing
> servants.

Others, like Murray's contemporary, G. R. Porter, viewed books in a quite
different light and welcomed any lowering in their price: "Books can no
longer be considered, as they were in bygone times, a luxury, to be provided for the opulent, who alone as a class, could read and enjoy them.
From year to year the circle is widening in which literature becomes almost
a necessary of life. . . ."[5] Since my early glimpses into these commercial
vicissitudes, I have felt increasingly impelled to relate changes in economic
conditions to corresponding ones in the publishing and marketing of
books. I do not for a moment regard myself an economic determinist but
rather an historian whose methods are eclectic. What follows is meant
more by way of suggestion than proof.

During the nineteenth century especially, one finds no lack of trade-cycle depressions. They occurred with monotonous and, for those who lived through them, devastating regularity. Following the Napoleonic Wars, there were major panics in 1819, 1825–1826, 1829–1832, 1837–1842, and 1847–1848. Then the cycle lengthened considerably. Almost ten years separated the crises of 1857, 1863, 1873, and 1893, although there were lesser dips in between.[6] The fact that there were political and social crises concurrent with these severe fluctuations in the economy both simplifies and complicates our task. Let us consider the circumstances first in England, then in the United States, and conclude with a few observations appropriate to both.

Nowadays we so take for granted the nineteenth-century trend toward lower book prices that we often forget that the opposite occurred during the first quarter of that century. This earlier trend was due partly to the inflation that accompanied Britain's involvement in war from 1793 to 1815, and partly to the government's policy of discouraging the production and distribution of cheap printed matter by taxing manufactured paper, advertisements, and political newspapers. Whereas the average price of a new novel in the 1780s was 3s 6d, it rose to 10s 6d by the 1820s.

Testifying before a Committee of the House of Commons in 1818, one printer observed: "Books are a luxury, and the purchase of them has been confined to fewer people. In general, those who would be disposed to purchase books, have not the means of so doing, and are obliged to be frugal."[7] If 10s 6d was considered a luxury in 1818, it is clear that only middle- and upper-class readers could own a volume costing 31s 6d, and then only occasionally. More tempting bargains were offered in the form of noncopyrighted works in special reprinted editions and drastically reduced "remainders."

Following the panic of 1819, a few book entrepreneurs (most notably the firms of Whittingham and Limbird) reduced prices on new or recently published works, but it was not until 1825 that a major publisher like Constable greatly extended his market by issuing works at 3s 6d. Unfortunately, before he could really launch his Miscellany he was forced into bankruptcy by the crisis of 1825–1826. However, Constable reasoned that during times of economic hardship such a project made even more sense, so he continued planning for it, with the result that the first of these nonfiction volumes appeared in January 1827, followed by others in the series at three-week intervals.

The scheme had to be abandoned shortly thereafter because Constable's finances were beyond salvaging, but the experiment intrigued other leading firms in London and Edinburgh. In 1829, with trade still stagnant, John Murray launched his Family Library of new or nearly new nonfiction works and sold each volume for 5s. At about the same time Longman &

Company began Lardner's Cabinet Cyclopaedia, Oliver & Boyd of Edinburgh came out with its Cabinet Library, and Colburn & Bentley inaugurated its National Library. In 1831 Colburn & Bentley even went so far as to take some of its backlist from five years or more, reissue the titles in attractive single volumes labeled Standard Novels, and sell them for 6s each. Other lesser known publishers imitated the prestigious houses and claimed that their new series, like the others, were meant to offer the reading public a windfall of current literature at greatly reduced cost. In his book, *The English Common Reader,* Richard Altick nicely captures the mood of provisional optimism: "Between 1827 and 1832, therefore, London and Edinburgh publishers behaved as if they stood on a peak in Darien, beholding for the first time a vast sea of common readers."[8]

Expectations of reaching a vast new readership were illusory for the very reasons that inspired them. In times of adversity middle-class book buyers were bound to retrench, and 5s or 6s a volume was still too dear. This held all the more true for artisans and clerks, whose salaries of two or three pounds a week could not possibly cover such purchases. Nonetheless, for every publisher like John Murray who had to give up his series after a few years, there was a Longman or a Bentley who carried on successfully, and their middle-class customers expected to be provided with new books at greatly reduced prices decade after decade.

For readers who were not willing to wait several years to sample the latest literary offerings, there was the option of subscribing to a circulating library. These libraries adjusted their fees depending upon the clientele, the class of books handled, and the frequency of borrowing, so that lower-class patrons might pay only a few shillings a year while middle-class borrowers were charged two guineas. There is little doubt that the number of circulating libraries grew steadily during the first half of the nineteenth century in response to high book prices, periodic trade slumps, and the recognition by the middle class that it was considered respectable to borrow in this fashion. The most successful of these lending libraries was begun by Charles Edward Mudie in the depression of 1842. His instincts directed him to offer new subscribers a tempting bargain in hard times, so he lowered his annual charge to one guinea instead of the usual two.

Hard-pressed middle-class readers also responded in increasing numbers to a form of installment buying that Charles Dickens made popular in 1836–1837 with *Pickwick Papers.* Publishing a work in weekly or monthly parts had been tried before by religious tract societies and producers of family Bibles, but *Pickwick Papers* was different in that those who put down a shilling for each part knew they had secured the latest number. People with greater financial resources had no particular advantage over those of more modest means. Many more families felt that they could afford an occasional shilling for the latest part-issue, and they regarded it a marvel of thrift to be able to save one pound for the completed version.

Part-issues were among the many instances of an innovation that began in a year of relative prosperity and continued undoubtedly to be profitable during subsequent years of depression. From 1837 to 1842 many firms cut back and printed smaller impressions of books on their regular lists, yet they increased the printing of part-issues by Dickens and other novelists. One obvious advantage of part-issues was that they brought in a steady flow of cash from weekly or monthly sales and thus helped to meet paper and print expenses.

Traveling by train was another phenomenon in which a great many middle-class readers indulged and for which they required reading matter to help pass the time. A solution was found in the depressed year of 1848, when W. H. Smith launched his first railway bookstall in London's Euston Station. Although a publisher himself, Smith found it more advantageous to sell cheap editions of popular works produced by others. Soon a market developed in "railway libraries" that stocked tried-and-true favorites and sold them for a few shillings each.

Throughout the first half of the nineteenth century one firm in particular prospered from the financial failures of others in the book trade: Thomas Tegg and Son. It dominated the remainder trade and acquired at vastly reduced prices the copyrights of works that had not sold well or whose proprietors had gone bankrupt. From 1825 to 1827 Tegg bought up some of Scott's copyrights in this way, and by 1834 he took over Murray's entire Family Library. By offering thousands of titles at only a few shillings per volume, Tegg created markets where none had existed before.

The aforementioned examples have illustrated ways in which publishers tried to lure middle- and upper-class readers into purchasing or borrowing books at significantly lower prices during times of economic distress. However, publishers and printers came increasingly to the realization that lower-middle-class and working-class readers might also become biblio-philes if the contents were to their liking and the price low enough. At the end of the eighteenth century, there were cheap tracts produced by moral-ists who wished to inculcate upright behavior and religion and were highly successful at publishing; at the other end of the spectrum tales of romance and adventure were produced in the form of chapbooks and ballad broad-sheets that sold for mere pennies. Literature designed for the mass market tended to fall into two broad categories: one that sought to improve, and another that was meant to pander. The pioneer efforts of Charles Knight, Henry Brougham, and other supporters of the Society for the Diffusion of Useful Knowledge produced literature of the first type. In the distressed conditions of the 1820s, they launched a Library of Useful Knowledge, each fortnightly issue of which cost 6*d*, and also a Library of Entertaining Knowledge, which sold for 2*s* per part. Sales of some part-issues reached 20,000 copies, and as time went on it became evident that the purchasers came from the ranks of the lower middle class more often than from the working class. The society launched two other ventures aimed at its humblest patrons: the *Penny Cyclopaedia* and the *Penny Magazine,* both of which were successful in spite of a general decline in the rest of the book trade. For more than a decade Charles Knight was able to sustain his vision of enlightening the masses through cheap and edifying publications, but eventually he was forced to concede defeat. A combination of government taxation and working-class indifference ultimately undermined his publishing enterprise.

A commercially more successful publisher who also provided "wholesome" literature for the lower class was William Milner of Halifax. As a printer he found his business going from bad to worse, and so he decided to launch a clothbound series of cheap fiction reprints. Known as the Cottage Library, the series sold for 1*s* per volume and soon attracted imitators. Milner extended the range of reprints to include such poets as Robert Burns, of whom he sold more than 10,000 copies in 1837 and more than 30,000 by 1839.[9]

Books were not the only means publishers used to attract the pennies of the lower classes. Following the success of Charles Knight's *Penny Magazine,* others soon recognized the sales potential of cheap periodicals in times of economic distress. William and Robert Chambers began to sell their *Edinburgh Journal* at three half-pence and, because they were not under any moral constraints, met with greater long-term success. As Richard Altick noted, 1832 was indeed the *annus mirabilis* for cheap periodicals. "Within a few months were born the *Half-Penny Magazine,* the *Christian's Penny Magazine,* the *London Penny Journal,* the *Girls' and Boys' Penny Magazine,* the *True Half-Penny Magazine, Dibdin's Penny Trumpet,* the *Penny Comic Magazine,* the *Penny Story Teller,* and the *Penny Novelist.*"[10]

Preparing the way for cheap periodicals were the Sunday newspapers of the late eighteenth and early nineteenth centuries. Soon after the Battle of Waterloo, Robert Bell launched his *Weekly Dispatch,* which sold more than 40,000 copies by 1840. Later that year the *Sunday Times* became dissatisfied with its circulation of only about 12,000 and began to serialize a novel by William Blanchard Rede entitled *The History of a Royal Rake.* This idea may well have been inspired by the depression-born weeklies published in America, *Brother Jonathan* and the *New World.* Serialization caught on quickly in Britain. Edward Lloyd soon introduced stories into his *Penny Sunday Times* and *Police Gazette* and, by eschewing politics, avoided the newspaper stamp duty.[11]

A Nottingham printer, Herbert Ingram, took the weekly publication one step further. He came to London in 1842 to start an illustrated weekly in which he could promote his own patent medicine. But the medicinal cure-all was rapidly eclipsed by the spectacular popularity of his new *Illustrated London News,* whose sales climbed steadily from 25,000 to 60,000 in its first year of publication. During the 1850s its circulation rose from 130,000 to 200,000 and a few years later to 300,000. Although the weekly sold at the relatively high price of 6*d,* it provided so many illustrations that customers could not resist;[12] it also appealed primarily to the family. Recognizing this, George Biggs started the *Family Herald* in 1842. Wholesome in tone, it combined cheapness with respectability and appealed to the lower middle class rather than to the working class.[13]

Almost every experiment calculated to lure middle-class readers into the market—remainders, library series, railway fiction, or cheap periodicals—had its counterpart in a cheaper version that sold for a penny or two and was aimed at the lower classes. Dickens's part-issues of *Pickwick Papers* were not only plagiarized in penny installments but the idea of part-issues also was extended to a whole new genre of fiction known as "penny bloods" or "blood and thunder" tales or, later still, "penny dreadfuls." Edward Lloyd (1815–1890) is generally acknowledged as the originator of "penny bloods" in their familiar eight-page, double-column form, which was adorned by a lurid woodcut illustration on the cover. By 1836 he had spawned four part-issue series: Lives of the Most Notorious Highwaymen; The Gem or Romance, or Tales of Intense Interest; The History of Pirates of All Nations; and the Calendar of Horrors.[14] Lloyd's talent lay in exploiting and imitating the product of others, by creating his own cheap versions of Sunday newspapers or illustrated weeklies. His publishing career commenced in the calm of 1836, but it prospered especially during the chaotic years of 1837–1842. While the British middle and upper classes fretted over the Corn Laws and Chartism, the lower classes sought escape in romance, gothic horror, highway robbery, and criminal intrigue.[15]

During the 1860s the authors of the "penny dreadfuls" substituted youthful heroes in place of the standard adult villains in order to appeal to a younger audience. The dozen or so juvenile magazines that featured violence and crime provoked a strong middle-class reaction of distaste and condemnation. To counteract the pernicious influence of these publications, the Religious Tract Society began the year 1879 with a new, illustrated weekly, *Boy's Own Paper.* Within six months it reached an incredible circulation of 500,000 copies, and the following year witnessed the appearance of *Girl's Own Paper.* Together the two weeklies vanquished many of their competitors.

On the surface it may not be apparent that these two weeklies originated in a depressed economy. However, what made them unusual was that they were publications of a society and not a trade publisher. This had not been the Society's intention, but no commercial firm would undertake the project because it was presumed no one could produce a juvenile weekly that combined wholesomeness and adventure. Other reasons commercial publishers may have had for declining to issue the new periodicals included the altogether discouraging economic climate—business was slow and credit scarce—coupled with the recognition that existing publishing patterns would be difficult to change. The Society, on the other hand, had no choice but to attempt the impossible, and it was not long before it congratulated itself for being able to further its overseas activities with income derived from the sale of its magazines.[16]

Viewed from a different perspective, the Society succeeded largely because it had sufficient resources to experiment with a new product in a highly competitive field. The history of the British and American book trade abounds with stories of firms that either perished or survived depending on their ability to make timely acquisitions or sell literary property. Thus, the timely extension or withholding of credit (or property) was integral to successful publishing. We have seen how Archibald Constable went bankrupt in the 1820s in spite of owning such a valuable asset as the *Encyclopaedia Britannica*. Adam Black's ability to raise enough money to acquire this encyclopedic work enabled him to reap its rewards for the rest of the century, which included the preparation and sale of the ninth edition during 1875–1888. An estimated half-million sets were sold in the British market, even though Black was unable to prevent at least twelve American piracies of part or all of the work. When the heirs of Adam and Charles Black decided to part with the *Encyclopaedia* at the end of the century, it was bought by the financially ailing London *Times* with help from an American, Horace E. Hooper. When *Times* subscribers were offered the whole set at half price, the sales that were realized immediately generated close to £500,000 in profit.[17]

Another example of the necessity of having adequate financial resources is the story behind Everyman's Library, which would have foundered had its owner, J. M. Dent, not been able to secure timely credit. Mindful of the risks of launching an extensive series of hardcover reprints, Dent set aside £10,000 to cover anticipated costs. From earlier years he had known all too well what it was like to be near bankruptcy; thus he was determined not to incur debt from financing the Everyman project. Ironically, the initial volumes sold so well that too much capital had to be tied up in reprinting new stock. Soon there were precious few funds left to publish additional volumes in the series. Furthermore, his bindery in London could not keep up with the demand due to a shortage of space, so Dent decided to move his plant as well as his work force 34 miles out of London to a new town in Hertfordshire. This was an added expense that had not been anticipated, but it was only the first of many such surprises. By moving the workers to the proposed site, he had hoped to improve their living conditions and enable them to go home for a midday meal. However, flats and houses in the new town were too small, so Dent was forced to build a number of cottages for his employees. It was then discovered that the land designated for the bindery was not level. The simplest solution was to dig a full basement under the building, a decision that then led Dent to install his printing works in the basement. Before he knew it, Dent had spent an additional £20,000. In his memoirs he mused:

> As paper was the cause of the large capital outlay, I resolved to lay the matter before my paper-makers, showing them what large sums I had owing to me and the necessity of keeping the books in print. They were very good and helped me by extended credit, and I was able to get on for twelve months without much difficulty.

Somewhat later he noted:

> My original £10,000 had long since disappeared, but money was beginning to come back, though of course it was inadequate for all of the undertakings which grew out of one another with such rapidity. In spite of myself I was forced to get money from the bank, and I also had to appeal to my good friends the paper-makers, who, becoming somewhat alarmed at the amount of my credit, refused to extend it.

Because Dent was a major customer he was able to take his business elsewhere and secure further credit, but his case reminds us that innovation depends upon solvency, whether the times are prosperous or hard.[18]

Let us now consider the great depression of the 1930s. Not surprisingly, this was a crucial formative period for book-trade development. Although the idea of book tokens had been suggested in the 1920s, it was not until 1932 that Harold Raymond of Chatto & Windus acted on it. There was perhaps nothing inherently depression-related about such a scheme, and yet its growing success during the 1930s suggested several underlying connections. Because only members of the Associated Booksellers could acquire tokens, there was some incentive to maintain a strong trade association at a time when business was slow. As more and more bookshops sold and redeemed the tokens, customers grew eager to have them and usually bought more than the value of their gift tokens. Given the tight money supply at the time, the tokens could be redeemed only for books. Although book tokens continued to flourish in prosperous times, their origin seems to be distinctly related to belt-tightening and modest expenditures.[19]

Another phenomenon that began during the 1920s but came into its own in the 1930s was the literary book club. The first such organization in

Britain was called the Book Society, no doubt inspired by the Book-of-the-Month Club and the Literary Guild in America. It followed the American example and avoided underselling, offered new titles at reduced prices made possible by its large-volume purchases, and thus enabled subscribers to feel they were keeping up with the latest and best literature of the day. Among the most successful of the British clubs was the Left Book Club. Begun in 1936 by Victor Gollancz, it was initially conceived as a vehicle for distributing some of its founder's own avant-garde publications. At the end of its first month, 6,000 subscribers had joined, and by 1939 there were 60,000 members. Not only did the club provide a new title each month, it also fostered discussion groups, lectures, and even group tours. As one historian noted:

> It coincided with the triumph of the Popular Front in France
> and with the beginning of British interest in the Spanish Civil
> War. The economic climate in 1936 also contributed to the
> Club's rapid success. The depression had passed its worst
> stage, and a scheme based on monthly contributions was work-
> able, while the constant danger of economic crisis kept the en-
> thusiasm of Club members at a high pitch.[20]

Gollancz recognized the potential for a special-interest club sooner than the rest of the book trade. Eventually many publishers followed suit by establishing clubs devoted to history, gardening, antiques, and recorded music.

Probably the most famous example of an innovation born of the depression was the founding of Penguin Books by Allen Lane in 1935. As one of Lane's business associates later recalled, there was little doubt as to his motivation:

> Allen Lane's decision to try his luck with paperback reprints of
> successful novels and biographies was little more than a rather
> desperate last throw to save the fortunes of a small publishing
> house, The Bodley Head, which had become famous in the
> 1890s, had run into financial difficulties during the 1920s . . .
> and was on the verge of bankruptcy after the slump of 1929
> and the great depression that followed.[21]

In stark contrast to Dent, who began his Everyman series with more than adequate equity but later found himself in debt, Lane started Penguin with a mere £100, and very soon began to see profits roll in.

What distinguished the early Penguin books was not their paper binding nor even their low selling price of 6*d*. Rather, they were remarkable in that they were reprints of other publishers' works that were still being sold in hardcover editions. Financially, the breakeven point fell somewhere between 15,000 and 20,000 copies for each title. The early success of Penguin books can be attributed in part to the 34,000-copy purchases of each of the first ten Penguin titles by the book buyer at F. W. Woolworth Company, whose wife happened to be present when Lane was trying to persuade him to stock the books. Because she was convinced that the average shopper at Woolworth would readily buy such book bargains, her husband agreed to carry them.

The shoestring operation that was Penguin books in its infancy had as its first business address the crypt of Holy Trinity Church on Euston Road. There the delivery vans would discharge their cargo in the church cemetery, from where it was conveyed by a drop chute to the office underground. As Ian Norrie described it, "The petty cash was kept in one empty tomb, the invoices in another. The packers pinned up nudes above their benches and the management arranged for blinds which could be quickly pulled down to obscure them when the Vicar paid a call to 'see how the dear boys were getting on.' "[22]

During its first year (1935), Penguin issued around 20 titles. Thereafter an average of 50 new titles appeared annually until the outbreak of the war. All were fiction reprints taken from the current lists of the leading publishers and, as a consequence, Lane was frequently put to the task of having to convince his professional colleagues that Penguin paperbacks would not jeopardize the hardcover market but rather would lure readers to buy what they had previously ignored or borrowed. In 1937 the Penguin editions were joined by 20 nonfiction titles that were called Pelicans, which were received equally well. Three years later a series of children's books, called Puffins, appeared. Penguin did make an occasional departure from strictly reprint publishing and would publish original material (usually dealing with a contemporary political or economic issue) as a so-called Penguin Special. World War II, far from hurting Penguin, opened up a vast market for cheap paperbacks among members of the armed forces.[23]

The situation in the United States during this period will be examined, somewhat briefly, as an existing work deals in considerable detail with the years 1837–1843.[24] Our discussion will begin with the depression of 1857 and will use case studies in an effort to establish a pattern.

The "dime novels" of Beadle & Adams first appeared in 1860 and seem to have been a by-product of the hard times immediately preceding their publication. Erastus Beadle began a publishing business with his brothers in Buffalo, New York, during the early 1850s, but it was not long before his brothers grew discouraged and left. Unable to carry on by himself, Erastus sold the printing plant in 1855 and headed west to speculate in land that was then being sold in the newly acquired Nebraska Territory. However, this venture failed and Beadle was forced to return to the printing trade in Buffalo. During the 1857 depression, he decided to risk moving to New York City, where he published miscellaneous cheap reprints until he finally hit upon the scheme that eventually made him famous. Beadle's Dime Novels often sold for a nickle and were roughly 100 pages long; decked in bright yellow or orange wrappers, they quickly became the rage. The conditions created by the Civil War substantially helped the sales of these tales of mystery and adventure, which had reached four million copies by 1865.

Of the three paperback revolutions in American history referred to by Tebbel, the first occurred in 1837–1843. The second started with the depression of 1873, and the firm generally credited with touching it off was R. R. Donnelley & Sons of Chicago.[25] Richard Robert Donnelley was one of several partners in a printing and publishing business that grew steadily from 1865 to 1870. Thus encouraged, they constructed a new plant and had already installed the presses when the great Chicago fire of 1871 destroyed everything. Two years later Donnelley tried again to expand his firm, but this time the depression struck. Printers had to be laid off and a skeleton crew of 42 workers carried on until the firm finally landed a contract to produce the Chicago City Directory. While this project was underway, the company could justify increasing its work force to more than 80, but upon completion of the directory Donnelley faced the problem of redundant employees. At this juncture Donnelley's partner, Alexander T. Loyd, proposed the now familiar solution of publishing cheap reprints, which would both keep the presses going and attract additional customers by their low prices. Typical of most American entrepreneurs, he appropriated noncopyrighted British and American works. Appearing first in January 1875, the opening numbers of the Lakeside Library had 24 three-column pages and appeared twice a month at a price of ten cents each. The prospectus promoted the series as follows:

> The great popular want of to-day is CHEAP, GOOD LITERATURE. There is enough and to spare of the CHEAP, and no lack of the GOOD, but a woeful poverty of both combined. Dime novels are issued by the million and good books by the thousand, but to the mass of readers the one is as distasteful as the other is inaccessible. The favored few accumulate extensive and costly libraries, but the many must content themselves with literary Weeklies, cheap, and equally poor, Novels, and, perhaps, the Magazines, with only occasional Books, which, after all, form not only the foundation but most of the superstructure of sound and desirable mental culture.
>
> Scarcely a week passes but the reader of this is reminded by a friend's praise of one book, or an extract in his local paper from another, that his library fails to keep even pace with his wants, and also, unfortunately, that the length of his purse forbids its desired extension.

The aim of the present series of publications is to cure this evil—to make the BEST BOOKS as cheap as the literary trash now flooding the country, to offer GOOD LITERATURE at the price of the poor and pernicious. It takes possession of the vast middle-ground, with dime novels and "blood and thunder" stories on the one hand, and costly, unattainable books on the other.

In brief, the theory of the omnipresent, inexpensive daily and weekly Newspaper, is carried into the hitherto exclusive domain of literature, and its treasures popularized and made free to all.

The second issue further extolled the virtues of cheapness.

Very few readers care for the expensive paper and elaborate binding that make the better class of novels, tales, travels, etc., so costly as to be beyond the means of the masses. What is wanted is simply the author's work, complete and unabridged as it leaves his pen, clearly printed on good paper, in a convenient form for perusal and preservation. This want the Library fully supplies.

By the end of its first year, the Lakeside Library showed distinct signs of having been accepted. A new installment came out every ten days, each containing 32 pages. Soon 40 pages appeared weekly, and efforts were made to persuade the post office that the issues could be classified as magazines and therefore qualify for reduced postal rates. Besides being sold by subscription, the installments were distributed through a large network of newsstands where many readers of modest means could buy them.

For a while the Lakeside Library dominated the market for cheap but respectable reprints, but before long rival series emerged. Most formidable among them was George Munro's Seaside Library, which was published in New York. It had much larger financial resources and produced three times as many volumes as did the Chicago competition, so that by the late 1870s Seaside boasted a list of 600 titles compared to Lakeside's 200. In the Lakeside Library's 98th number (1877) the following note of concern was issued:

The various publishers of dime novels, sensational trashy weekly papers, etc., finding no market for their pernicious stuff since the inauguration of "The Lakeside" cheap reprints of good reading, are now seeking by formidable imitations of the Lakeside editions to steal the benefits of our widespread advertising and the popularity ensuing, from the cheap publications of good literature.

By the time Lakeside issued number 192 (1878) this note of apprehension had become far more shrill:

> We would caution our readers against counterfeits and imitations of our popular The Lakeside Library put forth by certain unscrupulous New York publishers. These counterfeits are published in miserably small, poor type on poor paper with only one coarse illustration. The unreadable fine type of these counterfeits will soon dim or even utterly destroy the strongest eyesight. Beware of them!

Alas, Donnelley was forced to concede the contest in the spring of 1879 and sold his Lakeside Library, numbering 270 issues, to his arch rival Munro. As was so often the case, the creator of the new product did not enjoy his achievement very long before competition became fierce and the market glutted.

The 1880s saw a change in the size of the popular paperback. Quartos gave way increasingly to the more convenient duodecimos, while the number of major firms producing them increased: There were 14 by the end of 1870, 23 by the end of the 1880s, and 50 on the eve of the 1893 depression. All the while that this tremendous expansion was taking place, one man, John Lovell, was trying to monopolize paperback production by buying the plates and stock of his competitors in the hope of controlling the market and putting a halt to the ruinous price-cutting. His failure, and the consequent bankruptcy of his United States Book Company in 1893, was the most spectacular of many similarly ambitious schemes.

By the twentieth century fewer than a half-dozen recognized paperback publishers remained, the largest being Street & Smith. Its success can be attributed in part to the failure of John Lovell and in part to its authors, who included Gilbert Patten, Edward Stratemeyer, and Horatio Alger, the creators of heroes such as Nick Carter, Frank Merriwell, the Rover Boys, the Motor Boys, and Tom Swift. The 1893 depression disgorged an estimated seven to eight million paperbacks onto the market, many of which were bought by Street & Smith and enabled that firm to savor the commanding market position for which Lovell had so longed.[26]

Of the American book clubs, we will discuss briefly the most famous, the Book-of-the-Month Club (BOMC), because it raises some rather puzzling questions regarding factors that either promoted or impeded survival and growth in the depression years. Begun in 1924, the BOMC attracted 45,000 subscribers during its first year. An impartial jury of literary experts would select one of the best books of the year as a monthly selection that would then be offered to subscribers, who were expected to purchase it at the moderate price of $3. Later this requirement was reduced to four books per year. By 1927 membership was up to 60,000 and two years later had risen to 110,000. With the 1929 crash, people cancelled subscriptions, and, because the cost of securing new members kept rising, prospects for growth looked dim. A low point was reached in 1932, when several of the club's leading executives resigned. By 1935, however, things had turned around, and by 1940 over 350,000 belonged to the club.

How does one account for such a reversal during the depths of the depression? Perhaps it can be explained better by the growing sense of confidence in the nation than by any specific policy changes made by BOMC. Yet planned purchasing was attractive in such times of retrenchment because it allowed people to avoid impulse buying and still commit themselves to a minimum of four worthwhile and popular books each year. The club itself also took measures to make its offerings more attractive and tempting. Opposed in principle to radical price-cutting, BOMC resorted to other incentives, such as offering a free book with every two purchases, allowing new subscribers to receive the current monthly selection free without obligation to join the club, or providing premiums in the form of especially costly and deluxe editions at cut-rate prices. The club also stopped buying its monthly selections directly from the publisher and began paying a royalty to acquire the printing plates from the original firm so that it could issue its own special club edition.[27]

In 1938 the U.S. post office gave a helping hand to book clubs by reducing their rates. While the charge had ranged previously from seven to fifteen cents per pound depending upon distance, the new regulations proclaimed a uniform one-cent postage. This change may have been largely in response to congressional and public pressure and contrasts markedly with the earlier policies of the post office that put cheap paperback reprints out of business in the 1840s and the 1870s.[28]

There was also an American version of the Penguin. Heedless of Allen Lane's success, most American booksellers and publishers were unenthusiastic about paperbacks in 1939, especially since the United States had comparatively few bookshops within easy reach of potential buyers. What did exist in every town and village, however, were newsstands, druggists, and cigar stores, and these became outlets for the new Pocket Book series. As with dime novels and Penguins, Pocket Books were bolstered enormously by the outbreak of war. Within six years over 100 million copies were published, many of which were contracted by the U.S. government for distribution to the armed forces. The logo of Pocket Books was a kangaroo, and as one historian noted: "They had highly attractive covers of the kind that appealed to readers of periodicals and comics."[29]

Now that we have cited examples and set forth illustrations, it is perhaps appropriate to draw one or two conclusions. If necessity *is* the mother of invention, as we suggested at the outset, it cannot be said to be the only stimulus to innovation. However, our purpose here has been to demonstrate that severe economic crises often encourage new directions and undertakings in spite of conditions of chaos and commercial devastation. Although lowering prices has been the usual response to economic depression and the hopeful strategy to attract the public's dwindling income, an alternative was found in raising prices for books aimed at a narrow but well-to-do clientele. Circulating libraries were a case in point, as was vanity subscription publishing, which is not dealt with here.

Experiments that began in times of comparative prosperity often managed to survive a subsequent downturn in the economy. This was especially true for part-issues, which allowed customers to spread payments over a long period of time. The same applied to magazine subscribers, who found they could "pay as they read," so to speak. Finally, we have noted instances in which individuals sought to improve their lot by launching bold undertakings that may or may not have been responses to trade depressions but that were innovations born of adverse circumstances. The ability to command credit and solicit customers simultaneously often made the difference between success and failure for many publishing ventures.

By emphasizing the economic impetuses to innovation, I have tended to ignore other factors, such as technological change, individual genius, shifts in popular taste, and relevant legal decisions. Yet it must be remembered that members of the book trade were first and foremost business people, and their decisions to act or to refrain from acting depended primarily on their perception of the economic climate.

NOTES

1. The notion of three paperback revolutions figures prominently in John Tebbel's four-volume *A History of Book Publishing in the United States* (New York, 1972–1981).

2. As quoted in J. J. Barnes, *Free Trade in Books: A Study of the London Book Trade Since 1800* (Oxford, 1964), pp. 113–114.

3. As quoted in S. Bennett, "John Murray's Family Library and the Cheapening of Books in Early Nineteenth Century Britain," *Studies in Bibliography* 29 (1976): 158.

4. Murray to Gladstone, 3 September 1851, as quoted in Barnes, op. cit., p. 79.

5. Ibid., p. 96.

6. For those who seek to correlate trade fluctuations with levels of political and social discontent, see W. W. Rostow, *British Economy of the Nineteenth Century* (Oxford, 1948), pp. 33, 124–125; and G. Rudé, "Protest and Punishment in Nineteenth-Century Britain," *Albion* 5 (1973): 1–23.

7. The subject of increasing book prices is dealt with briefly by Graham Pollard in his unpublished Sandars lectures of 1959; lecture no. 4, typescript p. 39. For the

years 1800–1824 and the printer's quotation of 1818, see R. D. Altick, *The English Common Reader* (Chicago, 1957), pp. 260–262.

8. Ibid., p. 274. For Murray's Family Library series, see Bennett, op. cit., passim. See also Barnes, op. cit., p. 111.

9. V. E. Neuburg, *Popular Literature* (Harmondsworth, 1977), pp. 177–178 and 184.

10. Altick, op. cit., p. 338.

11. For a discussion of Sunday newspapers, see H. Hobson et al., *The Pearl of Days: An Intimate Memoir of the Sunday Times, 1822–1972* (London, 1972), pp. 3–25; and L. James, *Fiction for the Working Man, 1830–50* (Harmondsworth, 1974), pp. 39–40.

12. C. Hibbert, *The Illustrated London News* (London, 1975).

13. James, op. cit., p. 44.

14. P. Haining, ed., *The Penny Dreadful* (London, 1976), pp. 14, 24, 30.

15. Concerning Edward Lloyd, see ibid., p. 30; Hobson, op. cit., p. 13, James, op. cit., pp. 29, 39–42, 51; and Neuburg, op. cit., pp. 170–171.

16. P. Dunae, "*Boys Own Paper:* Origins and Editorial Policies," *Private Library* 9 (1976): 123–158

17. Barnes, op. cit., p. 147; F. A. Mumby and I. Norrie, *Publishing and Bookselling* (London, 1974), pp. 221–222; P. Kruse, "Piracy and Britannica," *Library Quarterly* 33 (1963): 313–328.

18. J. M. Dent, *The Memoirs of J. M. Dent, 1849–1923* (London, 1928), pp. 124–131; E. Rhys, *Everyman Remembers* (New York, 1931), pp. 234–236.

19. Book tokens are discussed in Barnes, op. cit., p. 151; Mumby and Norrie, op. cit., p. 315; and T. Joy, *The Truth about Bookselling* (London, 1964), pp. 96–99.

20. S. Samuels, "The Left Book Club," *Journal of Contemporary History* 1 (1966): 65–86.

21. H. Schmoller, "The Paperback Revolution," in *Essays in the History of Publishing,* ed. A. Briggs (London, 1974), p. 297.

22. Mumby and Norrie, op. cit., p. 365.

23. For further information about Penguin Books, see *Penguin's Progress, 1935–1960* (Harmondsworth, 1960); and W. E. Williams, *The Penguin Story, 1935–1956* (Harmondsworth, 1956). I am indebted to Robin Myers for calling my attention to these and other sources used in the preparation of this article.

24. See J. J. Barnes, *Authors, Publishers and Politicians: The Quest for an Anglo-American Copyright Agreement, 1815–54* (London and Columbus, 1974), especially Chap. 1.

25. I would like to acknowledge my gratitude to the Donnelley Company for permitting me to examine the extant archives in its memorial library. Although the

evidence is fragmentary, a fairly clear picture emerges as to how and why Richard Robert Donnelley began to issue cheap reprints in the 1870s.

26. For background on John Lovell and on Street & Smith, see Tebbel, op. cit., Vol. 2, pp. 487–507.

27. Book of the Month Club, "Special 50th Anniversary Supplement," *Book of the Month Club News*, April 1976; Tebbel, op. cit., Vol. 3, pp. 386–390, 493–498; C. Madison, *Book Publishing in America* (New York, 1966), pp. 393–394.

28. For some discussion of postal rates and how they have affected publishing ventures in the United States, see Barnes, *Authors, Publishers and Politicians*, pp. 18–23; Tebbel, op. cit., Vol. 2, p. 496. For information about rates for mailing books in the 1930s, I am indebted to the director, Office of Rates, U.S. Postal Service.

29. Madison, op. cit., p. 548.

III

Library History and the History of Books: Two Fields of Research for Librarians

Paul Raabe

[FEW PEOPLE HAVE done as much as Dr. Paul Raabe to further study of the history of the book. In addition to his own numerous studies—an instance of leading by example—he has turned the Herzog August Bibliothek in Wolfenbüttel into a center of research. Dr. Raabe has done this in part by making that library's rich holdings widely known and accessible. He has also transformed the library into a body that sponsors a large number and a wide variety of publications, meetings, and research organizations. Thus, it was highly appropriate that Dr. Raabe should give not a detailed research paper but an evening talk in the Boston Public Library on research by librarians. It is hoped that this summary of his address preserves, above all, Dr. Raabe's intense feeling that research by librarians is important, not just because of the information unearthed or the insights gained but because all will suffer if librarians are only technocratic managers.—*Ed.*]

In Europe, librarians have traditionally been, in the truest sense of the word, scholars, fully familiar with the content and form of the books in their care. Numerous examples come readily to mind, from Callimachus in Alexandria, to the monks of the Middle Ages, to the learned librarians of early modern times—Bernard de Montfaucon, the founder of paleography;

Richard Bentley, the classical philologist, at Cambridge; the German philosopher, Gottfried Wilhelm Leibniz; the Italian historian, Lodovico Antonio Muratori; and the brothers Grimm, among many others. All perpetuated learning, not only as curators of books but also as active scholars.

But the profession has changed today, along with the rest of society. The reading of books has long since ceased to be a privilege of the upper classes. On the contrary, the ability to read is taken for granted, and books have become a medium of instruction, mass education, and entertainment. Consequently, libraries are no longer exclusively enclaves devoted to scholarship; they are also institutions that supply books to all groups in the population, and those books are used for a wide variety of reasons.

Changes in readership have resulted in the formation of various types of libraries, ranging from huge, national libraries to highly specialized collections in business firms. Although it might be expected that the diversity in types of libraries would foster different types of librarians, this, by and large, has not happened. Librarians in all types of institutions increasingly see themselves as suppliers of information or purveyors of data, and the book is viewed not so much as an intrinsically valuable object but rather as one element of a system, even as one medium among others. Moreover, the complex nature of libraries and the great demands placed upon them have transformed librarianship into a profession in which the work is increasingly administrative and far removed from productive academic endeavor. Increasingly, librarians have become alienated from the book and, by the same token, from academic pursuits of their own. This has often led to a rupture of the bond between the librarian and the scholar, to the detriment of scholarship, for the librarian who is not a scholar cannot effectively promote scholarship.

Scholarship of one's own and the promotion of scholarship are inextricably related. Librarians who see themselves as links in a long scholarly tradition will not stop at promoting and transmitting learning by assisting others in their efforts. They themselves will seek to contribute directly, and that direct contribution will better enable them to promote the scholarship of others. Of course, it would be anachronistic to ask that the librarians of today be polymaths like their great predecessors, but it is by no means anachronistic to plead that librarians be active as scholars. Every librarian has at hand the source materials for library history and the history of the book.

Few libraries have the wealth of sources that my own library, the Herzog August Library in Wolfenbüttel, has. There one can trace the library's collecting policies since the seventeenth century. From the catalogs of a number of private collections acquired en bloc, one can do research on the nature of private libraries. The old catalogs have been preserved, and the lending records since 1666 are complete. The visitors' books, the correspondence files, pictorial material, even such objects as old book trucks—all have been preserved at Wolfenbüttel. But all libraries have records, and by writing library history librarians contribute not just to library history but to the broader field of the history of academic and cultural institutions. Even more, library history enriches the history of scholarship, the history of education, and aspects of social history.

Just as all libraries have records that can be source material for library history, so do all libraries have the basic materials needed for research in the history of the book. Such research is needed in many specialized fields of book history, particularly in the following:

1. *The history of the writing of books:* This discipline, which is today the prerogative of philologists, should be approached to a greater extent from the viewpoint of book history. It should consider how book manuscripts for the printer came into being and the nature of relationships between authors and publishers.

2. *The history of book production:* The classic field among the many areas of study in book history, this is often equated with the history of the art of printing, but more than technical aspects should be considered. In addition to compositorial practices and proofreading, typography should be included. This field must also cover descriptive bibliography and involve the comparative examination of various copies of the same book.

3. *The history of book illustration and decoration:* Although closely connected with book production, the history of illustration, ornamentation, initial letters, vignettes, and publishers' marks are topics of research in their own right and are particularly dependent upon a thorough knowledge of the books themselves.

4. *The history of materials used in printing, especially paper:* Although this is an independent discipline that is often studied without reference to book history, various types of research into the history of books cannot be pursued without knowledge of the materials.

5. *The history of bookbinding:* This is another classic field of research by librarians. In addition to aesthetic questions raised by this topic, the history of binding casts light on the activities of artisans and relates to sales techniques over the centuries.

6. *The history of the book trade:* One of the major fields of book history, this can be pursued from various points of view. Individual firms can be studied, or the trade of a particular city, region, or country can be analyzed over a period of time. In addition, the means of distribution—bookshops, book clubs, book-trade organizations, plus the antiquarian book trade—can be examined.

7. *The history of reading:* This is a more recent branch of studies in book history. It examines reading habits, particularly among various classes of readers, and seeks to shed light on the various purposes for which books were used by different groups.

The wide range of possibilities for research becomes clearer if one keeps in mind that the term "history of the book" is meant to include all forms of reading matter—periodicals, almanacs, newspapers, broadsides. Similarly, it is meant to embrace all types of reading matter in terms of content and genre: literary works, schoolbooks, dictionaries, Bibles, hymnals, prayer books, children's books, how-to books—the list could go on. Each type of book has undergone change over the centuries, and the investigation of those changes is one of the tasks of the history of the book.

To be sure, the librarian who wishes to pursue research must gain a basic knowledge of the history of the book and specialized knowledge in some aspect of the field, but the task can be done. Generally, librarians will not produce all-encompassing syntheses that review a vast body of secondary literature, but they are ideally situated to pursue detailed studies, such as the work already done on medieval manuscripts and early printed books— two domains in which the contribution of librarians has been outstanding. Now librarians need to examine other periods, more diverse types of material, and more aspects of the history of the book.

At the same time that I know librarians can do such research, I fear that few will. Those who have resisted the trend toward alienation from the book are in danger of becoming outsiders in the profession: Such people are tolerated more than respected and are sometimes even objects of ridicule. It is easy to understand that not all would wish to join such a group, particularly when society at large measures one's worth largely in material terms.

Yet librarians need to resist the general trend precisely because those values that do not further economic self-interest are endangered. Librarians need to pursue historical research not just to contribute to our understanding of the past but to preserve and defend human values and traditions. As Goethe said, "Libraries are the memory of mankind." Librarians, then, are the preservers and guardians of that memory, and a world buffeted by change needs that memory more than ever. Let us not be timid about asking those who control financial resources to support libraries and research by librarians. Even though lofty sentiments are not fashionable, I cannot refrain from saying that we have a responsibility to raise our voices in public and to labor in quiet rooms, not out of an obligation to the past but rather to those yet unborn. Their lives will be narrower if the past is not a part of their present. We want the future as well to live in the consciousness expressed by a writer in ancient times: "bibliotheca docet"— the library is our teacher.